Revised Printing

Multicultural Psychology

Reflecting Humanity

Trude Cooke Turner
La Keita Carter
Azar Etesamypour-King

Kendall Hunt

publishing company

Kendall Hunt
publishing company

www.kendallhunt.com
Send all inquiries to:
4050 Westmark Drive
Dubuque, IA 52004-1840

ISBN 978-1-4652-4858-9

Printed in the United States of America
10 9 8 7 6 5 4 3 2

Contents

About the Authors

TRUDE COOKE TURNER, PH.D.

Dr. Trude Cooke Turner is chair of the Behavioral Sciences Department at the Community College of Baltimore County and an assistant professor of psychology. She has served as a faculty member, coordinator of multicultural affairs, and assistant dean of student services at various institutions. She is a graduate of the University of Minnesota—Twin Cities where she earned a bachelor's degree in English; and Arizona State University, where she completed a master's degree in counseling and a doctorate of philosophy in counseling psychology. Dr. Cooke Turner enjoys membership in the American Psychological Association where she is a consulting editor for the Journal of Diversity in Higher Education. She lives in Baltimore County, Maryland, with her husband and three children.

AZAR ETESAMYPOUR-KING, PH.D

Dr. Azar Etesamypour-King is an assistant professor of psychology at the Community College of Baltimore County in Catonsville, Maryland. She is an Iranian-born, naturalized American citizen and a French-educated experimental /neuropsychologist. She received her bachelor's, master's, and doctorate degrees in psychology from the Rennes II University (France); she also completed a postdoctorate fellowship in neuropsychology and neurotoxicology from the Neurology Department, Neuropsychology Diagnostic and Research Laboratory, at the University of Maryland School of Medicine. Etesamypour-King's experience includes the research supervision of undergraduate and graduate students. Her classes include both face-to-face and online instruction. Her teaching experience includes classes in Experimental Psychology, Neuropsychology, Introduction to Psychology, Physiology of the Nervous System, Adolescent Psychology, Social Experimental Psychology, Life-Span Developmental Psychology, Psychology of Early Childhood, Educational Psychology, and Multicultural Psychology. She is a member of several professional organizations, including the American Psychological Association (APA), and the Jean Piaget Society (JPS). She lives in Baltimore County, Maryland, with her husband, her daughter (Armita), and her twin boys (Armin & Aryan).

LA KEITA CARTER PSY.D.

Dr. La Keita Carter is the director of the Psychology Division at Loyola Clinical Centers (of Loyola University Maryland) and assistant professor of psychology at the Community College of Baltimore County on the Essex campus. After receiving her undergraduate degree from Temple University, she earned her master's and doctoral degrees from Loyola University Maryland. As a licensed psychologist who was trained in clinical psychology, Dr. Carter splits her professional time between training graduate students in psychology and teaching psychology. She has taught a myriad of online and face-to-face classes at the undergraduate and graduate levels including Introduction to Psychology, Health and Wellness, Group Counseling, Psychometrics, Personal Life and Career Planning, Personality Psychology, Psychology of Learning, Social Psychology, Advanced Issues in Eating Disturbances, Human Relations in a Culturally Diverse Society, and Diversity Issues in Psychology. She has also worked as a psychotherapist in a number of clinical settings including hospitals, community mental health agencies, college counseling centers, and school systems. She is a member of the Maryland Psychological Association (MPA), Association for Psychology Training Clinics (APTC) and American Psychological Association (APA). She lives in Baltimore, Maryland, with her husband and two children.

Preface

In the constantly changing world in which we operate as humans, family and community members, consumers, workers and retirees, one fact is notably clear: there are differences among and between us. Within the transitory human landscape exists a cadre of individuals coexisting though often unaware of how each influences the other. As we have occupied the same scenery, some have noted a change in the scenery; others have argued for the scenery to remain as they remember it. So it has been within the discipline of psychology.

Traditionally, psychology has been a scientific representation of the standard measures by which the human mind interposes, interprets, and interacts with the environment. From its earliest theories to present day, there has been a mental dance around the relevance of certain characteristics, traits, expectations, explanations, goals, and regarding affect, behavior, and cognition. In some instances, the dance has been halted in an effort to not engage polarity or differing opinions. From this halted stance, however, a new "dance" emerged—multicultural psychology.

Multicultural psychology as a social science discipline continues to develop and broaden its focus on individual and human interactions. As such, this scientific paradigm originally concentrated on the racial and ethnic disparities commonly researched around the world. Multicultural psychology has often been considered a derivation of other social sciences, including anthropology and sociology. With this view, critics of multicultural psychology have not looked favorably on research practices, curricular advancements, or textbook creation. However, the argument for the necessity of a broader perspective within psychology lies in the reality that what was once considered "traditional" in psychology has undergone a paradigm shift.

This latest textbook on multicultural psychology focuses on the growing understanding of how "culture" is viewed and understood. Within the term *multicultural* come those with physically "disabilities," those from various religious sects, racial and ethnic backgrounds, socioeconomic groups, and others who were not previously included in the discussions on culture influences on behavior, feelings, and thoughts. Similarly, the focus of this text is not solely with the individual, but on how the individual's presence and activity in society affects the social environment at large.

Written with the novice psychology student in mind, *Multicultural Psychology: Reflecting Humanity* intends to be a primer for those with little-to-no background in psychology. Ideally, students who have had an introductory psychology course would benefit from being able to associate the history of psychology with the paradigm shift that includes multicultural psychology as the "fourth force." Those students who have never been exposed to the more full composition of the history of psychology and its current practices will be able to ascertain how multicultural psychology adds to the historical framework of the psychological science. Students need not have prior knowledge about the underpinnings of psychological theory before reading this textbook because psychology, as a science, is continually being reviewed with respect to the standards used in practical application of psychology.

In order for students to be better prepared for graduate education in psychology, they need to have a background that emphasizes the importance of multicultural psychology as a paradigm within the broader realm of the discipline. This text will, also, provide cross-disciplinary information from science (biology), mathematics (economics), literature, and language communities (i.e., American Sign Language, slang, and jargon). Therefore, this text is written in a format that requires students to think critically; consider their values, traditions, and beliefs; and apply novel concepts in conventional and contemporary society.

Trude Cooke Turner, Ph.D.
La Keita Carter, Psy.D.
Azar Etesamypour-King, Ph.D.

Acknowledgments

This text would not have been possible without the unwavering support of our former dean of the School of Business, Social Science (BSSWE), Wellness and Education at the Community College of Baltimore County (CCBC), Dr. Avon H. Garrett; and our current dean of the School of Wellness, Education, Behavioral and Social Sciences (WEBSS), Dr. Timothy O. Davis. We appreciate your celebration of multicultural scholarship, our professionalism, and desire to make learning a continual enjoyment for our students through your examples.

Dedication

Dedicated to all of the underserved, underprivileged, under-resourced populations of the world . . . You aren't invisible.

AND

This text honors the spiritual being who has created me and placed great earthly beings in my path to shape me. Written in memory of Alice Coleman, a woman of grace, sophistication and humility. (LDC)

This book is dedicated to my parents, Dr. Reza and Akram Etesamypour who have supported and loved me all these years, & to my husband (Dr. Theodore King), and my children (Armita Yeuneko, Armin Matthew, &Aryan Theodore) for their love and support. (AEK)

This book, my knowledge of cultural experiences, nor my life could have been possible without the guidance and love of Jesus Christ, Who has made all that makes "me" me. (TCT)

CHAPTER 1

Refining Multicultural Psychology: History and Metamorphosis

"A man is not what he thinks he is, but what he thinks, he is."

—*Max Hickerson*

In a story of dramatic proportions, the news accounts of the murder and dismemberment of a woman in South Dakota initially got little national media attention (Setrakian & Singh, 2007). When Daphne Wright was convicted of the murder of Darlene VanderGeisen, more attention was paid to the question of how she could have committed such an act. The news reported the crime as the result of a love triangle between Ms. Wright and another woman with whom the deceased was also said to have had a relationship. Also key to the puzzle was Ms. Wright's early childhood and adolescence. Underneath all of the "what-ifs" and "how-coulds" remained the fact that Daphne Wright could not only be viewed as a lesbian woman, but also as a woman of African American descent with learning disabilities who is deaf or hearing disabled ("Deaf Woman Sentenced to Life in Prison," 2007). Daphne Wright, like all humans, is multicultural.

How would psychology as a science and a profession address an individual such as Daphne Wright—using one way to describe them, or as a person with a collection of different cultural identities? Wright's complex characteristics—woman, African American, lesbian, learning disabled, deaf—taken separately, would require specific attention and skills from a professional trained in one of the many fields within the psychology. In order to understand fully the complexity of issues, a few questions immediately surface: What is psychology? If there are different fields within psychology, what are they, and how would they attempt to respond to the question?

In the quote opening this chapter, Hickerson suggests that humans are not composed simply of thoughts and opinions, but of something much less tangible—the inner workings of the human mind. Although people may define one another in terms of "good" or "bad," "successful" or "failure," "happy" or "sad," these terms serve only to focus on short-term experiences. Instead, the focus of every human, according to Hickerson, is on becoming whatever is possible for him or her to imagine. If an individual were to only focus on immediate issues, she or he might miss the possibilities of what could become.

This textbook is written to unravel some of the queries about how psychology as both a science and a profession deals with human beings as they interact with those who are similar to and dissimilar from them. In this ever-increasingly diverse world, it has become necessary to learn more about others while at the same time learning more about humanity. The term *diverse* simply means

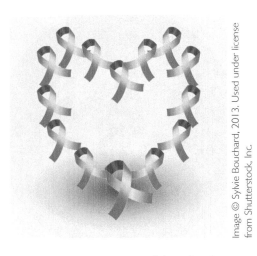

varied or "having distinct qualities" (Merriam-Webster, 2013). In some cases, diversity is referred to in terms of race. However, this is a limited view of the term, as it simply suggests that when things are diverse, there are a number of varieties. When people go out to eat at a fine restaurant, they typically find a diversity of choices on the menu. This may be one of the reasons for selecting that restaurant, because of its diverse options.

EVERYBODY KNOWS WHAT CULTURE IS, RIGHT?

In essence, humans develop their sense of how to do things based on culture. Culture can be defined as *shared, organized, historically reproduced symbolic practices that facilitate meaningful human existence* (Gone, 2011, p. 235). (Chapter 4 will provide a more full discussion of "culture," but for the purpose of introduction, what people often refer to as an individual's "background" is viewed synonymously as "culture.") When people talk about where they come from, they are talking about their culture. Someone from Baltimore, Maryland, for instance, has certain shared experiences with someone else from Baltimore. Culture in Baltimore includes, but is not limited to certain foods like crabs, Old Bay® seasoning, the Orioles, the Ravens, and Berger® cookies. So, those native to Baltimore are familiar with a lifestyle and value system where art, music, language, and geography are distinct to them as Baltimoreans. Can you think of some other examples?

In their book *Multicultural Psychology: Understanding Our Diverse Communities*, Mio, Barker, Tumambing (2012) argue that the term *culture* is complicated and encompasses a broad set of characteristics that are not universally accepted. Similarly titled books on multicultural psychology (Matsumoto & Juang, 2012; Hall, 2010; Rosenblum & Travis, 2008; Myer, 2007) refer to the idea that the term *multicultural* takes on new meaning with the recognition of previously ignored groups in society. So, one can easily note that some of the reasons why the subject is so complicated is that cultures evolve. The manner in which individuals communicate, learn, and work is different than it was a few decades ago (Turkle, 2011). The emergence of computer technology has dictated that people are living in a time that contradicts the Industrial Revolution of the 18th and 19th centuries (in England and the United States, respectively). Our language, expectations, and lifestyles are dissimilar to those of the earlier period.

One of the hallmarks of social psychology is the belief that behavior takes place within a cultural context. This suggests that actions that take place are directed by the values, beliefs, history, and expectations of one's culture. The audience for this textbook, for instance, is expected to be a part of the college student culture. Within the collegiate culture are beliefs, expectations, rules, and other principles that differentiate the college student from someone who is not a college student. That is your culture. That is just one aspect of your culture, however. Whereas you are a college student, you may also be a female, someone's child, an athlete, a member of a particular faith, a 24-year old, an employee, or more. Each facet of your being is considered part of your cultural makeup. Can you think of other cultures? How do these cultures affect how you do what you do throughout your day? How do they affect how you see your life?

Multicultural psychology is the scientific study of how groups identify, create, and engage in cultural activities and values (Hall, 2005 when they are in the same group or in different groups. In 2002, the **American Psychological Association (APA)**, the professional organization responsible for regulating and training in psychological practices, acknowledged the need

> ### THINK ABOUT IT
>
> How does your culture (pick any one of your multicultural entities) affect where you live? Whom you date? What major you have selected? How you view money? What you do with your spare time? Your view of people who are different from you? Your choice of food, friends, or fun?
>
> Write a two-page, double-spaced paper with 1-inch margins discussing one aspect of your culture in response to these questions.

for comprehensive guidelines for working with and conducting research on multicultural populations (Franklin, 2009; Comas-Diaz, 2009; Matsumoto & Juang, 2012). While early psychologists researched and remarked on the relationship between culture and mental processes (Sue, Bingham, Porsché-Burke, & Vasquez, 1999; Hothersall, 1995; Ponterotto, Casas, Suzuki, & Alexander, 1995), very little attention or training was developed to research multicultural populations until the 20th century, 100 years after the introduction of psychology as a science. While the APA created "[g]uidelines on multicultural education, training, research, practice and organizational change for psychologists" in 2003, deeper discussions continue about the role of culture in psychological science (Ponterotto, 2010; Franklin, 2009; American Psychological Association, 2003).

What psychology as a science has come to understand is that there are many diverse perspectives in the world. These perspectives help individuals, groups, and communities better understand how the world operates. Some perspectives allow individuals to look at the world with a narrow lens, focusing only on particular details in the world and allowing those details to inform their daily interactions in the world. Still others use a wider lens to explore possibilities available in the world, with creativity and purpose for finding nuances that could broaden their experience in the world. It is this search for perspective and potential that is at the core of scientific inquiry. It was in this space that traditional psychology developed.

Multicultural Psychological research considers not simply that there are 3 women in this photo, but that each of these women has learned something about herself (age, musical talent, marital status) through her involvement in society.

In returning to the previous discussion about Daphne Wright, we would note that the deaf community, for instance, has a language—American Sign Language (ASL)—that is, their main mode of communication. Without ASL, Ms. Wright's lawyers, family members, and friends would not be able to tell her "side" of the story nor would they be able to help her understand what others thought about her behavior or the outcome of the case. The deaf culture not only has a language, but an extensive history, values, and beliefs that are vividly demonstrated by those who both belong to the culture and others who appreciate it (Leigh, Corbett, Gutman, & Morere, 1996; Padden & Humphries, 2009). The human experience for the deaf community is different—not better or worse—from the hearing culture, but the differences often get dramatized while the similarities (e.g., expression of love, attention, displeasure) are often ignored.

TRADITIONAL PSYCHOLOGY: IN PERSPECTIVE

A lab in Leipzig, Germany, at the University of Leipzig, would be the springboard for questions and answers to human behavior that would revolutionize the reason and logic behind the human condition (Wade & Tavris, 2011; Weiten, 2012). Here, Wilhelm Wundt (pronounced in German "Vilhelm Vunt"), a medical doctor, would develop the first laboratory for the study of psychology. (See box "Why Make a Big Deal About the Pronunciation of Wilhelm Wundt's Name?") The focus of his studies was the basic dimensions of human behavior that underlie conscious interactions. In other words, Wundt wanted to be able to measure and articulate what people understood about their own behavior, thoughts, and feelings. From here, psychology took its place in the scientific community where measurement, description, control, and prediction were highly regarded as absolute and logical.

Students who take introductory psychology courses typically learn that psychology has traditionally been viewed as the "study of the mind and mental processes" (Ardilla, 2007; Weiten, 2012). It was Wundt who believed that the only way to truly understand the human condition was to study it through experiments and to base conclusions or theories on the results (Hothersall, 1995). Years of research (or measurable scientific study) has led to many theories about how people think, act, and feel. However, early psychologists and psychological researchers did not spend a great deal of time exploring differences among cultural groups, which can be most clearly

---

BOX 1.1   Why Make a Big Deal About the Pronunciation of Wilhelm Wundt's Name?

The purpose behind multicultural psychology is to legitimize the diversity that exists in the world. Traditional psychology might suggest that a name is a name; however, the cultural relevance and historical significance of one's name and its origin are not easily disregarded. This distinction is made about Wundt's name because the mispronunciation of the name speaks the lack of importance that is placed on proper acknowledgement of a culture and its practices. When someone pronounces the name Wundt as if he were from the United States (thus saying "Wunt"), there is an implicit assumption that only those from the United States are literate, important, or capable of creating historical or linguistic significance. Though not spoken, the assumption is clear and could be offensive to a German citizen.

---

seen in their desire to define stability (mental health) and a process of standardization that would define as "deficient" any deviation from the norm (Sue & Arredondo, 1992).

Psychology is both a science and a profession (American Psychological Association, 2003). As a science, psychology attempts to study both normal and abnormal human and animal behavior, thoughts, and feelings (Weiten, 2012). As both a science and a profession, psychology seeks to understand how human behavior and mental processes affect one's biological processes, mental state, and physical environment (Wade & Tavris, 2011; Cauce, 2011). Say, for instance, a person has a fear of dogs. Each time that person encounters a dog, there will be a physiological response which causes the person's heart to pound, makes the breathing more labored, and creates the desire to run (or simply to have the dog go away). Each of these processes involves the biological mechanisms that naturally occur in humans. At the same time, the biological response may be followed by or coexist with the mental state that leads the individual to believe that danger is present. It is that state that may cause the person to consider running. All of these, though individually significant, are tied to the psychological process of what can happen when one is afraid. Yet, biological processes are only one part of the equation when it comes to looking into the field of psychology.

Image © Bill Ragan, 2013. Used under license from Shutterstock, Inc.

THE SCIENCE OF PSYCHOLOGY

Early philosophers saw psychology as a field that concentrated on the metaphysical (outside of the realm of what can be seen, touched, known) study of the soul, the mind, and the interaction between them. In its infancy, psychology sought answers to how to gauge the interaction between the physical, physiological (i.e., neural processes), philosophical, and practical. For this reason, the majority of early psychological theorists had medical degrees and backgrounds in the study of biological processes.

Generally speaking, **psychology** is the scientific study of mental processes (Morris & Maisto, 1998; Rathus, 1999; p. 2). These mental processes include how individuals see and makes sense of the world and their interaction in it. This includes the actual order of what came first: Does someone have a thought first, then act on it? Does someone feel something and then think about what the feeling meant? Does someone do something and then think about the consequences. This is all a part of what psychology seeks to discover. So, it is widely known that the goal of psychology is to be able to describe, explain, predict, and control behavior and mental processes (Smith, Sarason, & Sarason, 1982; Wade & Tavris, 1998; Weiten, 2012). The overarching goal of the discipline, however, is to standardize sensations, performance, and thought patterns for two sectors in society: the mentally healthy and the mentally ill. Ultimately, psychology attempts to uncover the method to maintain mental health according to a prescribed standard.

Traditional psychology teaches about the creation of psychology as the unfolding of a science dedicated to the study of how people think, act, and feel. The development of psychology as a science came about as the result of questions about how humans act and interact in the world, which came from early Greek philosophers. These philosophers were interested in the relationship between the exploration of living things and the function of those things. In fact, the word *psychology* comes from the Greek words *psyche,* which means soul and *logos* or the study of a subject (Hothersall, 1995).

Psychological professionals are those who are trained to study human and animal behavior and mental processes (American Psychological Association, 2010). Historically, the science focused on the study of the psyche or soul and what it meant to think, behave, and feel "human." These three characteristics of being human—thoughts, behavior, and feelings—are also referred to as the **ABCs of psychology**.

The *A* stands for **affect,** which means *feeling.* Each human is expected to be able to express him or herself in a way that demonstrates being able to emotionally connect with him or herself and the environment. Whether the individual's emotional capacity is fully functional (being able to laugh appropriately when a situation requires or to cry when a situation requires) or not sets the stage for social judgment about his or her mental health. (This will be discussed in subsequent chapters.)

Psychology emphasizes not only the feelings and thoughts that individuals have, but the behaviors that may manifest what the person is feeling or thinking. This term is referred to simply as the *B* in the ABC model, **behavior**, or *actions*. Psychological researchers who believe that human behavior is the cornerstone of the human condition are called behavioral theorists or behaviorists (Ramnerö & Törnecke, 2008). Their studies in human behavior are partially responsible for how we understand happiness, mental disorders, love, criminal behavior, and cultural practices (Franklin, 2009).

In addition to concentrating on one's feelings, psychology also focuses on one's thoughts. The term used for *thoughts* in the ABC model is **cognition**. When psychologists study human thought patterns, they are interested not only in what the thought is, but why it comes about at a certain time; how much energy is placed on the thought (i.e., in trying to answer a complicated math problem); and its possible meaning to the individual. These researchers who study the process of thoughts are called cognitive psychologists.

As psychology began to develop as a science, many views were shared among the psychological community about how human behavior could be explained. These views are referred to as **paradigms**. Wundt's initial view of the explanation of human behavior was that it could be explained by simply asking the individual about his or her consciousness—in other words, the things of which the person is *aware*. It was later found that people are not always aware of what they are doing. Ever had a daydream during class? What happened? Several researchers considered this, but **Sigmund Freud**, an Austrian medical doctor decided to research what a person was thinking when unaware that he or she is thinking. Freud's research led to a change of assumption about human behavior, referred to as a paradigm shift. Freud later referred to this experience as the **unconscious**. He found that the unconscious was responsible for behavior that oftentimes could not be easily explained.

Paradigm shifts continued to include behavioral theorists such as **John B. Watson** and **B. F. Skinner,** who believed that human behavior was not unconscious but clearly orchestrated and intentional. Behaviorists believe that all behavior is purposeful, such that everything humans do is done with a point in mind. Even when mistakes are made, they are originally intentional, but get called "mistakes" because society disapproves of them. **Abraham Maslow** and **Carl Rogers**, critics of this paradigm, created another way to view human behavior, calling it **humanism**. Humanists believe that all humans are created with exceptional potential. Their potential becomes watered down only when people buy into the notion that they are not as good as others. Take, for instance, when a baby enters the world from the mother's womb. The baby, according to humanist theorists, has unlimited potential. Society then labels the baby "girl," "boy," "blue-eyed," "brown-eyed," "fat," or "thin," labels that get characterized as strengths or weaknesses. It is this kind of thinking and behavior that compromises the individual's ability to achieve to his or her fullest capabilities.

"Missing in Action" (Psychologists Not Mentioned in Early Psychology Textbooks)	
Mary Whiton Calkins (1863–1930)	First female elected as president of the American Psychological Association (APA), although Harvard would not confer a Ph.D. to her when she met the academic requirements for the degree.
Christine Ladd-Franklin (1847–1930)	Awarded a Ph.D. 40 years after completing the degree, Christine Ladd-Franklin did not let that deter her from making invaluable contributions to psychology with her theory of color vision perception in humans.
Francis Cecil Sumner (1895–1954)	Commonly referred to as the "father of Black psychology", Sumner was a counterpart of noted psychologist G. Stanley Hall. In fact, Hall was a mentor to Sumner, who was the first African American to be conferred (or granted) a PhD in psychology. (The PhD or doctorate of psychology is the highest—or *terminal*—degree offered from colleges and universities in scientific study.) While he did not achieve as much acclaim as his contemporaries, he is credited with explaining that Black Americans experience psychology differently than was previously researched by early Western psychologists.
Jorge ("George") Sanchez (1906–1972)	Considered the "father of Chicano (Mexican American) psychology" (Lahey, 2004), Sanchez' pivotal research and advocacy on the appropriateness of culture-fair testing revolutionized how tests are constructed, especially with relation to intelligence testing of nonnative English-speaking children.
Kenneth Clark (1914–2005) and **Mamie Phipps Clark** (1917–1983)	Psychological researchers who were also husband and wife, the Clarks produced award-winning research that was used during the 1954 Supreme Court ruling in *Brown v. Board of Education* of Topeka, Kansas. The Clarks' research on self-esteem and self-perception of Black American and European American children was used in the landmark case regarding the integration of U.S. public schools. Kenneth Clark was the first Black president of the APA (Lahey, 2004; Rathus, 1999).

Most students taking an introductory psychology course would be expected to be familiar with the theoretical and practical contributions of the early psychologists. However, students might be less familiar with the following psychologists: **Francis Cecil Sumner, Jorge Sanchez, Mary Whiton Calkins, Kenneth and Mamie Clark,** and **Christine Ladd-Franklin**. While the Freuds and Maslows are commonly discussed in traditional psychology courses, their **multicultural** peers, or people who come from various backgrounds, are not as widely discussed in such courses, yet their contributions are evident. Even more important to consider are the contributions of multicultural psychologists in order to get a more complete understanding of the science of psychology.

If Francis Cecil Sumner is considered the "father of Black psychology," then **Robert Guthrie** (1930–2005) is a close second. His book, *Even the Rat Was White: A Historical View of Psychology* (1976), was an incredible exposé into how few U.S. students of color (also referred to as "ethnic minority") were pursuing psychology degrees. As a result of this seminal work, more funding and resources for research on African Americans and other minority groups grew (O'Connor, 2001; Williams, 2005).

A New Way of Thinking

General psychology textbooks (Wade & Tavris, 2011; Weiten, 2012; Carter & Seifert, 2013) discuss very similar views of how human behavior can be predicted and controlled but only from a perspective (or way of thinking) that suggests there is one way to do and view people and research correctly. Anthropologists—scientists who study the role of culture on human behavior (including values and traditions, music, art)—refer to this perspective as the **emic** approach (Lett, 1996). The emic approach assumes that there is one way to do things because the particular "thing" comes from the perspective of members of the same group who have determined that their way is the right way.

In traditional psychology, groups who do not meet or conform to the expectations of a society have been considered abnormal. Their thoughts, behavior patterns, and emotions are neither welcomed nor validated (seen as "real") by those who are not members of their specific groups. The emic perspective is contrasted with the **etic** perspective. In the etic perspective, it is the outsider (oftentimes an interested observer or, possibly, a student) who attempts to bring universal understanding to a particular issue. An example of the etic perspective might be exchanging gifts at Christmas. Not everyone celebrates Christmas, but people do celebrate each other by giving and receiving gifts. So while some may not practice the Christian holiday of Christmas, they might still engage in a gift exchange during that time as a sign of relationship and solidarity within a family or among friends.

It should be noted that research with diverse populations has been referred to as "cross-cultural," "ethnic," "cultural," "multicultural" research. These terms are, for the most part, synonymous.

Multicultural Psychology Emerges

Here in the early 21st century, it is becoming increasingly clear that institutions and professional organizations require respectful and equitable treatment for all people regardless of ethnic/racial, socioeconomic, gender, and sexual orientation—in other words, culture (Sue et al., 1999; Flowers & Richardson, 1996; Boysen, Vogel, Cope, & Hubbard, 2009). In an attempt to explain what is seen as abnormal behavior, psychologists explain that Daphne Wright probably encountered what is referred to as an "intersection between [several] aspects" (Kich, 1996, p. 275) of her identity or human experience (Nettles & Balter, 2012). This experience, however, in traditional psychology often gets overlooked in order to understand the person as an organism, instead of as a multicultural being. The organism is, simply, a living thing. Yet, people are not simply living things but things that have feelings and experiences that are specific to them as individuals. This is the basis behind the development of multicultural psychology as the "fourth force" in psychology.

Within the field of multicultural psychology, there are multicultural counseling, cross-cultural psychology, social psychology, and other fields that focus on examining group behavior and development within cultural groups, unlike anthropology. Multicultural psychologists are not interested solely in group behavior but in how the group behavior affects individuals within the group as well as those who are not members of the group. *Multicultural counseling* focuses on the types of psychological **interventions** or strategies to assist people from different backgrounds. These interventions include face-to-face discussions that lead people to make changes in their behavior, thoughts, or feelings. This is also referred to in psychology as **therapy**.

Now, cross-cultural psychology (which has been used synonymously with multicultural psychology) and social psychology are interested in finding out how culture influences behavior. For the purposes of clarification throughout this book, multicultural psychology examines all aspects of human behavior based on cultural factors (e.g., age, spirituality, economics, gender, ethnicity, ability, and education) that can be seen when similar and dissimilar groups meet. Within these cultural factors are traditions and rituals that are native to the cultural group. These include art, music, foods, language, and communication.

One of the criticisms about multicultural psychology has been its proximity to anthropology, namely cultural anthropology. The difference between the two can be seen in that psychology is the scientific study of the mind and mental processes. Multicultural psychology studies these processes as they emerge when people who are similar and dissimilar from one another interact. Anthropology is the scientific study of the human origins and their development over time. Cultural anthropology is the scientific study of human technologies, economies, beliefs, and values within the larger umbrella of anthropology (Pauketat, 2001). While multicultural psychology focuses on the internal and external mental and behavioral forces that define a person's human experience, cultural anthropology concentrates on what makes the dimensions of humanity "human" regardless of mental process.

Each of the chapters in this textbook will call attention to specific aspects of multicultural psychology as they affect different cultural groups. While this textbook is not intended to give a complete discussion of each culture in the world, it will present a broad scope of the values, behaviors, language, and other dimensions of various cultures.

Chapter 1 calls the reader's attention to the history of multicultural psychology within the broader scientific study of human behavior, thoughts, and feelings. In this chapter, the changes of a vibrant society are discussed as giving way to growth of groups that did not previously exist (i.e., "hackers"). With the rise of these groups comes an increase in the need to know how to associate, integrate, and even separate one group from/with another.

Image © Ivonne Wierink, 2013. Used under license from Shutterstock, Inc.

Chapter 2 discusses the importance of research in discovering the elements that make investigation of cultures fascinating and valid. Without the information obtained through rigorous, intentional research, it is difficult to understand human behavior. Therefore, historical measurements of human interactions, influence of intelligence testing and personality assessments, and other sociocultural evaluations are discussed in this chapter.

Chapter 3 addresses culture from a more broad perspective. What individuals often think of as "background" is examined under the microscope of history, science, and group behavior to explain what culture is and how it gets carried on from generation to generation.

Multicultural psychology studies the elements that contribute to individual thoughts, feelings and behaviors. This young boy's multicultural identity is composed of biological, environmental and social conditions that affect how he engages the world.

Chapter 4 considers how communication and language affect human engagement. Simple terms or beliefs can be misconstrued from culture to culture, making the exchange of information not only difficult, but can lead to the creation of stereotypes, violence, or distancing between cultural groups. Difficult dialogues are encouraged in this chapter so that readers learn not only to engage others in communication patterns that may be unfamiliar, but necessary in order to improve human interactions.

Chapter 5 focuses on how stereotypes, prejudices, racism, and other forms of discrimination decrease human interactions. While many governments, agencies, and individuals may be able to identify discriminatory acts, this chapter discusses the origin of discrimination and the psychological factors that lead them to continue.

Chapter 6 compels the reading audience to think about gender and sexual orientation. These terms have, historically, been used interchangeably, causing there to be confusion about what it means to be a member of a particular gender or to have a certain sexual orientation. The chapter includes research on how what science knows about gender and sexual orientation contributes to a better understanding of the psychological experiences of people in those cultural groups.

Chapter 7 recognizes keen differences between immigrant and refugee cultures. These groups have often been categorized as having the same experiences regardless of whether they enter another country voluntarily or legally. Throughout the chapter, discussion about the process of immigration and the psychological impediments to full citizenship are contained in this chapter.

Chapter 8 looks at the incorporation of family and parenting styles as they affect cultural values, expectations, beliefs, and the other dynamics discussed throughout the chapters. Central to Chapter 8 is the psychological role of group dynamics, becoming an individual, and investment in relationships.

Chapter 9 considers the role of spirituality in cultural groups. While there are groups whose spirituality includes religions that are orthodox, uniform, and having existed for centuries, there are also groups where there is lack of clarity about the presence and practicality of organized spiritual belief systems. Both a sociological and psychological explanation of the role in cultural identity and stability are addressed in this chapter with a view toward the spiritual contribution to cultural groups.

Chapter 10 demonstrates the diversity of health concerns related to age, gender, socioeconomic background, and other cultural factors. The chapter concentrates on the fact that physical, mental, and social health is intertwined. Each is affected by the other. The statistical measures and qualitative data from individuals and the media all recognize disparities regarding health and healthcare, specifically in the United States.

Chapter 11 invites the readers to consider the previous 10 chapters and consider how social, environmental, and individual forces have affected human interaction both positively and negatively. With attention to the growing need for increased dialogue among cultural groups, Chapter 11 challenges readers to recapture the reality that each culture brings to the world.

FROM THERE TO HERE

As the study of multicultural psychology continues, it explores what is known about diverse groups using various research formats. Psychological research points to the fact that some people tend not to explore the world because of what they might find in it. The search might lead to **cognitive dissonance**, or an uncomfortable feeling one gets when holding two or more contradictory beliefs about something. That dissonance, the individual believes, could cause a shaking of the values and virtues attributed to the person's culture. Instead, individuals prefer to stay within their comfort zones by applying a **top-down approach** to thinking. This method employs the belief that "if it walks like a duck and quacks like a duck, it must be a duck." It is the type of thinking that does not want to be challenged, but instead to use what is known when making decisions. Using the top-down approach to social interaction typically ends badly because it suggests that what a person knows is real, authentic, and unchanging.

This same mind-set has prevailed throughout the centuries and continues today, where people are placed in certain social groups based on a limited understanding of ethnic, religious, gender, sexual orientation, socioeconomic, and other statuses. Here is where a vibrant, elderly man who is going blind as the result of a degenerative visual disorder may no longer be considered an asset to the human social order. Instead, he may be expected to leave his job or career, accept government assistance for his daily needs, and assume a position of obscurity in society. Yet, this man may choose to continue in his job or career, seek assistance in learning how to increase his awareness of the tools that are available to assist the visually impaired in their daily interactions, and become an advocate for the visually impaired. Instead of viewing the individual as a changed person, those in the field of multicultural psychology would see his visual impairment not as something negative, but as bringing a new sense of understanding to him as an individual.

A better method of understanding culture comes from a **bottom-up approach** (Maxwell, 2005; Ponterotto, 2010). This is the multicultural method that looks for opportunities to better understand situations and people. It is the bottom-up approach that says, "Teach me. I don't know everything." It is the mind-set that people use when they attempt to learn something for the first time: driving a car; falling in love; enrolling in college courses.

When a student begins to learn a new language, does that change who the student is or does it broaden his/her awareness of a new way to communicate? Does it make the student less able to think or socialize with his/her peers? Introductions to cultural milieus tend to enhance one's ability to engage with people who are similar and dissimilar from him or her. Yet, there is a difference between this student's ability to learn and apply these new words in context.

MAKING THE MOST OF THIS CHAPTER

Research demonstrates that as humans grow, they change (Okami, 2013; Weiten, 2013). Change is an inevitable part of the human experience and one that can be difficult to transcend if the individual chooses to be frustrated by it. When at all possible, humans prefer to be comfortable rather than uncomfortable. In science, this is referred to as *homeostasis* or the point at which balance between internal conditions and the external environment is achieved even when the external environment changes (Merriam-Webster, 2013). One expectation in reading and using the material in this book is that the reader will gain a better understanding of the interaction between people who are similar and dissimilar from one another; there may be resistance to change the way one thinks, feels, or behaves toward others.

Start with a more intentional look at what constitutes culture. What is clear when the reader begins the search for understanding is that many things become clearer, even those things for which the person was not searching. In this case, the elements of culture include all of those factors that make one who one is, whether owing to geographic location, visual acuity, speech patterns, or one's place among his or her generation. Each of these groups are composed of people who may share the values, traditions, histories, and language. So, what does it feel like to acknowledge being a part of a culture? One who wears glasses, for instance, is someone who has a problem with visual acuity. When that person goes to see the ophthalmologist, it is because this issue has limited the person's ability to see clearly. In talking with the ophthalmologist, it becomes clear that there is a shared language about the visual problem through use of terms such as 20×200 vision, astigmatism, bifocals, and frame shapes. Those who do not have these concerns are typically not used to using such language in their daily communications.

The reader is encouraged to acknowledge the feelings of being a member of a particular culture. (After all, this is a psychology course.) A few thoughts to consider when these feelings arise are the following:

- What types of cultures are there?
- Why is this hard for me [to read about or relate to the information in this chapter/book] about culture?
- Will acknowledging that this information may be true affect my interactions with people who are like me? Different from me? My parents/children? My significant other? My work associates? Those who work at my favorite restaurant/store?
- What can I do to explore (and validate) my own cultural awareness?
- Think about how you communicate with people who are similar to /different from you.

As you read this textbook, spend some time considering the psychological, historic, economic, and even biological reasons why people may feel similarly about change. While the intent of the book is not to change opinions, it is hoped that realities will be broadened; questions will be considered; and improvement will be made with respect to human interactions.

SUMMARY

Psychology, as a science and profession, has studied the thoughts, feelings, and behaviors of human beings. Traditional psychology specifically studies the thoughts, feelings, and behaviors of individuals in society, often without attention to other dimensions such as culture or health. Multicultural psychology is the scientific study of how groups identify, create, and engage in cultural activities and values. These values result in feelings, thoughts, and behaviors that distinguish one culture from another.

THINK ABOUT IT

What is your "cultural autobiography?"

Write a two-page cultural autobiography detailing one aspect of your culture. There are a number of cultural choices from which to choose. A few examples could include, being

- the eldest member of your family
- the only one of your gender in your family
- an athlete
- an "A" student
- an employee
- a glasses-wearer
- married/single
- a college student
- from a particular geographic location
- from a certain socioeconomic background
- a parent
- spiritual/religious

CHAPTER 2

Reviewing Scientific Research with Diverse Populations

One of the points we tried to make in Chapter 1 was that most findings in psychology are limited to the parameters of the research that generated them, and cultural psychology examines the boundaries of that knowledge by altering *one* of those methodological parameters-the cultural background of the participants in the studies. Yet, cross-cultural research is conducted within its own set of parameters. Thus not only is it important to be able to read cross-cultural research and understand its contributions to knowledge; you also need to be able to evaluate it on its own merits. As active consumers of research in your everyday and academic lives, you need to review cross-cultural research with a critical but fair and open mind, accessing the literature directly and evaluating it with established criteria for quality. And you should be able to evaluate the research that we present in this book.

This chapter describes some of the most important issues that determine the quality of cross-cultural research. Let's begin by discussing the types of studies that exist in cultural psychology.

TYPES OF CROSS-CULTURAL RESEARCH

Method Validation Studies

All researchers are concerned with issues concerning **validity** and **reliability** of measurement. Validity refers to whether or not a scale, test, or measure accurately measures what it is supposed to measure. Reliability refers to whether it measures it consistently. These concepts are extremely important to all researchers, cross-cultural or not.

One of the things that we have learned is that cross-cultural researchers *cannot* simply take a scale or measure that was developed and validated in one culture and use it in another. This is because even if that scale was validated in one culture, there is no reason to assume that it is equally valid in any other culture. It would have to be equivalently valid in all the cultures it was to be used; else, data derived from its measurement would not be comparable across cultures.

Because cross-cultural researchers are concerned with equivalence in validity, and because they know that just translating a measure does *not* ensure measurement equivalence (we will discuss this concept more below), there is a need to conduct studies to test the reliability and validity of measures in different cultures in order to be sure they can be used in the various cultures, thereby ensuring the cross-cultural measurement equivalence of the measure used. **Cross-cultural** validation studies do so. They examine whether a measure of a psychological construct that was originally generated in a single culture is applicable, meaningful, and most importantly psychometrically equivalent (that is, equally reliable and valid) in another culture. These studies do not test a specific hypothesis about cultural differences; rather, they test the equivalence of psychological measures and tests for use in other cross-cultural comparative research, and they are important to conduct *before* cross-cultural comparisons.

Indigenous Cultural Studies

Another type of study conducted by cultural psychologists is **indigenous cultural studies**. These are characterized by rich descriptions of complex theoretical models of culture that predict and explain cultural differences. A basic philosophy underlying this approach is that psychological processes and behavior can only be understood within the cultural milieu within which it occurs; thus to understand mental processes and behavior requires an in-depth analysis of the cultural systems that produce and support those processes and behaviors, linking them to each other. Mesquita (Mesquita, 2001; Mesquita & Karasawa, 2002), for instance, describes how cultural systems produce different concepts of the self, which in turn produce different types of specific concerns. According to her framework, individualistic cultures encourage the development of independent senses of self that encourage a focus on personal concerns and the view that the emotions signal internal, subjective feelings; collectivistic cultures, contrastingly, encourage the development of interdependent senses of self that encourage a focus on one's social worth and the worth of one's ingroup and the notion that emotions reflect something about interpersonal relationships.

This type of research has its roots in anthropology, such as in the works of Margaret Mead or Ruth Benedict. Early cross-cultural researchers such as John Berry and Beatrice Whiting made use of such methods. More recently, this methodology has been used to explain cultural differences in a number of psychological processes including morality (Shweder, 1993), attributional style (Nisbett, Peng, Choi, & Norenzayan, 2001), eye movements when viewing scenes (Masuda & Nisbett, 2001), the nature of unspoken thoughts (Kim, 2002), the need for high self-esteem (Heine, Lehman, Markus, & Kitayama, 1999), and many others. We will be discussing much of this research throughout the book.

Cross-Cultural Comparisons

Cross-cultural comparisons are studies that compare cultures on some psychological variable of interest. Cross-cultural comparisons serve as the backbone of cross-cultural research and are the most prevalent type of cross-cultural study. Several writers have referred to the different phases through which cross-cultural research has evolved over the years (Bond, 2004b; Matsumoto & Yoo, 2006). Different types of cross-cultural studies are prominent at different times, each with its own set of methodological issues that have an impact on its quality. Below we'll discuss the issues most relevant to the conduct of valid and reliable cross-cultural comparative research today.

TYPES OF CROSS-CULTURAL COMPARISONS

Exploratory vs. Hypothesis Testing

There are four important dimensions that underlie and characterize different types of cross-cultural comparisons. The first involves the distinction between **exploratory** and **hypothesis-testing studies**. Exploratory studies are designed to examine the existence of cross-cultural similarities and differences. Researchers tend to stay "close to the data" in exploratory studies. Hypothesis-testing studies are designed to examine why cultural differences may exist. Thus they make larger inferential jumps by testing theories of cross-cultural similarities' and differences. Unfortunately, the validity of these inferential jumps is often threatened by cross-cultural biases and inequivalence (see below). The methodological strengths and weaknesses of exploratory and hypothesis-testing studies mirror each other. The main strength of exploratory studies is their broad scope for identifying cross-cultural similarities and differences, which is particularly important in under-researched domains of cross-cultural psychology. The main weakness of such studies is their limited capability to address the causes of the observed differences. The focused search of similarities and differences in hypothesis-testing studies leads to more substantial contribution to theory development and explicit attempts to deal with rival explanations but is less likely to discover interesting differences outside of the realm of the tested theory.

Presence or Absence of Contextual Factors

The second dimension refers to the presence or absence of **contextual factors** in the design. Contextual factors may involve characteristics of the participants (such as socioeconomic status, education, and age) or their cultures (such as economic development and religious institutions). From a methodological perspective, contextual factors involve any variable that can explain, partly or fully, observed cross-cultural differences (Poortinga, van de Vijver, Joe, & van de Koppel, 1987). Including such factors in a study will enhance its validity and help rule out the influence of biases and inequivalence (more below) because an evaluation of their influence can help to (dis)confirm their role in accounting for the cultural differences observed. For example, administering a measure of response styles can help to evaluate the extent to which cross-cultural differences on extroversion are influenced by these styles. Hypothesis-testing studies generally need to include contextual variables.

Structure vs. Level Oriented

What is compared across cultures is addressed in the third dimension, which is the distinction between **structure-** and **level-oriented studies.** The former involve comparisons of constructs (e.g., Is depression conceptualized in the same way across cultures?), their structures (Can depression be assessed by the same constituent elements in different cultures?), or their relationships with other constructs (Do depression and anxiety have the same relationshipin all countries?). The latter involve the comparisons of scores (Do individuals from different cultures show the same level of depression?). Structure-oriented studies focus on relationships among variables and attempt to identify similarities and differences in these relations across cultures. Level-oriented studies ask whether people of different cultures have different mean levels of different variables.

Individual vs. Ecological (Cultural) Level

A fourth dimension underlying cross-cultural comparisons concerns individual vs. ecological (cultural) levels of analysis. Individual-level studies are the typical type of study in psychology, in which individual participants provide data and are the unit of analysis. **Ecological-** or **cultural-level studies** use countries or cultures as the unit of analysis. Data may be obtained from individuals in different cultures, but they are often summarized or averaged for each culture and those averages are used as data points for each culture. Or country data are obtained from other sources (such as population statistics, average temperature or rainfall). Table 2.1 gives an example of how data are set up in an individual-level study, which is the typical way psychology studies are conducted, compared with an ecological-level study.

Ecological-level studies comprise an important part of studies in cultural psychology. Many cross-cultural researchers have come to realize that just showing a difference between two cultural groups does not demonstrate that the difference occurs because of any cultural difference between them. After all, differences between two cultural groups could occur because of many factors, including and not including culture. Thus researchers became interested in identifying the kinds of psychological dimensions that underlie cultures in order to better understand cultures on a subjective level (as opposed to an objective level; see Triandis, 1972) and to explain differences better when observed in research.

Individual-Level Study			Ecological-Level Study		
Level of Analysis	Self-Esteem	Academic Performance	Level of Analysis	Self-Esteem	Academic Performance
Participant 1	Participant 1's score on self-esteem	Participant 1's score on academic performance	Country 1	Country 1's mean on self-esteem	Country 1's mean on academic performance
Participant 2	Participant 2's score on self-esteem	Participant 2's score on academic performance	Country 2	Country 2's mean on self-esteem	Country 2's mean on academic performance
Participant 3	Participant 3's score on self-esteem	Participant 3's score on academic performance	Country 3	Country 3's mean on self-esteem	Country 3'5 mean on academic performance.
Participant 4	Participant 4's score on self-esteem	Participant 4's score on academic performance	Country 4	Country 4's mean on self-esteem	Country 4's mean on academic performance
Participant 5	Participant 5's score on self-esteem	Participant 5's score on academic performance	Country 5	Country 5's mean on self-esteem	Country 5's mean on academic performance
Etc.	Etc.	Etc.	Etc.	Etc.	Etc.

Table 2.1 A Comparison of the Data Used in an Individual-Level Study, Typical in Psychology, vs. an Ecological-Level Study, Comparing the Relationship Between Self-Esteem and Academic Performance

The most-well-known ecological-level study of culture is Hofstede's seminal work. In his original work, Hofstede (1980) reported data from 40 countries, and soon thereafter from an additional 13 (Hofstede, 1984). Most recently, he has reported data from 72 countries involving the responses of more than 117,000 employees of a multinational business organization, spanning over 20 languages and seven occupational levels to his 63 work-related values items (Hofstede, 2001). Respondents completed a 160-item questionnaire; 63 were related to work values. Hofstede conducted ecological-level analyses on the country means of the 63 items and generated three dimensions that he suggested could describe the cultures of the countries sampled. Hofstede split one of the dimensions into two, based on theoretical reasoning and the fact that controlling for country-level gross national product produced a different set of scores. This resulted in his well-known set of four dimensions, introduced in Chapter 1: Individualism versus Collectivism, Power Distance, Uncertainty Avoidance, and Masculinity versus Femininity. Later Hofstede incorporated a fifth dimension called "Long- versus Short-Term Orientation" (Hofstede, 2001; Hofstede & Bond, 1984), which was derived from Bond's work on Asian values (Connection, 1987).

In recent years, individual- and cultural-level data have been combined in what are known as **multi-level studies**. These are studies that use data from two (or even more) levels, and incorporate the use of sophisticated statistical techniques that examine the relationship of data at one level to later at another. For example, multi-level studies can examine how individual differences in performance on a cognitive task (level 1) may be related to personality traits of those individuals (level 2) and how those personality traits may be related to cultural values or other ecological variables (level 3). We predict that most cross-cultural comparisons in the future will involve this type of multi-level approach.

DESIGNING CROSS-CULTURAL COMPARATIVE RESEARCH

Getting the Right Research Question

By far the most important part of any study, cross-cultural or not, is knowing what research questions to ask in the first place. Because cultural differences are relatively easy to obtain, especially the greater the cultural distance between the groups being compared, researchers should remember that the purpose of conducting research is to contribute to a body of knowledge (the literature), and any consideration of research designs starts first with a comprehensive and functional knowledge of that literature so that one understands what gaps in the knowledge exist and what research questions should be addressed to contribute to that knowledge. It happens all too often that researchers exclusively focus on designing the methodology of a study without considering adequately what research question should be addressed in the first place. Sophisticated statistical techniques and elegant research designs cannot "salvage" studies that are neither novel nor insightful.

Understanding why any study is to be conducted in the first place leads to questions about how to conduct it, which is a discussion in the realm of research methodology. Questions related to the taxonomy described above apply here. Is the study exploratory in nature or hypothesis testing? Does it or should it include contextual variables? Is it structure oriented or level oriented? And what is the level of analysis? Of course, no one study can do everything, and it's usually better to do something of limited scope very well than to try to conduct a study that addresses too much not so well at all.

With regard to studies that are designed to document cultural differences, it is important to keep in mind that the field has gone much beyond the need to merely document differences between two or more cultures on any psychological variable. Indeed, because of cultural distance, it is fairly easy to document differences on something, provided the cultures being compared are disparate enough. Instead, one of the major challenges that faces cross-cultural researchers today concerns how to isolate the source of such differences, and identify the active cultural (vs. noncultural) ingredients that produced those differences. It is in the empirical documentation of those active cultural ingredients that cross-cultural research designs need to pay close attention to.

In doing so, researchers need to pay attention to a number of theoretical and empirical issues (see Matsumoto & Yoo, 2006, for a more complete discussion). For example, is the source of the differences to be explained cultural or not? Examining these questions forces researchers to have a definition of what culture is and to find ways of objectively measuring it. Once the active cultural ingredients that produce differences are identified, there is a level of analysis issue. Cultural variables exist on the group and individual levels, and studies themselves can be entirely 011 the individual or cultural level, or involve a mixture of the two in varying degrees with multiple levels. Different variables at different levels of analysis bring with them different theoretical and methodological implications, and require different interpretations of the research literature. When individual-level cultural variables are incorporated in a study, researchers need to distinguish between them and non-cultural variables on the individual level such as personality. Certainly a variable is not "cultural" just because a researcher says so; there needs to be a well thought-out rationale that is based in theory and data that supports the identification and distinction of such variables.

THINK ABOUT IT

Consider one of the cultural research studies below. What cultures are being studied? Discuss the hypotheses of the study; the ethical implications of the study; and the findings.

1. Auschwitz Twin Experiments (Mengele, 1943)
2. The Stanford Prison Experiment (Zimbardo, 1971)
3. Doll Experiments (Clark, 1940's)
4. Tuskegee Syphilis Experiments (1932–1972)

Another question that researchers must face in designing studies concerns their theoretical model of how things work. A commonly held view that culture "produces" differences in a fairly top-down fashion is a theoretical bias held by many. But how do we know that to be true, and more importantly, how does one demonstrate that empirically? It may very well be that individual-level psychological processes and behavior produce culture in a bottom-up fashion, or that both top-down and bottom-up processes occur simultaneously. Regardless of how one believes things are put together, it behooves researchers to adopt research design strategies that are commensurate with their beliefs and models.

Designs that Establish Linkages Between Culture and Individual Mental Processes and Behaviors

As mentioned above, a study that merely documents differences between cultures on some psychological variable does not say anything about whether the source of the differences is cultural or not (thus there are severe limitations to exploratory studies in the types of interpretations that can be made from data). Thus most researchers have come to realize that it's important to empirically establish linkages between the contents of culture and the variables of interest in the study. This has led to the emergence of a class of studies called **linkage studies** that attempt to do just that. There are two types of linkage studies conducted in the field today: unpackaging studies and experiments.

Unpackaging Studies

Unpackaging studies are extensions of basic cross-cultural comparisons, but include the measurement of a variable (contextual factor) that assesses the contents of culture that are thought to produce the differences on the variable being compared across cultures. The underlying thought to these studies is that cultures are like onions, for which layer after layer needs to be peeled off until nothing is left. Poortinga, van de Vijver, Joe, and van de Koppel (1987) expressed the view this way:

> "In our approach culture is a summary label, a catchword for all kinds of behavior differences between cultural groups, but within itself, of virtually no explanatory value. Ascribing intergroup differences in behavior, e.g., in test performance, to culture does not shed much light on the nature of these differences. It is one of the main tasks of cross-cultural psychology to peel off cross-cultural differences, i.e., to explain these differences in terms of specific antecedent variables, until in the end they have disappeared and with them the variable culture. In our approach culture is taken as a concept without a core. From a methodological point of view, culture can be considered as an immense set of often loosely interrelated independent variables."

In unpackaging studies, "culture" as an unspecified variable is replaced by more specific variables in order to truly explain cultural differences. These variables are called **context variables**, and should be measured to examine the degree to which they can account for cultural differences. When measured, researchers then examine the degree to which they statistically account for the differences in the comparison. If the context variables do indeed statistically account for differences, then the researchers are empirically justified in claiming that that specific aspect of culture-that is, that context variable-was related to the differences observed. If they do not, then researchers know that that specific context variable did *not* produce the observed differences. In either case, researchers are empirically justified in making claims about aspects of culture being related to the variables of interest.

Individual-Level Measures of Culture

Over the past few years, one of the more common types of context variables used in research has been **individual-level measures of culture**. These are measures that assess a variable on the individual level that is thought to be a product of culture. To date, a number of different types of such measures have been used. By far, the most common dimension of culture operationalized on the individual level is Individualism versus Collectivism (IC). As mentioned in Chapter 1, this dimension was first coined by Hofstede (2001). Thereafter, Harry Triandis, a noted cross-cultural scientist, championed the cause for this dimension and argued that the IC framework organizes and explains many different types of cultural differences (Triandis, 1994, 1995), many of which we will discuss throughout this book.

Because of the large emphasis on IC as a grounding theoretical framework of culture, scientists have developed a number of ways to measure it on the individual level (in order to use it as a context variable in hypothesis-testing research). Triandis himself was a leader in this movement, producing many different types of individual-level measures of IC. Hui (1984, 1988), for example, developed the Individualism-Collectivism (INDCOL) scale to measure an individual's IC tendencies in relation to six collectivities (spouse, parents and children, kin, neighbors, friends, and coworkers and classmates). Later Triandis, Leung, Villareal, and Clack (1985) used items from the INDCOL and further broadened them by adding senarios and other ratings. Triandis et al. (1986) used items from Hui (1984, Triandis et al. (1985), and items suggested by colleagues in other cultures to measure IC, Triandis et al. (1988) used items from the INDCOL and U.S.-originated items to measure IC. Triandis, McCusker, and Hui (1990) used a multiple-method approach to measuring IC that represented an evolution not only in method but also in thinking. These researchers viewed IC as a cultural syndrome that includes values, beliefs, attitudes, and behaviors (see also, Triandis, 1996); they treated the various psychological domains of subjective culture as an entire collective rather than as separate aspects of culture. Their multiple-method approach included ratings of the social content of the self, perceptions of homogeneity of ingroups and outgroups, attitude and value ratings, and perceptions of social behavior as a function of social distance. Participants were classified as either individualist or collectivist on the basis of their scores on each method. On the individual level, Triandis refers to individualism and collectivism as **idiocentrism** and **allocentrism**, respectively (Triandis et al., 1986).

Triandis and his colleagues (Singelis, Triandis, Bhawuk, & Gelfand, 1995) developed measures that include items assessing a revised concept of individualism and collectivism they call "horizontal and vertical individualism and collectivism," representing yet further advances in the conceptual understanding of Ice. In horizontal collectivism, individuals see themselves as members of ingroups in which all members are equal. In vertical collectivism, individuals see themselves as members of ingroups that are characterized by hierarchical or status relationships. In horizontal individualism, individuals are autonomous and equal. In vertical individualism, individuals are autonomous but unequal.

Matsumoto, Weissman, Preston, Brown, and Kupperbusch (1997) also developed a measure of IC for use on the individual level that assesses context-specific IC tendencies in interpersonal situations—the IC Interpersonal Assessment Inventory (ICIAI). Matsumoto, Consolacion, Yamada, Suzuki, Franklin, Paul et al. (2002) used it in an unpackaging study examining American and Japanese cultural differences in judgments of emotion. They showed that Americans and Japanese differed in how strongly they perceived facial expressions of emotion. More importantly, however, they also demonstrated that these differences were linked with differences in individual-level measurement of IC (using the ICIAI), and that this linkage empirically accounted for the cultural differences in judgment of faces. Thus, they were empirically justified in claiming that IC accounted for this difference, exemplifying the utility of an unpackaging study.

A meta-analysis of 83 studies examining group differences on Individualism versus Collectivism (IC) and the possible contribution of IC to various psychological processes reported that European Americans were more individualistic and less collectivistic than others in general (Oyserman, Coon, & Kemmelmeier, 2002). But they were not more individualistic than African Americans or Latinos, nor were they less collectivistic than Japanese or Koreans, contrary to common stereotypes. In addition, this review indicated that IC had moderate effects on self-concept and relationality and large effects on attributions and cognitive styles across the studies examined. These findings in some way challenged researchers notions about how IC may be the source of cultural differences and spurred the way to the search for other kinds of context variables.

Self-Construal Scales

Spurred on by the IC framework, Markus and Kitayama (1991b) proposed that individualistic and collectivistic cultures differed in the kinds of self-concepts they fostered, with individualistic cultures encouraging the development of independent self-construals, and collectivistic cultures encouraging the development of interdependent self-construals (we will discuss these more fully in Chapter 13). This theoretical advance led to the development of scales measuring independence and interdependence on the individual level, most notably the Self-Construal Scale (Singelis, 1994). Using this scale, cultural differences in self-esteem and embarassability were empirically linked to individual differences on these types of self-construals, again exemplifying the utility of unpacking studies (Singelis, Bond, Sharkey, & Lai, 1999).

Personality

Any variable that is thought to vary on the cultural level and that may be thought to affect psychological processes can be used as context variables. One such possibility is personality. There are differences in aggregate personality traits across cultures. The United States, Australia, and New Zealand, for example, are noted for their relatively high degrees of extraversion, while France, Italy, and the French Swiss are associated with high levels of neuroticism. Thus, cultural differences may be a product of different levels of personality traits in each culture.

For instance, Matsumoto (2006a) measured emotion regulation—the ability that individuals have to modify and channel their emotions—in the United States and Japan, and demonstrated the existence of cultural differences in emotion regulation. He also measured several personality traits, and demonstrated that the personality traits known as extraversion, neuroticism, and conscientiousness were linked to emotion regulation, and accounted for the cultural differences in it. Thus, what were apparent "cultural" differences on a variable could be explained by differences in aggregate levels of personality between the two cultures studied.

Cultural Practices

Another important type of context variable that is important in linkage studies are those that assess cultural practices such as child-rearing, the nature of interpersonal relationships, or cultural worldviews. Heine and Renshaw (2002), for instance, showed that Americans and Japanese were different in their liking of others, and that differences in liking were linked to different cultural practices. Americans liked others they thought were similar to them or shared, their own views. For Japanese, liking was related to familiarity and interdependence with others.

Experiments

Another major type of linkage study is experiments. Experiments are studies in which researchers create conditions to establish cause-effect relationships. Participants are generally assigned randomly to participate in the conditions, and researchers then compare results across conditions. These studies are fundamentally different from cross-cultural comparisons because in cross-cultural comparisons, researchers cannot create the cultural groups, nor can they randomly assign participants to those groups. (Cross-cultural comparisons are generally examples of what are known as quasi-experimental designs.) True experiments, however, differ because researchers create the conditions and assign participants to those conditions.

There are different types of experiments conducted in cross-cultural psychology today. Here we cover two types: priming studies and behavioral studies.

Priming Studies Priming studies are those that involve experimentally manipulating the mindsets of participants and measuring the resulting changes in behavior. These are interesting because researchers have attempted to manipulate mindsets supposedly related to culture in order to see if participants behave differently as a function of the primed mindset. If they do, researchers can infer that the primed cultural mind set caused the observed differences in behavior, there by providing a link between a cultural product (the mindset) and a psychological process (the behavior).

One of the first studies that primed culitural contents of the mind was that by Trafimow, Triandis, and Goto (1991). In this study, American and Chinese participants were primed to think in either a private or collective, group-oriented way. Participants primed in the private way read instructions that stated:

> For the next two minutes, you will not need to write anything. Please think of what makes you different from your family and friends.

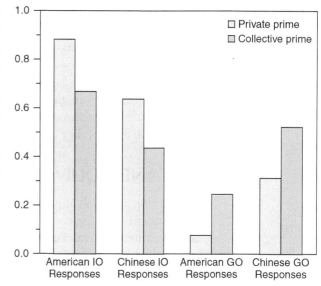

Figure 2.1 Amount of Individually Oriented (IO) and Group-Oriented (GO)

Source: Responses for Americans and Chinese in Trafimow et al. (1991).

Participants primed in the collective, group-oriented way, however, were primed with these instructions:

> For the next two minutes, you will not need to write anything. Please think of what you have in common with your family and friends. What do they expect you to do?

Then all participants were asked to complete a self-attitude instrument that involved their completing a series of incomplete questions that started "I am." Their responses were then coded according to whether it was individually oriented or group oriented. The findings indicated that, as expected, Americans as a whole produced more individually oriented responses than the Chinese, while the Chinese produced more group-oriented responses. But, the results also showed that the priming worked. Individuals who were primed privately—that is, to think about how they were different from others—produced more individually oriented responses, regardless of whether they were American or Chinese. Likewise, individuals who were primed collectively—that is, to think about how they were similar to others—produced more group-oriented responses, regardless of whether they were American or Chinese (Figure 2.1).

Behavioral Studies Perhaps the most stringent experiments involve manipulations of actual environments and the observation of changes in behaviors as a function of these environments. For example, it is commonly thought that members of collectivistic cultures cooperate more with each other because cooperation is necessary for groups to function effectively and because of the group-oriented nature of collectivism. Two classic studies on cooperative behavior will elucidate the importance of experiments in identifying what about cultures produce such differences. In the first study, Yamagishi (1986) used a questionnaire to categorize Japanese participants who were high trusters and low trusters; all of the participants then participated in an experiment in which they could cooperate with others by giving money to them, either with a sanctioning system that provided for punishments or without such a system. The conditions, therefore, were the presence or absence of the sanctioning system. The results indicated that high trusters did indeed cooperate more than low trusters without the sanctioning system; when the sanctioning system was in effect, however, low trusters cooperated more than did the high trusters.

Yamagishi (1988) then replicated this study in the United States and compared American and Japanese responses. He found the same results for Americans as he did for the Japanese; when there was no sanctioning system, high-trusting Americans cooperated more than low-trusting Americans. When there was a sanctioning system, the findings reversed. Moreover, there were no differences between the Americans and the Japanese when the sanctioning system was in effect. This suggests, therefore, that the greater cooperation observed in Japanese culture exists because of the sanctioning system within which individuals exist; when Americans were placed in that same type of system, they behaved in the same ways.

BIAS AND EQUIVALENCE

In designing and, evaluating cross-cultural research, no concepts are more important than equivalence and bias. **Bias** refers to differences that do not have exactly the same meaning within and across cultures. **Equivalence** is a state or condition of similarity in conceptual meaning and empirical method between cultures that allows. comparisons to be meaningful. These constructs go hand in hand; bias refers to state of non-equivalence, and equivalence refers to a state of no bias.

In its strictest sense, if there is any bias in any aspect of a cross-cultural comparative study, then the comparison loses its meaning (and may in fact be meaningless). Bias (or lack of equivalence) in a cross-cultural study creates the proverbial situation of comparing apples and oranges. Only if the theoretical framework and hypotheses have equivalent meaning in the cultures being compared—and if the methods of data collection, management, and analysis have equivalent meaning–will the results from that comparison be meaningful. Apples in one culture can be compared only to apples in another.

Thus it's important for cross-cultural researchers to understand the many aspects of their studies that may be culturally biased and work to establish equivalence in them. Below we discuss five major areas of bias: conceptual bias, method bias, measurement bias, response bias, and interpretational bias.

Conceptual Bias

A major concern of cross-cultural research is the equivalence in meaning of the overall theoretical framework being tested and the specific hypotheses being addressed in the first place. If these are not equivalent across the cultures participating in the study, then the data obtained from them are not comparable because they mean different things. If, however, the theoretical framework and hypotheses are equivalent across the participating cultures, the study may be meaningful and relevant.

For example, people trained to do research in the United States or Europe may be bound by a sense of "logical determinism" and "rationality" that is characteristic of such formal and systematic educational systems. In addition, because we are so used to drawing two-dimensional theories of behavior on paper, that medium affects the way we think about people and psychology. People of other cultures who have not been exposed to such an educational system or who are not used to reducing their thoughts about the world onto a two-dimensional space may not think in the same way. If this is the case, then a real question arises as to whether a theory created within a Western European or American cultural framework is meaningful in the same way to people who do not share that culture. If the theory is not meaningful in the same way, then it is not equivalent.

Method Bias

Sampling Bias

There are two issues with regard to sampling bias, which refers to whether cross-cultural samples can be compared. One concerns whether the samples are appropriate representatives of their culture. Most cross-cultural studies are, in fact, not just cross-cultural; they are cross-city, and more specifically, cross-university studies. A "cross-cultural comparison" between Americans and Mexicans may, for instance, involve data collected in Seattle and Mexico City. Are the participants in Seattle representative of American culture? Would they provide the same responses as participants from Beverly Hills, the Bronx, or Wichita? Would the participants in Mexico City provide the same results as those in San Luis Portosi, Guadalajara, or the Yucatan Peninsula? Of course the answer is "we don't know," and it is important for cross-cultural researchers, and consumers of that research (you) to recognize that sound cross-cultural comparisons would entail the collection of data from multiple sites within the same cultural group, either in the same study or across studies, to demonstrate the replicability of a finding across different samples within the same culture.

A second question concerning sampling bias concerns whether the samples are equivalent on noncultural demographic variables, such as age, sex, religion, socio-economic status, work, and other characteristics. For example, imagine comparing data from a sample of 50 Americans from Los Angeles with 50 individuals from Bombay, India. Clearly, the Americans and the Indians come from entirely different backgrounds-different socioeconomic classes, different educational levels, different social experiences, different forms of technology, different religious backgrounds, and so on.

To deal with this issue, researchers need to find ways of controlling these non-cultural demographic factors when comparing data across cultures. They do this in one of two ways: experimentally controlling them by holding them constant in the selection of participants (e.g., conducting studies in which only females of a certain age can participate in the study in all cultures) or statistically controlling them when analyzing data.

A conceptual problem arises in cross-cultural research in that some noncultural demographic characteristics are inextricably intertwined with culture such that researchers cannot hold them constant across samples in a comparison. For example, there are differences in the meaning and practice of religions across cultures that make them oftentimes inextricably bound to culture. Holding religion constant across cultures does not address the issue because being Catholic in the United States does not mean the same thing as being Catholic in Japan or Malaysia. Randomly sampling without regard to religion will result in samples that differ not only on culture but also on religion (to the extent that one can separate the influences of the two). Thus presumed cultural differences often reflect religious differences across samples as well. The same is often true for socioeconomicstatus (SES), as there are vast differences in SES across cultural samples from around the world.

Linguistic Bias

One arena in which potential bias in cross-cultural research becomes quickly apparent is in language. Cross-cultural research is unique because it often involves collecting data in multiple languages, and researchers need to establish the linguistic equivalence of the research protocols. **Linguistic bias** refers to whether the research protocols—items on questionnaires, instructions, etc.—used in a cross-cultural study are semantically equivalent across the various languages included in the study.

There are generally two procedures used to establish linguistic equivalence. One is known as **back translation** (Brislin, 1970). Back translation involves taking the research protocol in one language, translating it to the other language, and having someone else translate it back to the original. If the back-translated version is the same as the original, they are generally considered equivalent. If it is not, the procedure is repeated until the back-translated version is the same as the original. The concept underlying this procedure is that the end product must be a semantic equivalent to the original language. The original language is **decentered** through this process (Brislin, 1970, 1993), with any culture-specific concepts of the original langooge eliminated or translated equivalently into the target language. That is, culture-specific meanings and connotations are gradually eliminated from the research protocols so that what remains is something that is the closest semantic equivalent in each language. Because they are linguistic equivalents, successfully back-translated protocols are comparable in cross-cultural hypothesis-testing research.

A second approach to establishing language equivalence is the committee approach, in which several bilingual informants collectively translate a research, protocol into a target language. They debate the various forms, words, and phrases that can be used in the target language, comparing them with their understanding of the language of the original protocol. The product of this process reflects a translation that is the shared consensus of a linguistically equivalent protocol across languages and cultures.

Researchers may combine the two approaches. A protocol may be initially translated and back-translated. Then the translation and back-translation can be used as an initial platform from which a translation committee works on the protocol, modifying the translation in ways they deem most appropriate, using the back-translation as a guideline.

Procedural Bias

The issue of bias and equivalence also applies to the procedures used to collect data in different cultures. For instance in many universities across the United States, students enrolled in introductory psychology classes are strongly encouraged to participate as research subjects in partial fulfillment of class requirements. American students generally expect to participate in research as part of their academic experience, and many American students are "research-wise."

Customs differ in other countries. In some countries, professors simply collect data from their students or require them to participate at a research laboratory. In some countries, students may consider it a privilege rather than a chore or course requirement to participate in an international study. Thus, expectations about and experience with research participation may differ.

All the decisions researchers make in any other type of study are made in cross-cultural studies as well. But those decisions can mean different things in different countries. Laboratory or field, day or night, questionnaire or observation—all these decisions may have different meanings in different cultures. Cross-cultural researchers need to confront these differences in their work and establish procedures, environments, and settings that are equivalent across the cultures being compared. By the same token, consumers need to be aware of these possible differences when evaluating cross-cultural research.

Measurement Bias

Perhaps the most important arena with regard to bias and equivalence may concern the issue of measurement. **Measurement bias** refers to the degree to which measures used to collect data in different cultures are equally valid and reliable. As mentioned above, validity refers to whether a measure accurately measures what it is supposed to measure; reliability refers to how consistently a measure measures what it is supposed to measure.

To be sure, one of the most important lessons to learn about cross-cultural research methods is that linguistic equivalence alone does not guarantee measurement equivalence. This is because even if the words being used in the two languages are the same, there is no guarantee that those words have exactly the same meanings, with the same nuances, in the two cultures. A successful translation gives the researcher protocols that are the closest linguistic equivalents in two or more languages. However, they still may not be exactly the same. In translating the English word *anger,* for example, we might indeed find an equivalent word in Cantonese or Spanish. But would it have the same connotations, strength, and interpretation in those languages as it does in English? It is very difficult to find exact translation equivalents of most words. Thus, cross-cultural researchers need to be concerned with measurement equivalence in addition to linguistic equivalence.

One way to think about measurement equivalence is on the conceptual level. Different cultures may conceptually define a construct differently and/or measure it differently. Just because something has the same name in two or more cultures does not mean that it has the same meaning

(Wittgenstein, 1953/1968, cited in Poortinga, 1989) or that it can be measured in the same way. If a concept means different things to people of different cultures, or if it is measured in different ways in different cultures, then comparisons are meaningless. Cross-cultural researchers need to be keenly aware of the issue of equivalence with regard to their conceptual definitions and empirical operationalization of the variables (the way researchers conceptually define a variable and measlJre it) in their study.

Past debates concerning cross-cultural studies-of intelligence highlight issues concerning conceptual equivalence, Intelligence typically is thought to consist of verbal and analytical critical-thinking skills and tests such as the Wechsler Adult Intelligence Scale (WAIS) have been widely used to assess IQ. Different cultures, however, may have a different conception of what constitutes intelligence. For example, a culture may consider nobility of character and sincerity to be markers of intelligence. Another culture may consider theiability to have smooth, conflict-free interpersonal relationships a marker for intelligence. Yet another culture may consider creativity and artistic abilities to be indices of intelligence. Comparisons of WAIS data from all of these cultures may not be a meaningful cross-cultural comparison of intelligence.

Another way to think about measurement equivalence is on the statistical level–that is, in terms of **psychometric equivalence**. Psychometric equivalence can be ascertained in several different ways. One of the most important ways, especially when using questionnaires to collect data (which is used in many cross-cultural studies), is to determine whether the questionnaires in the different languages have the same structure. For example, researchers often use a technique called factor analysis to examine the structure of a questionnaire. Factor analysis creates groups of the items on a questionnaire based on how the responses to them are related to each other. The groups, called factors, are thought to represent different mental constructs in the minds of the participants responding to the items. Scores are then computed to represent each of these mental constructs.

When using questionnaires across cultures, one concern that arises is whether the same groups of items, or factors, would emerge in the different cultures. If so, then the measure is said to have **structural equivalence**. If not, however, the measure is structurally nonequivalent (biased), which suggests that people of different cultural groups have different mental constructs operating when responding to the same questionnaire. Thus, their responses may not be comparable to each other.

Another way in which psychometric equivalence can be ascertained is by examining the internal reliability of the measures across cultures. **Internal reliability** can be assessed by examining whether the items on a questionnaire are all related to each other. If they are supposed to be measuring the same mental construct, then items should be related to each other; that is, they should have high internal reliability. If the items are working in the same way across cultures, then they should have high internal reliability in each of the cultures being tested.

Response Bias

In addition to the methodological issues concerning bias and equivalence described above, cross-cultural researchers need to be aware of the fact that different cultures can promote different types of response biases. A **response bias** is a systematic tendency to respond in a certain way to items or scales. If response-biases exist, then it is very difficult to compare data between cultures because it is not clear whether differences refer to "true" differences in what is being measured or are merely differences in how people respond using scales.

There are, in fact, several different types of response biases. **Socially desirable responding**, for instance, is the tendency to give answers that make oneself look good (Paulhaus, 1984), and it may be that people of certain cultures have greater concerns that lead them to respond in socially desirable ways than people of other cultures. There are two facets of socially desirable responding, which include *self-deceptive enhancement-seeing* oneself in a positive light—and *impression management.* Lalwani, Shavitt, and Johnson (2006) demonstrated that European

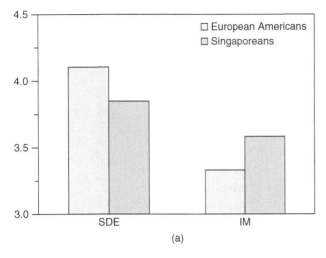

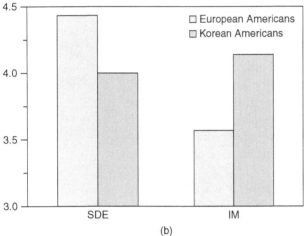

Figure 2.2 Socially Desirable Responding

(a) Comparison of European Americans and Singaporeans, (b) Comparison of European Americans and Korean Americans. SDE = self-deceptive enhancement; IM = impression management.

(Source: Adapted from Lalwani et al., 2006.)

American university students score higher on self—deceptive enhancement than both Korean Americans and students from Singapore, but the latter score higher on impression management than do European Americans (Figure 2.2).

Lalwani et al. (2006) also demonstrated that individuals with more individualistic cultural orientations engaged in more self-deceptive enhancement, while individuals with more collectivistic orientations engaged in more impression management. In a related vein, Matsumoto (2006b) showed that differences between Americans and Japanese university students' individualistic versus collectivistic cultural orientations disappeared once socially desirable responding was statistically controlled.

Two other types of response bias are **acquiescence bias**, which is the tendency to agree rather than disagree with items on questionnaires, and **extreme response bias**, which is the tendency to use the ends of a scale regardless of item content. Van Herk, Poortinga, and Verhallen (2004) examined responses on marketing surveys regarding household behaviors (e.g., cooking, use of products, shaving, washing clothes) in six European countries. They reported that countries near the Mediterranean (Greece, Italy, and Spain) exhibited more of both acquiescence bias and extreme response bias than countries in northwestern Europe (France, Germany, and the United Kingdom). Interestingly, their degree of the two response biases were *not* correlated with national differences in actual behaviors with regard to the issues raised. (If there were differences in rates of actual behaviors, it could be argued that the response styles were not biases, but were reflective of actual differences in behaviors, but this was not the case.)

A final type of response bias is the **reference group effect** (Heine, Lehman, Peng, & Greenholz, 2002). This idea is based on the notion that people make implicit social comparisons with others when making ratings on scales, rather than relying on direct inferences about a private, personal value system (Peng, Nisbett, & Wong, 1997). That is, when completing rating scale's, people will *implicitly* compare themselves to others in their group. For example, Japanese individuals may appear to be fairly individualistic on questionnaires, even more so than Americans. But Heine et al. (2002) argue that this may be because the Japanese implicitly compare themselves to their own groups, who are actually fairly collectivistic, when making such ratings, and thus inflate their ratings of individualism. Likewise, Americans may inflate their ratings of collectivism because they implicitly compare themselves to others, who are actually fairly individualistic. Peng et al. (1997) examined four different value survey methods: the traditional ranking, rating, attitude scaling procedures, and a behavioral scenario rating method. The only method that yielded reasonable validity estimates was the behavioral scenario rating method, the most uncommon of all the measures tested.

What aspects of culture account for response biases? Johnson, Kulesa, Cho, and Shavitt (2004) examined these biases in 19 countries around the world and correlated indices of the biases with each country's score on Hofstede's cultural dimensions. (This study is an example of an ecological-level study.) On one hand, extreme response bias occurred more in cultures that encourage masculinity, power, and status. They suggested that this response style achieves clarity, precision, and decisiveness in one's explicit verbal statements, characteristics that are valued in these cultures. On the other hand, respondents from individualistic cultures were less likely to engage in acquiescence bias, probably because maintaining harmony and conveying agreeableness and deference are less emphasized in these cultures.

In the past, response biases were viewed as methodological artifacts that need to be controlled in order to get to "true" responses. Today, however, there is a growing view of them as an important part of cultural influence on data. Regardless of how researchers choose to view this issue, their effects should be acknowledged and incorporated in data analysis in cross-cultural comparisons.

Interpretational Bias

Analyzing Data

In testing cultural differences on target variables of interest, researchers often use inferential statistics such as chi-square or analysis of variance (ANOVA) and engage in what is known as null hypothesis significance testing. These statistics compare the differences observed between the groups to the differences one would normally expect on the basis of chance alone and then compute the probability that the results would have been obtained solely by chance. If the probability of obtaining the findings they did is very low (less than five percent), then researchers infer that the findings did not occur because of chance—that is, that the findings reflect actual differences between the cultural groups from which their samples were drawn. This "proof by negation of the opposite" is at the heart of the logic underlying hypothesis testing and statistical inference.

In the past, researchers were quick to take "statistically significant" results and interpret them as if they were "practically meaningful to all or most members of the groups being compared." That is, researchers (and consumers of research) often assume that most people of those groups differ in ways corresponding to the mean values. Thus, if a statistically significant difference is found between Americans and Japanese, for instance, on emotional expressivity such that Americans had statistically significantly higher scores than the Japanese, people often conclude that all Americans are more expressive than all Japanese.

But the fact that the differences between group means are statistically significant does not by itself give an indication of the degree of practical meaningfulness of the difference between the groups. Group means may be statistically different even though there is considerable overlap among the scores'bf individuals comprising the two groups. The tendency to make glossy, broad-sweeping statements based on "statistically significant" results is a mistake in interpretation that is fueled by the field's fascination and single-minded concern with statistical significance and perhaps stereotypes.

Fortunately, statistical procedures are available that help to determine the degree to which differences in mean values reflect meaningful differences among individuals. The general class of statistics is called "effect size statistics"; when used in a cross-cultural setting, Matsumoto and his colleagues call them "cultural effect size statistics" (Matsumoto, Grissom, & Dinnel, 2001). There are a number of different types of such statistics that can help researchers and readers get an idea of the degree to which the between-group cultural differences actually reflect differences among the individuals tested, helping to break the hold of stereotypic interpretations based on group difference findings.

Dealing with Nonequivalent Data

Despite the best attempts to establish equivalence in theory, hypothesis, method, and data management, cross-cultural research is often inextricably, inherently, and inevitably nonequivalent. It is nearly impossible to create any cross-cultural study that means exactly the same thing to all participating cultures, both conceptually and empirically. What cross-cultural researchers often end/up with are best approximations of the closest equivalents in terms of theory and method in a study. Thus, researchers are often faced with the question of how to deal with nonequivalent data. Poortinga (1989) outlined four different ways in which the problem of nonequivalence of cross-cultural data can be handled:

1. *Preclude comparison.* The most conservative thing a researcher could do is not make the comparison in the first place, concluding that it would be meaningless.
2. *Reduce the nonequivalence in the data.* Many researchers take steps to identify equivalent and nonequivalent parts of their methods and then refocus their comparisons solely on the equivalent parts. For example, if a researcher used a 20-item scale to measure anxiety in two cultures and found evidence for non-equivalence on the scale, he or she might then examine each of the 20 items for equivalence and rescore the test using only the items that are shown to be equivalent. Comparisons would then be based on the rescored items.
3. *Interpret the nonequivalence.* A third strategy is for the researcher to interpret the nonequivalence as an important piece of information concerning cultural differences.
4. *Ignore the nonequivalence.* Unfortunately, what many cross-cultural researchers end up doing is simply ignoring the problem, clinging to beliefs concerning scale invariance across cultures despite a lack of evidence to support those beliefs.

How researchers handle the interpretation of their data given non-equivalence depends on their experience and biases and on the nature of the data and the findings. Because of the lack of equivalence in much cross-cultural research, researchers are often faced with many gray areas in interpreting their findings. Culture itself is a complex phenomenon, neither black nor white but replete with gray. It is the objective and experienced researcher who can deal with these gray areas, creating sound, valid, and reliable interpretations that are justified by the data. And it is the astute consumer of that research who can sit back and judge those interpretations relative to the data in their own minds and not be unduly swayed by the arguments of the researchers.

Interpreting Findings

Just as culture can bias formulation of the research questions in a cross-cultural study, it can also bias the ways researchers interpret their findings. Most researchers inevitably interpret the data they obtain through their own cultural filters, and these biases can affect their interpretations to varying degrees. For example, for years American-Japanese cultural differences in emotionality were interpreted by researchers as indicative of Japanese suppression of emotion (Matsumoto & Ekman, 1989). Later studies, however, provided evidence that it may not be so much that the Japanese suppress, but that Americans exaggerate their emotional responses (Matsumoto, Kasri, & Kooken, 1999). Thus, our own interpretations of the data were biased in implicitly considering the American data as the "true" responses and non-American data as somehow different.

In hypothesis-testing cross-cultural studies, cultural groups are often treated as independent variables in research design and data analysis, making these studies a form of quasi-experiment. Data from such studies are basically correlational, and inferences drawn from them can only be correlational inferences. For example, if a researcher compared data from the United States and Hong Kong on social judgments and found that Americans had significantly higher scores on a person-perception task, any interpretations of these data would be limited to the association between cultural membership (American or Hong Kong Chinese) and the scores. Cause-effect inferences (for example, being American *causes* one to have higher person-perception scores) are unwarranted. For such causal statements to be justified, the researcher would have had to: (1) create the conditions of the experiment (the cultural groups) and (2) randomly assign people to each of the conditions. These experimental conditions cannot apply in any study in which one of the main variables is cultural group. It makes no more sense to assume a causal relationship between cultural membership and a variable of interest than it does to assume such a relationship on the basis of sex, hair color, or height.

A related type of mistaken interpretation is to suggest specific reasons why cultural differences occurred even though the specific reasons were never measured in the study. Matsumoto and Yoo (2006) call these **cultural attribution** fallacies, which occur when researchers claim that between-group differences are cultural when they really have no empirical justification to do so. For instance, a researcher might take the significant American-Hong Kong differences found in the previous example and suggest that these differences occurred because of differences between individualism and collectivism in the two cultures. Unless the researchers actually measured individualism and collectivism in their study, found that the two cultures differed on this dimension, and showed that it accounted for the cultural-group differences on social judgments, the interpretation that this construct (IC) is responsible for the group differences is unwarranted. Linkage studies (discussed above) address this problem.

SUMMARY

Cross-cultural research is tough. As you read above, there are many threats to the validity of any cross-cultural study, including threats to theoretical frameworks (construct bias), methods of data collection (method bias), measurement (measurement and item bias), responses (response bias), and analyzing data and interpreting findings (interpretational bias). Even when cultures are compared correctly, there is the additional problem of how we can link the differences to meaningful aspects of culture.

All in all, the issues discussed in this chapter are so daunting that you may well wonder whether any cross-cultural study can tell us anything. All studies have at least some imperfections, arid every study has its limitations. But that does not necessarily mean we cannot learn something from those studies. The real question is whether the flaws of a study so outweigh its procedures as to-severely compromise the trust you place in its data. If a study is so compromised that you don't trust the data, you shouldn't believe it, whether it is cross-culturalor not, even if you agree with its nebulous conclusions. But if a study's problems are less serious, you should be able to glean information from it about 'cultural differences.' If you can do this over a number of studies in an area, they might cumulatively or collectively say something about that area, even though any single study might not.

Despite all the inherent difficulties, cross-cultural research offers a number of exciting and interesting opportunities not available with traditional research approaches. Through cross-cultural research, we can test the limits and boundaries of our knowledge in psychology and about human behavior. We can push the envelope of knowledge and understanding about people in ways that are impossible with traditional research approaches. The cross-cultural enterprise itself offers a process by which scientists and laypersons from disparate and divergent cultures can come together and work toward common goals, thereby improving human relations across what otherwise may seem a considerable chasm. The findings from cross-cultural research offer scientists, scholars, and the public ways to further our understanding. of human diversity that can serve as the basis for renewed personal and professional interrelationships and can help to focus public and social policy. Methodologically, cross-cultural studies offer researchers a way to deal with empirical problems related to the conduct of research, such as confounding variables present in traditional research approaches.

This process of evaluating the merits of each study in terms of the trust you would place in the data and then accumulating bits and pieces of information across the studies you trust is integral to learning about a field. In this chapter, we have tried to provide a solid basis for developing and practicing these skills. The material presented in this chapter is just the tip of the iceberg. Many excellent resources, other than those cited throughout this chapter, explain cross-cultural research issues in greater detail for specialists in the field (see Matsumoto & van de Vijver, 2011). And there are many things researchers can do before and after collecting data to ensure their studies reduce bias and establish equivalence.

It is this cumulative process that we went through in selecting studies and findings from the various fields of cross-cultural psychology to present, to you in the remainder of this book. But do not take our word for it; you can evaluate that research for yourself. It is a skill that takes practice in order to do well, but like many skills, it can be learned. Hopefully the issues we have discussed above can serve as a platform by which you can conduct your own evaluations of cross-cultural research. As you read and evaluate the studies presented in this book and elsewhere, we hope you will find that while cross-cultural research has its own problems and limitations, it has advantages and potentialities that far outweigh the difficulties.

CHAPTER 3

Rethinking Culture

"I don't mean to be rude, but what are you?" Amy, a high school teacher with a multicultural background, gets this question a lot from her students during the first few weeks of school. Depending on your own unique physical characteristics, you may also get this question, too. The assumption is that culture is being questioned, but what do people really mean when they ask, "What are you?"

The field of psychology is tasked with studying the mental processes and behaviors of people (Ciccarelli & White, 2011); therefore, psychologists should know and be able to articulate the differences between race, ethnicity, and culture. Unfortunately, as Markus (2008) points out, psychologists still are not unified on the definitions of these words. Research for race is published in journals completely separate from research on ethnicity and culture. Therefore, not only do laypeople use the terms *race*, *ethnicity,* and *culture* incorrectly, but psychologists do too sometimes! Despite the fact that people use these terms interchangeably, they are three different words with three distinct definitions. Let's tease them apart to get a deeper understanding of what they really mean.

RACE

The term *race* is thrown about everywhere. It's used in politics, entertainment, academia, and social settings. For example, in 2008 Senator Barack Obama made headlines and national history when he became the first Black man to be elected to the highest public office in the nation, the President of the United States of America. In another example, both Latinos and women celebrated as Sonia Maria Sotomayor (pictured, right) was nominated and confirmed as the first Hispanic and as only the third woman to serve as a Supreme Court Justice. Fewer people know that, after finishing her undergraduate work at Howard University, Dr. Mamie Phillips Clark was the first Black woman to graduate from Columbia University with a PhD in psychology (her husband, Kenneth Clark, was the first Black person to graduate from Columbia).

Image © K2 Images, 2013. Used under license from Shutterstock, Inc.

Think about what it means to be considered "the first" (e.g., first child or the first to graduate from college). What does this suggest in terms of the individual, society, and successors to be "the first?"

DOES RACE REALLY MATTER?

When you use the words *Black* or *White*, what do you mean? Most people, when asked to define it, believe that race has to do with heritage or lineage. However, when some people ask about race, they are really interested in understanding nationality (we will discuss this term shortly). *Race* is a very confusing term partly because everyone has a different definition about what another person's race is. Just ask Maddie Jagger, a former student at Trinity University. She describes herself as "lightly tanned year-round" and points out the ambiguity in her complexion as she is too light to be considered African American, and "not the right shade" to be classified as Latina (Jagger, 2008, p. 1). Obviously, people ask questions and make assumptions about race, but really, what is race?

> 66 *The term race only gets you as far as the differences that you can see between people. It doesn't account for the differences that you can't see between people.* 99

Race is the arbitrary categorization of the human species based on observable physical differences. This definition highlights two important points. First, it emphasizes that race is based only on "observable physical differences." These differences include complexion, eye color and shape, hair color and texture, and even bone structure. In other words, the term *race* only gets you as far as the differences that you can see between people. It doesn't account for the differences that you can't see between people. It is for this reason that the American Anthropology Association (AAA) refers to race as "a body of prejudgments that distorts our ideas about human differences and group behavior" (aaanet.org, para. 8). When we use race to categorize and judge people, we are not entertaining what is below the surface.

Second, and just as important, this definition highlights the randomness of racial categories. In fact, this term has been scientifically researched for many decades, and scientists have never been able to find any genes that are directly linked to race. The bottom line is that if you look at the genes of two people who come from two different races, such as a Japanese American woman and an European American woman, you can't find any indicator of racial difference. In 1998 AAA developed a contemporary statement on race confirming that "human populations are *not* unambiguous, clearly demarcated, biologically distinct groups" (aaanet.org, para 1). Simply put and biologically speaking, there are no racial groups.

Would you be surprised to know that racial groups have more variation, or difference, *within* the group than between other groups? Markus (2008) notes that some of our country's most notable educational leaders believed in the notion that some races are just superior to others. However, studies indicate that about 94% of the physical characteristics that we think help us determine differences between racial groups actually occur within groups more frequently (aaanet.org). That means that African Americans have more differences *within* the African American "race" than with other "races" like European Americans or Chinese Americans, for example.

WHY USE *RACE* AT ALL?

Because science has not been able to prove genetically that different races exist, the term is no longer in technical use. A quick dictionary search of *race* will uncover a definition followed by one important word—obsolete. However, we still use the term socially to categorize people. Most social scientists (i.e., psychologists, sociologists, anthropologists to name a few) will agree that race is a socially constructed term. A socially constructed term is one that has been created and maintained for social purposes. At this point, you may be wondering, if race is no longer in technical use, what "social purposes" do we have for the word? Why are we still using the term *race*? This multifaceted question is one worthy of deep consideration. However, there are three overarching reasons that we still use the term *race*, despite the evidence that indicates there is really no such thing.

1. We use *race* because we don't understand the true definition of the word and don't understand other, more accurate ways of categorizing people.

    Oftentimes we hear words and, without understanding them fully, we repeat them. Children definitely aren't born understanding the differences between races; someone has to teach them what it means to be "Black" or "White." When the wrong information is passed along, we have the breeding ground for generations of people to be misled and uninformed. Furthermore, it is not enough that we understand the definition of race. We also need to understand other important words related to race, such as *ethnicity* and *culture* so that we know when and how to use them.

2. We use *race* because we think it's the easiest way to categorize people.

Imagine that you are standing in line on Black Friday at 3 a.m. waiting for your local electronics store to open. You are in the market for a 50-inch flat-screen television for only $400 when you see a White man running alongside the line of people. Then you notice that he snatches a woman's purse and runs off. You call 911 immediately and explain what you saw. "I just saw a man run up to a woman and snatch her purse outside of ABC Electronics." Typically, you will be asked to describe the perpetrator and your first response would most likely be to disclose the race of the man (and perhaps what he is wearing). Telling the police officer the race of the criminal is helpful because, as she is patrolling the surrounding area, she can immediately rule out people who belong to other races.

Although using racial categories can be a quick way to communicate information, they can be extremely inaccurate. The police officer's definition of a White man and your definition, as a witness to the crime, may be totally different. One of the problems with socially constructed words is that they can only be used effectively when people speak the same social language. For example, your great grandmother might look at you strangely if you said, "Darn, I just broke my mouse." In her social world, mice are pests that easily find their way into your home, but have a harder time finding their way out. However, your best friend might naturally assume that you were referring to your computer hardware. As people, we don't just communicate with others who speak the same social language as we do: We are forced to communicate with people who function outside of our social context.

While *Black* or *White* seem like quick, simple words to use to communicate information effectively, the reality is that you may be conveying misleading and inaccurate information by using words that mean different things to different people.

3. We use *race* because we want to maintain the social structure of our society.

American society was born out of a caste system, a system of the haves and have-nots. If you think back to your American history lessons on how and why early Americans broke away from their English rulers, you will remember that, simply put, Americans believed that the English were mistreating them. They believed that the English were taking advantage of the natural resources on American soil and the labor of Americans without proper compensation. In other words, Americans were treated as the "inferior race." How interesting it is that those same early Americans who fought so desperately to separate from the English in the American Revolution turned around and created the same superior/inferior social system with Africans. There is no doubt that, from America's inception, race has been used to exclude people from social privileges, economic growth, academic/professional development, and personal enrichment.

Sociologists' **conflict perspective** contends that members of society function best when they are in competition with each other instead of in cooperation. According to this perspective, society maintains its balance because people are always competing for advantages over others. This can be found at the macro and micro levels. **Macro** is Greek for "big," and it means on a large scale or the big picture. In America, we can see groups of people competing with each other to make sure that their group remains superior. In fact, our political system is set up so that Republicans, a group of conservative people, compete with Democrats, a group of liberal people, to determine which group will make decisions for our local cities or towns, states, and the country as a whole. **Micro,** on the other hand, is Greek for "small," and it means on a minor scale. We compete on a small scale in sports (e.g., singles tennis and pool) as well as academically. As you look back on your college admissions process, did you realize that you were competing against other individuals for a spot? Every year, colleges and universities around the country figure out how many students they can accommodate based on the number of resources that they have. Some students get in, and some don't.

From this perspective, it is clear to see that one of the reasons we still use the term *race* is to maintain the social order of our society. Despite the term's lack of a scientific foundation, we need to remain in conflict (or competition) with others so that some people can be winners, thus getting more than enough access to goods, resources, and services, while others can be losers and not receive access to those things.

TYPES OF RACIAL GROUPS

Despite the fact that there are no pure races, our country still officially uses race to classify people. The U.S. Office of Management and Budget (OMB), the office that oversees the development, preparation, and implementation of the federal budget, also determines standard policies for other federal offices, including the U.S. Census Bureau. The OMB has required that the Census Bureau maintain at least five racial categories on the census. They are White, Black or African American, American Indian or Alaska Native, Asian, and Native Hawaiian or Other Pacific Islander. Nearly every American (97%) who provided census information in 2010 reported that they were **uniracial**, or belonging to one race, which is very interesting considering that migration has made it increasingly harder to prove that there is any pure race left in America. Consider the White race for example. There are varying skin tones within that race, so much so that sometimes the "obvious physical differences" aren't that obvious. Let's take a look at the five racial categories recognized by the United States.

Image © Konstantin Sutyagin, 2013. Used under license from Shutterstock, Inc.

White

Typically, when you think of a White person, you think of someone whose ancestry points toward European countries like Italy, France, and Denmark. However, the U.S. government defines the White race as anyone whose original people were from Europe, the Middle East, or North Africa. Seventy-two percent of Americans (223.6 million) identified racially as White and, according to our government, the term *White* includes people from at least 71 different countries.

Black or African American

According to the Census, a Black or African American person is anyone who has origins from Africa. Depending on what part of the country you live in, it may seem like Blacks are half of our population or more; however, only 13% (38.9 million) of Americans identify as members of this category. As with the government's definition for the White race, the definition of who is considered Black is very vague. Additionally, the definition stated above is not consistent with who is considered Black socially. For example, socially speaking, Jamaican Americans are considered Black as are Haitian Americans and West Indian Americans. Despite the fact that Jamaica (an island in the Caribbean Sea) and Africa (the second largest continent in the world) are two different places, we socially group people from these countries together.

Image © michaeljung, 2013. Used under license from Shutterstock, Inc.

American Indian or Alaska Native

The census defines this group as having origins in any of the original peoples of North and South America (including Central America) and who maintains tribal affiliation or community attachment. The term *American Indian* is indeed a misnomer, or wrong name. Legend has it that when Christopher Columbus set out to explore the New World, he reached North America but thought that he was in the Indies. Once he encountered the people of the land, he referred to them as Indians and, despite the fact that Columbus was mistaken, the name has stuck. The Native American community has been torn on the issue of their politically correct name for years. Some Native Americans feel insulted to be called *Indian*, a name that was given to them out of, at the least, a mistake, and at the most, ignorance. Some Natives don't care either way, and others actually prefer the term *Indian*. A **native** is someone or something that was the original. Therefore, when we refer to the group of people who were on American soil before other explorers "found" it, we call them Native Americans. Another word for *native* is **indigenous** (they will be used interchangeably throughout this textbook).

There is debate about the use of tribal symbols in college and professional sports teams. What do these discussions suggest about the importance of symbols in culture (Native American and sports cultures)?

Some Native Americans have tried to dissociate themselves with the term *Indian* for years with no success, while others believe that the term *Native American* is too Americanized. In the face of the social confusion surrounding the correct term for this group of people, there has been no official change in how we address Native Americans from the government or the private sector. The Bureau of Indian Affairs (BIA), a federal government agency, has never attempted to change its name, nor has the American Indian College Fund (AICF) or the American Indian Movement (AIM). The best way to refer to a member of this race is to use his or her tribal name. Of course, the problem with this idea is that most Americans have a limited understanding of what it means to be a part of a tribe and even less of an understanding of tribal names. Currently, the U.S. government recognizes 566 Native American tribes.

Asian

An Asian is considered to be a person having origins in any of the original peoples of the Far East, Southeast Asia, or the Indian subcontinent. When most people consider the term *Asian*, they think Chinese or Japanese because these two groups have the longest history in the United States (Schaefer, 2012). However, *Asian* is an umbrella term used to catch a number of people including Vietnamese, Korean, Filipino, and Pacific Islanders people. According to Schaefer (2012), Asian Americans, despite having their own experiences with racism and discrimination, feel that Americans don't see their experiences as detrimental to the Asian American community because they have succeeded in spite of them. In fact, this group is often referred to as the model minority because, despite the hardships they encoun-

tered, they have succeeded economically, educationally, and socially without sociopolitical confrontations with White Americans. Did you know that only 30% of the American population (25 years and older) holds a bachelor's degree compared to 50% of Asian Americans? This may not seem like a lot; however, when compared to other racial groups, as depicted in Figure 3.1, they far exceed all other races educationally, including Whites (Ying, et al., 2001). With that being said, the term *model minority* only adds to the problems of prejudice and discrimination for two reasons. First, the term doesn't consider all aspects of life. According to Ying and colleagues (2001), the "model minority" label doesn't consider that Asian Americans may not be as successful socially.

Americans 25+ Years Old with a Bachelor's Degree

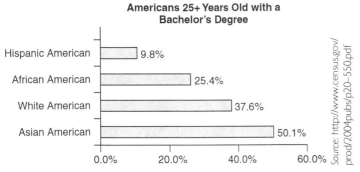

Hispanic American	9.8%
African American	25.4%
White American	37.6%
Asian American	50.1%

0.0% 20.0% 40.0% 60.0%

Source: http://www.census.gov/prod/2004pubs/p20–550.pdf

Figure 3.1 Americans 25 Years and older with a Bachelor's Degree

Image © Deborah Kolb, 2013. Used under license from Shutterstock, Inc.

Not only have Asian Americans felt ignored because they haven't resorted to such acts as speaking on Capitol Hill like the Native Americans or staging sit-ins like African Americans, but they believe that their successes in this country have sent the implicit message that they are not struggling for social equality.

Native Hawaiian and Other Pacific Islander

This group comprises people who have a biological connection to the original people of Hawaii, Guam, Samoa, and other Pacific Islands, such as Fiji, Polynesia, Melanesia. Even though there are over one million people in the country who identify in this category, they still make up only 0.2% of the population. According to the U.S. Census Bureau (2010), about one third of people who classify themselves in this racial category live in Hawaii. In terms of education, this group yields a comparable number of high school graduates when compared to Whites. That is, 89% of Native Hawaiian and Other Pacific Islanders graduate from high school, while 91% of Whites graduate. However, the education gap widens at the college level where only 20% of this race have college degrees compared to 31% of Whites. Furthermore, this education gap directly affects the socioeconomic status of Native Hawaiians and Other Pacific Islanders as 17% of them live below the poverty line as opposed to 11% of Whites (DeNavas-Walt, Proctor, & Smith, 2011).

Berry's Model of Acculturation

You may not have seen the term *acculturation* before, but you most likely have seen an example of it. **Acculturation** is the contact between individuals from different cultures and the changes that take place as a result of that contact (Schwartz & Zamboanga, 2008). There are four categories within Berry's model, and each category represents a different level of acculturation. Someone who is *integrated* is someone who truly recognizes the importance of maintaining important aspects of his or her cultural identity while incorporating parts of the dominant society's culture. For example, Jaime might embrace the celebration of Thanksgiving, an American holiday, as well as Rosh Hashanah, the Jewish New Year. Someone who is *marginalized* is the opposite of an integrated person. If you are marginalized, then you don't feel connected to your cultural group or the dominant society's culture. If Yin doesn't feel "Asian enough" because he was born in America and is rejected by the children at school because he looks different, he is marginalized.

	Person feels close to cultural group	Person *doesn't* feel close to cultural group
Person feels close to dominant culture	Integration	Assimilation
Person *doesn't* feel close to dominant culture	Separation	Marginalization

Figure 3.2 Depiction of Berry's Acculturation Theory (1997)

The last two categories are assimilation and separation. *Assimilation* is the act of taking on all of the characteristics of the dominant culture and not identifying at all with other cultural identities. For example, Ericka may choose to completely ignore her Native American heritage and celebrate more Americanized traditions. Ignoring the cultural demands of the dominant society and identifying only with one's own cultural identity despite living in the dominant society is an example of *separation*. For example, Zaid only speaks to Americans when he has to and only shops at stores that are owned by people of his culture.

Berry's (1997) Acculturation Model was meant to be applied to immigrants; however, it can certainly be applied to other cultures. For example, let's say you had a professor who would meet with you only in person or on the phone. The dominant culture contends that people should be connected electronically; therefore, if the professor refused to check email

What examples of Berry's Model can be depicted here? Discuss your rationale.

or engage with you electronically, that professor would be considered a separatist. In this case, the professor is adhering to his own cultural identity and not incorporating the practices of the dominant culture. In the same example, if the professor provided in-person office hours as well as virtual office hours (via videoconferencing), then he would be considered an integrationist.

MAJORITY RULES (NOT REALLY)

One of the principles on which the United States was built is the principle of fairness. According to our founding fathers, in order to determine the direction our country should take, we should look to the people. More specifically, our political process allows the people to vote on who should run our country and how. This process implies that the majority rules, right? While we like to believe that the majority rules, the majority doesn't rule in our country. **Majority** is the group that makes up more than half of the population. With respect to race, Whites make up 72% of our population; therefore, they are the majority. Conversely, a **minority** is the group that makes up less than half of the population. Since all of the other races in America make up 28% of the population combined, they represent the minority.

While some groups may be the quantitative majority in America, they may not be the social majority. A **social majority** is the group that holds the most social power, and this has nothing to do with the number of people in the group. For example, not only are Whites the physical majority, they are also the social majority. In other words, people who look White have the most social power in our country. It is important to note that you don't have to identify with being White to get social power. You only have to be perceived by others as being White. As a Latina little girl who looked White and came from a well-to-do family, Arendale (2008) asserts, "I was a privileged member of the top socioeconomic class, [but] in [other minority member's eyes] I have become white." This former Trinity University student who self-identifies as a White Venezuelan demonstrates how, even though she personally identifies as Latina American, she is perceived to be a member of the social majority because of the wealth of her family and her skin tone. If you don't think that Whites are the social majority in the country, consider our congressional demographics. Despite the fact that Whites make up only 72% of the population, they make up 85% of Congress, the group that is charged with leading the country politically.

In this picture two children are praying for an adult. What does this picture suggest about majority or minority? age? power?

The **social minority**, on the other hand, is the group that holds less social power. Again, this has nothing to do with the number of people who represent the group. It's important to distinguish between a majority and a social majority because the majority rules theory is an illusion. In our country, the majority doesn't rule; the social majority rules. Sometimes it works out that the physical majority and the social majority are the same group. Let's consider religion. Christians are the majority in our country. According to the Pew Research Center (2007), 78.4% of the country identifies religiously as Christian. Christians are also the social majority and have been since our country began. Patrick Henry, an early American leader, is quoted as saying, "It cannot be emphasized too strongly or too often that this great Nation was founded not by religionists, but by Christians; not on religions, but on the Gospel of Jesus Christ." This quote demonstrates that, from its very inception, the United States of America consisted of mostly Christians, who have maintained social power to this day. That power can be seen throughout our history as we have struggled to give voting rights to Blacks, equal pay to women, and marriage rights to gays.

Now let's consider gender. Women make up 50.8% of our country's population; therefore, they are the majority. However, they are not the social majority. While there are physically more women than men in the country, women are not the people with the most power. Congress is composed of 444 men (83%), while only 94 women. Additionally, in the over 200-year history of our country, we have never had a female president.

RACIAL IDENTITY MODELS

As mentioned previously, even though race doesn't matter biologically, it definitely matters socially. **Racial identity**, as defined by Helms (1993), is the degree to which one identifies with other people who have been socially categorized in the same racial group. Additionally, racial identity has to do with how much one identifies with the different cultural aspects of one's race (i.e., clothing, history, literature, customs, and traditions). Several theorists have hypothesized and researched theories about how people come to identify racially; however, we will specifically discuss the racial identity models of Cross (1971), Helms (1984), and Sue & Sue (1999).

Cross' Black Racial Identity Development Model (1971)

Bill Cross (1971) was interested in understanding how Blacks came to appreciate, respect, and be proud of their Blackness in America where the dominant race was European American. Therefore, he hypothesized that Blacks progressed through four stages of racial identity development, the pre-encounter, encounter, immersion-emersion, and internalization stages, in his Negro to Black (Nigresence) or Black Racial Identity Development Model. When a Black person is at the *pre-encounter stage*, she or he assimilates to the dominant culture, "devalue[s] Blackness and endorse[s] Eurocentric notions of Blackness" (Stith-Williams & Haynes, 2007, p. 29). In other words, at this stage Blacks are only interested in taking on aspects of European American culture (the dominant culture in America) and diminishing African American culture.

According to Cross, an individual may remain at the pre-encounter stage unless or until that person experiences a catalyst that prompts him or her to view race differently. Cross specifically called this a "catalytic event," or an event that sparks an internal reaction. He further believed that this event was not enough to move onto the second stage, the *encounter stage.*

BOX 3.1   Cross' Black Racial Identity Development Model
Stage 1: Pre-encounter Stage 2: Encounter Stage 3: Immersion/Emersion Stage 4: Internalization

The individual must also see the event as threatening to already-established ideas about Blacks. This event could be a racial injustice or "exposure to a new aspect of African American culture" (Stith-Williams & Haynes, 2007, p. 29). Examples of a catalytic event may include being called a racial slur or meeting someone who disproves your theory that "all Blacks are —." During the *immersion-emersion stage*, the Black person is ostentatiously committed to displaying Black pride. This may be done through choosing Afro-centric clothes and hairstyles, exploring Black culture and literature, shifting political affiliation, and desiring to only be in the company of other like-minded Blacks. Additionally, the person sees White people as the enemy, and feels intense anger at Whites as a whole for perpetuating negative stereotypes about Blacks. Lastly, there is shame and guilt surrounding the person's own actions and beliefs during previous stages of development.

Internalization is the last stage of Cross' model. Generally speaking, this stage ushers in a healthy appreciation for Blackness as well as an appreciation for parts of the dominant culture. At this stage anger toward Whites dissipates. Cross specifies that there are three internalization identity types: the nationalist, biculturalist, and multiculturalist. The nationalist comes to an internalization of Black identity by focusing primarily on issues affecting the Black community. This is not to say that the nationalist doesn't like members of the dominant society; however, the nationalist finds it important to concentrate attention on this part of his or her identity. The biculturalist, on the other hand, integrates Black identity with mainstream American identity, while the multiculturalist integrates Black identity with at least two other identities. For example, Joyce may integrate her Blackness with her American culture and her Muslim culture.

It is important to note that this model of racial identity has been critiqued over the years. Parham (2000) points out that people don't necessarily progress through these stages in a linear way. In other words, some people move nicely from stage 1 to 2 to 3 to 4. Parham further explains that people experience a "catalytic" event at multiple points in their lives, which prompts them to move back through the stages and continually develop Black identity.

Helms' White Racial Identity Development Model (1984)

Janet Helms (1984) posits that Blacks weren't the only race to go through psychological and emotional changes in an effort to identify with Black people and culture. She hypothesized and researched the notion that Whites also experienced changes, which she calls statuses, that helped them transition from having negative opinions and beliefs about people of color to having a nonracist identity. Contact, disintegration, reintegration, pseudo-independence, immersion/emersion, and autonomy are her six statuses.

During the first status, contact, Whites are oblivious to issues of racism. Typically, people at this status will contend that they don't see color. People at this status "either have an uncritical acceptance of White racism [unconsciously], or they regard racial differences as unimportant (Stith-Williams & Haynes, 2007, p. 31). The next status, disintegration, is comparable to Cross' encounter stage. At this point, the White person experiences something that conflicts with the "race doesn't matter" attitude. This experience could be internal or external. For example, the

BOX 3.2　Helms' White Racial Identity Development Model

Status 1: Contact
Status 2: Disintegration
Status 3: Reintegration
Status 4: Pseudo-Independence
Status 5: Immersion/Emersion
Status 6: Autonomy

White person may think negative thoughts about people of color based on the actions of one person ("I knew he would be late for the interview. Black people are always late."). This would be an internal experience of disintegration. An external experience may be laughing at a coworker's racist joke. In this example, although the conflict didn't start internally, it still conflicts with the White person's view of himself as a color-blind person. This conflict produces feelings of shame and guilt, which lead the White person to avoid people of color as well as to avoid thinking about issues with race.

The *reintegration* status is next. The conflict of the second status is so great that the White person regresses back to a state of White idealization. Additionally, the person feels anger and indifference toward people of color. By the fourth status, the *pseudo-independence* status, the person is not comfortable ignoring racism and starts to identify with people of color. There is still an ignorance surrounding the social power and privilege that she has as a White person. At this status, the White person wants to understand people of color more, but fails to see that understanding people of color means understanding them in their social context. Simply put, Whites at this status understand the social inequities of people of color at an intellectual level, but they don't understand at an emotional or psychological level.

The questioning of whiteness marks the fifth status. At the *immersion/emersion* status, the person is starting to investigate all of the privilege and power that he has simply based on skin tone. The person legitimately makes an effort to confront racism in his life and questions biases that have long been held and taught to Whites. This quest continues the process of understanding what it means to be a person of color in America at a psychological and emotional level.

Lastly, the *autonomy* status is characterized by a decrease in guilt and shame for being White. The person recognizes that there are racial differences, values diversity among people, and is no longer threatened by topics related to racism.

Sue and Sue's Racial/Cultural Identity Development Stages (1999)

This model of identity development isn't specific to any group of color, unlike the Cross model. This model is focused on how people of color come to identity with their race while living in a society where they are not the physical and social majority and subjected to racism, prejudice, and discrimination.

BOX 3.3　Sue & Sue's Racial/Cultural Identity Development Model

Stage 1: Conformity
Stage 2: Dissonance
Stage 3: Resistance and Immersion
Stage 4: Introspection

According to Sue and Sue, the *conformity* stage is typified by a preference toward the dominant culture and feelings of shame and embarrassment about one's own race. At the next stage, the person of color experiences cognitive dissonance as the person is faced with an experience or information that challenges previously held beliefs. This is the *dissonance* stage. "For many, the dissonance stage is the first time they actually consider positive aspects of their racial/cultural group" (Stith-Williams & Haynes, 2007, p. 34). At the *resistance and immersion* stage, the person starts to reject White social norms as "the way to be" and replaces them with social norms that are specific to one's own race and culture. This stage produces a number of vivid feelings that include a sense of connection to and appreciation for one's own racial and cultural group. Unfortunately, it is also marked with feelings of shame, guilt, and anger for not having had more pride in one's racial or cultural group earlier.

During the *introspection* stage, the person is starting to question whether she needs to adhere to all racial and cultural norms in order to be connected with one's race and culture. In addition, it becomes psychologically difficult to maintain the notion that all parts of the dominant culture are bad. The *integrative awareness* stage brings about a sense of connection to one's own race or culture without denigrating the dominant race or culture.

Our racial identity affects a lot of things such as our attitudes, behaviors, feelings, and performance (Markus, 2008), and the models previously summarized are not the only identity development models focused on how people come to identify with their race or culture. However, notice that all of them start with a person, regardless of race, assuming that race doesn't matter or that the dominant race or culture is superior. Then, at some point, the person starts to question this. Additionally, all of the models indicate that a complete and healthy identification with one's racial identity doesn't include hating other races or cultural groups. In fact, healthy identification with one's race and culture includes integrating it with aspects of the dominant race or culture into self. As we move toward understanding how *ethnicity* is a separate concept from *race*, think about how you came to appreciate being a member of your race, keeping in mind that you may not yet fully identify with your race. Also, remember that life circumstances can cause you to revisit different stages of development so that you may feel a deeper connection and appreciation for your race, whatever it may be.

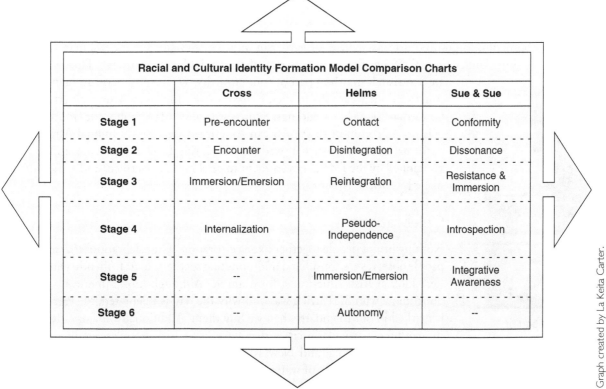

Racial and Cultural Identity Formation Model Comparison Charts			
	Cross	**Helms**	**Sue & Sue**
Stage 1	Pre-encounter	Contact	Conformity
Stage 2	Encounter	Disintegration	Dissonance
Stage 3	Immersion/Emersion	Reintegration	Resistance & Immersion
Stage 4	Internalization	Pseudo-Independence	Introspection
Stage 5	--	Immersion/Emersion	Integrative Awareness
Stage 6	--	Autonomy	--

Graph created by La Keita Carter.

Figure 3.3 Racial and Cultural Identity Formation Model Comparison Chart

ETHNICITY

As mentioned previously, although *race* and *ethnicity* are terms often used interchangeably, they actually have two different definitions. **Ethnicity** is a term used to describe a group of people who share a common trait like values, customs, language, traditions, beliefs, or rituals. Markus (2008) asserts that ethnicity "can be a source of meaning, action, and identity . . . and confers a sense of belonging, pride, and motivation" (p. 654). This term, unlike race, has proved to be more useful because it is based on things that connect people at deeper levels.

European American students have reported feeling very left out and devoid of culture when they are students in diversity/cultural studies classes. In other words, they are concerned that their whiteness doesn't matter. However, the truth of the matter is that people of color aren't the only people who belong to ethnicities. Irish Americans, Italian Americans, British Americans—all of these groups are ethnicities, and the ethnic differences between them vary greatly. There are too many ethnicities to begin to list for this chapter; however, let's review some of the traits that bring people together. As you work to have a better understanding of ethnicity, consider language, traditions, beliefs, and rituals.

Language

Language is one aspect of ethnicity that unites groups of people. For instance, while outsiders may view all Native Americans to be the same, Native Americans and allies know that there are many differences between tribes, and one of those differences is language. Historically, the Cherokee tribe has spoken a different language than the Navajo tribe. Spanish is another example of a language that unites people. The term *Hispanic* refers to people who are historically or culturally connected to Spain. Keep in mind that there are several countries that are connected to Spain; therefore, this term references millions of people. However, one thing that brings people from different Spanish cultures is language.

Traditions

Dress

Sometimes a group's customary dress, or garb, can indicate ethnicity. Consider a man dressed in a skirt. Under normal circumstances in America, that may look pretty strange. However, if you are Scottish, it may be a part of your ethnicity. While most Scottish men living in America don't wear kilts in their everyday lives, they may wear their ethnic dress for formal events like weddings. Similarly, in an effort to honor the "motherland," it is not uncommon to see African Americans wearing traditional African garb to formal ceremonies such as weddings or during Black History month, a month sanctioned by the federal government to celebrate the sacrifices and achievements made by African Americans.

Image © Anthony Ricci, 2013. Used under license from Shutterstock, Inc.

Dress is an important part of tradition. What does the dress here suggest? Does the style of dress say something about the groups represented?

Celebrations

Nothing brings people together like a celebration. The celebrations that a group of people observes are considered traditions that set them apart from other ethnicities. Let's look at Irish Americans, for example. Although most Americans probably don't know who St. Patrick was and why the day is celebrated, St. Patrick's Day is marked in our calendars when we buy them. Additionally, major cities around the country, particularly cities that have large Irish populations like Chicago, Boston, Philadelphia, and New York, celebrate the day with parades and even dyeing the town's body of water green. While most Americans don't do anything special to celebrate the day, as we would at Thanksgiving with a special dinner, for

Irish Americans the day is about being proud of their heritage and ethnicity.

Native Americans offer another example of ethnicities. To outsiders, our country's native peoples are grouped by one term—Native Americans. However, within that label are nuances that make up the different ethnicities within the group. For instance, different tribes have different customs and tribal dances. Some tribes paint facemasks for their celebrations, while some celebrate with intricate headdresses and clothing. Even the dances that celebrate different moments are varied among the tribes. As you can see, these traditions break up the umbrella term of *Native American* into smaller ethnicities.

Image © Salim October, 2013. Used under license from Shutterstock, Inc.

Beliefs, Rituals, and Customs

Beliefs, rituals and customs also unite people. Blacks tend to believe that funerals are a time of celebration of the life of the deceased, not the death; therefore, funerals in this community often include joyous singing and dancing, flowers (a sign of life) and colors, not just black. A **quinceañera,** the Latin American celebration of the transition from childhood to womanhood, is another example of a custom that is ethnic specific. The event resembles what Americans would expect to find at an American wedding reception (i.e., dancing, eating, toasting, cutting cake). It also includes ritualistic moments that are unique to the ethnicity, like the Tree of Life ceremony in which the guest of honor gives a candle to the 15 most influential people in her life over the past 15 years. As you can imagine, each quinceañera is different depending on the family's ethnicity (e.g., Dominican, Cuban, Ecuadorian).

Image © Thoman Barrat, 2013. Used under license from Shutterstock, Inc.

CULTURE

We've discussed how race is related to obvious physical differences and how ethnicity refers to the differences between groups that lie below the surface. So, what is culture? **Culture** is the "shared, patterned, and historically reproduced symbolic practices that . . . facilitate . . . meaningful human existence" (Gone, 2011, p. 235). Cooper and Leong (2008) add that culture includes a way of living that is influenced by the "historical, economic, ecological and political forces on a group" (p. 133). Notice that this definition doesn't specifically include anything about skin tone, language, eye shape, nationality, heritage, beliefs, and the like. Culture pertains to the common things that people do that unite them. Simply put, no one is without culture, and everyone is multicultural. Let's break this definition down even further.

Image © Pavel L. Photo and Video, 2013. Used under license from Shutterstock, Inc.

Why is culture "shared?" Culture is shared because practices that maintain the culture are engaged in by most of the people who identify with the culture (Gone, 2011. For example, a common, but difficult, practice in gay culture is coming out (this will be discussed in more depth in Chapter 6, "Responding to Gender and Sexual Orientation"). In fact, Rosario, Schrimshaw, and Hunter (2004) indicate that part of gay cultural identity is "feel[ing] more comfortable with others knowing about [your] sexual identity [and] disclos[ing] that identity to others" (p. 216).

Image © Patryk Kosmider, 2013. Used under license from Shutterstock, Inc.

Image © Blend Images, 2013. Used under license from Shutterstock, Inc.

It is frowned upon in this culture to be 'in the closet' forever. The gay culture walks a fine line between being empathic and understanding of how difficult coming out can be and being "out and proud," and the majority of the culture shares this sentiment.

What does "patterned" mean and why is it used to describe culture? In this context, *patterned* means distinctive and unique. "Culture is *patterned* because the practices of interest are organized and utilized systematically in order to be intelligible to others—they are not randomly recreated with each usage" (Gone, 2011, p. 235). Judaism is an example of religious culture as there are common religious practices that are passed down from generation to generation. Jewish faith (and culture) holds certain beliefs about the death process that dictate specific funeral customs. According to Jewish law, the time period between death and a funeral is a time of limbo for the soul of the deceased, as the soul is departed from the body but has not reached its final resting place until the body has been committed back to the earth (Goldstein, n.d.). Therefore, it is customary for Jewish people to be buried as soon as possible after death. In this example, it is clear that the practices surrounding burying the Jewish deceased are systematic and ritualistic.

Lastly, how is culture "historically reproduced"? The practices of cultures are historically reproduced because they are passed onto future generations so that they can carry on the practices that keep the culture united (Gone, 2012). You may have come to realize by now that being a Black American means that you belong to the Black race in that you have distinct and obvious physical features that set you apart (i.e., skin tone). It also means that you may have African American ethnicity with its beliefs, traditions, and customs that unite people based on heritage or origin. Being a Black American may also mean that you ascribe to Black culture. Spanking is an example of how a practice is historically reproduced in the Black culture. Research in the 1980s and 1990s demonstrated that Blacks used spanking as a disciplinary tool at some point during their parenting lifetime (Day, Peterson, & McCracken, 1998; Straus & Gelles, 1986). Additionally, Blacks are more prone to support the use of spanking as an appropriate disciplining technique than their White counterparts (McLoyd, Kaplan, Hardaway, & Wood, 2007). Generally speaking, Blacks spank their children under the theory that "I was spanked, and I am better for it." Furthermore, this ideology holds true for Blacks across socioeconomic statuses (McLoyd et al., 2007). This is an example of a historically reproduced practice. It is important to note that these practices are oftentimes difficult to break within cultures. Despite the mounting research that supports the use of disciplining behaviors outside of spanking and the social pressure to stop spanking, it is still widely accepted in Black culture.

CHARACTERISTICS OF CULTURES

As you consider culture in your life, pause to think. More than likely, you were holding a definition of culture that was incomplete. The fact is that being multicultural is not something that only people of color experience. We all belong to different cultural groups; we are all multicultural, not because we belong to difference races and ethnicities, but because we belong to different races, ethnicities, genders, sexual orientations, age groups, tribes, religions, ability groups, and more.

Five characteristics of culture are important to discuss. First, cultures are fluid. In other words, cultures are ever-changing. For example, the telephone used to be the most used communication tool; however, the explosion of social media has changed how the culture communicates. Now over 164 million Americans use Facebook, which amounts to 53% (socialbakers.com), and over 340 million tweets are sent every day on Twitter (Lunden, 2012). Obviously, these media have changed the culture of how Americans and the world communicate. It goes without saying that not every part of your culture is fluid. Your race and ethnicity are pretty stable throughout your life. However, you will learn in Chapter 6, "Responding to Gender and Sexual Orientation," that gender, an aspect of culture that we assume is stable, isn't stable for everyone.

Additionally, cultures are not mutually exclusive. In other words, belonging to one culture doesn't necessarily mean that you can't belong to another culture. Just like someone can be Black *and* White, you can identify with deaf culture and French culture. Some cultures may seem to be opposites, but in fact, they may not be. For example, a teenager may chronologically be a part of the youth culture because of her age; however, she may identify with older age groups. Therefore, she may not engage is the practices associated with being a teenager. The same could be true for an older adult.

Third, sometimes our cultures can conflict. For example, American culture has attached itself to the idea that you may not be selfless in life, but you should be in death. That is, it is highly promoted in American culture that you "don't take your organs with you." This is so much a part of the culture that you can get a symbol placed on your driver's license that indicates that you would like to donate your organs should you ever be in a fatal car accident. Jewish law, however, conflicts with this practice since the entire body (and its contents) must be buried (Simmons, 2000). Cultural practices in this religion stress that because the body was once the dwelling place for the soul, it must be treated with the highest level of respect before and after death. The exception to this rule is if someone who can spare an organ donates it to a specific person in need. However, it would be considered disrespectful to contribute to an organ bank where there is no urgent need or intended beneficiary. Additionally, "it is … forbidden to donate [the human body] for general medical research or for students to dismember in medical school" (Simmons, 2000, para. 7). Obviously, the expectations of one culture in this example conflict with the demands of another and, in these moments, each person has to decide which cultural practice to follow.

Also, culture can control what and how you think about yourself (Oyserman & Lee, 2008). According to Guan, Lee, and Cole (2012), when you strongly identify with your culture it is more likely that you will accept and internalize the beliefs, practices, and values associated with that specific culture. For example, research shows that Black American women who have internalized more American values tend to value a thinner body ideal, whereas Black American women who have internalized Black culture tend to value a thicker body ideal (Guan, Lee, and Cole, 2012).

The last characteristic of culture is that we decide to which cultures we belong. Unlike ethnicity, which is part of our makeup at birth, we decide whether we want to be active members in the culture. For example, no one is born in the hip-hop culture, yet some make a decision to identify with it. That identification may manifest obviously in the music you buy and listen to;

BOX 3.4   Five Characteristics of Culture

1. Culture is fluid.
2. Cultures are not mutually exclusive.
3. Cultural demands can conflict.
4. Culture influences how we perceive ourselves.
5. People self-admit into specific cultures.

Image © Blend Images, 2013. Used under license from Shutterstock, Inc.

Green ribbon

Organ transplant and organ donation awareness
Traumatic Brain Injury awareness and support
Cerebral Palsy awareness and support
Kidney Cancer aka Renal Cell Carcinoma awareness

Image © spline_x, 2013. Used under license from Shutterstock, Inc.

Image © Vladimir Mucibabic, 2013. Used under license from Shutterstock, Inc.

Cultural Group	Social Majority	Social Minority
Age/Generation	Early to middle-aged adults	Children, adolescents, and older people
Developmental Disabilities	Able-bodied people	People with developmental disabilities
Disability Acquired Later in Life	Able-bodied people	People with developmental disabilities
Religion	Christians	Non-Christians
Ethnicity/Race	European/White Americans	Non-Europeans/people of color
Socioeconomic Status	People of high class (wealth), education, income, and occupational levels	People of lower class, education, income, occupational levels
Sexual Orientation	Heterosexual people	Bisexuals, homosexual, transgendered people
Indigenous People	European/White Americans	Indigenous and Native people
National Origin	Natural-born Americans	Immigrants, refugees, international students
Gender	Men	Women; intersex people

Table 3.1 ADDRESSING Model   Adopted from Dr. Pamela Hayes's Addressing Model

however, it may also manifest in your clothing and hairstyle choice, where you decide to live, friend choices, and the like. Every deaf person doesn't belong to the deaf culture. There are some deaf people who view their deafness as a disability and would trade it to be hearing-abled at a moment's notice. Others, however, identify with deaf culture so much that they refuse treatment for their curable hearing loss. Similarly, being raised Catholic doesn't necessarily mean that you ascribe to that culture. You could go through the motions and rituals without feeling connected to them at all.

Consider the different cultures to which you belong. Maybe you identify with the Asian culture or American culture. Perhaps you feel connected to the social media culture or the youth culture. Pamela Hayes (2007) developed a model to understand cultural groups called the ADDRESSING Model. This model provides you with a mnemonic device to help you understand the over-arching groups that hold hundreds of cultures within them.

SUMMARY

After this chapter you should have a clear understanding as to the differences between *race, ethnicity,* and *culture.* Race pertains to the physical differences between people, whereas ethnicity refers to the values, beliefs, traditions, and languages that unite people. Culture, on the other hand, has to do with the behaviors in which people engage that unite them. Notice that your culture is not just about the color of your skin or the country from which your ancestors originated. Your culture is about your connection to lots of different people in many different ways.

Why is it important to understand the differences between these concepts? First, we need to understand them so we can use them correctly. Second, knowing that there is a difference between your race and your many cultures reaffirms the notion that you are a complex animal with many facets. In other words, you aren't "just White" as some students say. You are multicultural in a number of ways. Remember that some of our cultures aren't as important to us as others. Additionally, oftentimes different aspects of your culture are important at different times in your life.

Some people feel more connected to their age and gender cultures when they are younger and, as they age, feel more connected to their ethnic and religious cultures. Others experience the exact opposite, and still others never feel connected to some cultural aspects of their lives.

The other chapters in this textbook will look deeper into the different cultures that exist in humanity. As you complete this chapter, rethink your definition of culture. Reconsider how you may have, before this chapter, seen people as unicultural instead of multicultural. Rethink your ideas about your own cultural makeup.

CHAPTER 4

Reconsidering Communication and Civility

Samantha had been anxiously awaiting her lunch break so she could finally grab the leftovers from her meal the prior evening. She had been daydreaming about how the savory sauce from the rice intertwined with the baked chicken and spices would taste. When she opened the community refrigerator—a haven for sandwiches, sodas, and scrumptious desserts that were shared among the staff at her job—she was surprised to find that her lunch was not there. She searched from front to back of the refrigerator, expecting that someone had simply moved it to make room for their own lunch. After several minutes passed, she realized that the food had been taken. "Who," she thought, "would eat someone else's food that they did not bring?"

This scenario may not be one that is familiar to those who have not shared a communal refrigerator at work, but it may be more familiar to those who share a household with others. It could be the last piece of bread; the last cup of milk; the last . . . you name it. What is it that makes others so quick to take things that do not belong to them when they know that the owner will be back to reclaim his or her property? The issue is one that has been around since the beginning of time and simply deals with the concept called **civility**. So, what is civility?

"Civility" is defined by Merriam-Webster Dictionary (2013) as "formal politeness." While civility has been a concern among groups, it wasn't until 2000 when P. M. Forni, a literature professor at the Johns Hopkins University in Baltimore, Maryland, cofounded the Johns Hopkins Civility Project (JHCP) that it was applied to particular groups. The JHCP researched the history of manners, politeness, and respect for others. The project's popularity resulted in several interviews and requests for more information. In 2003, Forni's popular book, *Choosing Civility: The Twenty-five Rules of Considerate Conduct,* was written with a look at how to improve everyday interactions by limiting thoughtless and/or inconsiderate behaviors. So, whether in the break room, bathroom, or boardroom, intentionally exercising courtesy was being studied.

The term *civility* has also been used synonymously with "manners" and "etiquette" (Dresser, 1996) although the specifics of the terms differ from culture to culture. In sports—often viewed as a subculture of the masculine culture—it is perfectly acceptable to scratch one's private areas

Image © Inga Marchuk, 2013. Used under license from Shutterstock, Inc.

in public. However, when in the company of other groups, such behavior may be considered rude or barbaric. In Muslim cultures, it is inappropriate for a woman to touch a man's hand if she is not related to him. This is considered lewd behavior not befitting a woman of character. So, when in a business meeting, a man extends his hand to a Muslim woman, it is expected that she will respectfully decline his offer for the handshake.

Civility, whether in behavior or communicated through language, is a form of communication. It is civil discourse that can lead to open dialogue that enriches and points toward clarity of the subject matter. However, when there is a lack of civility, what tends to occur is a distancing that limits openness to interactions. As a result, what can often be seen is a tendency for individuals and groups to intentionally segregate themselves from uncivil or insulting encounters.

FUNDAMENTALS OF COMMUNICATION

So, what is communication? Many introductory speech classes expose students to the fundamentals of communication. When trying to convey information from one person to another, the individuals will engage in the art of **communication**, the process by which information is exchanged (Merriam-Webster Dictionary, 2013); or simply, the sending and receiving of messages (Mio, Barker, & Tumambing, 2012; Wilson & Sperber, 2002) in order to convey a message from one person to another. For the purposes of discussion, the text will distinguish between the "sender" (one who sends a message) and the "receiver" (one who receives the message).

The purpose of the communication is to transmit information (Beebe, Beebe & Ivy, 2012; Neuliep, 2012; Park & Kim, 2008: Thomas, 1998). However, the message being sent and received is only understood within the context of the culture of the person sending or receiving the message. (See Figure 4.1.) In his 1940 work on linguistics, Whorf explains that one reason for miscommunications is that people tend to communicate based on their own realities (Bennett, 2008) or worldviews. Oftentimes, miscommunication between parents and children, employers and employees, service professionals and customers occur because there are different realities and, therefore, expectations for the way messages are sent and received both within and between cultural groups (Bennett, 2008; Cardemil & Battle, 2003). Here, the interpretation of the message, however, is not the responsibility of the sender, but of the receiver. However, when the sender and receiver use different methods of getting and receiving messages, the outcome can result in miscommunication.

WORLDVIEW AND COMMUNICATION

Worldviews can be defined as cultural perspectives that determine how people perceive and respond to what happens around them (Beebe et al., 2012). One's cultural worldview is based on one's perception of events and understanding of the individual's role in society; it determines how the person interacts with society. Worldviews develop from cultural values—or what is seen as important, valuable, powerful—and belief system (Mio et al., 2012). These cultural values are taught from infancy throughout one's life and result in one's beliefs about how the world operates.

Both Harry Triandis (1995) and Geert Hofstede (1980) performed research on worldviews identified as individualistic or collectivistic. The **individualistic** perspective is a cognitive

Communication Model

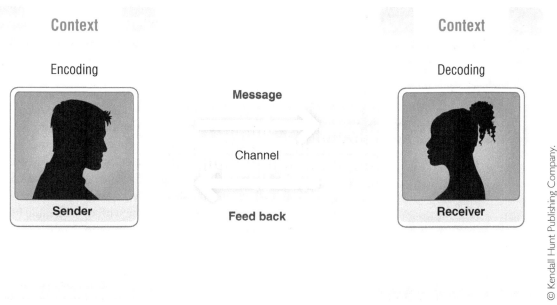

Figure 4.1 The communication model is based on transmission of information from one person (sender) to another person (receiver). This model is used with all human cultures to include hearing cultures, deaf cultures, and blind cultures, and is irrespective of language cultures.

appreciation for individual achievement and personal success that becomes a part of the behavior of the culture. Countries such as the United States, Denmark, Canada, and Italy, for instance, place high value on a person's ability to "climb the corporate ladder"; "pull oneself up by the boostraps"; and come in first place. Those with this worldview do not hold teamwork in high regard. Consider, for instance, professional sports teams. In individualistic cultures, the team is important, but greater emphasis is placed on the individuals on the team who are considered the stars (e.g., the NBA's Michael Jordan, soccer's David Beckham, star Olympic athletes like Michael Phelps). Simply put, individualistic cultures adhere to the "me before we" motto. One way to view this privilege with respect to college students is to see how the A student often responds to the D student who wants to use her notes. What is often evident is that the A student does not feel compelled to share her notes because she believes the D student does not deserve to have access to good notes. Instead, the A student may feel that the D student deserves to fail because of her poor work ethic. Are faces and names coming to mind here?

Countries that value the importance of group achievement are said to have a **collectivistic** perspective. In this perspective, "the whole is greater than the sum of its parts" (Weiten, 2011). This Gestalt philosophy suggests that collaboration and teamwork are keys to a culture's success because everyone benefits. The Amish are an example of a collectivistic culture whose worldview centers around the needs of the entire group instead of the individual's needs within the group. This is one reason that a particular style of dress or position is suited to that group so that no one, in particular, receives more attention than another. Contrary to individualistic cultures, collectivistic cultures support the "we before me" principle. It is most important in collectivistic cultures that everyone is taken care of without particular attention paid to one person. Another example of a collectivistic culture is a sports team. A sports team has to have its players work

Amish culture is an example of a collectivistic culture where the needs and concerns of the group outweigh those of an individual.

together to achieve a goal. When one player scores a winning goal, the entire team wins. So, those from collectivistic cultures see the importance of working together in harmony to achieve success for the group.

According to collectivistic cultures such as the Amish, the needs of the community supercede the needs of an individual because the group takes care of its needs for every member. Research on such populations points to the simplicity and closeness of the collectivistic culture (Triandis & Suh, 2002; Leninger & McFarland, 2006). Therefore, when an Amish couple considers marriage, the process is one that is done with considerable input from the elders of the community. Unlike in individualistic cultures where the attention for the marriage is often placed on the physical attraction of the couple, their finances (i.e., obtaining an engagement ring), and so on, collectivistic cultures focus on how the community can come together to assist the new couple in their union.

Idiocentrism and Allocentrism

As has been previously discussed, culture is learned (Mio et al., 2012). Trandis (Triandis & Suh, 2002; Armstrong & Swartzman, 2001; Mio et al., 2012) referred behavior from an individual who is more concerned with his interest being met than that of others as **idiocentric** ("idio" = *me*; "centric" = *center*). (Another word that has been used synonymously with idiocentric is *egocentric*.) When a group of individuals holds this belief, the group is referred to as **individualistic** (Mio et al., 2012). This idiocentric practice, also known as "me before we," has resulted in individuals simply responding to his/her own needs. When individuals act or feel that the needs of their group are more important than their individual needs, this is referred to as **allocentric**. The group that is interested in maintaining the best outcome for the group is referred to as **collectivistic**.

Americans are often viewed as an example of the individualistic culture, where the needs of the individual outweigh the needs of the group. For instance, Black Friday is a day after Thanksgiving when consumers take advantage of daylong savings on holiday giftware. In a nonverbal way, the individualistic perspective says, "I will get the best gift bargain for my family although I will miss the opportunity to enjoy being with my family during the Thanksgiving holiday." Research suggests that individualistic cultures are complex and relate more loosely to one another (Triandis & Suh, 2002).

The elderly are among the group considered collectivistic. As a group, throughout history, they were revered for their wisdom and viewed as custodians of culture (Mio et al., 2013). This group tends to emphasize cooperation (e.g., between their children and grandchildren) and building community (e.g., maintaining post-retirement relationships). Their stories communicate experience in times gone by that are intended to assist the younger generation in making good choices and learning from faulty ones. It has only been recently that their experience and knowledge have been discounted to the extent that the seniors in many individualistic communities are considered a burden.

Nelson's (2005) research shows that idiocentric individuals younger than the elderly tend to use exaggerated tone (p. 209), baby talk, and overaccommodation when addressing the elderly. In terms of overaccommodation, this suggests being overly polite, speaking louder or slower, and speaking in exaggerated tones. This is in sharp contrast to the way that those in collectivistic societies communicate with their elderly. In such cases, deference is given to the senior adult with special attention given to the value of the elder's knowledge, background, and station.

> **THINK ABOUT IT**
>
> Can you think of other examples of collectivistic or individualistic cultures?

WORLDVIEW MODELS

These kinds of considerations toward particular cultural groups caused researchers like Kluckhohn and Strodtbeck (1961) to examine particular perspectives that different cultures hold. They referred to these as **value orientations**. Values orientations are not described in terms of things that are "good" or "bad" but in ways that support how individuals and cultures view their experiences in the world. Their research provided clarity to the suggestion that everyone sees the world the same way. Instead, according to Kluckhohn and Strodbeck, there are five common concerns that human have and three possible responses to each of the concerns. (See Table 4.1.)

Concerns/Orientations	Possible Responses		
Human Nature. What is the basic human nature?	**Evil.** Most people can't be trusted. People are basically bad and need to be controlled.	**Mixed.** There are both evil people and good people in the world, and you have to check people out to find out which they are. People can be changed with the right guidance.	**Good.** Most people are basically pretty good at heart; they are born good.
Man–Nature Relationship. What is the appropriate relationship to nature	**Subordinate to Nature.** People really can't change nature. Life is largely determined by external forces, such as fate and genetics. What happens was meant to happen.	**Harmony with Nature.** Man should, in every way, live in harmony with nature.	**Dominate over Nature.** It the great human challenge to conquer and control nature. Everything from air conditioning to the "green revolution" has resulted from having met this challenge.
Time Sense. How should we best think about time?	**Past.** People should learn from history, draw the values by which they live from history, and strive to continue past traditions into the future.	**Present.** The present moment is everything. Let's make the most of it. Don't worry about tomorrow: enjoy today.	**Future.** Planning and goal setting make it possible for people to accomplish miracles, to change and grow. A little sacrifice today will bring a better tomorrow.
Activity. What is the best mode of activity?	**Being.** It's enough to just "be." It's not necessary to accomplish great things in life to feel your life has been worthwhile.	**Becoming.** The main purpose for being placed on this earth is for one's own inner development.	**Doing.** If people work hard and apply themselves fully, their efforts will be rewarded. What a person accomplishes is a measure of his or her worth.
Social Relations. What is the best form of social organization?	**Hierarchical.** There is a natural order to relations, some people are born to lead, others are followers. Decisions should be made by those in charge.	**Collateral.** The best way to be organized is as a group, where everyone shares in the decision process. It is important not to make important decisions alone.	**Individual.** All people should have equal rights, and each should have complete control over one's own destiny. When we have to make a decision as a group, it should be "one person one vote."

Table 4.1 Description of Five Common Human Concerns and Three Possible Responses (Kohls, 1981).

While the study of humans within cultures was growing, **Geert Hofstede** (1980) researched the culture of business throughout the world. His research, mainly with the IBM (International Business Machines) Corporation, found that the business culture is typically viewed as individualistic: the goal of corporations is to manufacture a product that successfully outpaces their competitors. As such, corporations do not focus on the group but on the individuals in the group who can independently achieve success. Countries that scored high on this cultural value include: Australia, Belgium, the United States, Canada, Sweden, and France (Beebe et al., 2012; Hofstede, 1980). (Table 4.2.)

Individualistic Versus Collectivistic Dimension	Power Dimension	Gender (Masculine/Feminine) Dimension
Reliance on self versus others	Emotion (little emotion vs. emotional)	Men more assertive; women, docile
Interest for self outweighs interests of others	Physical distancing (distance versus closeness)	Men concerned with maintaining power; women, with outcome for all
Focus on getting things (done) versus people	Trust (mistrust versus trust)	Gender roles defined versus fluid (overlapping)

Table 4.2 Hofstede Model From Hofstede (1980) Worldview Model

Harry Triandis (1989, 1995), who had been doing research with cultural populations in the early 1960s, further examined worldview and found that not only were two worldviews represented in the world, but that within each worldview could be seen other factors that contributed to each group's perspective. He referred to these factors as "dimensions"—vertical and horizontal. (See Table 4.3.) In the horizontal dimension, Triandis (2000; 1995; 1989; Triandis & Gelfand, 1998) explained that both individualistic and collectivistic cultures operate using horizontal and vertical dimensions. The *horizontal dimension* suggests harmony and equality with others while the *vertical dimension* is equated with power and status. For instance, people who are horizontally individualistic (HI) would prefer to be left alone although they may not want to be recognized for any specific achievements. Those who are vertically individualistic (VI), however, want to be recognized for their own accomplishments. In situations where individuals "go along to get along," they may be said to behave in a horizontally collectivistic (HC) manner. The behavior they display insinuates that they are no different from anyone else, so they should simply follow the actions of the others. On the other hand, the vertically collectivistic (VC) individual will sacrifice personal opinion to maintain the integrity of the cultural group (Triandis & Gelfand, 1998).

Worldview	**Horizontal** (relationship)	**Vertical** (power)
Individualism	Self-reliant; unique *Example:* ■ "I pulled myself up by my own bootstraps." ■ "I don't need anybody's help."	Highly competitive *Example:* ■ "I won't let them win."
Collectivism	Cooperative *Example:* ■ "I'm a Baltimore Ravens fan." ■ "I'm from the West side."	Respects [community] norms by demonstrating cohesion *Example:* ■ "I will sacrifice my wants to ensure that everyone's needs get met."

Table 4.3 Triandis (1995) Worldview Model

Derald Wing Sue (Mio et al, 2012), however, cautioned that when considering the models of power and gender, these did not always align with the experiences of people of races other than Caucasian. Sue's research explains that in Western society, a person who is individualistic is looked upon favorably (Chung, 2006). Those who have been discriminated against or who have been dominated by systemic practices (i.e., racial and ethnic minorities, women, disabled populations) are not viewed as highly because their worldviews do not match those of Europeans. In research on the worldview of ethnic populations, they found, instead, that there were indeed two dimensions to worldview, but both had a different focus (Sue & Sue, 2003). In the Sue worldview model (Figure 4.2) are four factors that play a role in a person's worldview: a locus of control, a locus of responsibility, internal dimension, and external dimension. The *locus of control* refers to the amount of control individuals have over their life (e.g., "I am an A student because I enjoy learning."), while the *locus of responsibility* expresses whether individuals believed that life occurrences happened to them or despite them (e.g., "I have to work a little harder if I want to get a promotion."). The *internal* dimension regards the person's distinct characteristics and personality (e.g., "Whatever happens to me happens because I allow it."). The *external* dimension has to do with the outside influences on the individual (e.g., "Whatever happens to me is out of my control.").

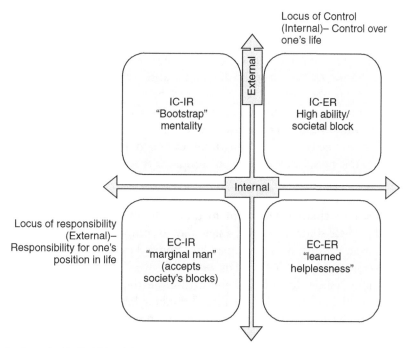

Figure 4.2 Sue (1978) Worldview Model

To view any of these models in isolation limits the value of their contribution to psychology. Each of them has unique dimensions that help to explore, expand, and understand the importance of values, distinctions, and situations that make each culture what it is. To better relate to the feelings, thoughts, and behaviors of the corporate culture, Hofstede's worldview model demonstrates why, for instance, the "dog-eat-dog" philosophy is maintained for that group. Similarly, one might better grasp how an elderly widow—who married during a time when women did not drive, but left the chore of driving to their husbands—feels depressed because her family has decided that she is too "needy" and "dependent" on them for her daily survival. She is an example of "learned helplessness" (EC-ER) in Sue's worldview model.

Communication Styles

There are many ways that individuals and groups communicate within their cultures and with other cultures (Sue, Bingham, Porsché-Burke, & Vasquez, 1999; Triandis, 1995). We refer to these as *communication styles*. According to Jones (2002), "It has even been demonstrated that people identify more with people who speak the same language than with people who share the same familial background." (p. 52). Research demonstrates that communication styles vary within a culture based on age, geographic location, and other variables that are present within a culture. For instance, two people may belong to a particular generation, but one may live in the West and the other in the East. What is typically noted is that while they share the culture of age, they will express certain words differentlyy whether in syntax or grammar. *Syntax* refers to the literal meaning or how sentences are constructed, while *grammar* refers to the proper use of words in a sentence.

Within each culture are words and phrases that are used to directly communicate a message within the group that may be misunderstood to those outside of the group. When people talk using abbreviated terminology like slang and jargon, these terms are typically intended to be relayed to and understood by a particular group. So, when a server in a restaurant gives an order to the chef to "Paint it red," what is being communicated here? It is called *jargon*. Jargon terms are those that are specialized and used in the world of work. Courses in colleges and university use jargon that is considered universal. When a student refers to a particular class, the name is abbreviated to "PSYC 105," which indicates that it is an introductory psychology course. Those who do not belong to the college culture may not understand these terms and are often confused by their meanings.

Sometimes what people hear does not match the message that was intended. This can lead to misinterpretation and miscommunication.

Image © Dan Kosmayer, 2013. Used under license from Shutterstock, Inc.

There are terms, however, that are not related to the workforce but are used within a particular cultural group. These shorthand terms are called *slang*. Often there is an assumption that slang terms are vulgar. While some slang can be vulgar, the common use for slang is to communicate a message in an abbreviated format between members of the same culture. When someone from the tattoo culture is discussing his tattoos, he will use slang terms like "ink" or "tat." To other members of the tattoo culture, these are ways to describe a tattoo, as in "I'm going to get some ink" or "I'm getting a tat." Slang terms can be found in all cultures but are examples of the emic perspectives, where the people of that culture understand the intent and the meaning of the terms.

When deaf schools were instituted in New England (Connecticut) in the early 1800s, deaf children were sent to these schools to learn to communicate in the world. These students learned a new way to communicate using the American Sign Language (ASL) system developed by Thomas Hopkins Gallaudet (Leigh, Corbett, Gutman, & Morere, 1996). For years, ASL was used as one of the main communications vehicles for the deaf and hard-of-hearing communities until the eugenics movement and "survival of the fittest" thinking began to take hold on the American society. This required that the deaf become more like the hearing and adjust their communication style in order to relay messages orally with the hearing. (This history on the deaf is quite expansive but is necessary to understand how critical the Sue worldview model is in multicultural psychology.)

After years of learning to lip-read and converse orally with the hearing population, the deaf community rebelled against this insistence to change their cultural values and traditions. In an exceptional demonstration of solidarity and pride, from March 6 to 18, 1988, the students at Gallaudet University in Washington, DC, held a campuswide protest to publically denounce the university's plans to hire the only "hearing" candidate in the bid for a university president when competitive deaf presidential candidates were not favorably considered. Elisabeth Zinser, though having been offered and accepted the presidency of Gallaudet, resigned amid the protests leading to the hiring of Dr. I. King Jordan as president. Jordan successfully served the university from 1988 to 2006.

Direct and Indirect Communication

There are two types of communication: direct versus indirect communication and high-context versus low-context communication. Direct communication involves sending messages that are literal, to the point, and explicit (Myers & Sadaghiani, 2010). When using direct communication, the sender intends to convey a message that tells the receiver exactly what the sender means. An example might be, "I said that I would meet you at 10:00. Can't you tell time?" Here, the sender is letting the receiver know that she is not pleased with the other person's tardiness. The message that is communicated clearly demonstrates this. In cases like this one, individualistic cultures as in America, Germany, and other Western countries tend to use direct communications styles although there are different levels of directness that each uses (Beebe et al., 2012).

On the other hand, cultural groups whose communication style is indirect tend to use more nonverbal methods to communicate their messages. Researchers have found that these cultures tend to be more collectivistic (group-focused) than individualistic (individual-focused). The goal of their interactions is to maintain a relationship with the receiver. In societies where indirect communication is preferred, there is often less conflict. However, when a person who is used to using a direct approach when communicating comes into contact with a person whose communication style is indirect, the outcome tends to be miscommunication.

Example

> *Beverly (using direct communication style):* **Let's go to the movies tonight.**
> *Leah (response using indirect communication style):* **If that's what you want to do.**

In this situation, Beverly is asserting her desire to go to the movies. Leah understands this and because she wants to maintain her relationship with Beverly—although she might have other ideas about how the two could be entertained that evening—she seems to agree with Beverly. In actuality, she is only agreeing that she wants to do what makes Beverly happy, not that she wants to go to the movies. This can be seen in what she does not say, or in-between the lines.

Returning to the example of the exchange at the beginning of the chapter, note that Samantha does not know who took the sandwich. However, someone was aware that s/he took the sandwich. This behavior suggests that the person probably knows that what s/he did was wrong. Even though the person may not realize that the sandwich belonged to Samantha, taking the sandwich is an example of *indirect* communication. The result of this behavior could lead to conflict whether at the moment or later turning into a disintegration of friendship or trust [of those in the workplace].

Verbal Communication

Traditionally, both linguistic and social science researchers agree that there are at least two types of information: verbal and nonverbal (Neuliep, 2012). In verbal communication, messages are transmitted using the voice from the sender to the receiver. Although words are used in verbal communication, the meanings of words can be construed differently depending on what is called *paralanguage* (*para* = "alongside" or "beside"). Paralanguage includes vocal utterances that are not considered "words" but that communicate a feeling, emotion, or sentiment about a topic. It can affect how information is transmitted. For instance, when a parent calls to his or her child from a distance, the interpretation of that call can be determined by elements that are referred to as paralanguage—*emphasis, tone, pronunciation,* and *rate of speed.*

Emphasis refers to the stress placed on words as they are being communicated. In the case of the deaf culture, emphasis is made in the form of facial gestures and body movement. There is a difference between "Derek, come here, please." and "De---rek, come here!" Emphasis signals the receiver to the intensity of the sender's intent.

The vocal quality of a message alerts the receiver to the nonverbal aspects of the message. This can be referred to as *tone*. If someone is whispering, this often suggests that the information being shared is for the receiver only, not for anyone else. However, if the sender whispers because he has laryngitis, this allows the receiver to know that the sender is not feeling well, which may require the receiver to pay closer attention to the message. Either way, the interpretation of the message can be determined by the sender's tone.

Early in a child's development, that child is taught to pronounce words clearly and correctly. This is referred to as "enunciation." *Pronunciation* is the sound one makes when saying a word; enunciation requires the person to state the word clearly (i.e., speak without mumbling or slurring the word). In *enunciation*, emphasis is used to stress either the consonant or vowels so that the "receiver" is clearly able to understand the word.

Example

> *Manny:* Where is Trisha?
> *Ana:* Ova daya.
> *Manny:* What?
> *Ana (pointing):* O-ver the-re.

Rate of speed (how quickly the message is relayed) may suggest the importance of the message or whether the individual is conveying a "double-message." At the end of television or radio promotions, the announcer typically speaks more quickly than when promoting the product. Oftentimes, the receiver has difficulty understanding what is being said because of the rapid rate of speed used. In Western societies, this is also referred to as the "fine print," a portion of a document that contains restrictions and suggests important information that—by the use of small printing style—is written in an attempt to dissuade the reader from reading it. These quick messages are critical elements in the sale of any product, but may contain information that could cause the sender" to reconsider purchasing of the product. Western cultures teach that when a person talks fast that the person is either nervous, unsure, or trying to deceive the receiver (Ekman, 2009).

Nonverbal Communication

Nonverbal communication includes information that is transmitted from the sender to the receiver without vocalization or formal words. This information includes body language, gestures, written documents (e.g., music, journal), artifacts (e.g., logos, jewelry, tattoos), touch and silence (Mio et al., 2012; Niels, Giles, & LePoire, 2003). When considering the deaf community, this cultural group tends to use nonverbal communication when sending and receiving messages. These nonverbal messages are communicated through sign language or even lip reading.

Research demonstrates that cross-cultural interactions that use nonverbal methods of communicating can lead to unintentional clashes (Mio et al, 2012). At issue with communication is the context of the message. Twenty-first century anthropologist **Edward T. Hall** (1976, 1990) introduced the concepts of *high-* and *low-context cultures* (Würtz, 2005). Here, context is the circumstance surrounding the message. Why was the message sent? What was the external environment like when the message was sent?

Those in low-context cultures tend to place less emphasis on verbal indicators (Beebe et al., 2012; Hall, 1990; Mio et al., 2012). In other words, the messages they transmit are direct or to the point. There is very little question about what the person in the low-context culture thinks; the speaker articulates the meaning as if there is only one way for the message to be interpreted (Park & Kim, 2008). Therefore, less time is spent creating an atmosphere of uncertainty. If a person from a low-context culture is asked for an opinion on a matter, that person might offer the opinion with the understanding that only one correct answer was possible.

Conversely, *high-context* cultures are those that combine verbal and nonverbal messages to convey meaning, reasonably placing more emphasis on nonverbal indicators (Beebe et al., 2012). When communicating with high-context cultures, more attention will be focused on what is not said, but is implied. Meaning is often determined by what is not said more so than what is said. In this type of culture, "reading between the lines" becomes a strategy for understanding the message that is sent or received. For instance, the act of bowing to a monarch or person of high social class is a high-context behavior. According to high-context communication, there is no need for verbal exchange in this case because the context of the situation calls for an acknowledgement of status and social power.

In the 1986 romantic drama *Children of a Lesser God*, the protagonist James Leeds (played by actor William Hurt) is an English teacher newly hired at a New England School for the deaf. Here, he meets Sarah Norman, a young deaf woman who is the school janitor at the school (Blankenship, 2006). The movie contains both high-context and low-context communication, with particular attention being paid to the ASL used throughout the move. ASL is an example of high-context communication. In the deaf community, ASL is learned before English is learned (Padden & Humphries, 2009; Leigh, 2012). So, for the deaf community, learning English is learning a second language, making this cultural group bilingual—able to communicate (read, write, relay messages) using two language formats.

Award-winning actress Marlee Matlin, deaf since birth, has been a visible advocate who had an instrumental role in closed captioning legislation.

In Eadie's (2010) research, he explains that communication in the gay and lesbian "co-cultures" is typically in indirect ways using high-context style. While many stereotypes suggest that the clothing a gay male or lesbian wears indicates sexual orientation, research has found this to be an unreliable measure (Kulick, 2000). At a time in history when one could be tried and convicted in court for "sex crimes" that included homosexuality (Nazi Germany, Victorian England; present-day Cameroon or West Africa), it became critical for members of the gay and lesbian communities to communicate their culture only to each other (Sodomy Violation of Basic Human Rights). Therefore, communication—as is often seen in any minority culture—focuses on slang or abbreviated language known only to members of the cultural groups.

COOPERATION IN COMMUNICATION

When discussing how to engage people from different cultures and backgrounds, Grice (1975) suggests that there are conversational rules for communicating in such groups. What Grice refers to as *cooperative principles* (Cardemil & Battle, 2003; Hughes & Gartsman, 2007; Mio et al., 2012; Sanchez-Burks, Lee, Choi, Nisbett, Zhao, & Koo, 2003) are assumptions that are made during conversations in order to understand the essence of the verbal or nonverbal communication. Whether the message is stated verbally or nonverbally, as with Sign Language or gestures, the principles can be applied. It is important to note that when discussing this topic, the terms *sender* and *receiver* are used to demonstrate that, whether the communication is made verbally or nonverbally, there is a person sending the message while there is another person receiving the message. (Using terms such as *speaker* and *hearer* could be considered offensive to the deaf community where the terms suggest that hearing and responding with the voice are the expected methods of communication.) Within these principles are *maxims* (Wilson & Sperber, 2002) or rules that guide how communication takes place regardless of the form of communication—either verbally or nonverbally.

Quality

The *quality* maxim suggests that during conversation, the sender is going to present clear and accurate information to the receiver. This is done with attention given to making sure that the receiver understands the message.

Example

> *Martha (across a college courtyard):* Is that you, Alex? (The sender wants confirmation of the receiver's identity.)
> *Alex (walking toward Martha):* Yes, Martha. How are you? (The receiver affirms that s/he is the person that the sender suspects.)

Quantity

The *quantity* maxim suggests that the information being communicated from sender to receiver is going to include the right amount of information and will allow both the sender and the receiver turns in the exchange.

Example

School principal: Now, you know that we have a rule in this school that all students must keep their hands to themselves and be respectful of others' property. Yet, several students saw you pick up Bobby's backpack and throw it across the playground during recess. Is this true? (Only the latter portion of the statement requires an exchange. The earlier information simply set the stage to prepare the receiver to respond. The principal's suggestion that the student was aware of the school's culture also refers to the *quality* maxim.)

Douglas (with downcast glance): Yes. (No further information is necessary. He responded to the request made of him for clarification. In this case, it was not only the verbal message that suggested *quantity*, but the nonverbal message of the downcast glance that suggested *quality*, as well.)

Relation

The *relation* maxim suggests that both the sender and receiver understand that, in order to communicate properly, both people need to remain on the topic being discussed and be relevant. When people are engaged in communication, it is necessary that they maintain the focus on the topic at hand so that there is clarity in the communication.

Example

Ann: Are you going to study this Saturday for the exam on Monday because I was hoping to go to the library?

Keith: Yes; I was going to go to the library on Saturday. Want to study together? (Keith responds to the question by staying on topic.)

Manner

The *manner* maxim focuses not on what is said, but how it is said. When communicating with another person, manner suggests that consideration be given to getting the message across in an orderly fashion. Manner also relates to a person's position, for instance, via age, class, or station (Bennett, 2008).

Example

Police officer (to person suspected of a driving at unacceptable speeds): I will need to see your driver's license and registration.

Driver (handing requested materials to officer): Here you are, Officer. (In this case, there is no need for discussion about being stopped for the suspected violation. What is expected is compliance with the officer's request because of her position. The driver communicates in an orderly and timely way that recognizes the officer's position.

Violations of Grice's Universal Maxims

According to Grice (1975), there are times in communicating that these maxims are violated. There are times during conversations when misunderstandings occur because of the way the individual communicates his or her thoughts or feelings. Some of these misunderstandings may occur because of individual characteristics, but often they can result from cultural communication factors (Cardemil & Battle, 2003).

Example 1

> *Beverly:* **Alex, did you eat my sandwich that I left in the refrigerator?**
> *Alex:* **That was yours?**

In this example, Alex is violating the maxim of relation. Here, he is trying to ignore the fact that he did eat the sandwich by switching the topic from the fact that he took the sandwich. What is demonstrated here is that there are two cultures: one of the sandwich owner, and the other of the sandwich taker. For the sandwich taker, his action suggests that he is neither interested in who owned the sandwich, nor in the fact that Beverly would return for her sandwich. More discussion of this type of communication is continued later in the chapter.

Example 2

> *Traveler driving in New Orleans, Louisiana, for the first time, asks pedestrian for directions.*
> *Traveler:* **Excuse me, could you tell me how to get to the Days Inn on Canal Street?**
> *Pedestrian:* **It's over by Tulane University.**

This violates the quantity maxim. Here, the traveler simply wants to obtain directions to a hotel. The pedestrian makes an assumption that the person must be more familiar with the setting and suggests a different landmark. This less informative information is a violation because it does not offer the receiver specific details addressing the question.

Example 3

> *Conversation between teenagers overheard in the back of a school bus.*
> *Teenager 1:* **What happened in Mrs. Finebush's class today? She ran out of the room as if there had been a fire or something.**
> *Teenager 2:* **I heard that she got fired. Nobody likes her anyway!**

While gossip is nothing new to the human condition, gossip is a violation of the quality maxim. Gossip often presents untruths as though they were fact. The statement, "I heard that she got fired" suggests that the speaker is not informed. Additional information, especially if not from a reputable source (one who had a first-hand account of the incident), would not be considered true. Be suspicious of blanket statements that include "nobody" and "anybody" because it is not possible to survey all humans in making such an assessment. Therefore, it is viewed as an untruth.

Example 4

> *Wife to husband:* **When are you going to finish all of these projects that need to be done around the house?**
> *Husband:* **When somebody stops spending all her time asking me about when I'm going to get the projects done.**

In this example, the husband is being ambiguous about his wife's question. Instead of giving her a particular date, time, or plan for tackling the household projects, he uses ambiguous language to suggest that if "someone" (referring to her) would stop asking him, he could complete the projects. This is a violation of the manner maxim, when the language used is either ambiguous, vague, or indicated by inappropriate speed or volume (Hughes & Gartsman, 2007; Khosravizadeh & Sadehvandi, 2011).

Researchers in both psychology and linguistics have learned that communication between people often serves different purposes for the sender and the receiver. In some cases, a conversational maxim will be violated in order to save a relationship:

Example 5

Person 1: **I feel as light as a feather. This diet is really working for me.**
Person 2 (with a smirk): **Good.**

Although this is a violation of the manner maxim (ambiguity), the receiver (Person 2) may not agree with the sender (Person 1), but does not want to negatively affect the relationship between the two. Instead of honestly stating that the person does not look as though he has lost weight, the short courteous response of "Good" allows Person 1 to make his own interpretation of the meaning of Person 2's statement.

As you read the following examples, can you detect which maxim is being violated and why? Is the example one of direct or indirect communication? High- or low-context communication?

Example 6

Martin: **How are you doing?**
Lisa: **Fine, and you?**

In this example, what has become commonplace in Western English-language communication is to keep details to a minimum. This has been suggested to demonstrate interest for the other person's time, but also allows the sender to monitor the amount of personal information one shares. The problem comes when the person is not doing "fine," but says so in order to limit access to one's actual experience. In some cultures, this limited information suggests a lack of trust (quality) and can determine the outcome of the strength of the relationship between the sender and the receiver.

THE ROLE OF LISTENING IN CULTURAL COMMUNICATION

When communicating in sign language, not only is the physical sign important, but also maintaining eye-to-eye contact between sender and receiver. In low-context cultures, eye-contact is not viewed as important.

Image © Vladimir Mucibabic, 2013. Used under license from Shutterstock, Inc.

As might be expected when attempting to communicate with another person, the art of listening is key in the interaction. Whereas most of this chapter has focused on *how* communication takes place, it is important to keep in mind how clearly someone receives the information. It has been said that the hearing culture does not listen very well. Interestingly, humans are taught to read, to speak, and to pay attention, but seldom are they taught how to listen. Truly listening requires a person to step out of him or herself in order to better understand what is being communicated by the sender.

Hearing has been said to occur without effort; listening occurs on purpose (Blatchford, 1997; Hornsby, 2013). Think about what is going on presently in the classroom. Are you aware of everything that is happening, or are you paying attention only to certain things? When paying attention, you are making an intentional attempt to gain understanding. This is often what is referred to as *learning*. However, it is clear that not everyone is listening when information is being transmitted. When sound waves are successful in transmitting information to the brain, biologically, this is called *hearing*. Listening is what happens when an individual makes a choice to get meaning from a situation.

It is believed that the penetration of the sound to the soul is what matters when listening takes place. Is that true?

Listening takes practice in any culture. Within the deaf community where nonverbal "listening" is required for successful communication, the high-context cues that are given and received are well defined based on how the sign is expressed. For instance, the sign for "father" is done with the thumb poised on the forehead; "mother," thumb positioned on the chin. Here, the intersection between gender roles and communication are visible. In the deaf community, therefore, it is necessary to "listen" to the message although the auditory signals are absent (Padden & Humphries, 1998, 2006; Jones, 2002). Research demonstrates, with respect to listening, that the deaf cultures "listen" differently from the hearing where facial expressions dictate the meaning of a conversation:

The use of sign language as a first language has been the foundation upon which much of the pro-Deaf culture advocacy has been based. Many people who use sign language even make a distinction between the sign language used by persons who acquire the language before the age of six, those who use "pure sign," and persons who acquire the language after early childhood (Wilcox, 1989). Pure signers say that they can recognize the approximate age at which a person acquired sign language by the way they use facial expressions (Jones, 2002, p. 52).

Think about a recent argument. Typically, in the individualized cultures, when an argument takes place, one person is supposed to be talking while the other is listening? According to Grice (1975), however, this does not always happen. In fact, instead of listening, the person on the receiving end of the sound waves is trying to articulate a defense. Hearing is taking place, but not listening. It could be said that those in individualized cultures may be better explained as "listening impaired" instead of "hearing impaired." How might this affect communication between couples? employees? in international negotiations?

> **THINK ABOUT IT**
>
> Discuss "healthy relationships." How does your culture inform you about "healthy" relationships? Talk with a close friend or relative about the role of communication in maintaining healthy relationships.

SUMMARY

Interaction between individuals is important to gain the other person's perspective. This interaction begins with civil engagement of respect between the parties. Lack of civility can lead to feelings, thoughts, and behaviors that negatively affect the intent of the exchange. Without civility, there can be a breakdown in communication; failure to want to communicate in the future; and a planned separation that can lead to systematic segregation.

Communication is more than just giving and receiving messages. Communication involves how the message is sent, what the intent of the message is, the proximity of one individual to another, and how the receiver makes sense of the message's intent—both verbal and nonverbal. Whether the message is being sent to between-age peers or among a group of people from diverse backgrounds, it is clear that words or gestures can be understood in different ways.

Psychological theorists who study human interaction are concerned not only about how a message is relayed, but also how the receiver interprets the message based on the receiver's culture. While there are those who believe that they simply state their message in a clear manner, it may not be received as such, and could lead to miscommunication and conflict. This is often the case when people from individualistic cultures engage those from collectivistic cultures. While the intent of the message may be positive and encouraging, depending on the value and translation of the message, the initial message could be construed as negative and demeaning.

CHAPTER 5

Revealing the "Isms"

As discussed in earlier chapters, the science of psychology is interested in the ABCs of humanity: why people feel what they feel (affect); do what they do (behavior); and think what they think (cognition). Our feelings, behaviors, and thoughts, which may be positive or negative, lead to bias. All people have a **bias**, which is the tendency to hold a particular view without exploration of other possibilities. Simply put, our biases help us to maintain prejudices (negative feelings), discrimination (negative actions) and stereotypes (negative thoughts), about different cultural groups.

No multicultural psychology dialogue would be complete without discussing the *'isms* as they are such a big part of any culture, but particularly American culture. While the word has a number of definitions, two of them apply specifically to multicultural psychology. *Ism* is a suffix that, when added to a root word, means a doctrine/belief system or the practice/action of doing something. Let's take classism as an example. Most people in Western society would not admit that they were *classist*, or a person who believes that the higher class is superior to the lower class. However, classist ideals can be seen in our lack of concern for the poor resources to which some people have access in our society. Classist feelings can be seen in our disdain for the homeless in America.

American society isn't the only society that contains deeply rooted beliefs about who is superior and who is inferior. In parts of Africa, for instance, being overweight is a sign of wealth, not an eating disorder. It is expected that a person who has access to capital and other resources is better off than someone who is economically deprived. Historically, this type of belief is grounded in philosophy and even movements like the *eugenics* movement. The prefix *eu* is Latin for "good," and the suffix *genic* refers to "genes." This early 20th-century social movement focused on advancing the biological traits of certain races while reducing the reproduction of those races that had lesser desirable traits (i.e., those who were disabled and racial minorities). This chapter reveals the role of categorization and "us versus them" thought patterns that often lead to prejudice, discrimination, stereotypes, and the "isms." More specifically, the focus of the chapter will be on how people are kept physically and emotionally separate from one another on purpose. Lastly, this chapter will discuss the progress being made to strengthen understanding about how such feelings, behaviors, and thoughts affect human relations in a culturally diverse society.

ANALYZING ABLEISM

© 2013 Shutterstock, Inc. paul prescott

Research estimates that about 20% of Americans have a disability (Freeman, Martin, & Schoeni, 2004). *Ableism* is a relatively new term that surfaced around the 1980s. Sometimes known as "disableism," ableism is the ideology that people who have developmental, emotional, physical, or psychiatric disabilities are inferior to those who have able bodies and minds. If you don't have any disabilities, you may not have noticed how our society is set up so that "normal" people can successfully navigate it. The next time you go to the grocery store, analyze how difficult it would be to access the products on the top shelf if you had a visual or height challenge. Ponder about how wheelchair-bound children can have fun at your state fair. Can they go through the House of Mirrors, or are the aisles too narrow to fit a wheelchair?

Stigma

© 2013 Shutterstock, Inc. migu77

There is a social stigma surrounding disabilities, and people who have disabilities are frequently faced with overt and/or covert messages that they are a burden to society. *Overt messages* are messages that are clear, intentional, and direct. There is no question when an overt statement is made regarding what the person said or meant. For example, an overt message may be, "He's an amputee! Of course he can't compete in the Olympic Games." (Reference to Oscar Pistorius, nicknamed "Blade Runner," because he uses J-shaped carbon-fibre prosthetics during athletic competitions. He became the first amputee to compete in the 2012 Olympic Games.) These types of messages are clear indications of 'ism thinking.

Covert messages are subtle, indirect, and oftentimes hidden. Therefore, they require the receiver of the message to "read between the lines." With covert messages, there are more opportunities from miscommunication because the message isn't explicitly stated. For instance, "You drew that pretty well for someone who wears glasses." The covert message here is that the person's visual impairment should make him or her less likely to perform visual activities well. It is worthy of note that these types of messages also convey 'ism thinking; however, they are harder to notice. In fact, some cultures may refer to the comment above as a *back-handed compliment*, which is a comment that was masked as a compliment, but is really an insult.

Moreover, people in the social majority (i.e., people without disabilities) tend to view members of this social minority as abnormal as opposed to different (Reid & Knight, 2006). Oftentimes students feel torn between making their disabilities known to their professors and keeping them a secret. Aside from the social stigma, the academic stigma is that the term *learning disability* is a code word for lazy. Therefore, students may feel a great deal of shame, anxiety, and self-doubt when it comes to advocating for themselves. The concern is that outing themselves invites judgment from others. However, keeping the disability a secret means that students can't get the proper accommodations on assignments and tests, which ultimately puts them at a disadvantage compared to students without disabilities. Students have disclosed their disabilities expecting support and guidance from teachers and received skepticism and suspicion. According to Smith, Foley, and Chaney (2008), "disability has not been widely recognized as a multicultural concern by the general public" (p. 304).

Social Movement

The *disability rights movement* started in the 1960s, inspired by both the women's rights (1920s) and the civil rights (1950s) movements. Advocates sought to establish, maintain, and safeguard equal rights, services, and opportunities for people with varying types of disabilities. More specifically, it was the civil rights movement that gave advocacy groups for the differently abled the formula by which to demand social benefits and equal rights (Pettinicchio, 2004). In other words, the leaders of the disability rights movement fashioned their movement after the civil rights movement, a method that worked in terms of changing the laws in the United States, so that they could move their agenda forward.

Prior to the disability rights movement, American society was designed with practically no thought to how people with physical disabilities could move about it independently. For example, architects and engineers created buildings where stairs were the only route of entry. Transportation authorities around the country failed to provide instructions on public transportation vehicles that would help people with visual or auditory disabilities travel without the aid of someone else. Public works departments didn't maintain walkways and curbs so that wheelchair-bound people could travel safely. This movement was determined to bring awareness to the plight of people with disabilities and to change society's mentality about being disabled. An important mental shift was that they were *differently abled,* not *disabled,* a term that literally means inoperative (or not working). Differently abled people are fighting to be more than an afterthought.

> ❝ *"Once social change begins, it cannot be reversed. You cannot uneducate the person who has learned to read. You cannot humiliate the person who feels pride. You cannot oppress the people who are not afraid anymore. We have seen the future, and the future is ours."*
> ~ César Chávez ❞

On the Legal Books

One of the first pieces of legislation addressing discrimination at the national level actually started on the desk of President Franklin D. Roosevelt, the only physically disabled (polio, in adulthood) and longest serving U.S. president (1933–1945). He signed into law Executive Order 8802, which created the Fair Employment Practices Committee (FEPC). Under this new law, the U.S. government was prohibited from discriminating against individuals seeking contracts with the government.

Most people believe that the civil rights movement and the legislation born out of that social movement (the Civil Rights Act of 1964) was about giving Blacks equal rights. The writers of the legislation were insightful enough to demand equal rights to other social minorities, not just Blacks. Section 504 of Title IV of the Civil Rights Act of 1964 specifically addresses rights of people with disabilities. This section prohibits discrimination against people with disabilities. It also provides children with disabilities equal access to education (Pettinicchio, 2004).

Interestingly, the Rehabilitation Act of 1973 (amended in 1992), signed by President Richard M. Nixon, was designed to ban discrimination in federal programs on the basis of any type of disability. For example, the United States Postal Service may not deny someone a job on the basis of a disability if, given reasonable accommodations, a prospective employee would be able to fulfill the duties of the job. Additionally, and most importantly, it prohibited discrimination on the basis of disability in any program that receives federal monies. With this legislation, Congress made sure that public schools and colleges and state and city agencies were compliant with this act. If they were not, they would no longer receive funding from the federal government.

In the summer of 1990, President George H. W. Bush signed the Americans with Disabilities Act (ADA) into law (Nettles & Balter, 2012). At this point, you may be thinking, why do we need two pieces of legislation to protect people with disabilities? According to Leuchovius (2003), although the Congress intended for the antidiscrimination provisions in the Rehabilitation Act of 1973 to be applied to cases liberally, it found that the federal courts were narrowly applying the legislation. ADA was intended to change how we view people with disabilities. "This is important because, prior to the ADA, government agencies providing rehabilitative services assumed that most people with severe disabilities were not employable. Now they must assume that individuals with even the most severe difficulties can work" (p. 1).

As mentioned, Congress used federal funding as the teeth in the Rehabilitation Act. ADA extended the Rehabilitation Act's bite to state and locally funded programs. That is, now any program that receives any government monies (whether it is federal, state, or local government) must adhere to the antidiscrimination practices set forth by both pieces of legislation. Lastly, ADA extended its reach to the private sector. It maintained that private businesses and nonprofit organizations, two types of business that don't depend on government funds, had to adhere to the policies set forth by both acts so long as 15 or more people were employed by the business or organization.

CONTEMPLATING CLASSISM

In a country that is viewed as a world power, it is important to understand the definition of *class*. What does it actually mean to be in the "low" socioeconomic class as opposed to the "high" socioeconomic class? Class is a position of status that is the product of one's income, wealth, education, status, and/or power. One's income and wealth are two different things. *Income* refers to the salary or wages that you receive for the services you provide at a place of employment. If you are a cashier at a grocery store, your income is the money that the store pays you for coming to work and doing your job. *Wealth*, on the other hand, refers to your assets (e.g., property, stocks, bonds, land, and other possessions). In other words, you can have no income, but be very wealthy or have an income with no wealth. Most people have to work to get paid for the things that they want. That's income. Sometimes income can lead to wealth if you manage your money correctly, however. For example, English author J. K. Rowling's only income was a welfare check at one point in her life. However, after writing seven best-selling books in the *Harry Potter* series, her financial focus has shifted from income to wealth.

Education also contributes to your class level, even if you aren't wealthy. In America, we view people with high levels of education such as doctors, engineers, judges, and lawyers, as people who have money or have the potential to make a lot of money. It can often be noted that social

power increases with class levels. For example, Ursula Burns grew up in "low" socioeconomic class. Raised in the projects of New York, her single mother ran a day care out of her home and ironed shirts to put Ursula through Catholic school. After graduating from Columbia University, one of the more prestigious private institutions in the United States, she became an intern at Xerox and worked her way up. Currently, she is Xerox's CEO and chairperson and holds the honor of being the first African American woman to lead a Fortune 500 company. She may have started barely making income as an intern, but in 2012 she was ranked the 17th most powerful woman in the world by *Forbes* magazine. Regardless of how much money she makes at her job, Burns' job title of CEO elevates her to a certain class level.

Classism refers to the belief that one economic class is superior to another class. Most times classism goes in one direction. That is, most times it is the belief that people who have lower levels of income, wealth, education, and power are inferior to those who have achieved or received higher levels. It is important to note that some

people do absolutely nothing to achieve higher levls of socioeconomic status, while others work tirelessly and achieve it. For example, Paris Hilton, the granddaughter of Conrad Hilton (founder of Hilton Hotels), was born into wealth. She dropped out of high school and only has a GED (low education), and she never had an income before T Management hired her as a model at the age of 19 (low income). Despite these factors, she has great wealth because of her grandfather's businesses, and even more social power because of her family heritage. Like Paris Hilton, Steve Jobs, founder and former CEO of Apple, had low education; he dropped out of Reed College in Portland after only six months. Additionally, he came from a modest family as his adoptive mother was an accountant and his adoptive father was a veteran of the Coast Guard and a machinist (middle-level income). However, after hard work he was charged with reinventing Apple products in the 1990s. At one point in Apple's history, Jobs received a self-imposed salary of $1 per year, and now the company is worth over $650 billion. Notably, Steve Jobs became one of the most powerful men in the world before his death in 2011.

The interesting thing about classism is that it is a cultural category within cultural categories. In other words, class is often seen in the context of race or ethnicity. Schaefer (2012) pointed out that to be poor and Black is different than to be poor and White. The American Dream is based on the idea that class doesn't have to matter. The American Dream is the idea that anyone, regardless of race, national origin, religion, ethnicity, age, gender, or disability, can be a success if they put enough work into the equation. Unfortunately, some of the 'isms, like racism and sexism, make it increasingly difficult for the American Dream to become a reality for certain groups of people. According to Smith, Foley, and Chaney (2008), of the persons living in poverty, people of color are overrepresented.

In 2009, African Americans had the lowest homeownership rate of all of the social minority groups surveyed in the United States (Schaefer, 2012). *Redlining*, or the practice of denying resources or overcharging those who live within a certain community because of income or other cultural factors, may affect this trend. Redlining literally means drawing a red line on a map pinpointing which areas of the town will not get access to resources. Examples of redlining include banks refusing to provide home loans to citizens wishing to buy homes in particular neighborhoods, credit companies turning down applications for lines of credit when they see an address in a certain area, or service providers refusing to provide services in certain areas of the city. Not only is redlining unfair and discriminatory, but it leaves residents in those areas at a disadvantage compared to residents in other areas who do get access to bank loans, credit lines, and luxuries such as food deliveries. Wells Fargo, a national bank, was accused of redlining some of

the citizens of Baltimore, Maryland, and Washington DC for six years (between 2004 and 2010). Specifically, the U.S. Justice Department found that "highly qualified black borrowers were four times as likely to receive a subprime loan as similarly qualified white applicants. Hispanic borrowers were three times as likely to get a subprime loan. Those mortgages carried higher interest rates and unfavorable terms that often resulted in borrowers falling behind on payments or losing their homes altogether" (Mui, 2012). In July 2012, Wells Fargo settled the case with Baltimore for $175 million dollars in homeowner assistance. Notably, Wells Fargo refuses any wrongdoing and contends that they settled the case to avoid a long and drawn-out legal process.

One of the factors in the lack in minority homeownership compared to White homeownership is the notion of income and wealth. Classism.org indicates that education is the key to class mobility. White Americans who often have more access to quality education have a higher probability of turning their income into wealth, even if it takes all of their lives. This provides a basis for the next generation to build on in White communities. Unfortunately, the antithesis is true for the social-minority communities. In these circles, hard-working citizens live their entire lives with barely enough income to support themselves and their families let alone leave something for the next generation.

Social Movement

As discussed previously, social movements create opportunities for change. The labor movement in the United States refers to the period of time when workers started to request that they be represented by a *union,* a collective organization that advocates for employee rights. This movement focused primarily on two things—better working conditions and better treatment from superiors. Prior to the labor movement, there was no limit on the number of hours that could be worked in a day. Additionally, whenever matters between employers and employees arose, the U.S. government almost always favored the employer. In fact, in the early 1800s a Massachusetts court found that it was illegal for employees to unite and protest in an attempt to increase their own pay.

On the Legal Books

Throughout the 1800s much legislation was enacted to keep workers from unionizing and striking if they thought that they were being treated unfairly. However, in 1935 things changed. As part of the President Roosevelt's New Deal initiative, the National Labor Relations Act (1935), also known as the Wagner Act, gave workers the right to organize into unions without being harassed or fired for doing such.

You may not understand the power of the Labor Movement because it isn't discussed as much as other movements in American History classes, despite that it is older than many other movements. However, minimum wage, paid holidays, and the two-day weekend (instead of just Sundays) are all products of this movement.

SCRUTINIZING SEXISM

Usually when the word *sexism* is used the implication is that a woman is being discriminated against; however, the word can be applied to any person who treats another differently because of gender. In other words, women can be sexist as well. **Sexism** is the belief that one gender is superior to others (Note here that "others" is plural. You will learn in Chapter 6, "Responding to Gender and Sexual Orientation" that there are more than just two genders.). *Feminism* is a term related to *sexism*. *Feminism* is the belief and practice of establishing, protecting, and promoting equal economic, political, educational, occupational, and social rights for women. It may sound like a silly idea now, but at the time of its birth, feminism was a radical idea.

It was both puzzling and disturbing to American men and some American women that women wanted equality. Patricia Heaton, the actress who played Deborah on the TV sit-com *Everybody Loves Raymond*, has been quoted as saying, "Men are very competent in their workplace—and this is going to sound sexist—women are better at running households and juggling lots of things, kids and scheduling and that kind of thing." In opposition, "Either you are a feminist or you are a sexist/misogynist. There is no box marked 'other'" is a quote from Ani DiFranco, an American musician. From these rather recent quotes, it is clear that women are still divided over feminism.

Social Movement

The women's movement (sometimes referred to as the feminist movement or the women's liberation movement) started earlier than most people think. Most believe that it started in the mid 1960s; however, nearly 100 years prior, women were galvanizing for equal rights. The first women's movement, which consisted mostly of White middle- and upper-class women, was dedicated to equal rights for women. It was called women's suffrage, and it started in the mid 1800s. At this point in history, women were concerned that they didn't have the right to vote, which meant that their male counterparts had the task of making the political, economic, and social decisions that affected them. Created by Susan B. Anthony and Elizabeth Cady Stanton, the National Woman Suffrage Association (NWSA) sought to amend the Constitution. More specifically, they campaigned that the 15th Amendment should not be passed until it extended the right to vote for women. As it was originally written, this amendment only maintained that states couldn't deny citizens the right to vote based on race, color, or previous status as a slave.

The women's movement died down and picked up momentum again in the 1960s. At this time, some women were questioning the traditional roles that women had filled for so long (Mahoney, 1975). In fact, many women who were involved in the movement believed that if discrimination against women were eradicated, women would be able to reach their full potential socially, economically, and politically (Stoloff, 1973). On the other hand, some women were not supporters of the movement. According to Agronick and Duncan (1998), homemakers who were 28 to 43-years old were less supportive of the movement as compared to women who had started a career by 28-years old.

Having secured the right to vote during the first wave of the women's movement, the goal became the social rights of women. For example, women fought for reproductive rights (i.e., the right to get an abortion) and sexuality rights (i.e., the right to deny your husband sex). Prior to this wave, it was considered impossible for a husband to rape his wife because she was considered his property. Aside from passionate female supporters, the movement had help from different sources in maintaining its momentum. For example, President John F. Kennedy employed a number of women in top White House roles. Additionally, the birth control pill, which was approved by the Federal Drug Administration (FDA) in 1960, hit the market in 1961, giving women more control over the decision to have children. Some 20 years later, however, the women's movement had lost the country's attention again.

Ten years later, in the 1990s, women who belonged to racial and economic minorities were revitalizing the women's movement. With this surge came the assertion that the women's movement had previously catered to gender equality for White middle- to upper-class women. *Womanism*, a term coined by Alice Walker, was born out of feminism, but is seen as a total separate thrust in women's struggles for equality in America. *Womanism* is the belief and practice of establishing, protecting, and promoting equal economic, political, educational, occupational, and social rights for women of color by considering the effects of social ills like slavery, segregation, and poverty. This ideology was in response to the concern that feminism addressed only the concerns of women through the lens of White privilege (we will discuss this term later in this chapter). For example, women of color were protesting and advocating for equal pay practices between women and men; however, there were unequal pay practices *within* the female gender. That is, oftentimes women of color in the workforce were not only making less than men, but they were making less than White women. The feminist movement didn't address equality *among* women, only equal pay *between* genders.

As with any other 'ism, there are stigmas associated with class levels. The poor often feel inadequate and invisible in a capitalistic society where money makes a lot of things happen. Parents with money can finance better education, afford healthier foods, bank roll social experiences like college tours and extensive family vacations and access superior healthcare services. Another stigma associated with being poor is the notion that poor individuals/families are supported totally by government funds, and they receive financial support for an extended period of time. However, according to the Department of Commerce (2014), only 20% of welfare recipients received funds for more than five years. The majority of welfare recipients, nearly 54%, received welfare between the time period of less than 7 months to 2 years. This means that, contrary to popular belief, the majority of poor people are not "living off of the system."

Poor people aren't the only people who fight stigmas associated with class. Rich people fight stigmas as well. For example, poor and middle class people often look at rich people as unrelatable and out-of-touch because they don't have to do the things that "regular people" do. People on the outskirts of wealthy culture also tend to see rich people as being "problem-free." In other words, there is an assumption that rich problems don't matter or that they are all solved with money. Interestingly, an Italian proverb speaks to this faulty idea. "After the game, the king and the pawn go into the same box." Of course, in a game of chess, no matter how much power the king piece has during the game, at the end of the game they both rest at the same level (in the game box). Comparing the game of chess of the game of life, no matter how much money or power you have during the game of life, problems still exist.

It should also be noted that rich people often go through the same problems that others go through. The powerful Kennedy family is a great example of how money and social power don't exclude you from tragedy. Other stars like Patrick Swayze and Farrah Fawcett, who both died of slow and painful cancers, are examples of how problems rest on the shoulders of all people. Finally, no matter how much money you have, you are still subject to life difficulties like addiction, as were Elvis Pressley and Michael Jackson. It is clear that this Italian proverb couldn't be more true because at the end of life all people rest at the same level, *literally*.

On the Legal Books

A number of laws pertain to equal rights for women, the first of which was the right to vote. Remember this was the major goal of the women's movement from the start. Over 40 years after Susan B. Anthony and Elizabeth Cady Stanton wrote the piece of legislation, it was ratified as the 19th Amendment to the Constitution. After women got the right to vote, the Equal Pay Act of 1963 guaranteed women equity in pay for completing the same job duties as men. While it is illegal to pay women and men differently for the same job, statistics indicate that this is still a problem. For instance, when looking at the salaries for women who are 35 years old and above, their weekly salaries are 75% to 80% of men's weekly salary in the same age group (U.S. Bureau of Labor Statistics, 2011).

As previously stated, the Civil Rights Act of 1964 also included equal rights for women. For example, it prohibited the discrimination of women in the workplace in hiring, advancing, and terminating practices. Later, this legislation was amended to include the prohibition of discrimination of pregnant women.

HONING IN ON HETEROSEXISM

When it comes to equality, the world is set up to tolerate only people who are romantically involved with members of the opposite sex. For example, despite being in a loving and committed relationship with his partner for 10 years, Anthony had no rights when it came to Jerry's wishes as he approached his final days in his battle against lung cancer. *Heterosexism* is the belief that

> **BOX 1.1   Heterosexist "Facts"**
>
> 1. Gay men (and women) aren't real men (and women).
> 2. Any sexual activity that is not heterosexual should remain hidden.
> 3. Anyone who wants to be in a sexual relationship with someone of the same sex must be mentally ill or have been traumatized as a child.
> 4. God does not condone acts of homosexuality.

heterosexuals and heterosexual behavior is superior to people who have other sexual orientations and behaviors associated with those orientations. This 'ism is set in the middle of a core belief system that holds a number of ideas as fact.

Of course, some of these facts can lead to homophobia. It is important to note that homophobia is not the same concept as heterosexism, although they can be related. *Homophobia* is defined as contempt, negative attitudes, and hatred and fear of people who identify as homosexual. According to Lee (1995), despite having similar jobs and education levels and belonging to the same age group, women who identified as lesbian earned 14% less than women who identified as heterosexual women.

Social Movement

Minor lesbian, gay, bisexual, and transgender (LGBT) movements can be seen through the 1800s in America. However, the 1960s ushered in more vocal movements from coast to coast. Gay people were marching in front of Independence Hall, while transgender (this term will be discussed in Chapter 6) prostitutes were rebelling against police persecution in San Francisco. Homosexual people were urged to free themselves from the walls of their sexual closets and "come out" as the gay liberation movement was underway. Within a few years, the gay liberation movement had lost its steam, but the gay rights movement was picking up momentum.

The gay rights movement got major footing in the political arena because it attached itself to the language of the civil rights movement. Simply put, advocates and activists contend that sexual orientation has no effect on any other part of a person's life except for what happens in the bedroom. Gays function in the same jobs, raise children, practice religiously—all of the things that a heterosexual person does.

On the Legal Books

You would have to have your head buried in sand to miss the uproar about what rights should be afforded to the LGBT community. Massachusetts was the first state to legalize gay marriage in 2004 and Connecticut followed in 2008. By 2009, Iowa and Vermont were added to the list. New Hampshire was the only state in 2010 to jump on board, but by 2011, New Yorkers passed the vote as well. In 2012, five states voted on gay marriage, and three of them passed laws in support of it—Maryland, Maine, and Washington State. As of fall 2013, nine states and the District of Columbia have legalized same-sex marriage. Fourteen states recognize civil partnerships or unions, which means that

© 2013 Shutterstock, Inc. Rostislav Glinksy

members of the LGBT community have some of the same benefits that are afforded to their heterosexual counterparts. However, most of the states in the union still ban gay marriage by virtual of their state constitutions.

REVIEWING RACISM

The United States is made up of a lot of different people from many different places. As mentioned, race is a categorization of someone based on obvious physical differences; therefore, *racism* is the ideology that a particular group of people with obvious physical differences is inferior to another group. From the time of the country's birth until the mid 1800s, racism was practiced overtly in the form of slavery. It wasn't until the 1800s that the country started to divide on the issue of slavery. The northern states wanted to end it, but the southern states wanted to maintain it. By 1860, things came to a head and the southern states were threatening to secede from the United States of America and make their own country, the Confederate States of America, so that they could maintain slavery. By 1861, the American Civil War had started, and President Abraham Lincoln warned the southern states that if they didn't end the war and rejoin the northern states, he would outlaw the practice of slavery on American soil.

One faulty notion of the federal government of the 1860s was that freeing slaves would force the hand of the southern states. Instead, the southern states continued to rebel and on January 1, 1863, the President signed the *Emancipation Proclamation*. Unfortunately, there was one major flaw with this executive order. The ultimate goal of the Emancipation Proclamation was not to free slaves, but to keep the country together. Ending slavery just happened to be the most direct way to do it. Lincoln knew that slavery was the South's biggest source of economic growth and that, without slavery, the southern states wouldn't be able to survive. Because Lincoln's actions were not fueled by the mistreatment and cruelty shown toward Africans, he freed only the slaves who were living in the 10 rebelling states. Of the four million slaves living in the United States in 1863, the Emancipation Proclamation freed 3.1 million of them. The slaves who lived in non-rebelling states (i.e., Maryland, Delaware, Kentucky, and Missouri) were still slaves.

There were some minor flaws of the Emancipation Proclamation as well. First, the order didn't make former U.S. slaves citizens; therefore, they still didn't have any of the rights or privileges of being Americans. They couldn't carry weapons, didn't have freedom of speech, and couldn't vote or marry. In fact, it was separate legislation, the Civil Rights Act of 1866, which affirmed that all people born in the United States, even if they were born to slave immigrants, were American citizens. The second minor flaw was that it didn't give slaves any support to survive on their own. Imagine that you have worked for your neighbor in his home and yard since you were a young child. You weren't allowed to learn how to read or count money, and the only job that you have ever known was planting his flowers and cooking for his family. Then someone says, "You don't have to work for your neighbor any more. You can leave." Where do you go? How do you buy a house when you don't know how to count money? How do you read street signs when you were never taught how to read? How do you start your own business when you have never been educated? The point here is that, even after President Abraham Lincoln signed the Emancipation Proclamation, Blacks were still being treated as less than human and racism was still alive and strong.

It is worthy of note that while Africans were the first immigrants to encounter the brutal realities of racism, they were not the last. Whereas Africans experienced a forced immigration to the

United States, several racial and ethnic groups that had opted to come to the United States had to combat racism. Irish families fled to the United States during the Great Famine (or the Great Potato Famine) after a fungus killed the potato crop in Ireland. During this time, it is estimated that one million people died from the famine and another one million emigrated from Ireland. However, the Irish people who decided to immigrate to the United States were met with social movements that were anti-Catholic and anti-immigrant. Additionally, Irish people were characterized as alcoholics and were frequently called White Negroes. "The Irish were worse than blacks, according to the dominant Whites, because unlike the slaves and the freed blacks who 'knew their place,' the Irish did not suffer their maltreatment in silence" (Schaefer, 2012, p. 126). In another example, Italian immigrants often settled in "decaying, crime-ridden neighborhoods that became known as Little Italy" (p. 128). Regrettably, because of their lack of education, adherence to Catholicism, cultural customs, and the small subset of Italians who did resort to violence to climb the social ladder, Italians were seen as people who were only good enough for blue-collar jobs.

© 2013 Shutterstock, Inc. Lee Reitz

Social Movement

It is hard to pinpoint when the civil rights movement (CRM) began; however, estimates indicate that it started sometime around 1954. There had been an undercurrent of uprising in the Black community since the turn of the 20th century. By the 1950s things had come to a boiling point. Some say that the CRM picked up momentum in 1955 when Rosa Parks, later known as the mother of the CRM, was arrested for refusing to move to the back of the bus. This arrest sparked the Montgomery Bus Boycott, a social movement that involved African Americans refusing to take segregated public transportation in Montgomery for 381 days. The loss in revenue eventually led the City of Montgomery to desegregate buses.

Others say that the landmark Supreme Court case, *Brown vs. Board of Education*, placed the CRM on the socio-political forefront. Linda Brown, a seven year-old Kansas-native, was denied the right to attend the elementary school that was four blocks from her home because it was for White students only. Instead, she had to attend the "colored school" that was nearly two miles away. With the help of the National Association for the Advancement of Colored People (NAACP) and The Honorable Thurgood Marshall (he was the lawyer for the NAACP at the time), Linda's father (Oliver Brown) and other Black parents brought suit against the Board of Education in Topeka, Kansas. After losing the district case in Kansas, the NAACP appealed to the U.S. Supreme Court. In May of 1954, the Supreme Court reached the decision that separate facilities for people of color was not equal—in fact, it was inherently unequal. See the direct quote from Chief Justice Earl Warren on the right.

The events described above were just two major events in the life of the CRM. There were other events that were just as big. Additionally, other events were much smaller in nature, but had a major impact. Regardless of the event, the CRM set the precedent for social change in America.

> ❝ We come then to the question presented: Does segregation of children in public schools solely on the basis of race, even though the physical facilities and other 'tangible' factors may be equal, deprive the children of the minority group of equal educational opportunities? We believe that it does. . . We conclude that in the field of public education the doctrine of 'separate but equal' has no place. Separate educational facilities are inherently unequal. Therefore, we hold that the plaintiffs and others similarly situated for whom the actions have been brought are, by reason of the segregation complained of, deprived of the equal protection of the laws guaranteed by the Fourteenth Amendment. ❞

On the Legal Books

The Civil Rights Act of 1964 was the product of the Civil Rights Movement. Despite the protests of southern Congressmen who tried to stop the legislation, President Lyndon B. Johnson signed the act into law in the summer of 1964. The act made two important legal changes. First, it prohibited discrimination based on cultural factors such as color of skin, race, religion, gender, or national origin in the public sector (i.e., in public services, offices, and employment). Second, it permitted the U.S. Attorney General to file lawsuits against individual states that refused to enforce the new law. Last, the act invalidated any state and local laws that continued discrimination.

People are complex animals, and one of the goals of psychology is to figure out why we do what we do. Dr. Ana Mari Cauce, the dean of the College of Arts and Sciences at the University of Washington, indicated that "We don't live in a homogeneous world, but one in which people differ from each other in important ways . . . For too long we have been a psychology in which the prototypical study groups have been white rats and white college students" (Farberman, 2011). Here, she discusses the history of racial preference that the field of psychology has used in researching and understanding human behavior. That preference, however, doesn't stop at race. Traditional psychology has preferred to understand the behaviors of White, heterosexual, able-bodied, able-minded, middle-class, relatively young men since it began and has mistakenly tried to extend those research findings to other groups. The research and theories of multicultural psychology won't replace traditional psychology. After all, there is great importance in understanding universal experiences. Multicultural psychology only contends that it is just as important to understand culture-specific experiences. What better way to analyze culture-specific experiences than to talk about the 'isms and how they manifest in our diverse cultural setting.

You may be wondering, is this all of the 'isms? Of course not! Unfortunately, the list of 'isms discussed above is not exhaustive. There are other 'isms that need to be explored more deeply and, quite honestly, an entire textbook chapter could be dedicated to each of them. The previous discussion is just a glimpse into the social constructs that influence how people, particularly Americans, relate. As you consider the 'isms revealed above, it should be clear that none of these 'isms stands alone as an isolated issue. Issues of race intersect with issues of class and sexual orientation, just as issues of ability intersect with gender and ethnicity. Now, let's turn our attention to how the 'isms are maintained.

PHENOMENA OF THE 'ISMS

We can't discuss the 'isms without also discussing the social phenomena that fuel them. Ableism, classism, heterosexism, racism, sexism, and the other 'isms aren't maintained on their own. There are important operational dynamics like privilege, prejudice, discrimination, and stereotypes working behind the social scene that support, motivate, and influence the 'isms.

Power and Privilege

Are you aware of the social power that you have as a member of certain cultural groups? What about your lack of social power—are you aware of that? In the world of multicultural psychology, power and privilege are sisters. *Power* is the ability to exercise influence over others, while *privilege* is the unique, preferential treatment that members of the social majority automatically receive just because they are members of that group. Do you have enough religious privilege that you are sure that when you stop to pray, you won't be harassed? Do you have enough economic privilege that you can buy your college textbooks *before* the semester starts? Do you have enough racial privilege that you can walk into any restaurant in your city and know that you will be treated fairly? Does your cultural group have enough power to make important decisions or laws for other cultural groups? All of these questions solicit information about your cultural power and privilege.

Liu, Pickett, and Ivey (2007) contend that people of privilege deem this preferential treatment to be the norm. However, this assumption is part of the privileged package. You see, people of privilege have so much social power that they often don't see their advantages as advantages. They see them as the opportunities or resources that are available to everyone or opportunities that *would* be available to everyone if others just worked harder. It is much easier for people who are underprivileged to see the power and privilege that they lack. "White Privilege: Unpacking the Invisible Knapsack" (McIntosh, 1987) is an article about racial privilege in America using the author's own experiences of privilege. Her opening and most powerful point throughout the piece is that she never knew the privilege she had as a White person until she noticed the privilege that she lacked as a woman in the workplace. Note that McIntosh (2003) refers to her privilege as an "invisible weightless knapsack of special provisions, maps, passports, codebooks, visas, clothes, tools, and blank checks" (p. 1). In other words, the privileged group isn't taught to understand, recognize, and look for ways in which they have unfair, unearned power or influence over other groups. In fact, they are taught to ignore those advantages and look down on the groups that don't have them. The author goes on to list 50 privileges that she has as a White person in American society, including:

- I can be pretty sure that my neighbors . . . will be neutral or pleasant to me.
- I can be sure that if I need legal or medical help, my race will not work against me.
- I can easily buy posters, postcards, picture books, greeting cards, dolls, toys, and children's magazine featuring people of my race. (p. 2–3)

If you think back to Chapter 3, "Rethinking Culture," you will recall that each cultural group has a social majority and a social minority. The members of the social majority are the people who have the most privilege and social power. For example, when it comes to gender, men are the social majority, which means that they have more privilege than other genders (e.g., women and intersex, transgender and transsexual people). When it comes to religion, Christians are the social majority, which means they have more power than other religious groups. Have you noticed that nearly every school district in America closes school during Christian holidays such as Christmas, Easter, and even Good Friday (the day that Jesus was crucified)? However, most school districts, regardless of the size of the Jewish student population, don't close schools for Yom Kippur, Rosh Hashanah, or Hanukkah. The same applies to Muslim holidays.

Think about your areas of privilege. If you are a 25-year-old, Black, Christian, female student from Ethiopia, then you only have age and religious privilege in American society. Your race, gender, and nationality are areas where you lack privilege. If you are a White, middle-aged, homosexual, atheist man, then you have racial, age, and gender privilege; however, you lack religious and sexuality privilege. There is no doubt that privilege carries a lot of weight in our society. Consider this: even though most teenagers don't make enough money to support themselves, teens whose parents have economic (or financial) privilege don't encounter the same educational and career challenges as teens whose parents have less economic privilege (Lapour & Heppner, 2009).

Privilege and power are important concepts to all of the 'isms. Without these two conceptual siblings, there would be no difference between the subgroups within cultures. That is, without privilege there would be no advantage to being heterosexual, male, White, able-bodied and minded, Christian, and middle class (at the least). As you will soon find out, the privilege that we hold onto contributes to prejudice.

Prejudice

As you have now learned, race, ethnicity, and culture are three distinct sociological terms that are often misused socially. This same social confusion exists among the use of the words *prejudice* and *stereotype*. *Prejudice* is the negative attitude toward a group of people based on their cultural identification. For example, one can have a prejudicial attitude toward Blacks, Asians, women, poor people, non-Americans, bisexual people, and more. We should be clear that prejudice has nothing to do with having a negative attitude toward someone because of his or her actions, behaviors, or remarks. That's just genuine dislike. Prejudice has to do with disliking an entire group of people based on what you believe to be true about that group or based on an experience that you had with a select few people from that cultural group.

Sometimes our attitudes can come out in how we talk about and label certain groups of people. *Ethnophaulisms* are ethnic slurs used to refer to groups of people in a disparaging and offensive way. Referencing someone in a derogatory or condescending way because of their cultural identification is also considered an ethnophaulism. For example, "Lakeisha, not bad for a girl" or "Hiro, I am surprised

Common Ethnophaulisms	
African Americans	nigger, jigaboo, tar baby
Arab Americans	turban head, rag head, sand nigger
Asian Americans	chink, gook, jap, slant
Biracial Americans	oreo (part African American/part European American descent), mut, half-breed
European Americans	honky, cracker, whitey
Hispanic Americans	spik (mostly Mexican Americans), wetback
Jewish American	jap ~ Jewish American Princess (young Jewish girls), yid
Native American	redskin, squaw (Native American women)
Immigrants	wop ~ without papers (mostly used for people who were suspected of being illegal immigrants)

Table 5.1 Common Ethnophaulisms for Racial Groups

© 2013 Shutterstock, Inc. charles taylor

© 2013 Shutterstock, Inc. SFC

at your math grade given your Asian descent" are examples of referencing others in a derogatory and condescending way because of their identification with a cultural group.

Stereotypes

The term stereotype has been a part of the national conversation since America began. Stereotypes are undependable and oversimplified generalizations about all members of a group that do not consider the individual differences within that group. If you consider just the last 100 years, you will find that stereotypes were the talk of the country in the early 1900s when suffragists rebelled against the stereotypes that women were only good enough to be wives and mothers with no ideas, creativity, and skills of their own. Then, in the mid-1900s African Americans launched a sociopolitical movement to gain access to equal rights. Since the World Trade Center attacks on September 11, 2001, Arab and Muslim Americans have fought stereotypes that they are religious extremists who are violent, without conscience, and threatening to all Americans.

Some people believe that, as long as stereotypes are good, they are not harmful. This is another faulty idea. For example, one stereotype of Asian Americans is that they are excellent students. Unfortunately, this "positive stereotype" is still harmful for Asians. Not only does it place undue pressure on Asian American students in the classroom, but it also isn't true. Not all Asians are good students: Some are average students, while others are poor students. As we think about undue pressure in the classroom, consider stereotype threat, a product of stereotyping.

Stereotype Threat

You may not know what stereotype threat is, but you may have experienced it. A *stereotype threat* is the experience of anxiety or worry that one's performance will confirm a negative stereotype about his or her cultural group (Steele & Aaronson, 1995). The original research on stereotype threat was done on race. It reviewed the impact of stereotype threat on test scores of Black and White students, and the results were astounding. Thirteen Black and White students were recruited for the research and given a test. Half of the students were told that the test was a measure of intelligence, while the other half was told that the test was a problem-solving test. Steele and Aronson found that changing the description of the test had no effect on the White students; however, it had a profound effect on the Black students. Black students who were told that they were taking an intelligence test scored much lower than the Black students who were told that they were taking a problem-solving test. The research found that "those in the verbal intelligence condition showed evidence of thinking and worrying about stereotypes about their group and correctly answered about half as many items as test takers in all other conditions of the study" (Aronson, Burgess, Phelan, & Juarez, 2013, p. 51).

While this research was groundbreaking and offered the opportunity to understand one aspect of the educational racial gap between Black and White students, stereotype threat applies to a number of cultural groups and social minorities, not just Blacks. For example, a Jewish customer may not want to haggle with a car salesperson for fear that he will confirm the stereotype that Jewish people are cheap. A businesswoman who feels overwhelmed trying to juggle work and home duties may not show her emotions at work for fear that they will confirm that women are "too emotional" for the business world. Steele and Aronson (1995) also pointed out that one doesn't have to believe the stereotype, the person just has to know it exists to be subject to stereotype threat. In other words, Karen doesn't have to believe that women are too emotional for business; she just has to know that others hold this idea to be true in order to be affected by this phenomenon.

Racial Profiling

Another important product of stereotyping is racial profiling. At the Strengthening Police-Community Relationships Conference in 1999 in Washington, DC, President Bill Clinton referred to racial profiling as "the opposite of good police work, where actions are based on hard facts, not stereotypes." He further stated that it was "morally indefensible [and a] deeply corrosive practice" (Ramirez, McDevitt, & Farrell, 2000, p. 1). This quote defines what racial profiling is *not* (i.e., good police work) and it furnishes descriptions of the term, but what is it? *Racial profiling* is any police-initiated action that relies on identifiable cultural factors (such as race, ethnicity, or national origin) to make judgments about criminal activity or the likelihood of criminal activity rather than an individual's behavior or verified information about that individual.

Throughout history, racial groups have complained about racial profiling, but little has been done to address concerns. African Americans have coined the term DWB (driving while Black) as a way of indicating that they were stopped by police officers because of race, not because of illegal driving behaviors. Dr. John Lamberth, a Temple University psychology professor, conducted research to compare the number of people who were stopped, searched, and arrested with the number of people who actually violated traffic laws on Maryland highways (Laney, 2004). He found that nearly 75% percent of speeders were White, while almost 18% percent were Black.

Disappointingly, 79% of the drivers who were searched were Black. This means that Black people were being stopped at a much higher rate than White people.

Racial profiling resurfaced as a hot topic right after the September 11th attacks. As early as nine months after the attacks on New York's World Trade Centers, five people of Middle Eastern or Asian descent filed lawsuits against airline companies for being taken off or stopped from boarding their flights after they were cleared by airport security checks. Nearly 12 years after that tragic day for the United States, the arguments for and against racial profiling still exist, and our government is still trying to find counterterrorism measures that will keep Americans safe and are legal.

Discrimination

Because prejudice is an attitude, it cannot be illegal. There is nothing stopping you from having negative attitudes about other groups of people. Nothing except the idea that you would preclude yourself from the rich experiences that having a diverse group people in your life brings. The problem with prejudicial attitudes is that those attitudes come out in our words, tones, and actions. That's where discrimination comes in; *discrimination* is an action. It is the refusal of opportunities and equal rights or privileges to individuals or groups because of arbitrary reasons like their cultural identification. For example, not allowing Debra to hold a religious leadership position based solely on her gender is discriminatory. Relegating Joseph "to the back of the bus" because he is African American or not hiring Sagar based on his age, even though he is fully capable of carrying out the duties of the job, are actions of discrimination.

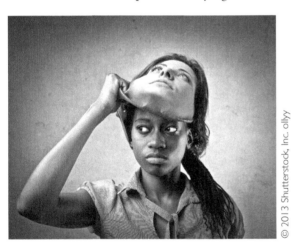

It is important to note that one way to circumvent discrimination is to pass. *Passing* involves purposefully engaging in behaviors so that one can be accepted as someone or something else. Passing is a behavior in which nearly all social minorities engage. For example, lighter-skinned Blacks have been known to "pass" as White to gain access to certain privileges and resources that their darker counterparts don't have. Passing is also seen in homosexual culture. Homosexuals who pass may change their voices, wear different clothing and/or associate (or not associate) with particular people to "pass" as a heterosexual. In both of these examples, do you see how the social minority member is attempting to avoid stigma, rejection of resources, or discriminatory acts against them by allowing others to think that they belong to the social majority?

Hate Crimes

One aspect of discrimination that goes beyond denying someone access to equal opportunities and resources is hate crimes. A *hate crime* (or bias-motivated crime) is any illegal behavior toward another person or group of people that is motivated by hatred of the person's cultural makeup. In other words, hate crimes take place against all social minority groups including ethnicities, genders, religions, sexual orientations, the differently abled, and the like. Hate crimes consist of physical attacks, verbal or physical harassment, rape or sexual assault, financial fraud, acts of vandalism and destruction of property belonging to social minorities.

About 5% (585 people) of homicide victims were at least 65-years old and nearly half of them were women (Federal Trade Commission, 2011). These statistics are startling when you consider that in other age groups, women make up fewer than one quarter of homicide victims. The older members of our society aren't the only age group affected by hate crimes. Children and young adults between the ages of 12 and 19 with disabilities have two times as many experiences with hate crimes as those without a disability (Rand & Harrell, 2010).

It goes without saying that race is at the root of the majority of hate crimes. In 2009, 71% of hate crimes were against Blacks, while 17% were crimes against Whites (Federal Bureau of Investigation, 2009). Unfortunately, the major problem with discussing hate crime statistics is that hate crimes are significantly underreported. Therefore, as bad as the numbers look in Black and White, they are worse in the real world.

Merton's Typology

Since prejudice and discrimination are two different concepts, it's possible that someone could be prejudiced or discriminatory, but not both, right? Right! This is exactly what Robert Merton, a sociologist dedicated to studying sociological phenomena, outlined when he developed his typology of prejudice and discrimination. He argued that people could be placed into four categories that depict situations where our attitudes and behaviors are prejudiced, discriminatory, both or neither.

- The *all-weather liberal* is a person whose attitudes and behaviors are consistent. That is, one who isn't prejudiced and whose behaviors are not discriminatory. For example, if Sara, a high school cheerleading coach, believes wholeheartedly that all of her cheerleaders, despite their race, have the potential to be successful and treats all of them fairly, then she is an all-weather liberal.
- Like the all-weather liberal, the *all-weather bigot* has attitudes that are consistent with behavior as well. However, there is one distinct difference between these two categories. People who fall into the all-weather bigot category are those who are prejudiced and whose behaviors are discriminatory. For instance, Sara believes that Asian American cheerleaders are naturally better at cheerleading than European American students and, because of these beliefs, she only selects Asian Americans to be on the team. In this example, she has a negative attitude toward a group of students based on their race and changes her behavior to match that attitude.
- The other two categories in Merton's Typology address attitudes and behaviors that are inconsistent. The person who falls into the *reluctant liberal* is one who, despite not having prejudiced attitudes, behaves in discriminatory ways. You may wonder, how does someone behave differently than how she or he feels? In the cheerleading example, let's say that Sara's athletic director really wants to win the cheerleading competition this year. Therefore, he pressures Sara to pick only Asian Americans because he believes that they have superior cheerleading skills. Even though Sara doesn't agree, she follows his instructions because she is worried that that if she doesn't, she could be fired from her job as head coach. In this case, Sara isn't prejudiced, but her actions are still discriminatory.
- The *timid bigot* is the exact opposite of the reluctant liberal. People who fall into this category have negative attitudes toward a specific group of people; however, their actions don't display those negative attitudes. If Sara, the high school cheerleading coach, believed that European Americans were inferior when it came to cheerleading skills but never acted on those beliefs because it's illegal and unethical to treat students differently based on race, she is considered a timid bigot.

Kohlberg's Theory of Moral Development

Discrimination, clearly a moral issue, has to do with how you treat people. Kohlberg (1973) contended that we are not born understanding moral laws, but that they develop in us as we mature psychologically. Additionally, he outlined a theory that specifically discusses how we come to understand what is morally right and wrong. His theory has three levels of morality with two stages in each level. The first level of morality is *pre-conventional*. At this level, one makes moral decisions based on avoidance of punishment and self-interest. For instance, Rosario doesn't like it when Muslims come into her restaurant. However, she treats all of her customers with respect, not because she believes they deserve it, but because she would get fired if she didn't. Additionally, she would lose tips if she didn't treat people well. Notice that in this example she is making a moral decision to treat others well to avoid punishment (i.e., the loss of her job) as well as feeding her own interests (i.e., getting good tips). Interestingly, Kohlberg suggested that young children made decisions at this level; however, studies have shown that adults can function at this level of moral development as well.

The *conventional level*, stage 2, also contains two stages. At this level, one makes moral decisions based on society's demands and attempts to maintain social order. That is, Rosario may decide to treat everyone fairly because legally she is required to do so. Additionally, her manager may have set up employee policies that prohibit discrimination against customers. Therefore, despite the fact that she doesn't believe Muslims should be treated fairly, she conforms to the rules of society and her place of employment.

Kohlberg's last level of moral development is the *post-conventional level*. At this stage, people make moral decisions based on universal principles of fairness and justice. This means that Rosario isn't treating people fairly to avoid being punished or to make good money. She also isn't treating people fairly because it's a rule written down somewhere. She is treating others fairly because it's the right thing to do. It is important to note that, according to Kohlberg, most adults' moral development is arrested at the conventional stage. In fact, he believed that only about 20% of adults actually develop fully and reach the post-conventional stage.

As with any theory, Kohlberg's ideas have some critics. In particular, he was criticized for studying only the moral development of men and then applying the research findings to women (Gilligan, 1982). Carol Gilligan contended that women make moral decisions differently than men do; however, research hasn't demonstrated this to be true (Ciccarelli, 2012).

SUMMARY

Regardless of when the social movements started for each of the 'isms, they have always been social, political, and economic problems for this country. For example, even though ableism has gotten a lot of attention since the disability rights movement in the 1980s, Americans have always been under the assumption that people with disabilities should be hidden and kept away from the general population. Americans have always assumed that those who were differently abled would have to learn how to navigate the world as well as those who have able-bodied and able-minded privilege. However, ableism got its start when a small few began to challenge these assumptions. If you think back to the other 'isms that were revealed in this chapter, you will find that they, too, have always been a part of the social, economic, and political downfalls of American history. However, changes didn't start happening until a relatively small few demanded those changes. Margaret Mead is quoted as saying, "Never doubt that a small group of thoughtful, committed citizens can change the world; indeed, it's the only thing that ever has." This quote couldn't be more applicable to this chapter.

When the social minorities affected by the 'isms and their phenomena united to change the social climate of the country, they were successful. Keep in mind that, as Blacks banded together to fight racism, torturous acts against them, and discrimination, they were (and still are) a small group of people compared to the non-blacks in the country. When women rallied to combat sexism, inequality, and discrimination, they were (and still are) a social minority (even though they are not the physical minority). As the LGBT community unites to battle heterosexism, unfair treatment, and inequality, they are the social and physical minority. While these and other 'isms are still practiced today on micro and macro levels, we are still working to make sure that we as a country practice the theoretical concepts outlined our country's Pledge of Allegience "with liberty and justice for all," not for some.

CHAPTER 6

Responding to Gender and Sexual Orientation

Very early in your childhood (probably from the time that you were about three-years old), you understood there was a difference between a girl and a boy (Turner & Gervai, 1995; Poteat & Anderson, 2012). You may not have understood what the terms meant completely, but you understood there was a difference. You also understood early on that you belonged to either of these categories. This is called "self-labeling" (Martin, Ruble, & Szkrybalo, 2004). It is around this time that parents and teachers stop focusing on generic social rules (i.e., saying please and thank you to everyone) and start applying gender-specific social rules. "Terrence, boys don't hit girls. It's not nice" or "Sharon, remember to sit ladylike when you are in a dress."

As you grew, you started to understand that there are more than physical differences that set boys and girls apart. In other words, girls are not just boys with longer hair or boys who happen to wear pink. They look, think, behave, respond, and react differently. As you read this chapter, rethink and reflect on your definitions of gender and how you respond to gender expectations in your life. Also, consider how you respond to those who belong to different sexual orientation groups than yours.

SEX CHARACTERISTICS AND CATEGORIES

The term *sex* has a lot of social definitions. According to Crooks and Baur (2002), sex is a category that describes the biological components of being female or male. In other words, your body contains a set of biological markers that indicate your sex. Additionally, there are psychological components of being male and female, and these components not only influence how people interact in social settings, but also determine how the individual sees him- or herself (Mooney, Knox, & Schacht, 2011).

This chapter will define and discuss the biological and psychological components of being male and female. Culture plays a large role in how gender is perceived and displayed; therefore, a discussion of the intersection between culture and gender is necessary. Lastly, we will discuss sexual orientation. More specifically, we will talk about the differences between sexual orientations, what it means to be a "sexual minority," and how sexual orientation overlaps with other important parts of our cultures. Let's first discuss the biology behind being male or female.

SEX AS A BIOLOGICAL LABEL

Often when you are completing forms or questionnaires, you are asked to indicate your sex. "Are you a girl (or woman) or boy (or man)?" In other words, you are being asked to self-categorize based on your body parts. Therefore, *sex* pertains to the physical differences between males and females. As male and female humans, our bodies are designed to function differently, but together, to continue the human species.

Introductory biology classes explain that there are two distinct aspects of biological sex—genetic sex and anatomical sex (Crooks & Baur, 2002)—and both of these aspects have specific markers that indicate one's sex. *Genetic sex* refers to one's sex chromosomes (Weiten, 2013). If you remember from biology or human sexuality class, everyone has a total of 46 chromosomes (23 chromosomes from each parent). Forty-four of those chromosomes, also called *autosomes*, determine things like height, personality, and eye color. Your sex chromosomes make up the last two chromosomes, and typically most people have two sex chromosomes (one from your mother and one from your father). The female sex chromosome is XX, and the male sex chromosome is XY. In other words, genetic sex is determined by the sex chromosome coding on your DNA (deoxyribonucleic acid), which is the set of genetic building blocks that determine each person's biological traits. *Anatomical sex,* the other aspect of biological sex, refers to the physical body parts (i.e., vagina and penis) that differentiate between males and females.

Normal Human Karyotype

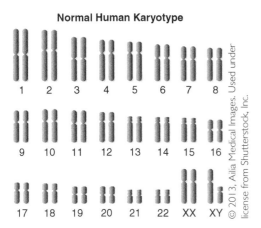

© 2013, Ailia Medical Images. Used under license from Shutterstock, Inc.

It is important to note that there are hormonal differences between genders as well (American Psychological Association, 2011), although these differences are not distinct. Both males and females have testosterone in their bodies; however, men have significantly more than women, which produces some of the secondary sex characteristics that are discussed below. In fact, males produce as much as 40 times more testosterone than women (Davis, 1999). Similarly, males produce female sex hormones, estrogen, but at much lower rates than women (Crooks & Baur, 2002).

Do You Know

Throughout history, females have been blamed when they did not "product" male heirs. In fact, the fact that the "Y" chromosome found in the male (Females only have "XX" chromosomes.) is the determiner of the sex of any baby. In patriarchal societies, the ability to divorce, beat into submission, or even kill women who did not produce male heirs is a matter of record.

Female Sex Characteristics

Sexual organs, while underdeveloped in both males and females, are present at birth (Ciccarelli & White, 2012), and each sex has primary and secondary sex characteristics. *Primary sex characteristics* consist of the sexual structures that create and/or carry offspring. Therefore, a female human is classified as one who has the primary female sex characteristics: a vagina, ovaries, and uterus. Simply put, when a person has the three characteristics above, she falls into the sex category of *female*. Females also have secondary sex characteristics. After onset of puberty, *secondary sex characteristics*, like menarche, or the first menstrual cycle, bodily hair (particularly pubic and underarm hair), and breasts surface. As you can see, all of these characteristics, with the exception of the menstrual cycle, support reproduction, but they aren't necessary for reproduction to occur.

Male Sex Characteristics

As with female sex characteristics, males have their own organs that facilitate or support reproduction. A male human is classified as one who has the primary male sex characteristics: testes, scrotum, penis, and prostate gland. Secondary sex characteristics for human males, which also occur after puberty, include bodily and facial hair, a deeper voice, increased muscle mass, and the literal development of thicker skin (Ciccarelli & White, 2012). Notice that secondary sex characteristics don't make the person a man. There are plenty of men who have high-pitched voices and no facial hair. It's their primary sex characteristics that categorize them as men.

Intersex Characteristics

The majority of babies that are born have very clear genitalia. In other words, there is a noticeable and fully formed penis or vagina at birth. However, 1 out of 1,500 children are labeled as intersex (Dreger, 1999). Before we discuss intersex, it is important to note the distinction between fully formed and fully developed. Most newborns are born with fully formed genitalia that will eventually reach full development. It takes years for human genitalia to fully develop, or reach its full size and shape; however, most are born with genitalia that is appropriate in size and shape given their age. *Intersex* (formerly called hermaphroditism), which literally means "between the sexes," is a third sex label that includes people who are born one of three ways (Ciccarelli & White, 2012, p. 380).

1. *Intersex people are sometimes born with ambiguous genitals.*
   That is, some individuals are born with genitals that resemble a penis or vagina, but are not developed well enough to be classified as either.
2. *Others are born with genitals that don't match their genetic makeup.* As we have seen in previous discussions, the female sex chromosome is XX. This chromosomal code typically translates to having a vagina, while the male sex chromosome, XY, typically translates to having a penis. In the case of intersex individuals, one may have XY chromosomes but have a vagina or vice versa. In other words, the intersex individual may have a conflict between the genes and the physical body parts of that individual.
3. *Some intersex people are born with both male and female genitals.* That is, some people have a partially formed penis and vagina. It is rare, according to Ciccarelli and White (2012), to have internal sexual organs of both sexes (i.e., ovarian and testicular material); however, both external genitals can be visible with intersex (or intersexual) individuals.

When a baby is born intersex, there are some options for the family. Some families choose to perform surgery to construct fully formed genitals or to remove one genital (in the case where there are two genitals). Other families decide to not perform any medical procedures, but still

---

The Story of Bruce/Brenda/David Reimer

In the historic case of "Brenda" Reimer (Mio, Barker,& Tumambing, 2013) sex reassignment surgery, the surgical option to construct genitals was one that occurred as the result of an accident, not because Brenda was born an intersex individual. In 1965, healthy, identical twins boys, Brian and Bruce, were born to Ron and Janet Reimer in Canada. A few months after birth, during a routine circumcision procedure, Bruce's penis was accidentally marred. After consultation and urging from a medical professional, his parents decided to raise Bruce as a girl so that he could live a normal life.

Ron and Janet changed Bruce's name to "Brenda", and the child was given a regular hormone regimen to ensure that she did not develop the sex characteristics of a male at the time of puberty. Throughout her life, however, Brenda did not feel like a girl and often wondered why her twin brother did not have to take the "vitamins" that she was required to take each day. All of this turmoil eventually led to an alcohol problem for Ron, depression for Janet, and ultimately, divorce. Only after a suicide attempt did Brenda's mother reveal the truth behind her gender turmoil. Eventually, Brenda made the decision to undergo sex reassignment surgery to regain the sexuality given her at birth. After the surgery, Brenda became David Reimer and began to experience life as a male. David later married a woman who already had children. Reimer became the subject of a *New York Times* best seller by John Colapinto, *As Nature Made Him: The Boy Who Was Raised as a Girl* (1995). In 2004, following the death of his twin brother and amidst financial problems and a troubled marriage, David shot himself while sitting in the parking lot of a grocery store.

choose a gender under which to raise the child socially. That is, they don't change the physical aspects of being intersex, but they do decide whether the child will be dressed and raised as a female or as a male and proceed accordingly. A small subset of parents decide against pursuing medical procedures and avoid injecting the social aspects of gender until the child is old enough to identify his or her own gender. Obviously, the latter option is the hardest to implement because society is set up to accept only those who fit into two gender categories.

The issue for David Reimer, and many people who do not fit the social expectations of gender or sex, is cognitive dissonance (Festinger, 1962). **Cognitive dissonance** (from *cognitive* meaning "thinking"; prefix, *dis* meaning wrong; *son* meaning "sound") is an uncomfortable feeling that comes about when a person holds two opposing beliefs or when one's beliefs conflict with his or her behaviors. David's cognitive dissonance pertained to him feeling like a boy, but being told that he was a girl. It is in studies of culture, therefore, that answers are sought about how to view, comprehend, and even reestablish a person's understanding of who s/he is in society.

GENDER CHARACTERISTICS AND CATEGORIES

Now that we have a foundational understanding of the physical differences between people, let's move on to the psychological differences between people. You may be puzzled about why gender is being discussed separately from sex. Well, the reason that sex and gender are being discussed separately is that they are separate. Although our society often uses them interchangeably, sex and gender are different concepts. Whereas *sex* is the physical aspects of being male or female, *gender* refers to the psychological aspects of being male or female. Sex has to do with the physical body parts that you have, while gender has to do with what you believe and feel about your sex.

Gender identity, a term sometimes used in place of gender, is your "internal sense of being male, female or something else" (American Psychological Association, 2011, p. 1). Kohlberg's (1966, 1969) research on cognitive development and gender identity found that for most people, their sex and their gender identity match. He reported that humans experience three stages of gender identity development: gender identity, gender stability, and gender constancy. The *gender identity stage*, which forms around the age of two, is a child's understanding of his or her sex. That is, at this point, a child understands "I am a boy" or "I am a girl." Most people who have penises feel and believe that they are men and were intended to be men. Most people who have vaginas feel and believe they are women. By the ages of four to six, humans experience **gender stability**. At this stage, children engage in individual and social interactions that match their sex (i.e., boys play with cars and trucks and girls play with dolls). By the age of 10, humans develop *gender consistency*, which is when children make life plans based on their sex and gender roles (e.g., I want to be a mommy when I grow up).

There is a small population of society, however, whose body parts don't match how they feel. These people don't identify with the sexual body parts that they were born with. In other words,

© 2013, Olga Besnand Used under license from Shutterstock, Inc.

there are some people who feel like they inhabit the wrong body (Ciccarelli & White, 2011). One way to deal with this conflict between their sex and gender identity is through gender expression. *Gender expression* refers to how a person conveys or expresses gender identity. Typically, people express their gender through their clothes, behavior, physical movement, hairstyles/cuts, and voice.

Transgender

Remember just reading that gender identity is your internal sense of being male, female, or something else? You may have been left wondering, what's the "something else"? Transgender people are the "something else." Just like we have racial and ethnic minorities living in America, we have sexual minorities. Transgender people are considered sexual minorities (Brewster, Velez, DeBlaere, & Moradi, 2012) and, while the term *transgender* has varying definitions, generally speaking, it is a term used for people who don't quite fit into society's already defined and inflexible gender categories of male and female. The American Psychological Association (2011) more specifically states that *transgender* is an umbrella term for those whose gender identity and gender expression are in conflict with the sex to which they were assigned at birth.

Let's consider Bob, a transgender male. Bob was born a woman but believes that he should have been born a male and has no psychological connection with being a woman (this means that his gender identity is different from his sex). Bob prefers to dress like a man and gets his hair cut by a barber to look like the man that he feels to be inside. These actions refer to his *gender expression*.

© 2013, s. bukley. Used under license from Shutterstock, Inc.

It is important to note that although the pronouns can get confusing, it is a sign of respect to refer to a transgender person using the pronouns with which the person is most comfortable. It is considered exceptionally rude and disrespectful to refer to transgender people as "he/she" or "it." Therefore, even though Bob may still have a vagina and ovaries, since he feels like a man, it is respectful to refer to Bob using the masculine pronouns *him* and *he*. It is important to note that a transgender person is not someone who simply prefers to dress differently from what society expects. Transgender people truly feel a psychological conflict between their body parts, how they are perceived versus how they want to be perceived, and how they feel about their gender.

A Social Minority

As mentioned previously, transgender people are a sexual minority just like those who identify as gay and lesbian (these terms will be discussed later in this chapter). Think back to Chapter 3, "Rethinking Culture," and recall that some cultures are physical *and* social minorities. The transgender culture is no exception. It is difficult to determine how much of the population identifies as transgender because typically scientists (usually psychologists and sociologists) who conduct research on the community, study the lesbian, gay, bisexual, and transgender (LGBT) community as a whole, and do not just isolate the transgender culture (Mooney et al., 2011; Louderback & Whitley, 1997; Slusher & Anderson, 1996). One can be safe in assuming, however, that they are not the physical majority. Not only are they the physical minority, but they also represent a social minority in that they have less power in our society (Mooney et al., 2011).

According to the National Center for Transgender Equality (2009), although 78% of American voters supported antidiscrimination measures for sexual minorities in 2008, 97% of transgender people report having been harassed at work and 26% have been fired because of their sexual minority status. Goldblum, Testa, Pflum, Hendricks, Bradford, and Bongar (2012) asserted that 45% of transgender people experienced "hostility" or "insensitivity" from school professionals such as teachers and administrators as well as their school-aged peers. These researchers further found that people who were exposed to gender-based violence at school were nearly four times as likely to attempt suicide than those who hadn't experienced gender-based violence. Additionally, 15% of transgender people were living below the poverty line ($10,000 per year) and another 21% were living just at the poverty line in 2011 ($20,000).

Unfortunately, the attempted suicide statistics among transgender people are even more startling than the aforementioned statistics. One study conducted by Clements-Nolle, Marx, and Katz (2006) found that 50% of transgender youth have attempted suicide at least once. Goldblum and colleagues (2012) discovered that suicide rates differ based on gender. More specifically, transgender men had a higher rate of suicide attempts (32%) compared to transgender women (27%).

Transsexuals

Upon reviewing of the definition of transgender, you will find that it is an "umbrella" term with other categories of people falling under it. What are the "other" categories? There are a lot of other categories that can't be fully explained in this text; however, *transsexual* is one category that falls under the term *transgender*. *Transsexuals*, according to APA (2011), are people who believe that they were put into the wrong body and who eventually undergo different treatments to "fully transition" to the other sex. Typically, transsexuals start their full transition by living as a member of the opposite sex and changing their identifying information slowly. For example, they may alert their places of employment about their name change and change their gender on any formal documentation (e.g., driver's license). They may also initiate hormone therapy. This process involves injecting the body with the hormones that are more prevalent in the body they believe they should have. For example, by injecting testosterone into her bloodstream, Katie's body will start to transition to a male's body. In other words, her voice will deepen, and facial and body hair may start growing. In addition to hormone treatments, some will decide to complete their transition to living in the most comfortable sex by undergoing *sexual reassignment surgery* (Ciccarelli & White, 2011). In other words, a plastic surgeon surgically changes Katie's unwanted genitalia to the preferred genitalia.

Cross-Dressers

Yet another category of people who fall under the transgender umbrella is *cross-dressers*. The major difference between cross-dressers and transgender and transsexual people is that cross-dressers do not believe they were born in the wrong body. Rather, they just enjoy dressing up in the clothing that is usually worn by people of the opposite sex. In other words, while the major issue in the lives of transgender and transsexual people is gender identity, the major issue in the lives of cross-dressers is gender expression (APA, 2011). It is worth noting that cross-dressing has not been related to sexual orientation. That is, people who cross-dress do not report a higher incidence of identification with homosexuality.

Drag Queens/Kings

Many people confuse drag queens and kings with cross-dressers because they have something in common—both groups of people wear clothes of the opposite sex. Although they may look the same, the motivation behind their behavior is different. As mentioned previously, the motivation for a cross-dresser to dress in clothes of the opposite sex is gender expression. That is, cross-dressers feel more comfortable (or just as comfortable) dressing in clothing of the opposite sex. A *drag queen* is a man who cross-dresses for entertainment purposes (APA, 2011), and a *drag king* is a woman who cross-dresses for the entertainment of others.

As you have read, society is made up of more than just males and females. We have people who were born between those two categories *(intersexuals)* and people who believe that they were born with the wrong physical characteristics (transgender). We have people who opt to make permanent changes to their bodies so that their physical bodies can be more aligned with their gender identity (transsexuals), and people who just enjoy expressing themselves in clothes traditionally worn by members of the opposite sex (cross-dressers) or to entertain others by dressing in opposite-sex clothing (drag kings and queens). Isn't the amount of privilege shared by those who identify as traditional males and females powerful? They share so much privilege that you may have never even heard of other sex categories or gender categories before reading this chapter. In fact, that's one of the privileges of being a social majority. You get to select who and what people are discussing.

THE INFLUENCES OF GENDER IDENTITY

Although it would be much easier if science could pinpoint one factor that is responsible for gender identity, science can't do that. Instead, there are lots of theories about what influences our gender identity. This chapter will discuss three of the major theories: evolutionary, biological/ hormonal, and sociocultural theories.

Evolutionary Theory

The evolutionary theory of gender identity development contends that the natural selection process influences gender differences. More specifically, this evolutionary theory asserts that, because female humans have to be more selective about their mates (female humans should be picking mates who will stick around to help protect offspring), male humans are at constant competition for sexual partners. This constant competition means that male humans have to be physically aggressive so that they can maintain social dominance over other male humans (Mooney et al., 2011; Weiten, 2013). Therefore, while most see aggressiveness as a negative personality characteristic, evolutionary theorists would say that this is just one example of how evolution influences gender identity.

Biological/Hormone Theory

The biological theory of gender identity influence contends that gender differences originate from the fetus's exposure or lack of exposure to hormones (Weiten, 2013). Berenbaum and Synder (1995) found that infant females who were prenatally exposed to medications that included androgens, male hormones (to decrease the mother's likelihood of a miscarriage) preferred to play with typical "boy" toys and enjoyed playing with the opposite sex more than the same sex. This research is stunning because most four- to six-year-old children engage in segregated play (i.e., boys play with boys and girls play with girls) when they have the option of playing with both sexes (Fabes, Martin, Hanish, Anders, & Madden-Derdich, 2003).

It is important to note that, despite being exposed to more male hormones, the girls in the Berenbaum and Synder's 1995 research eventually grew to be "typical" females who were interested in feminine things such as motherhood. In other words, this exposure to male hormones during prenatal development didn't have a long-lasting effect on the girls' gender identity.

Sociocultural Theory

While evolution and biology have made some convincing arguments about what influences gender differences, they aren't more convincing than the sociocultural arguments of gender identification. A host of researchers, psychologists, and other scientists have scientifically studied the effect of our many cultures on gender roles. *Gender roles* are externally set expectations about what is appropriate for the different sexes. Multicultural psychology contends that gender roles, which are taught and imposed on us by our cultures, significantly influence our gender identity. For example, Wade and Coughlin (2012) maintained that social expectations of American men include "antifemininity, homophobia, emotional restrictiveness, competitiveness, toughness, and aggressiveness" (p. 326). Additionally, there have been studies that indicate that women benefit from attending religious services and helping others more than men do. According to Rayburn (2004), men are much more likely to see themselves as religious, but not spiritual, whereas women are much more likely to see themselves as both spiritual and religious or as more spiritual than religious. This research demonstrates that the other parts of your culture have to do with how you come to internalize your gender. As you know from Chapter 3, we are all multicultural; therefore, according to this theory, all of the cultures to which we belong have some influence over how we identify in terms of gender. The assumption that there is one way to be male or female is shortsighted and biased (Norwalk, Vandiver, White, & Englar-Carlson, 2011) and leaves out the importance of culture in our lives.

SEXUAL ORIENTATION

Now that we have discussed sex as it pertains to the physical body, let's discuss sex as a label that classifies romantic and intimate attraction. This definition of sex has to do with sexuality and sexual orientation. *Sexual orientation* is defined as a long-lasting pattern of emotional, sexual, or romantic attractions to men, women, or both (APA, 2008), and is usually described using three categories: *heterosexual, homosexual, and bisexual.* Think back to the ADDRESSING Model discussed in Chapter 3, "Rethinking Culture," and note that if one's sense of identity is based on sexual orientation, then sexual orientation could be a salient cultural factor for the individual. In other words, if you strongly identify with being bisexual (which will be discussed in-depth below), then bisexuality is a part of your cultural makeup, just as your ethnicity or religion would be. As you read this section of the chapter, rethink your preconceived notions about sexual orientation and those who identify with each category.

Heterosexuality

The root word of *heterosexual* is "hetero," which means other or different (Dictionary.com, 2013). Therefore, the literal meaning of a *heterosexual* is someone who is romantically, emotionally, and sexually attracted to opposite-sex partners. Of course, just like identifying as female or male puts you in the physical and social majority of gender, identifying as heterosexual makes you a part of the physical and social minority when it comes to sexuality. Approximately, 93% of U.S. citizens self-identify as heterosexual; however, it is important to note that 4% of surveyed people labeled themselves as unsure of their sexual orientation (Frank & Newport, 2012).

Sexuality, in general, wasn't researched until the 1940s. Before this, sex was too taboo of a research topic. American biologist Alfred Kinsey (1943) was the first to conduct large-scale

© 2013, Alan Bailey. Used under license from Shutterstock, Inc.

research about the sexual practices, behaviors, and patterns of Americans, and what he found was truly remarkable. His colleagues and he found that, while the collective society looked at sexuality in categories (heterosexual, bisexual, and homosexual), individual Americans didn't categorize sexuality this way. In fact, he found that, even though Americans considered themselves to be heterosexual, a significant portion of them had experienced homosexual encounters. Moreover, his research purported that, even though some Americans considered themselves to be homosexual, they, too, had experienced heterosexual encounters.

Thus, Kinsey came to the conclusion that individual Americans viewed sexuality on a continuum. He devised a seven-point scale that depicted sexual orientation and contended that very few people were 0, which meant exclusively heterosexual with no homosexual experiences, and very few people were 6, which meant exclusively homosexual with no heterosexual experiences. Before Kinsey, it was assumed that sexuality was an either/or system. You are either a 0 (heterosexual) or a 6 (homosexual). Kinsey argued that most people didn't fall *on* 0 or 6, they fell *between* 0 and 6 in terms of their sexuality. In fact, Kinsey's original 1948 and 1953 studies found that nearly 12% of white men between the ages of 20 and 35 placed themselves at a 3 on his scale. In terms of women, 7% of single women and 4% of previously married women in the same ethnic and age group labeled themselves as a 3 on Kinsey's scale.

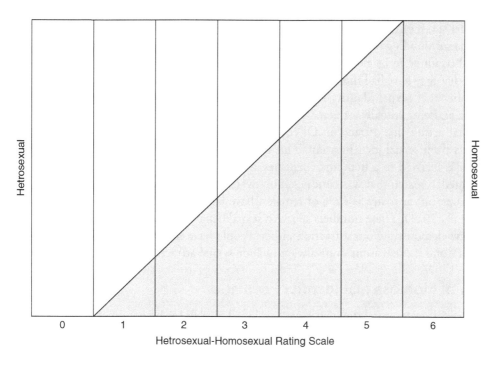

Hetrosexual-Homosexual Rating Scale

It must be acknowledged, however, that not everyone believes that sexual orientations should be categorized. Sell (1997) argued that the Kinsey Scale depicts homosexuality and heterosexuality as polar opposites on a sole dimension instead of as a complex and involved part of life that moves along several dimensions. Others have argued that Kinsey conducted his research using sexual deviants of society (i.e., child molesters and male prostitutes), which is why he got such significant findings. Kinsey disputed these claims, however.

Homosexuality

Of course, if "hetero" means different or other, then you have probably correctly assumed that "homo," which is Greek, means same. Therefore, a *homosexual* is someone who is roman-tically, emotionally, and sexually attracted to same-sex partners. Interestingly, most people think that homosexuals make up 10% of the population. This notion came from two Kinsey reports from 1948 and 1953. According to a Kinsey study entitled "Sexual Behavior in the Human Male" (1948), 10% of males had lived an exclusively homosexual life for three years between the ages of 16 and 55. A subsequent report, "Sexual Behavior in the Human Female" (1953), asserted that 8% of females were exclusively homosexual for at least three years between the ages of 16 and 55. Since these initial reports, it has been widely accepted that about 10% of the population was homosexual. However, newer research has indicated that this is a number that has been inflated since its inception.

In 2011, Chandra, Mosher, Copen, and Sionean found that 2–4% of males self-identify as homosexual, while 1–2% of females self-identify as lesbian. Therefore, at most only about 6% of the population identifies as homosexual. However, a recent Gallup poll (2012) conducted with over 120,000 people found that only 3–4% of the American population identifies as lesbian, gay, bisexual, or transgender (LGBT). With that being said, this number has and will continue to be skewed based on the stigma surrounding homosexuality and bisexuality. That is to say that all sexual identification statistics will continue to be clouded by people's reluctance to admit that they identify as a sexual minority or that they have had thoughts or experiences that deviate from the sexual majority.

Remember that sexual identity is different from sexual attraction, which is different from sexual behavior. Being sexually attracted to someone doesn't necessarily mean that you have sexual behaviors that act on that attraction. Of course, sexual attraction and sexual behavior are separate concepts from sexual identification. This means that Melissa could be sexually attracted to women, but is married to a man and identifies as a heterosexual woman. With those concepts being separated, research that was conducted on over 13,00 Americans indicates that only about 4–6% of males, but as many as 12% of females, have had some type of homosexual experience (Chandra et al., 2011). These numbers speak to sexual behavior. Keep in mind that our behavior doesn't always demonstrate our attraction either. People have sex for a number of reasons (e.g., money, guilt), and those reasons don't always include sexual attraction.

Theories of Homosexual Identity Formation

As with other cultures, several theorists have developed models for how individuals come to identify as homosexual. Next, we will summarize three theories of homosexual identity formation: the Cass (1979), Coleman (1982), and Troiden (1989) models. We will also discuss Lipkin's model; however, it is important to note that Lipkin views his model as an amalgamation of the previous three models.

Homosexual Identity Formation Model
Vivienne Cass (1979) Stage 1: Identity Confusion Stage 2: Identity Comparison Stage 3: Identity Tolerance Stage 4: Identity Acceptance Stage 5: Identity Pride Stage 6: Identity Synthesis

Cass's Theoretical Model of Homosexual Identity Formation (1979)

Vivienne Cass was the first to posit a theory of homosexual identity formation and to view the development of a homosexuality identity as normal. Fashioned after Cross's (1973) theoretical model of Black racial identity development (discussed in Chapter 3), Cass contended that homosexuals progress through a series of stages that help them "acquire an identity of 'homosexual' [and] fully integrate [it] within the individual's overall concept of self" (Cass, 1979, p. 220).

According to Cass, at the *Identity Confusion* stage of development individuals are able to objectively view their behavior, thoughts, and/or feelings and question whether they may be classified as homosexual. With this increase in awareness comes confusion about their sexuality. In order for individuals to approach stage 2 of Cass's model, *Identity Comparison*, they must recognize that there is a possibility of homosexual orientation. However, understanding this possibility produces a sense of "differentness" for the person, and this differentness can be felt on a societal level ("I am different from other Americans"), a familial level ("I am different from my siblings"), and on a social level ("I am different from my friends."). Stage 2 is about comparing self to others, noticing the differences between heterosexuals and homosexuals and navigating the sense of separation that the person feels because of these differences.

Identity Tolerance is the third stage. At this stage, the person has come to the realization that, "I am probably homosexual." Unfortunately, with this secret acknowledgment comes costs. While the individual experiences a decrease in confusion, his or her differentness is still palpable; therefore, the person is merely tolerating a homosexual identity, not accepting it. Making positive social contacts with other homosexuals helps to decrease social alienation on some levels, but the person still feels alienated from formerly close, heterosexual others. At the next stage, *Identity Acceptance*, the individual has started to internally accept his or her homosexual identity but is still apprehensive about whether that identity should be revealed publicly. If the person decides to "come out" with his or her homosexual identity, it will create a considerable amount of tension, and an attempt to resolve this tension will lead to stage 5. Cass argues that the homosexual may contemplate "passing as a heterosexual" as a way to reduce tension. This is particularly true in American culture where the assumption is that everyone is heterosexual.

Those who are at the fifth stage of Cass's homosexual identity development, *Identity Pride*, have already accepted their homosexual orientation and recognize that society as a whole is not accepting of their differentness. They view the world as "us" and "them" and develop a strong dedication to homosexual culture and people known as an "activist" stance. Unfortunately, homosexuals still live in a world where heterosexuals have the most privilege. Homosexuals' lack of privilege can spark anger and frustration. Lastly, in the *Identity Synthesis* stage, homosexuals understand that their extreme way of viewing people of different orientations is just that—extreme. In other words, they recognize that not all heterosexuals are enemies. Cass adds that social interactions between homosexuals and supportive heterosexuals solidify this idea. If synthesis happens, then the person no longer sees sexual orientation as his or her sole identity. Rather, sexual orientation is just one of many cultural groups that is fully incorporated into his or her sense of self.

Coleman's Theoretical Model of Homosexual Identity Formation (1982)

Shortly after Cass published her model of identity formation for homosexuals, Eli Coleman (1982) created a new identity model. His biggest concern with Cass's model was that it was a linear model. In other words, Cass contended that most people would move through these stages progressively. Coleman, on the other hand, argued that people often work on tasks for several different stages. One of the major drawbacks of this model is that it was never empirically validated (Eliason & Schope, 2006).

The first of Coleman's stages is the *Before Coming Out* stage. This stage of development is marked by feelings of differentness and a sense that others notice these differences. He contends that the person may act out to avoid dealing with these overwhelming feels and that this could result in mental illness or suicide. At the *Coming Out* stage, the individual has inwardly acknowledged being gay, although, a disclosure to even close family and friends may or may not follow. Furthermore, Coleman maintains that coming out to self doesn't necessarily mean that the person is ready to live openly gay.

The third stage, *Exploration*, is typified by testing out this new identity socially and sexually. "Promiscuity, infatuation, courtship, and rejection" are major parts of this stage (Houston,

---

Theoretical Model of Homosexual Identity Formation

Eli Coleman (1982)
Stage 1: Before Coming Out
Stage 2: Coming Out
Stage 3: Exploration
Stage 4: First Relationship
Stage 5: Integration

2007). The person evenually transitions to the fourth stage because of the desire to have deeper relationships with both friends and intimate partners. Adding depth to interpersonal relationships is part of stage 4, *First Relationship*. The last of Coleman's stages is *Integration*. The hallmark of this stage is congruence. At this point, the private and public homosexual self become congruent, or one. Coleman points out that while the individual may experience some rejection, the person is mature enough and secure enough in her or his sexuality that it isn't devastating.

Troiden's Theoretical Model of Homosexual Identity Formation (1989)

Yet another model of identity development for homosexuals comes from Richard Troiden (1989), a former student of Vivienne Cass. He developed his model based on the information gathered from interviewing gay men and believed that his model was an ideal-typical representation of gay identity development (Troiden, 1989).

The first stage of his model, *Sensitization,* pops up before puberty. According to Troiden (1989), at this stage the individual feels different but hasn't labeled those feelings, responses, and behaviors in a sexual context. Therefore, the assumption is that he or she is heterosexual. The *Identity Confusion* stage contains confusion about the possibility of being homosexual. Troiden points out that there are a lot of things that contribute to this confusion, including the stigma associated with being homosexual. At this stage, the individual no longer assumes that the heterosexual label applies to him or her.

Identity Assumption, the next stage, includes taking on the homosexual identity privately and publicly. The individual explores the social scene of homosexual subculture as well as the romantic scene. Like Cass, Troiden believes that a homosexual identity is only tolerated at this point, not accepted. Once the individual starts to fully adopt a homosexual identity, the individual has reached the last stage, *Commitment*. At this stage, the homosexual sees his or her sexuality as an important part of his or her identity.

Theoretical Model of Homosexual Identity Formation

Richard Troiden (1989)
Stage 1: Sensitization
Stage 2: Identity Confusion
Stage 3: Identity Assumption
Stage 4: Commitment

Lipkin's Theoretical Model of Homosexual Identity Formation (1999)

As mentioned previously, Arthur Lipkin's model was never intended to be a model that was based on his own research about homosexual identity formation. Instead, its purpose was to pull out pieces of the previous three (Cass, Coleman, and Troiden) models and combine them into one big model.

The first of Lipkin's stages is the *Pre-Sexuality* stage. At this stage, the individual feels different but doesn't attribute these feelings to sexual orientation. The second stage is *Identity Questioning* and consists of unclear sexual feelings toward the same sex. At this stage, the individual tries to avoid being labeled as homosexual to avoid the stigma. Lipkin's *Coming Out* stage, the third stage, is depicted by tolerance, not acceptance, and the sexual and social exploration of homosexual subculture. Finally, the fourth and fifth stages are *Pride* and *Post-Sexuality*, respectively. Pride occurs when the individual integrates his or her sexuality into self, starts to disclose identity to others (aside from other homosexuals), and deals with the stigma of being a sexual minority in

Homosexual Identity Formation Models				
	Cass	**Coleman**	**Troiden**	**Lipkin**
Stage 1	Identity Confusion	Before Coming Out	Sensitization	Presexuality
Stage 2	Identity Comparison	Coming Out	Identity Confusion	Identity Questioning
Stage 3	Identity Tolerance	Exploration	Identity Assumption	Coming Out
Stage 4	Identity Acceptance	Integration	Commitment	Pride
Stage 5	Identity Pride	Identity Synthesis	—	Post-sexuality
Stage 6	Identity Synthesis	—	—	—

a healthy way. At this point, the individual "diminish[es the] centrality of homosexuality in self-concept and social relations" (Lipkin, 1999, p. 104). In other words, the individual see his or her homosexual identity as a part of the cultural fabric of his or her life, not the only important factor.

It is important to note that there are a number of models of homosexual identity development. In fact, some theorists have even teased out lesbian identity development and created models that are specific to how women come to identify as lesbians. While all of the models mentioned and those left unmentioned focus on how homosexuals come to identify as *homosexual* and despite the social stigma that is associated with it, these models do have some commonalities that are important to understand. First, all of the models start with the person feeling different. Also, they all mention that, along the way of homosexual identity development, the person must disclose his sexual orientation. Therefore, no model infers or indicates that she can be "in the closet" and also be at an advanced stage in her sexual development. Additionally, at some point the individual needs to develop a sense of pride surrounding his identity. Lastly, the final or highest stage of most models requires that gender and sexual identities become integrated into the whole personality, so they are no more and no less important than any other aspect of identity.

Bisexuality

Bisexuality literally means having two ("Bi" means two) sexual orientations. More specifically, *bisexuality* is being romantically, emotionally, and sexually attracted to same- and opposite-sex partners. One to three percent of males, according to Chandra and colleagues (2011) identify as bisexual, while 2–5% of females do. Again, remember that these findings include only people who identify as bisexual and are willing to confirm this identification. It doesn't include people who are attracted to both sexes but have never acted on that attraction. It also doesn't include people who are not comfortable with admitting their bisexual identification. Third, it doesn't include people who are in denial about their sexuality. Crooks and Baur (2002) note that most bisexuals establish heterosexuality first in their lives and, over the years, realize that they are attracted to members of the same sex as well. They also indicate that there are three subtypes that fall under the category of people.

Bisexuality as a Real Orientation

One of the biggest misconceptions about bisexuality is that it is not a real sexual orientation. Past researchers in this area have argued that bisexuality is only an intermediary (or transitional) period of sexual identity development in LGBT individuals and that some people just get trapped there and are unable to continue on with sexual identity development to fully identify as homosexual (Worthington & Reynolds, 2009). However, Weinberg, Williams, and Pryor (1994) refute this claim, asserting that bisexuality is a legitimate sexual orientation where some people are sexually attracted to and get sexual gratification from both sexes.

Bisexuality as a Transitional Orientation

There are three ways in which people can be transitory bisexuals. First, bisexuality is transitory when it is purely experimentation (Dykes, 2000). For example, some people identify as bisexual as a way to figure out if they are homosexual. They may engage in bisexual experiences to "test" whether they are sexually satisfied with sex with a same-sex partner. Secondly, bisexuality can also be transitory when it is used to transition to homosexuality (Crooks & Baur, 2000). In these cases, bisexuality is just a stop along the long road of the coming out process.

Lastly, transitory bisexuality includes engaging in bisexual activities for reasons other than intrinsic romantic interest. "Transitory same-sex behavior may occur in single-sex boarding schools and prisons, yet the people involved resume heterosexual relationships when the opportunities are again available" (Crooks & Baur, 2002, p. 263). Additionally, some people who trade sex for money may be willing to participate in bisexual experiences only for extrinsic purposes (i.e., money) and consider themselves to be heterosexual or homosexual in their personal lives.

Bisexuality as a Denial of Homosexuality

Some people may identify as bisexual only as a way of evading the full stigma of being homosexual (MacDonald, 1981). This plan, however, can backfire because research shows that heterosexual and homosexual people have often pressured those who identify as bisexual to pick one sexual orientation (Patrick, 2000).

Sexual Orientation as a Culture

As was discussed in Hayes's ADDRESSING Model in Chapter 3, sexual orientation is a part of one's culture. The second S in ADDRESSING represents sexual orientation. But, why is sexual orientation considered a part of culture? If you review the five characteristics of a culture, you will find that sexual orientation has the characteristics of a culture.

The first characteristic of culture is *fluidity*. As with other cultural groups to which you may belong, your sexual orientation may not be a fixed part of your life. As mentioned previously, the vast majority of people who identify as bisexual start their sexual lives identifying as heterosexual.

The second characteristic of a culture is that it is *not mutually exclusive*. Of course, sexual orientation is only one of many salient factors for people. In other words, being a part of gay culture doesn't exclude a person from being a part of ethnic, religious, or disability cultures. Kevin can identify as homosexual as well as Jewish (religious culture), Irish (ethnic culture), and deaf (disability culture). Being a part of a culture can be titular (in name only), or it can be an integrated part of life. Therefore, the most salient parts of Kevin's culture may be his ethnicity and sexual orientation, which means that his religious and disability cultures may be a part of his culture in name only.

The third characteristic of culture is that the *demands of one culture can conflict with the demands of another*. This couldn't be more evident than with sexual orientation and religion. It is widely understood that homosexuality has been viewed negatively, to say the least, by Judeo-Christian religions. According to (Crooks & Baur, 2000), "laws against homosexual behaviors, which stem from biblical injunctions against sex-sex contact, have historically been exceedingly punitive" (p. 269). They further contend that Western societies have tortured and killed people who identify as homosexual. For example, it was common practice in the early days of American history to drown and

Matthew Shepard Story

On a late night in October of 1998, Aaron McKinney and Russell Henderson offered Matthew Shepard, a 21-year-old college student, a ride home. Instead of taking him home, however, they drove him to a secluded rural area to rob and torture him. After pistol-whipping him, they tied him to a fence and left him there to die. Shepard was found unconscious 18 hours later by a passerby and taken to the hospital. Unfortunately, his injuries were so severe that, five days after the attack, he died in the hospital. The attack was believed to be initiated because Shepard identified as gay.

Reprinted by permission of The Matthew Shepard Foundation.

Adapted from Megan Hodge of the *Anderson Edition* (2007)

burn homosexuals (Crooks & Baur, 2000). However, it was Thomas Jefferson who suggested that, instead of killing homosexuals, they should be castrated (Fone, 2000). It's clear that we, as a society, have been intolerant of sexual minorities. Although we have become more tolerate of this cultural group, we still have a long way to go. (See the accompanying Matthew Shepard Story).

If you think that harassing homosexuals is a thing of the past, think again. In September 2010, a roommate and roommate's friend secretly taped via webcam Tyler Clementi, a Rutgers University student, kissing another man. After finding out about the invasion of privacy, Clementi did his best to deal with his concerns by requesting a room change as well as meeting with the resident assistant for the dorm. (tylerclementi.org). However, after hearing that there was another webcam "viewing" planned for a group of people, the shame and embarrassment were too great and, three days after the initial incident, Clementi jumped off the George Washington Bridge, leaving the following note on Facebook: "jumping off the gw bridge sorry" (Curry, 2012).

Reprinted by permission of The Tyler Clementi Foundation, tylerclementi.org

It's terrible when anyone is harassed based on cultural identification, and Crooks and Baur (2000) contend that sexual and ethnic minorities have an even harder time because they have to live in three different communities—their ethnic community, their sexual community, and the larger society. Gays and lesbians who are also members of ethnic minorities may find it easier to hide their sexual orientation than face alienation and shame from their families (Morris, 2001). For example, despite the fact that 4% of Hispanic people identify as LGBT and nearly 6% "don't know," Latino men may keep their sexual orientation hidden from their families and friends because of the "cultural emphasis on 'machismo'" (Crooks & Baur, 2000, p. 282). The same is true for Asian Americans, but for different cultural reasons. Being "macho" isn't nearly as important in Asian culture as is conforming and respectfully representing one's family. Therefore, it would be considered shameful to be openly homosexual or bisexual. Additionally, Asians tend to put the good of their families before their own interests. Thus, not being able to create heirs to continue the family name would be seen as a selfish act in this community (Crooks & Baur, 2000).

Another characteristic of culture is that it influences how we perceive ourselves. Despite the desire to be and feel "like everyone else," homosexuals are inundated with messages that carry negative connotations about themselves. Stereotypes about homosexuals persist despite the diversity within this cultural group. If you consider the other cultural groups to which one can belong, you will notice that, just as heterosexuals can belong to different socioeconomic cultures, so can homosexuals. Just as heterosexuals can belong to different ethnicities and nationalities, so can homosexuals. Therefore, it is likely that homosexuals see themselves the same way that hetero-sexuals see themselves, with the only difference being the social stigma surrounding their sexual orientation. In spite of these similarities, homosexuals are still stereotyped based on their physical appearance (Terry, 1990). Whereas some homosexuals display feminine mannerisms (Crooks & Baur, 2000), these are the minority of homosexuals (Herek, Kimmel, Amaro, & Melton, 1991). In fact, Berger (1990) conducted research that demonstrated that neither homosexuals nor heterosex-uals could, with any accuracy, predict the sexual orientation of others as they watched videotaped interviews of them. Homosexual people see themselves just as heterosexual people see themselves.

What is most noteworthy here is how these stereotypes about sexual minorities influence how they see themselves. In fact, research shows that sexual minorities start to internalize some of the negative ideas about themselves, which ultimately allows them to perpetuate those stereotypes. *Internalized homophobia* is defined as sexual minorities having negative attitudes about themselves because of sexual minority status. Meyer and Dean (1998) contend that internalized homophobia can lead people to reject their sexual orientation. However, it is important to note that theorists have found that internalized homophobia is a natural part of lesbian, gay, and bisexual identity development. According to Cass (1979), this phenomenon can start as early as stage 1 of her model when people recognize homosexual thoughts, feelings, and behaviors in themselves, but refuse to accept them.

The last characteristic of culture creates a lot of debate when it is applied to sexual orienta-tion. This characteristic of culture is that people self-admit to cultures. Keep in mind that the last characteristic doesn't apply to all cultural groups. For example, people don't self-admit to racial cultures; they are born into them. Some people are born with disabilities; therefore, they didn't self-admit to a disability culture. Some argue that, just as racial and disability cultures are excep-tions to this last characteristic of culture, so is sexual orientation. That is, some people contend that sexual orientation is not a culture to which you self-admit. They argue that belonging to this cultural group is a biological process like racial culture.

While research in this area is still ongoing, there is some evidence that prenatal hormone levels as well as genetics have an impact on homosexual orientation. With that being said, there have been a number of people who have come out and asserted that they are gay because of their preferences or life choices, not because they were "born gay." In fact, in 2005, WNBA star Sheryl Swoopes made headlines when she "came out" as being gay after being married to and having a child with a man. When asked during an interview with *ESPN* magazine, "Do [you] think [you were] born this way?" her reply was no. She further added, "And that's probably confusing to some, because I know a lot of people believe that you are." It's clear that this debate sparks heated conversation no matter which side of the fence you fall on.

> **THINK ABOUT IT**
>
> Compare and contrast each of the theories on gender identity. What do they all have in common?

SUMMARY

Clearly, this chapter is replete with important information to consider when you think of culture. Yes, your gender is a part of your culture as is your sexual orientation. However, depending on your level of privilege, it can be very hard to acknowledge and celebrate these parts of your culture. In other words, only the gender majorities (people who identify as male or female) and the sexual majority (heterosexuals) get to live without fear of discrimination or worse (Poteat & Anderson, 2012). They are confident that when they present themselves, others will correctly assume the sexual orientation category to which they belong (Mooney et al., 2011). Some people, on the other hand, walk into a room knowing that others will assume incorrectly (Slusher & Anderson, 1996). The next time you are asked to identify yourself on a form as male or female, think about those who must check a box that really doesn't describe them so that they can move on with completing the form. The next time you are looking at a magazine, reflect on how many implicit messages we send about who should be attracted to whom. Hopefully, this chapter has made you think about your culture and how gender and sexual orientation are a part of it and reflect on how you respond to members of the gender and sexual minority groups.

CHAPTER 7

Recognizing Immigrants and Refugees

IMMIGRATION

The diversity of the American people is unmistakable evidence of the variety of places from which immigrants have come. Yet each succeeding generation of immigrants found itself being reluctantly accepted, at best, by the descendants of earlier arrivals. The Chinese were the first immigrant group to be singled out for restriction, with the passage of the 1882 Exclusion Act. The initial Chinese immigrants became scapegoats for America's sagging economy in the last half of the nineteenth century. Growing fears that too many non-American types were immigrating motivated the creation of the national origin system and the quota acts of the 1920s. These acts gave preference to certain nationalities until the passage of the Immigration and Nationality Act in 1965 ended that practice. Today in the United States many immigrants are transnationals who still maintain close ties to their countries of origin, sending money back, keeping current with political events, and making frequent return trips. Concern about both illegal and legal immigration continues with renewed attention in the aftermath of the September 11, 2001, terrorist attacks. Restrictionist sentiment has grown, and debates rage over whether immigrants, even legal ones, should receive services such as education, government-subsidized healthcare, and welfare. The challenges to an immigrant household upon arrival are not evenly felt, as women play the central role in facilitating the transition. Controversy also continues to surround the policy of the United States toward refugees.

The Caribbean immigrant Joseph E. Joseph was just doing what he felt was his civic duty when he registered to vote in Brooklyn back in 1992 when he came across some volunteers signing people up to vote. A legal permanent resident, he worked toward naturalization and it was then that he learned he violated federal law by registering to vote and now faces deportation.

Mohammed Reza Ghaffarpour is willing to adjust and is not against assimilating. The Iranian-born engineering professor aced his citizenship test in 2003 but had to wait until 2008 to gain citizenship. His trips from his Chicago home to Iran for academic meetings and tending to ailing parents led to scrutiny by the U.S. authorities. The 53-year-old man felt discriminated against but is not bitter; although he waited to become a citizen, he feels the "system is working" (Glascock 2008; Semple 2010).

Lewiston, Maine, a town of 37,000, was dying. A once bustling mill town, jobs and people began leaving in the 1970s. A family of Somali refugees found housing very cheap and after settling there in 2001 shared the good news to immigrant friends and relatives. Initially the greeting was hardly positive as the town's mayor wrote an open letter to the Somali community begging them to stop encouraging their fellow Somalis to come. They kept coming, some 5,000 accompanied by Sudanese, Congolese, and other Africans. The economy has been transformed by the sophisticated trading skills the Somalis brought with them, importing fabric and spices (Sharon 2010).

Faeza Jaber is a 48-year-old single mother in her first months in the United States with her 7-year-old son, Khatab. When she arrived in Phoenix, Arizona, it was 114 degrees, which is hotter than her home in Baghdad. She was granted her refugee status after her husband, who was an office manager and interpreter for *Time* magazine, was murdered in 2004 on his way to work at a time when Iraqi interpreters for foreign companies were being targeted. Previously a computer programmer at the Baghdad airport, Jaber has found the transition difficult. She now works as a part-time teacher's assistant at Khatab's elementary school. She is striving to learn English and is encouraged by the knowledge that of the 600 Iraqi refugees who pass annually through Phoenix, 91 percent find a job and are able to support themselves without any state and federal subsidies within five months of arrival (B. Bennett 2008).

These dramas being played out in Brooklyn, Chicago, Lewiston, and Phoenix among other places, illustrate the themes in immigration today. Immigrant labor is needed, but concerns over illegal immigration persist and, even for those who arrive legally, the transition can be difficult. For the next generation it gets a little easier and, for some, perhaps too easy as they begin to forget their family's heritage. Many come legally, applying for immigrant visas, but others enter illegally. In the United States, we may not like lawbreakers, but we often seek services and low-priced products made by people who come here illegally. How do we control this immigration without violating the principle of free movement within the nation? How do we decide who enters? And how do we treat those who come here either legally or illegally?

© 2013, ZouZou. Used under license from Shutterstock, Inc.

The world is now a global network, with the core and periphery countries, described in world systems theory (see page 19 in Chapter 1), linking not only commercial goods but also families and workers across political borders. The social forces that cause people to emigrate are complex. The most important have been economic: financial failure in the old country and expectations of higher incomes and standards of living in the new land. Other factors include dislike of new political regimes in their native lands, the experience of being victims of racial or religious bigotry, and a desire to reunite families. All these factors push people from their homelands and pull them to other nations such as the United States. Immigration into the United States, in particular, has been facilitated by cheap ocean transportation and by other countries' removal of restrictions on emigration.

IMMIGRATION: A GLOBAL PHENOMENON

Immigration, is a worldwide phenomenon and contributes to globalization as more and more people see the world as their "home" rather than one specific country, as shown in Figure 7.1. People move across national borders throughout the world. Generally, immigration is from countries with lower standards of living to those that offer better wages. However, wars and famine may precipitate the movement of hundreds of thousands of people into neighboring countries and sometimes permanent resettlement.

Scholars of immigration often point to *push* and *pull factors*. For example, economic difficulties, religious or ethnic persecution, and political unrest may push individuals from their homelands. Immigration to a particular nation, the pull factors, may be a result of perceptions of a better life ahead or a desire to join a community of their fellow nationals already established abroad.

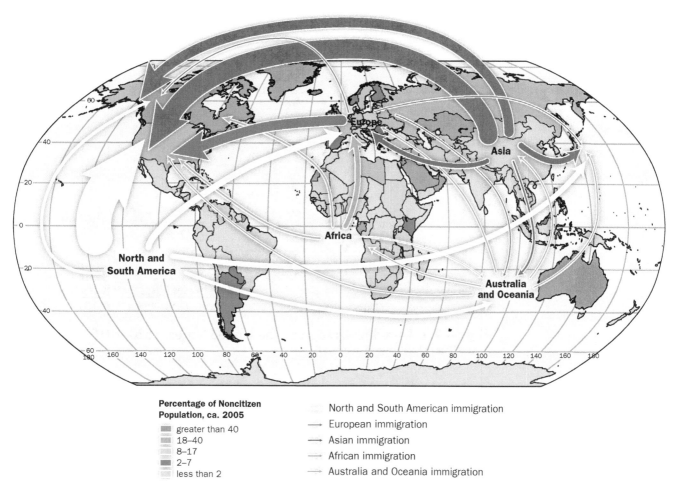

Percentage of Noncitizen
Population, ca. 2005

- greater than 40
- 18–40
- 8–17
- 2–7
- less than 2

North and South American immigration
→ European immigration
→ Asian immigration
→ African immigration
→ Australia and Oceania immigration

Figure 7.1 International Migration
Source: Fernandez-Armesto 2007:1006.

A potent factor contributing to immigration anywhere in the world is chain immigration. **Chain immigration** refers to an immigrant who sponsors several other immigrants who, on their arrival, may sponsor still more. Laws that favor people who desire to enter a given country who already have relatives there or someone who can vouch for them financially may facilitate this sponsorship. But probably the most important aspect of chain immigration is that immigrants anticipate knowing someone who can help them adjust to their new surroundings and find a new job, place to live, and even the kinds of foods that are familiar to them. Later in this chapter, we revisit the social impact of worldwide immigration.

PATTERNS OF IMMIGRATION TO THE UNITED STATES

There have been three unmistakable patterns of immigration to the United States: (1) the number of immigrants has fluctuated dramatically over time largely because of government policy changes, (2) settlement has not been uniform across the country but centered in certain regions and cities, and (3) the source of immigrants has changed over time. We first look at the historical picture of immigrant numbers.

Vast numbers of immigrants have come to the United States. Figure 7.2 indicates the high but fluctuating number of immigrants who arrived during every decade from the 1820s through the beginning of the twenty-first century. The United States received the largest number of legal immigrants during the first decade of the 1900s, which is likely to be surpassed in the first decade

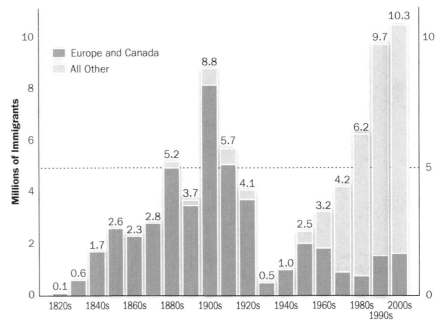

Figure 7.2 Legal Immigration to the United States, 1820–2010
Source: Office of Immigration Statistics 2011.

of the twenty-first century, but because the country was much smaller in the period from 1900 through 1910, the numerical impact was even greater then.

The reception given to immigrants in this country has not always been friendly. Open bloodshed, restrictive laws, and the eventual return of almost one-third of immigrants and their children to their home countries attest to some Americans' uneasy feelings toward strangers who want to settle here. Opinion polls in the United States from 1999 through 2011 have never shown more than 18 percent of the public in favor of more immigration, and usually about 43–50 percent want less (J. Jones 2011).

TODAY'S FOREIGN-BORN POPULATION

Before considering the sweep of past immigration policies, let us consider today's immigrant population. About 12–13 percent of the nation's people are foreign-born; this proportion is between the high figure of about 15 percent in 1890 and a low of 4.7 percent in 1970. By global comparisons, the foreign-born population in the United States is large but not unusual. Whereas most industrial countries have a foreign population of around 5 percent, Canada's foreign population is 19 percent and Australia's is 25 percent.

As noted earlier, immigrants have not settled evenly across the nation. As shown in the map in Figure 7.3, six states—California, New York, Texas, Florida, New Jersey, and Illinois—account for two-thirds of the nation's total foreign-born population but less than 40 percent of the nation's total population.

Cities in these states are the focus of the foreign-born population. Almost half (43.3 percent) live in the central city of a metropolitan area, compared with about one-quarter (27 percent) of the nation's population. More than one-third of residents in the cities of Miami, Los Angeles, San Francisco, San Jose, and New York City are now foreign-born.

The source of immigrants has changed. The majority of today's 38.5 million foreign-born people are from Latin America rather than Europe, as it was through the 1950s. Primarily, they are from Central America and, more specifically, Mexico. By contrast, Europeans, who dominated the early settlement of the United States, now account for fewer than one in seven of the foreign-born today (Camarota 2007; Grieco and Trevelyan 2010).

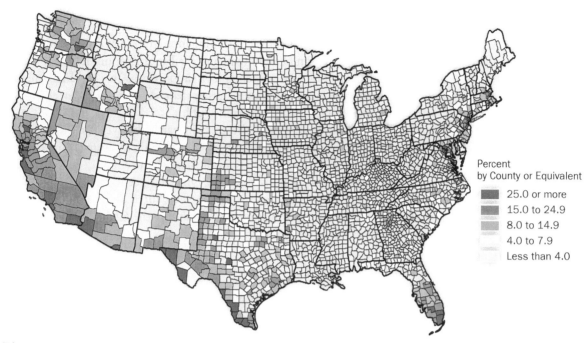

Percent
by County or Equivalent

■ 25.0 or more
■ 15.0 to 24.9
■ 8.0 to 14.9
■ 4.0 to 7.9
□ Less than 4.0

Figure 7.3 Foreign-Born Population by Counties
Source: American Community Survey 2006–2009 at www.census.gov.

EARLY IMMIGRATION

European explorers of North America were soon followed by settlers, the first immigrants to the Western Hemisphere. The Spanish founded St. Augustine, Florida, in 1565, and the English founded Jamestown, Virginia, in 1607. Protestants from England emerged from the colonial period as the dominant force numerically, politically, and socially. The English accounted for 60 percent of the 3 million White Americans in 1790. Although exact statistics are lacking for the early years of the United States, the English were soon outnumbered by other nationalities as the numbers of Scotch-Irish and Germans, in particular, swelled. However, the English colonists maintained their dominant position, as Chapter 5 examines.

Throughout American history, immigration policy has been politically controversial. The policies of the English king, George III, were criticized in the U.S. Declaration of Independence for obstructing immigration to the colonies. Toward the end of the nineteenth century, the American republic itself was criticized for enacting immigration restrictions. In the beginning, however, the country encouraged immigration. Legislation initially fixed the residence requirement for naturalization at five years, although briefly, under the Alien Act of 1798, it was 14 years, and so-called dangerous people could be expelled. Despite this brief harshness, immigration was unregulated through most of the 1800s, and naturalization was easily available. Until 1870, naturalization was limited to "free white persons" (Calavita 2007).

Besides holding the mistaken belief that concerns about immigration are something new, we also assume that immigrants to the United States rarely reconsider their decision to come to a new country. Analysis of available records, beginning in the early 1900s, suggests that about 35 percent of all immigrants to the United States eventually emigrated back to their home country. The proportion varies, with the figures for some countries being much higher, but the overall pattern is clear: About one in three immigrants to this nation eventually chooses to return home (Wyman 1993).

The relative absence of federal legislation from 1790 to 1881 does not mean that all new arrivals were welcomed. **Xenophobia** (the fear or hatred of strangers or foreigners) led naturally to **nativism** (beliefs and policies favoring native-born citizens over immigrants). Although the term *nativism* has largely been used to describe nineteenth-century sentiments, anti-immigration views and organized movements have continued into the twenty-first century. Political scientist Samuel P. Huntington (1993, 1996) articulated the continuing immigration as a "clash of civilizations" that could be remedied only by significantly reducing legal immigration, not to mention to close the border to illegal arrivals. His view, which enjoys support, was that the fundamental world conflicts of the new century are cultural in nature rather than ideological or even economic (Citrin, Lerman, Murakami, and Pearson 2007; Schaefer 2008b).

Historically, Roman Catholics in general and the Irish in particular were among the first Europeans to be ill-treated. We look at how organized hostility toward Irish immigrants eventually gave way to their acceptance into the larger society in the next chapter.

However, the most dramatic outbreak of nativism in the nineteenth century was aimed at the Chinese. If there had been any doubt by the mid-1800s that the United States could harmoniously accommodate all and was some sort of melting pot, debate on the Chinese Exclusion Act would negatively settle the question once and for all.

The Anti-Chinese Movement

Before 1851, official records show that only 46 Chinese had immigrated to the United States. Over the next 30 years, more than 200,000 came to this country, lured by the discovery of gold and the opening of job opportunities in the West. Overcrowding, drought, and warfare in China also encouraged them to take a chance in the United States. Another important factor was improved oceanic transportation; it was actually cheaper to travel from Hong Kong to San Francisco than from Chicago to San Francisco. The frontier communities of the West, particularly

© 2013, wong sze yuen. Used under license from Shutterstock, Inc.

in California, looked on the Chinese as a valuable resource to fill manual jobs. As early as 1854, so many Chinese wanted to emigrate that ships had difficulty handling the volume.

In the 1860s, railroad work provided the greatest demand for Chinese labor until the Union Pacific and Central Pacific railroads were joined at Promontory Summit, Utah, in 1869. The Union Pacific relied primarily on Irish laborers, but 90 percent of the Central Pacific's labor force was Chinese because Whites generally refused to do the back-breaking work over the Western terrain. Despite the contribution of the Chinese, White workers physically prevented them from attending the driving of the golden spike to mark the joining of the two railroads.

With the dangerous railroad work largely completed, people began to rethink the wisdom of encouraging Chinese to immigrate to do the work no one else would do. Reflecting their xenophobia, White settlers found the Chinese immigrants and their customs and religion difficult to understand. Indeed, few people actually tried to understand these immigrants from Asia. Although they had had no firsthand contact with Chinese Americans, Easterners and legislators were soon on the anti-Chinese bandwagon as they read sensationalized accounts of the lifestyle of the new arrivals.

Even before the Chinese immigrated, stereotypes of them and their customs were prevalent. American traders returning from China, European diplomats, and Protestant missionaries consistently emphasized the exotic and sinister aspects of life in China. **Sinophobes,** people with a fear of anything associated with China, appealed to the racist theory developed during the slavery controversy that non-Europeans were subhuman. Similarly, Americans were beginning to be more conscious of biological inheritance and disease, so it was not hard to conjure up fears of alien genes and germs. The only real challenge the anti-Chinese movement had was to convince people that the negative consequences of unrestricted Chinese immigration outweighed any possible economic gain. Perhaps briefly, racial prejudice had earlier been subordinated to industrial dependence on Chinese labor for the work that Whites shunned, but acceptance of the Chinese was short-lived. The fear of the "yellow peril" overwhelmed any desire to know more about Asian peoples and their customs (Takaki 1989).

Employers were glad to pay the Chinese low wages, but laborers came to direct their resentment against the Chinese rather than against their compatriots' willingness to exploit the Chinese. Only a generation earlier, the same concerns had been felt about the Irish, but with the Chinese, the hostility reached new heights because of another factor.

Although many arguments were voiced, racial fears motivated the anti-Chinese movement. Race was the critical issue. The labor market fears were largely unfounded, and most advocates of restrictions at that time knew that. There was no possibility that the Chinese would immigrate in numbers that would match those of Europeans at that time, so it is difficult to find any explanation other than racism for their fears (Winant 1994).

From the sociological perspective of conflict theory, we can explain how the Chinese immigrants were welcomed only when their labor was necessary to fuel growth in the United States. When that labor was no longer necessary, the welcome mat for the immigrants was withdrawn. Furthermore, as conflict theorists would point out, restrictions were not applied evenly: Americans focused on a specific nationality (the Chinese) to reduce the overall number of foreign workers in the nation. Because decision making at that time rested in the hands of the descendants of European immigrants, the steps to be taken were most likely to be directed against the least powerful: immigrants from China who, unlike Europeans seeking entry, had few allies among legislators and other policymakers.

In 1882, Congress enacted the Chinese Exclusion Act, which outlawed Chinese immigration for 10 years. It also explicitly denied naturalization rights to the Chinese in the United States; that is, they were not allowed to become citizens. There was little debate in Congress, and discussion concentrated on how suspension of Chinese immigration could best be handled. No allowance was made for spouses and children to be reunited with their husbands and fathers in the United States. Only brief visits of Chinese government officials, teachers, tourists, and merchants were exempted.

The rest of the nineteenth century saw the remaining loopholes allowing Chinese immigration closed. Beginning in 1884, Chinese laborers were not allowed to enter the United States from any foreign place, a ban that also lasted 10 years. Two years later, the Statue of Liberty was dedicated, with a poem by Emma Lazarus inscribed on its base. To the Chinese, the poem welcoming the tired, the poor, and the huddled masses must have seemed a hollow mockery.

In 1892, Congress extended the Exclusion Act for another 10 years and added that Chinese laborers had to obtain certificates of residence within a year or face deportation. After the turn of the century, the Exclusion Act was extended again. Two decades later, the Chinese were not alone; the list of people restricted by immigration policy had expanded many times.

RESTRICTIONIST SENTIMENT INCREASES

As Congress closed the door to Chinese immigration, the debate on restricting immigration turned in new directions. Prodded by growing anti-Japanese feelings, the United States entered into the so-called gentlemen's agreement, which was completed in 1908. Japan agreed to halt further immigration to the United States, and the United States agreed to end discrimination against the Japanese who had already arrived. The immigration ended, but anti-Japanese feelings continued. Americans were growing uneasy that the "new immigrants" would overwhelm the culture established by the "old immigrants." The earlier immigrants, if not Anglo-Saxon, were from similar groups such as the Scandinavians, the Swiss, and the French Huguenots. These people were

more experienced in democratic political practices and had a greater affinity with the dominant Anglo-Saxon culture. By the end of the nineteenth century, however, more and more immigrants were neither English speaking nor Protestant and came from dramatically different cultures.

The National Origin System

Beginning in 1921, a series of measures were enacted that marked a new era in American immigration policy. Whatever the legal language, the measures were drawn up to block the growing immigration from southern Europe (from Italy and Greece, for example) and also were drawn to block all Asian immigrants by establishing a zero quota for them.

To understand the effect of the national origin system on immigration, it is necessary to clarify the quota system. The quotas were deliberately weighted in favor of immigration from northern Europe. Because of the ethnic composition of the country in 1920, the quotas placed severe restrictions on immigration from the rest of Europe and other parts of the world. Immigration from the Western Hemisphere (i.e., Canada, Mexico, Central and South America, and the Caribbean) continued unrestricted. The quota for each nation was set at 3 percent of the number of people descended from each nationality recorded in the 1920 census. Once the statistical manipulations were completed, almost 70 percent of the quota for the Eastern Hemisphere went to just three countries: Great Britain, Ireland, and Germany.

The absurdities of the system soon became obvious, but it was nevertheless continued. British immigration had fallen sharply, so most of its quota of 65,000 went unfilled. However, the openings could not be transferred, even though countries such as Italy, with a quota of only 6,000, had 200,000 people who wanted to enter. However one rationalizes the purpose behind the act, the result was obvious: Any English person, regardless of skill and whether related to anyone already here, could enter the country more easily than, say, a Greek doctor whose children were American citizens. The quota for Greece was 305, with the backlog of people wanting to come reaching 100,000.

By the end of the 1920s, annual immigration had dropped to one-fourth of its pre-World War I level. The worldwide economic depression of the 1930s decreased immigration still further. A brief upsurge in immigration just before World War II reflected the flight of Europeans from the oppression of expanding Nazi Germany. The war virtually ended transatlantic immigration. The era of the great European migration to the United States had been legislated out of existence.

The 1965 Immigration and Nationality Act

The national origin system was abandoned with the passage of the 1965 Immigration and Nationality Act, signed into law by President Lyndon B. Johnson at the foot of the Statue of Liberty. The primary goals of the act were to reunite families and to protect the American labor market. The act also initiated restrictions on immigration from Latin America. After the act, immigration increased by one-third, but the act's influence was primarily on the composition rather than the size of immigration. The sources of immigrants now included Italy, Greece, Portugal, Mexico, the Philippines, the West Indies, and South America.

The lasting effect is apparent when we compare the changing sources of immigration over the last 190 years, as shown in Figure 7.4. The most recent period shows that Asian and Latin American immigrants combined to account for 81 percent of the people who were permitted

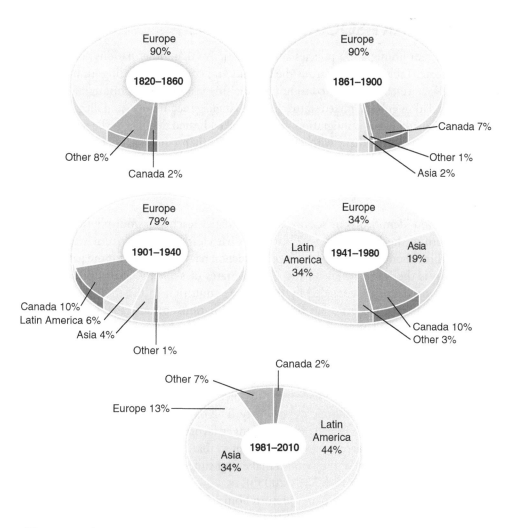

Figure 7.4 Legal Immigrants Admitted to the United States by Region of Last Residence, 1820–2010
Source: Office of Immigration Statistics 2011.

entry. This contrasts sharply with early immigration, which was dominated by arrivals from Europe.

The nature of immigration laws is exceedingly complex and is subjected to frequent, often minor, adjustments. In 2000 and 2010, between 840,000 and 1,270,000 people were legally admitted each year. For 2010, people were admitted for the following reasons:

Relatives of citizens	57%
Relatives of legal residents	9%
Employment based	14%
Refugees/people seeking political asylum	13%
Diversity (lottery among applications from nations historically sending few immigrants)	5%
Other	2%

Overall, two-thirds of the immigrants come to join their families, one-seventh because of skills needed in the United States, and another one-seventh because of special refugee status (Monger and Yankay 2011).

CONTEMPORARY SOCIAL CONCERNS

Although our current immigration policies are less restrictive than other nations', they are the subjects of great debate. Table 7.1 summarizes the benefits and concerns regarding immigration to the United States. Now we consider five continuing criticisms relating to our immigration policy: the brain drain, population growth, mixed status, English language acquisition, and illegal immigration. All five, but particularly illegal immigration, have provoked heated debates on the national level and continuing efforts to resolve them with new policies. We then consider the economic impact of immigration, followed by the nation's policy toward refugees, a group distinct from immigrants.

The Brain Drain

How often have you identified your science or mathematics teacher or your physician as someone who was not born in the United States? This nation has clearly benefited from attracting human resources from throughout the world, but this phenomenon has had its price for the nations of origin.

Brain drain is the immigration to the United States of skilled workers, professionals, and technicians who are desperately needed by their home countries. In the mid-twentieth century, many scientists and other professionals from industrial nations, principally Germany and Great Britain, came to the United States. More recently, however, the brain drain has pulled emigrants from developing nations, including India, Pakistan, the Philippines, and several African nations. They are eligible for H-1B visas that qualify them for permanent work permits.

One out of four physicians in the United States is foreign-born and plays a critical role in serving areas with too few doctors. Thousands of skilled, educated Indians now seek to enter the United States, pulled by the economic opportunity. The pay differential is so great that, beginning in 2004, when foreign physicians were no longer favored with entry to the United States, physicians in the Philippines were retraining as nurses so that they could immigrate to the United States where, employed as nurses, they would make four times what they would as doctors in the Philippines (Mullen 2005; *New York Times* 2005b).

Many foreign students say they plan to return home. Fortunately for the United States, many do not and make their talents available in the United States. One study showed that the majority of foreign students receiving their doctorates in the sciences and engineering remain here four years later. Critics note, however, that this foreign supply means that this country overlooks its own minority scholars. Currently, for every two minority doctorates, three foreign citizens are receiving this degree. More encouragement needs to be given to African Americans and Latinos to enter high-tech career paths.

Potential Benefits	Areas of Concern
Provide needed skills	Drain needed resources from home country
Contribute to taxes	Send remittances home
May come with substantial capital to start business	Less-skilled immigrants compete with those already disadvantaged
Maintain growth of consumer market	Population growth
Diversify the population (intangible gain)	Language differences
Maintain ties with countries throughout the world	May complicate foreign policy by lobbying the government
	Illegal immigration

Table 7.1 Immigration Benefits and Concerns

Conflict theorists see the current brain drain as yet another symptom of the unequal distribution of world resources. In their view, it is ironic that the United States gives foreign aid to improve the technical resources of African and Asian countries while maintaining an immigration policy that encourages professionals in such nations to migrate to our shores. These are the very countries that have unacceptable public health conditions and need native scientists, educators, technicians, and other professionals. In addition, by relying on foreign talent, the United States is not encouraging native members of subordinate groups to enter these desirable fields of employment (National Center for Education Statistics 2009:Table 319; Pearson 2006; Wessel 2001; West 2010).

Population Growth

The United States, like a few other industrial nations, continues to accept large numbers of permanent immigrants and refugees. Although such immigration has increased since the passage of the 1965 Immigration and Nationality Act, the nation's birthrate has decreased. Consequently, the contribution of immigration to population growth has become more significant. As citizen "baby boomers" age, the country has increasingly depended on the economically younger population fueled by immigrants (Meyers 2007).

Immigration, legal and illegal, is projected to account for nearly 50 percent of the nation's growth in from 2005 to 2050 with the children and grand-children of immigrants accounting for another 35 percent. That leaves just 18 percent of the next half-century of growth coming the descendants of thodse born and living here in 2005. To some observers, the United States is already overpopulated. Environmentalists have weighed in the immigration issue questioning immigration's possible negative impact on the nation's natural resources. We consider that aspect of the immigration debate later in this chapter. Thus far, the majority of the club's members have indicated a desire to keep a neutral position rather than enter the politically charged immigration debate (Kotkin 2010).

The patterns of uneven settlement by immigrants in the United States are expected to continue so that future immigrants' impact on population growth will be felt much more in certain areas, say, California and New York rather than Wyoming or West Virginia. Although immigration and population growth may be viewed as national concerns, their impact is localized in certain areas such as Southern California and large urban centers nationwide (Camarota and Jensenius 2009; Passel and Cohn 2009).

Mixed-Status Families

Very little is simple when it comes to immigration, and this is particularly true to the challenge of "mixed status." **Mixed status** refers to families in which one or more members are citizens and one or more are noncitizens. This especially becomes problematic when the noncitizens are illegal or undocumented immigrants.

The problem of mixed status clearly emerges on two levels. On the macro level, when policy debates are made about issues that seem clear to many people—such as whether illegal immigrants should be allowed to attend state colleges or whether illegal immigrants should be immediately deported—the complicating factor of mixed-status families quickly emerges. On the micro level, the daily toll on members of mixed-status households is very difficult. Often the legal resident or even the U.S. citizen in a household finds daily life limited for fear of revealing the undocumented status of a parent or brother or even a son.

About three-quarters of illegal immigrants' children were born in the United States and thus are citizens. This means that perhaps as many as half of all adult illegal immigrants have a citizen in their immediate family. This proportion has grown in recent years. This means that some of the issues facing illegal immigrants, whom we discuss later, will also affect the citizens in the families because they are reluctant to bring attention to themselves for fear of revealing the illegal status of their mother or father (Gonzalez 2009; Passel and Cohn 2009).

Language Barriers

For many people in the United States, the most visible aspect of immigration are non-English speakers, businesses with foreign-language storefronts, and even familiar stores assuring potential customers that their employees speak Spanish or Polish or Chinese or some other foreign language.

About 20 percent of the population speaks a language other than English, as shown in Figure 7.5. Indeed, 32 different languages are spoken at home by at least 200,000 residents. As of 2008, about half of the 38 million people born abroad spoke English less than "very well." This rises to 74 percent among those born in Mexico. Nationally, about 64 percent of Latino schoolchildren report speaking Spanish at home (American Community Survey 2009:Tables S0501 and S0506; Shin and Kominski 2010).

The myth of Anglo superiority has rested in part on language differences. (The term *Anglo* in the following text is used to mean all non-Hispanics but primarily Whites.) First, the criteria for economic and social achievement usually include proficiency in English. By such standards, Spanish-speaking pupils are judged less able to compete until they learn English. Second, many Anglos believe that Spanish is not an asset occupationally. Only recently, as government agencies have belatedly begun to serve Latino people and as businesses recognize the growing Latino consumer market, have Anglos recognized that knowing Spanish is not only useful but also necessary to carry out certain tasks.

Until the last 40 years, there was a conscious effort to devalue Spanish and other languages and to discourage the use of foreign languages in schools. In the case of Spanish, this practice was built on a pattern of segregating Hispanic schoolchildren from Anglos. In the recent past in the Southwest, Mexican Americans were assigned to Mexican schools to keep Anglo schools all-White. These Mexican schools, created through de jure school segregation, were substantially underfunded compared with the regular public schools. Legal action against such schools dates back to 1945, but it was not until 1970 that the U.S. Supreme Court ruled, in *Cisneros v. Corpus Christi Independent School District,* that the de jure segregation of Mexican Americans was unconstitutional. Appeals delayed implementation of that decision, and not until September 1975 was the de jure plan forcibly overturned in Corpus Christi, Texas (Commission on Civil Rights 1976).

Is it essential that English be the sole language of instruction in schools in the United States? **Bilingualism** is the use of two or more languages in places of work or educational facilities, according

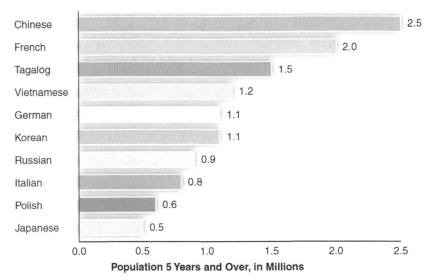

Figure 7.5 Ten Languages Most Frequently Spoken at Home, Other Than English and Spanish
Source: Data for 2007 in Shin and Kominski 2010.

each language equal legitimacy. Thus, a program of **bilingual education** may instruct children in their native language (such as Spanish) while gradually introducing them to the language of the dominant society (English). If such a program is also bicultural, it will teach children about the culture of both linguistic groups. Bilingual education allows students to learn academic material in their own language while they are learning a second language. Proponents believe that, ideally, bilingual education programs should also allow English-speaking pupils to be bilingual, but generally they are directed only at making non-English speakers proficient in more than one language.

In Listen to Our Voices, journalist Galina Espinoza of *Latina* magazine considers the role the English language has played in her own life as well as her chosen profession in the mass media.

Do bilingual programs help children learn English? It is difficult to reach firm conclusions on the effectiveness of the bilingual programs in general because they vary so widely in their approach to non-English-speaking children. The programs differ in the length of the transition to English and how long they allow students to remain in bilingual classrooms. A major study analyzed more than three decades of research, combining 17 different studies, and found that bilingual education programs produce higher levels of student achievement in reading. The most successful are paired bilingual programs—those offering ongoing instruction in a native language and English at different times of the day (Slavin and Cheung 2003; Soltero 2008).

Listen to Our Voices

That Latino "Wave" Is Very Much American

In 1990, I had just started my senior year at an Ivy League college when my political science professor asked me to come see her about the first paper I had turned in. While she complimented me on how much work I had put into it, she went on to explain that writing a college paper must be especially difficult for someone for whom English was not her first language.

I don't remember anything else she said after that, so consumed was I with trying to understand how she could have made this assumption. I was, after all an English major. Was it my accent I picked up during my childhood in Queens, N.Y.? Or my last name?

I find myself asking the same question now, with the release of the 2010 U.S. Census figures. Today, Hispanics number more than 50 million strong and account for 1 out of every 6 adults. Some politicians and pundits see our country besieged by a wave of non-English speaking immigrants coming through a porous border. Here's why they—like my professor—are wrong. What accounts for the dramatic rise in the Latino population are births: 1 out of every 4 children born in the U.S. today is Hispanic. In turn, that means most Latinos speak English as their first language. According to a 2007 analysis by the Pew Hispanic Center, "nearly all Hispanic adults born in the United States of immigrant parents report they are fluent in English," a percentage that rises "among later generations of Hispanic adults."

Of course, like many Americans of different cultural backgrounds, Latinos identify strongly with their roots. But even if many of us are bilingual, or want our children to learn Spanish, our true link to Hispanic identity is not through language. It's through culture. We like to know how to cook the foods of our home countries and what our traditional holiday celebrations are. We like to see authentic portrayals of ourselves. Our favorite TV series, according to *Advertising Age*, are *Grey's Anatomy* and *Desperate Housewives*, which prominently feature Latino characters.

And when it comes to politics, we like leaders who understand that Cubans in Miami just might vote differently from Mexicans in Chicago. It is in the ways that our cultural identity begins to reshape the national one that the true social impact of Latinos will be felt. And so if you want to understand who your new Latino neighbors really are, know this: We want to eat our rice and beans. But our apple pie, too.

Galina Espinoza is editorial director of Latina *magazine and co-president of Latina Media Ventures.*

Source: Espinoza 2011:9A.

Path to Get Green Card (Permanent Residence)

When one obtains lawful permanent residency in the United States of America, the individual is known as having "Green Card" status. A Green Card authorizes an individual to resident and work in the U.S. on a permanent basis. There are different steps for immigrants to take to become a Green Cardholder (permanent resident). These steps depend on where the individual currently resides (inside or outside of the United States), and may vary by category. The main categories are as follows:

1. **Obtaining Green Card through Family**
   Many people become permanent residents through their family members.

   a. Being a family member of a U.S. citizen.

   "Immediate relatives" of a U.S. citizen—defined as one's spouse, one's unmarried children under the age of 21, and one's parents may immigrate to the United States.

   If a person does not qualify as an immediate relative of a U.S. citizen, then the person may be eligible under the "family preference category," which includes relatives of U.S. citizens who are:

   ■ Unmarried sons or daughters over the age of 21.
   ■ Married child(ren) of any age.
   ■ Brothers and sisters (if the U.S. citizen petitioner is over the age of 21).

   Owing to federal limits on the number of relatives in the "family preference category" who can immigrate, there is usually a long waiting period before an immigrant visa number becomes available.

   b. Green Card for a family member of a permanent resident.

   In order to promote family unity, the permanent resident of the United States may apply to petition for certain eligible relatives (his/her spouse and unmarried child(ren) of any age) to come and live permanently in the United States. There is generally a long waiting period for this category (family preference category).

   c. Green Card through special categories of family.

   Individuals who meet particular qualifications and/or apply during certain time frames may apply to become a permanent resident through a special family situation.

   A member of a special category may *include:*

   i. A battered spouse, child, and parents of U.S. citizens and permanent residents may apply for a permanent residency card under the Immigration and Nationality Act (INA), as amended by the Violence Against Women Act (VAWA) without the abuser's knowledge.

   ii. Fiancé, the K-VISA categories for fiancé(e)s of U.S. citizens and their accompanying minor children (K-1 and K-2 visas) which were created to speed up the immigration process for these individuals.

   iii. A person born to a foreign diplomat in the United States may apply to be considered a permanent resident at birth. Any individual born in the United States is considered a U.S. citizen; however, a person born in the United States to a foreign diplomatic officer (such as ambassadors, ministers, charges d'affaires, counselors, secretaries, and attachés of embassies and legations, members of the delegation of the Commission of the European Communities) cannot be considered a U.S. citizen at birth under the 14th Amendment to the U.S. Constitution.

   iv. A spouse or child of a permanent resident may apply for the V nonimmigrant category that allows him or her to live and work in the United States while waiting to obtain immigrant status. The V nonimmigrant category was created by the Legal Immigration Family Equity (LIFE) Act in 2000.

   v. Persons legally married to a deceased U.S. citizen who were entered the marriage in good faith may apply for a green card under the Immigration Nationality Act (INA).

2. **Green Card through a Job and Employment**
   If there are not enough U.S. workers who are able, willing, qualified, or available in a specific geographic area, immigrants could be employed and become permanent residents through a job or offer of employment. The main immigration categories based on a job offer or employment is as follow:

   a. Green Card through a job offer: Individual could become a permanent resident based on an offer of permanent employment in the United States.

   b. Green Card through investment: Investors/entrepreneurs may become a permanent resident, if their investment creates new U.S. jobs.

   c. Green Card through self–petition: "Aliens of Extraordinary Ability" or certain individuals granted a National Interest Waiver may apply for a permanent residency as a self-petitioner.

Path to Get Green Card (Permanent Residence) (Continued)

3. **Green Card through Refugee or Asylee Status**
   People leaving their original country for fear of political or religious persecution may apply to become a permanent resident of the United States.

4. **Other Ways to Get a Green Card**
   In addition to the family sponsorship, employment, refugee status, or job offer, there are special programs for individuals meeting particular qualifications and/or applying during certain time to become permanent residents.

DREAM Act (Development, Relief, and Education for Alien Minors)

The DREAM Act is American federal legislation that would legalize the status of several million undocumented youth, was first proposed in the U.S. Congress in 2001, and the last bill was introduced in both the Senate and House in 2011. The 2013 Dream Act is expected to be reintroduced by both chambers of Congress in 2013.

Under current immigration law, the immigrant children who immigrate to the United States from another country can only obtain a Green Card status through their parents and might not apply for a permanent residency as a "self-petitioner." These individuals who were brought to the United States by their parents are allowed to attend and complete public education. Upon graduation from high school, these individuals *are not allowed* to attend college in many states. Furthermore, such children *are not generally allowed* to get their driver's licenses, Social Security cards, or cannot legally work in the United States without proof of legal immigration status.

Under the 2011 DREAM Act, which died in the Senate in December 2011, such immigrants could qualify for conditional permanent residency in the United States.

The general requirements to qualify for conditional permanent residency under the 2011 DREAM Act are that an individual:

- Must be between the ages of 12 and 30 at the time the law is enacted.
- Must have arrived in the United States before the age of 16.
- Must have resided continuously in the United States for a least five consecutive years since the date of their arrival.
- Must have graduated from a U.S. high school, or obtained a General Education Diploma (GED).
- Must have "good moral character" (no criminal convictions).

(Adapted from DREAM Act Bill of 2011)

As of November 2012, there are 12 states with their own versions of the DREAM Act (Texas, California, Illinois, Utah, Nebraska, Kansas, New Mexico, New York, Washington, Wisconsin, Massachusetts, and Maryland) which mostly deal with the state universities' financial aid and tuition prices. The Maryland DREAM Act was one of the last DREAM Acts approved by statewide ballot, winning 59% of the statewide vote on November 6, 2012.

Deferred Action for Childhood Arrivals

In June 2012 the Obama administration announced it would accept requests for Deferred Action for Childhood Arrivals (DACA). This initiative was designed to temporarily suspend the deportation of illegal immigrants who were brought to the United States as children. "Deferred Action" offers a two-year, renewable reprieve from deportation to illegal immigrants brought as children who are under the age of 31.

The general requirements to qualify for Deferred Action for Children Arrivals (DACA) are that an individual:

- Entered the United States before age 16.
- Lived continuously in the country for at least five years.
- Has "good moral character" (no criminal convictions).
- Is currently in school, or has graduated from high school, or obtained a GED.
- Has served in the U.S. military.

(Adapted from the Department of State 2013)

As of 2013, there are about 1.8 million illegal young immigrants who were brought to the United States by their parents as children and who might be, or might become, eligible for the Obama administration's "Deferred Action."

Path to Citizenship: Naturalization

The United States is the land of immigrants from all parts of the world. The United States has been welcoming these individuals who have immigrated to the land of freedom and opportunity from different nations with different backgrounds and cultures. The United States values immigrants and their involvement in the enrichment of this country.

As of 1776, the first U.S. citizenship statuses were granted retroactively without any required application or any Oath of Allegiance due to the adoption of the U.S. Constitution in 1787. These first immigrants just needed to be in the United States at the time that independence was declared and that they remained loyal to the new government and they would protect the government.

Since 1790, naturalization requirements gradually have changed. The Naturalization Act of 1790 put in place uniform regulation for naturalization and a common oath of allegiance. Additionally two years of residency in the United States and a good moral character were required of all naturalization applicants.

The Naturalization Act of 1798 required longer residency than the previous Act (1790), and two years of residency was increased to 14 years.

Then Naturalization Act of 1802 reduced the residency from 14 years to five years, which still stands today for immigrants who are not married to a U.S. citizen. Immigrants who are married to a U.S. citizen are required to have three years of residency before they can apply for naturalization.

An immigration act of 1906 required more standardized measures and knowledge of the English language for citizenship applicants. The Bureau of Immigration and Naturalization was established under the Act of 1906.

The Immigration and Nationality Act (INA), also known as the McCarran-Walter bill of 1952, put together and organized many existing naturalization requirements and reorganized the structure of immigration law. Even though the Immigration and Nationality ACT (INA) is still the basic frame of U.S. immigration law, it has been amended many times over the years.

In the United States, citizenship is granted in order to bring together all persons from different backgrounds, whether native or foreign born, to have a role in the future of the United States.

Individuals born in the United States or in certain territories, or individuals who have a U.S. citizen parent or parents at the time of their birth if born outside of the United States, and meet other requirements will become a U.S. citizen.

There are different ways for a foreign-born permanent residency cardholder to become a U.S. citizen through the process of naturalization. These naturalized citizens will have the same benefits as native-born U.S. citizens. However, naturalized citizens cannot become the president of the United States.

General Eligibility Requirements to Become a Naturalized U.S. Citizen

1. The applicant must be aged 18 or older at the time of filing for naturalization.
2. The applicant must be a Green Cardholder for at least five consecutive years.
3. The applicant must be physically present in the United States for at least 30 months out of these five years.
4. The applicant must show good moral character for five years before filing for naturalization.
5. The applicant should show respect to the principles of the U.S. Constitution, and follow the laws of the United States during his or her residency in the United States.
6. The applicant should be able to read, write, and able to communicate in English, in addition to having knowledge of U.S. history and government.

(Adapted from the Department of the Homeland Security, U.S. Citizenship and Immigration Services, 2013)

Members and veterans of the U.S. armed forces and their dependents may be entitled special requirements.

Most naturalization applicants are asked to take English, U.S. history, and government (civics) tests.

The cost of filing the naturalization form (Form N-400) has increased dramatically over the last few years. In 2013, the filling fee for the naturalization process is $595, and an additional $85 is required for applicants under the age of 75 years for biometric services.

Each year the number of applicants for becoming a naturalized U.S. citizen increases. In 2008, a record number of 1,046,539 immigrants submitted the naturalization application and became American citizens. Mexico, India, and the Philippines were the leading countries of origin of the immigrants within the United States who went through the naturalization process.

The United States values dual or multiple citizenship; therefore, individuals becoming naturalized citizens can keep their citizenship of origin.

© 2013 Shutterstock, Inc. Patrick Poendl

Attacks on bilingualism in both voting and education have taken several forms and have even broadened to question the appropriateness of U.S. residents using any language other than English. Federal policy has become more restrictive. Local schools have been given more authority to determine appropriate methods of instruction; they have also been forced to provide more of their own funding for bilingual education. In the United States, as of 2011, 30 states have made English their official language. Repeated efforts have been made to introduce a constitutional amendment declaring English as the nation's official language. Even such an action would not completely outlaw bilingual or multilingual government services. It would, however, require that such services be called for specifically as in the Voting Rights Act of 1965, which requires voting information to be available in multiple languages (U.S. English 2010).

Non—English speakers cluster in certain states, but bilingualism attracts nationwide passions. The release in 2006 of "Nuestro Himno," the Spanish-language version of "The Star-Spangled Banner," led to a strong reaction, with 69 percent of people saying it was appropriate to be sung only in English. Yet at least one congressman who decried the Spanish version sang the anthem himself in English with incorrect lyrics. Similarly, a locally famous restaurant owner in Philadelphia posted signs at his Philly steak sandwich diner announcing he would accept orders only in English. Passions remain strong as policymakers debate how much support should be given to people who speak other languages (Carroll 2006; Koch 2006b).

ILLEGAL IMMIGRATION

The most bitterly debated aspect of U.S. immigration policy has been the control of illegal or undocumented immigrants. These immigrants and their families come to the United States in search of higher-paying jobs than their home countries can provide.

Because by definition illegal immigrants are in the country illegally, the exact number of these undocumented or unauthorized workers is subject to estimates and disputes. Based on the best available information in 2011, there are more than 11.2 million illegal or unauthorized immigrants in the United States. This compares with about 3.5 million in 1990. With employment opportunities drying up during the economic downturn beginning in 2008, significantly fewer people tried to enter illegally and many unauthorized immigrants returned to their countries (Passel and Cohn 2011).

Illegal immigrants, and even legal immigrants, have become tied by the public to almost every social problem in the nation. They become the scapegoats for unemployment; they are labeled as "drug runners" and, especially since September 11, 2001, "terrorists." Their vital economic and cultural contribution to the United States is generally overlooked, as it has been for more than a hundred years.

The cost of the federal government's attempt to police the nation's borders and locate illegal immigrants is sizable. There are significant costs for aliens—that is, foreign-born noncitizens—and for other citizens as well. Civil rights advocates have expressed concern that the procedures used to apprehend and deport people are discriminatory and deprive many aliens of their legal rights. American citizens of Hispanic or Asian origin, some of whom were born in the United States, may be greeted with prejudice and distrust, as if their names automatically imply that they are illegal immigrants. Furthermore, these citizens and legal residents of the United States may be unable to find work because employers wrongly believe that their documents are forged.

In the context of this illegal immigration, Congress approved the Immigration Reform and Control Act of 1986 (IRCA) after debating it for nearly a decade. The act marked a historic change in immigration policy compared with earlier laws, as summarized in Table 7.2. Amnesty was granted to 1.7 million illegal immigrants who could document that they had established long-term residency in the United States. Under the IRCA, hiring illegal aliens became illegal, subjecting employers to fines and even prison sentences. Little workplace enforcement occurred

Policy	Target Group	Impact
Chinese Exclusion Act, 1882	Chinese	Effectively ended all Chinese immigration for more than 60 years
National origin system, 1921	Southern Europeans	Reduced overall immigration and significantly reduced likely immigration from Greece and Italy
Immigration and Nationality Act, 1965	Western Hemisphere and the less skilled	Facilitated entry of skilled workers and relatives of U.S. residents
Immigration Reform and Control Act of 1986	Illegal immigrants	Modest reduction of illegal immigration
Illegal Immigration Reform and Immigrant Responsibility Act of 1996	Illegal immigrants	Greater border surveillance and increased scrutiny of legal immigrants seeking benefits

Table 7.2 Major Immigration Policies

for years, but beginning in 2009 federal agents concentrated on auditing large employers rather than raiding workplaces (Simpson 2009).

Many illegal immigrants continue to live in fear and hiding, subject to even more severe harassment and discrimination than before. From a conflict perspective, these immigrants, primarily poor and Hispanic or Asian, are being firmly lodged at the bottom of the nation's social and economic hierarchies. However, from a functionalist perspective, employers, by paying low wages, are able to produce goods and services that are profitable for industry and more affordable to consumers. Despite the poor working conditions often experienced by illegal immigrants here, they continue to come because it is still in their best economic interest to work here in disadvantaged positions rather than seek wage labor unsuccessfully in their home countries.

Amidst heated debate, Congress reached a compromise and passed the Illegal Immigration Reform and Immigrant Responsibility Act of 1996, which emphasized making more of an effort to keep immigrants from entering the country illegally. The act prevented illegal immigrants from having access to such programs as Social Security and welfare. Legal immigrants would still be entitled to such benefits, although social service agencies were now required to verify their legal status. Another significant element was to increase border control and surveillance.

Illegal aliens or undocumented workers are not necessarily transient. One estimate indicates 60 percent had been here for at least five years. Many have established homes, families, and networks with relatives and friends in the United States whose legal status might differ. These are the mixed-status households noted earlier. For the most part, their lives are not much different from legal residents, except when they seek services that require citizenship status to be documented (Passel 2005).

Policymakers continue to avoid the only real way to stop illegal immigration: discourage employment opportunities. This has certainly been the approach taken in recent years. The Immigration and Customs Enforcement (ICE) notifies major companies that it will soon audit its employment records looking for illegal immigrants who, if found, can lead to both civil and criminal penalties against the business This has led corporations such as American Apparel and Chipotle Mexican Grill to look closer and fire hundreds of employees lacking sufficient documentation. Just in the period from October 2010 through March 2011 over 260,000 people have been deported (Jordan 2011).

The public often thinks in terms controlling illegal immigration of greater surveillance at the border. After the terrorist attacks of September 11, 2001, greater control of border traffic took on a new sense of urgency, even though almost all the men who took over the planes had entered the United States legally. It is very difficult to secure the vast boundaries that mark the United States on land and sea.

Numerous civil rights groups and migrant advocacy organizations expressed alarm over people crossing into the United States illegally who perish in their attempt. Some die in deserts, in isolated canyons, and while concealed in containers or locked in trucks during smuggling attempts. Several hundred die annually in the Southwest, seeking more and more dangerous crossing points, as border control has increased. However, this death toll has received little attention, causing one journalist to liken it to a jumbo jet crashing between Los Angeles and Phoenix every year without anyone giving it much notice (Del Olmo 2003; Sullivan 2005).

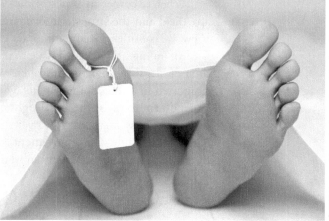

The immigration policy debate was largely absent from both the 2008 presidential race and 2010 midterm elections, having been replaced by concerns over the economy and the war in Afghanistan. Locally concerns continued. Erecting a 700-mile-long double concrete wall hardened the Mexico—United States border. This action, which was heavily supported by the general public, still brought concerns that desperate immigrants would take even more chances with their lives in order to work in the United States. Legal measures to make unauthorized crossings more difficult are being augmented by self-appointed border guards such as the Minuteman movement. Sometimes these armed volunteers engage in surveillance that leads to more violence and an atmosphere of suspicion and incidents of racial profiling along the United States-Mexican border.

A Global View

Immigration and South Africa

With its over 50 million people, the Republic of South Africa is not rich by global standards, but its economy is very attractive to most of the African continent. For example, South Africa has a gross national income per person of $9,780, compared to well under $1,000 in neighboring Zimbabwe. Even when South Africa was ruled by a White-supremacist government, Black Africans from throughout the continent came to the country fleeing violence and poverty in their home countries and to work, often in the mining of coal and diamonds. In the post-apartheid era, the numbers of immigrants, legal and illegal, have skyrocketed. Today's government is caught between compassion for those seeking entry and the growing inability of the economy to absorb those who seek work and shelter.

In 2008, the world took notice as riots broke out between poor South Africans taking out their rage on even more impoverished foreigners. The growing xenophobia took the government, which advocates racial harmony, by surprise as it tried to quell violence among Black Africans divided by citizenship status and nationality. In a matter of months in early 2008, some 32,000 immigrants had been driven from their homes, with attackers seizing all of their belongings. Some immigrants returned to their home countries—including Burundi, Ethiopia, Ghana, Malawi, Mozambique, and Zimbabwe—but most settled temporarily in camps.

South Africa, with limited government resources, deported 260,000 in 2006–2007, a proportion nearly comparable to that of the United States (with six times the population), which reported 1.2 million deportations during the same period. However, estimates of the total number of illegal immigrants in South Africa range from 3 million to 5 million—a much higher proportion than estimated in the Untied States.

The scapegoating of immigrants, or "border jumpers" as they often are called in South Africa, is not unique to this nation, but for the global community that still relishes Nelson Mandela's peaceful ascent to power, it has been a reminder of immigration's challenge throughout the world.

Sources: Dixon 2007; Forced Migration Studies Programme 2009; Koser 2008; Nevin 2008; Office of Immigration Statistics 2007; Roodt 2008; South African Institute of Race Relations 2007.

When it comes to issues of race and ethnicity, South Africa usually evokes past images of apartheid and the struggle to overcome generations of racial separation. However, in A Global View, we consider the contemporary challenge of dealing with immigration.

An immigration-related issue that begins to be raised in 2010 has been concern over the children of illegal immigrants born here who then are regarded as citizens at birth. These concerns, supported in public opinion polls by about half of the population, seek to alter the Fourteenth Amendment to revise the "birthright citizenship" that was intended for children of slaves but has since been long interpreted to cover anyone born in the United States regardless of their partners' legal status. While such a movement is unlikely to succeed it is yet another example of a relatively minor issue that sidetracks any substantive discussion of immigration reform (Gomez 2010).

THE ECONOMIC IMPACT OF IMMIGRATION

There is much public and scholarly debate about the economic effects of immigration, both legal and illegal. Varied, conflicting conclusions have resulted from research ranging from case studies of Korean immigrants' dominance among New York City greengrocers to mobility studies charting the progress of all immigrants and their children. The confusion results in part from the different methods of analysis. For example, the studies do not always include political refugees, who generally are less prepared than other refugees to become assimilated. Sometimes, the research focuses only on economic effects, such as whether people are employed or are on welfare; in other cases, it also considers cultural factors such as knowledge of English.

Perhaps the most significant factor in determining the economic impact of immigration is whether a study examines the national impact of immigration or only its effects on a local area. Overall, we can conclude from the research that immigrants adapt well and are an asset to the local economy. In some areas, heavy immigration may drain a community's resources. However, it can also revitalize a local economy. Marginally employed workers, most of whom are either themselves immigrants or African Americans, often experience a negative impact by new arrivals. With or without immigration, competition for low-paying jobs in the United States is high, and those who gain the most from this competition are the employers and the consumers who want to keep prices down (Steinberg 2005; Zimmerman 2008).

The impact of immigration on African Americans deserves special attention. Given that African Americans are a large minority and many continue to be in the underclass, many people, including some Blacks themselves, perceive immigrants as advancing at the expense of the African

---

Try these sample questions from the naturalization test (answers below)

1. What do the stripes on the flag represent?
2. How many amendments are there to the Constitution?
3. Who is the chief justice of the Supreme Court?
4. Who was president during World War I?
5. What do we call the first 10 amendments to the Constitution?
6. What are two rights in the Declaration of Independence?
7. Name one right or freedom from the First Amendment.
8. When was the Constitution written?

Answers: (1) The first 13 states; (2) 27; (3) John Roberts; (4) Woodrow Wilson; (5) Bill of Rights; (6) life, liberty, and the pursuit of happiness; (7) The rights are freedom of speech, religion, assembly, and press, and freedom to petition the government; (8) 1787.

Table 7.3 So You Want to Be a Citizen?

Source: Department of Homeland Security 2009.

American community. There is evidence that in the very lowest paid jobs—for example, workers in chicken-processing plants—wages have dropped with the availability of unskilled immigrants to perform them, and Blacks have left these jobs for good. Many of these African Americans do not necessarily move to better or even equivalent jobs. This pattern is repeated in other relatively low-paying, undesirable employment sectors, so Blacks are not alone in being impacted; but given other job opportunities, the impact is longer lasting (Borjas, Grogger, and Hanson 2006; Holzer 2008).

About 70 percent of illegal immigrant workers pay taxes of one type or another. Many of them do not file to receive entitled refunds or benefits. For example, in 2005, the Social Security Administration identified thousands of unauthorized workers contributing about $7 billion to the fund but that could not be credited properly (Porter 2005).

Social science studies generally contradict many of the negative stereotypes about the economic impact of immigration. A variety of recent studies found that immigrants are a net economic gain for the population in times of economic boom as well as in periods of recession. But despite national gains, in some areas and for some groups, immigration may be an economic burden or create unwanted competition for jobs (Kochhar 2006).

What about the immigrants themselves? Considering contemporary immigrants as a group, we can make the following conclusions that show a mix of successes and challenges to adaptation.

Less Encouraging Signs

- Although immigrants have lower divorce rates and are less likely to form single-parent households than natives, their rates equal or exceed these rates by the second generation.
- Children in immigrant families tend to be healthier than U.S.-born children, but the advantage declines. We consider this in greater detail later in this chapter.
- Immigrant children attend schools that are disproportionately attended by other poor children and students with limited English proficiency, so they are ethnically, economically, and linguistically isolated.

Positive Signs

- Immigrant families and, more broadly, noncitizen households are more likely to be on public assistance, but their time on public assistance is less and they receive fewer benefits. This is even true when considering special restrictions that may apply to noncitizens.
- Second-generation immigrants (i.e., children of immigrants) are overall doing as well as or better than White non-Hispanic natives in educational attainment, labor force participation, wages, and household income.
- Immigrants overwhelmingly (65 percent) continue to see learning English as an ethical obligation of all immigrants.

These positive trends diverge among specific immigrant groups, with Asian immigrants doing better than European immigrants, who do better than Latino immigrants (Capps, Leighton, and Fix 2002; Farkas 2003; Fix and Passel 2001; Myers, Pitkin, and Park 2004; Zimmerman 2008).

One economic aspect of immigration that has received increasing attention is the role of **remittances,** or the monies that immigrants return to their countries of origin. The amounts are significant and measure in the hundreds of millions of dollars flowing from the United States to a number of countries where they provide substantial support for families and even venture capital for new businesses. Although some observers express concern over this outflow of money, others counter that it probably represents a small price to pay for the human capital that the United States is able to use in the form of the immigrants themselves. Immigrants in the United States send billions to their home countries and worldwide remittances bring about $325 billion to all the world's developing countries, easily surpassing all other forms of foreign aid. While this cash inflow is integral to the economies of many nations, it also means that during the global economic recession that occurred recently, this resource drops off significantly (Migration News 2011).

The concern about immigration today is both understandable and perplexing. The nation has always been uneasy about new arrivals, especially those who are different from the more affluent and the policymakers. In most of the 1990s, we had paradoxical concerns about immigrants hurting the economy despite strong economic growth. With the economic downturn beginning in 2008, it was clear that low-skilled immigrants (legal or illegal) took the hardest hit and, as a result, remittances immediately declined.

WOMEN AND IMMIGRATION

© 2013, Ryan Rodrick Beiler. Used under license from Shutterstock, Inc.

Immigration is presented as if all immigrants are similar, with the only distinctions being made concerning point of origin, education, and employment prospects. Another significant distinction is whether immigrants travel with or without their families. We often think that historical immigrants to the United States were males in search of work. Men dominate much of the labor migration worldwide, but because of the diversified labor force in the United States and some policies that facilitate relatives coming, immigration to the United States generally has been fairly balanced. Actually, most immigration historically appears to be families. For example, from 1870 through 1940, men entering the United States exceeded women by only about 10–20 percent. Since 1950, women immigrants have actually exceeded men by a modest amount. This pattern is being repeated globally (Gibson and Jung 2006; A. Jones 2008).

Immigration is a challenge to all family members, but immigrant women must navigate a new culture and a new country not only for themselves but also for their children, such as in this household in Colorado.

The second-class status women normally experience in society is reflected in immigration. Most dramatically, women citizens who married immigrants who were not citizens actually lost their U.S. citizenship from 1907 through 1922 with few exceptions. However, this policy did not apply to men (Johnson 2004).

Immigrant women face not only all the challenges faced by immigrant men but also additional ones. Typically, they have the responsibility of navigating the new society when it comes to services for their family and, in particular, their children. Many new immigrants view the United States as a dangerous place to raise a family and therefore remain particularly vigilant of what happens in their children's lives.

Caring for the health of their households falls mainly on women in their social roles as mother, wife, and caregiver for aging parents. In Research Focus, we consider the most recent research on how immigrants are doing in the United States in terms of health. The outcome may not be what one expects.

Male immigrants are more likely to be consumed with work, leaving the women to navigate the bureaucratic morass of city services, schools, medical facilities, and even everyday concerns such as stores and markets. Immigrant women are often reluctant to seek outside help, whether they are in need of special services for medical purposes or they are victims of domestic violence. Yet immigrant women are more likely to be the liaison for the household, including adult men, to community associations and religious organizations (Hondagneu-Sotelo 2003; Jones 2008).

Women play a critical role in overseeing the household; for immigrant women, the added pressures of being in a new country and trying to move ahead in a different culture heighten this social role.

Research Focus

Assimilation May Be Hazardous to Your Health

Immigrants come to the United States seeking a better life, but the transition can be very difficult. We are familiar with the problems new arrivals experience in finding good jobs, but we may be less aware of how pervasive the challenges are.

Researchers continuously show that immigrants often encounter health problems as they leave behind old health networks and confront the private-pay system of medical care in the United States. The outcome is that the health of immigrants often deteriorates. Interestingly, this occurs with Puerto Ricans, who are citizens upon arrival and obviously do not experience as much culture shock as other new arrivals. Scholars Nancy Landale, R. S. Orapesa, and Bridget Gorman looked at the implications for infant mortality of migration from Puerto Rico to the United States. Their analysis showed that children of migrants have lower rates of infant mortality than do children of mainland-born Puerto Rican women. This means that babies of Puerto Rican mothers who are born in the United States are more likely to die than those of mothers who migrated from Puerto Rico.

Why does this happen? Immigrants generally are still under the protection of their fellow travelers. They are still networked with other immigrants, who assist them in adapting to life in the United States. However, as life in a new country continues, these important social networks break down as people learn to navigate the new social system—in this example, the healthcare system. They are more likely to be uninsured and unable to afford medical care except in emergencies. The researchers do note that Puerto Ricans in the United States, regardless of recency of arrival, still experience better health than those in Puerto Rico. Of course, this finding only further indicates the legacy of the colonial relationship of Puerto Rico to the United States and the healthcare system there on the island.

Sources: Meredith King 2007; Landale, Ogena, and Gorman 2000; Lara, Gambosa, Kahramanian, Morales, and Bautista 2005; Read and Emerson 2005.

THE GLOBAL ECONOMY AND IMMIGRATION

Immigration is defined by political boundaries that bring the movement of peoples crossing borders to the attention of government authorities and their policies. Within the United States, people may move their residence, but they are not immigrating. For residents in the member nations of the European Union, free movement of people within the union is also protected.

Yet, increasingly, people recognize the need to think beyond national borders and national identity. **Globalization** is the worldwide integration of government policies, cultures, social movements, and financial markets through trade, movement of people, and the exchange of ideas. In this global framework, even immigrants are less likely to think of themselves as residents of only one country. For generations, immigrants have used foreign-language newspapers to keep in touch with events in their home countries. Today, cable channels carry news and variety programs from their home countries, and the Internet offers immediate access to the homeland and kinfolk thousands of miles away.

Although it helps in bringing the world together, globalization has also highlighted the dramatic economic inequalities between nations. Today, people in North America, Europe, and Japan consume 32 times more resources than the billions of people in developing nations. Thanks to tourism, media, and other aspects of globalization, the people of less-affluent countries are aware of such affluent lifestyles and, of course, often aspire to enjoy them (Diamond 2003).

Transnationals are immigrants who sustain multiple social relationships that link their societies of origin and settlement. Immigrants from the Dominican Republic, for example, not only identify themselves with Americans but also maintain very close ties to their Caribbean homeland. They return for visits, send remittances, and host extended stays of relatives and friends. Back in the Dominican Republic, villages reflect these close ties, as shown in billboards promoting special long-distance services to the United States and by the presence of household appliances sent by relatives. The volume of remittances worldwide is easily the most reliable source of foreign money going to poor countries, far outstripping foreign aid programs.

The presence of transnationals would be yet another example of pluralism, as illustrated in the Spectrum of Intergroup Relations.

SPECTRUM OF INTERGROUP RELATIONSHIPS

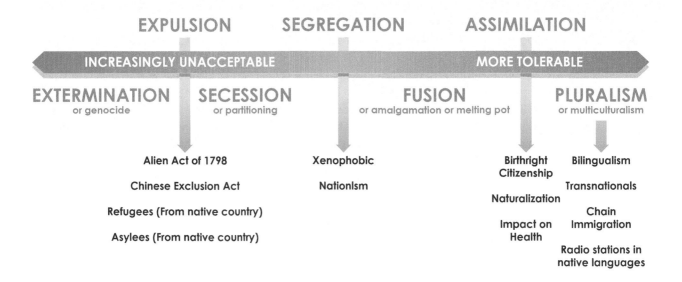

The growing number of transnationals, as well as immigration in general, directly reflects the world systems analysis we considered in Chapter 1. Transnationals are not new, but the ability to communicate and transfer resources makes the immigration experience today different from that of the nineteenth century. The sharp contrast between the industrial "have" nations and the developing "have-not" nations only encourages movement across borders. The industrial haves gain benefits from such movement even when they seem to discourage it. The back-and-forth movement only serves to increase globalization and help create informal social networks between people who seek a better life and those already enjoying increased prosperity.

The transnationals themselves maintain a multithreaded relationship between friends and relatives in the United States, their home country, and perhaps other countries where relatives and friends have resettled. Besides the economic impact of remittances described above, scholars are increasingly giving attention to "social remittances" that include ideas, social norms, and practices (religious and secular) throughout this global social network (Levitt and Jaworsky 2007).

THE ENVIRONMENT AND IMMIGRATION

At the beginning of the twenty-first century, the public expressed growing concern on a variety of environmental issues, from water quality to global warming. As with so many other aspects of life, the environment and immigration are tightly linked.

First, environmental factors are behind a significant amount of world migration. Famine, typhoons, rising sea levels, expanding deserts, chronic water shortages, earthquakes, and so forth lead to cross-border migration of what has been termed *climate refugees.* One estimate suggests up to 200 million people may move due to environmental factors between 2005 and 2050.

A particularly deadly aspect of this forced movement is that overwhelmingly the migration is by vulnerable poor people to developing countries ill-suited to accept the arrivals (International Organization for Migration 2009; Meyers 2005; Stern 2007).

Second, some environmentalists favor reducing or even ending United States population growth by imposing a much more restrictive immigration policy. The respected environmentalist group Sierra Club debated for several years whether to take an official position favoring restricting immigration. Thus far, the majority of the club's members have indicated a desire to keep a neutral position rather than enter the politically charged immigration debate.

Yet others still contend for the United States to finally address environmental problems at home and become global environmental citizens and for the United States to stop population growth. Critics of this environmentalist approach counter that we should focus on consumption, not population (Barringer 2004; CaFaro and Staples 2009).

Refugees

Refugees are people living outside their country of citizenship for fear of political or religious persecution. Enough refugees exist to populate an entire "nation." There are approximately 11 million refugees worldwide. That makes the nation of refugees larger than Belgium, Sweden, or Cuba. The United States has touted itself as a haven for political refugees. However, as we shall see, the welcome to political refugees has not always been unqualified.

The United States makes the largest financial contribution of any nation to worldwide assistance programs. The United States resettles about 70,000 refugees annually and served as the host to over one million refugees between 1990 and 2008. The post-9/11 years have seen the procedures become much more cumbersome for foreigners to acquire refugee status and gain entry to the United States. Many other nations much smaller and much poorer than the United States have many more refugees, with Jordan, Iran, and Pakistan hosting more than one million refugees each (Martin 2011; United Nations High Commission on Refugees 2008).

The United States, insulated by distance from wars and famines in Europe and Asia, has been able to be selective about which and how many refugees are welcomed. Since the arrival of refugees uprooted by World War II, through the 1980s the United States had allowed three groups of refugees to enter in numbers greater than regulations would ordinarily permit: Hungarians, Cubans, and Southeast Asians.

Despite periodic public opposition, the U.S. government is officially committed to accepting refugees from other nations. In Table 7.4 we consider the major sources of refugees. According to the United Nations treaty on refugees, which our government ratified in 1968, countries are obliged to refrain from forcibly returning people to territories where their lives or liberty might be endangered. However, it is not always clear whether a person is fleeing for his or her personal

2000		2010	
1 Bosnia-Herzegovina	22,699	Iraq	18,016
2 Yugoslavia (former)	14,280	Burma	16,693
3 Vietnam	9,622	Bhutan	12,363
4 Ukraine	8,649	Somalia	4,884
5 Russia	4,386	Cuba	4,818
Total:	85,076		73,293

Table 7.4 Top Sources of Refugees

Source: Martin 2011; Office of Immigration Statistics 2009:Table 14.

safety or to escape poverty. Although people in the latter category may be of humanitarian interest, they do not meet the official definition of refugees and are subject to deportation.

Refugees are people who are granted the right to enter a country while still residing abroad. **Asylees** are foreigners who have already entered the United States and now seek protection because of persecution or a well-founded fear of persecution. This persecution may be based on the individual's race, religion, nationality, membership in a particular social group, or political opinion. Asylees are eligible to adjust to lawful permanent resident status after one year of continuous presence in the United States. Asylum is granted to about 12,000 people annually.

© 2013, ajfi. Used under license from Shutterstock, Inc.

Because asylees, by definition, are already here, the outcome is either to grant them legal entry or to return them to their home country. It is the practice of deporting people who are fleeing poverty that has been the subject of criticism. There is a long tradition in the United States of facilitating the arrival of people leaving Communist nations, such as the Cubans. Mexicans who are refugees from poverty, Liberians fleeing civil war, and Haitians running from despotic rule are not similarly welcomed. The plight of Haitians has become one of particular concern.

Haitians began fleeing their country, often on small boats, in the 1980s. The U.S. Coast Guard intercepted many Haitians at sea, saving some of these boat people from death in their rickety and overcrowded wooden vessels. The Haitians said they feared detentions, torture, and execution if they remained in Haiti. Yet both Republican and Democratic administrations viewed most of the Haitian exiles as economic migrants rather than political refugees and opposed granting them asylum and permission to enter the United States. Once apprehended, the Haitians are returned. In 1993, the U.S. Supreme Court, by an 8–1 vote, upheld the government's right to intercept Haitian refugees at sea and return them to their homeland without asylum hearings.

The devastating 2010 earthquake in Haiti has caused the government to reconsider this policy. Indeed, the United States halted all deportations of the 30,000 Haitians that was about to occur for at least 18 months. This moratorium would also apply to the more than 100,000 Haitians believed to be living in the United States. As more residents of Haiti with U.S. citizenship or dual citizenship arrived in the aftermath from the island nation, the Haitian community rose to 830,000 by 2009. Despite the continuing obstacles, the Haitian American community exhibits pride in those who have succeeded, from a Haitian American Florida state legislator and professional athletes to hip-hop musician Wyclef Jean. In fact the initial earthquake refugees tended to come from the middle class or higher and even expressed annoyance at the quality of the public schools their children now attended compared to the private ones in Haiti (Buchannan et al. 2010; Office of Immigration Statistics 2011; J. Preston 2010; Winerip 2011).

New foreign military campaigns often bring new refugee issues. The occupation of Iraq, beginning in 2003, had been accompanied by large movements of Iraqis throughout the country and the region. Hopefully, most will return home,

THINK ABOUT IT

- What are the distinctions between an immigrant and a refugee? Knowing the differences between the two, why are they often treated the same when they reach their destination countries?
- Elaborate on the reasons for which an immigrant or a refugee would leave his/her country to move to a new place with no or very few social supports.
- Based on the research on immigrants and refugees, think about the adjustment that they have to make to the culture of the "adoptive country."
- Do you think immigrants, and/or refugees had knowledge about the language, and/or the culture of the new country before their immigration?
- Imagine that you were forced or had to leave your hometown and had to immigrate to another country where you are not familiar with the language, costume, norms, values, and their beliefs. Discuss how well you think you would adjust to this new environment and why you believe so?

but some clearly are seeking to relocate to the United States. As was true in Vietnam, many Iraqis who have aided the U.S.-led mission have increasingly sought refuge in the West, fearing for their safety if they were to remain in Iraq or even in the Middle East. Gradually, the United States has begun to offer refugee status to Iraqis; some 18,000 arrived in 2010 to join an Iraqi American community of 90,000. The diverse landscape of the United States takes on yet another nationality group in large numbers (Martin 2011).

SUMMARY

The immigrant presence in the United States can often be heard on the streets and the workplace as people speak in different languages, Check out your radio. As of 2011, radio stations broadcast in 35 languages other than English including Albanian, Creole, Welsh, Yiddish, and Oji- a language spoken in Ghana (Keen 2011).

Throughout the history of the United States, as we have seen, there has been intense debate over the nation's policies that brings the immigrants that speak these and other languages to the country. In a sense, this debate reflects the deep value conflicts in the U.S. culture and parallels the "American dilemma" identified by Swedish social economist Gunnar Myrdal (1944). One strand of our culture—epitomized by the words "Give us your tired, your poor, your huddled masses"—has emphasized egalitarian principles and a desire to help people in their time of need. One could hardly have anticipated at the time the Statue of Liberty was dedicated in 1886 that more than a century later Barack Obama, the son of a Kenyan immigrant, would be elected President of the United States.

At the same time, however, hostility to potential immigrants and refugees—whether the Chinese in the 1880s, European Jews in the 1930s and 1940s, or Mexicans, Haitians, and Arabs today—reflects not only racial, ethnic, and religious prejudice but also a desire to maintain the dominant culture of the ingroup by keeping out those viewed as outsiders. The conflict between these cultural values is central to the American dilemma of the twenty-first century.

The current debate about immigration is highly charged and emotional. Some people see it in economic terms, whereas others see the new arrivals as a challenge to the very culture of our society. Clearly, the general perception is that immigration presents a problem rather than a promise for the future.

Today's concern about immigrants follows generations of people coming to settle in the United States. This immigration in the past produced a very diverse country in terms of both nationality and religion, even before the immigration of the last 60 years. Therefore, the majority of Americans today are not descended from the English, and Protestants are just more than half of all worshipers. This diversity of religious and ethnic groups is examined in Chapter 5.

CHAPTER 8

Reinvigorating Family/Parenting Styles

FAMILY STRUCTURES

From the sociological perspective, the family can be viewed as the basic unit of kinship consisting of a man and a woman who are bound by a socially recognized contract and includes any children that they may have. Many variations of the **family** exist in American society today, including such nontraditional family units as occur in same-sex marriages, mutual cohabitation, and group marriages.

In American society, a man and a woman can formalize a marital relationship by means of a civil contract, a religious ceremony, or a combination of these socially acceptable means of bonding. The family structure that results is referred to as the **nuclear family,** or sometimes as the conjugal family.

The **conjugal family** consists of two generations, as the husband and wife are considered the first generation and their children constitute the second generation. By definition, the conjugal family is limited to two generations (i.e., the parents and their immediate children), although several augmented nuclear family forms are possible. While children view their parents as their *family of orientation*, when they marry and have children, they establish a *family of procreation*. The **family of orientation** is the family into which you were born and is the social unit that formed the basis for your early socialization into the community and society. On the other hand, the **family of procreation** is the family that you form when you get married. It is referred to as the family of procreation because the traditional expectation is that when a couple gets married, they procreate. Of course, in a sociological sense, the marital expectation of procreation is satisfied by adoption or even by marrying someone who has children already. This development cycle starts over when the children marry and start their own families of procreation.

In terms of increased complexity in social organization, we can move from the basic nuclear family structure and observe that a more complex form of social organization occurs in the **extended family.** By definition, the traditional patrilineal extended family consists of three or more generations and includes grandparents, unmarried children, married sons, their spouses, and their children. See Table 8.1.

In a traditional society, such as in Mexico, the extended family may consist of four generations, although it usually only contains three generations, namely the grandparents, their children, and their grandchildren. The extended family may be residentially consolidated (in which case family members would live on the same plot of land or even share household structures, for

■ Nuclear (Conjugal)
■ Extended (Consanguine)
Affinal Kin Relations
Fictive Kin Relations
■ Family of Orientation (First Generation)
■ Family of Procreation (Second Generation)

Table 8.1 Recognized Family Structures

example) or it can take a nonresidential form, wherein the extended family members simply live in the same neighborhood or community. The extended family is sometimes referred to as a **consanguine family.** Consanguine simply means that a group of individuals are related by blood, as the term derives from the Latin word *sanguine*, meaning "of the same blood."

CROSS-CULTURAL MARRIAGE PATTERNS

Cultural norms, social expectations, and established laws in American society today hold that one man should only be married to one woman at any given time. This cultural expectation is referred to as marital **monogamy.** However, widowed persons and, as occurs more frequently today, divorced persons are allowed to remarry. In more recent times, the term **serial monogamy** is used to describe the tendency of people to remarry following divorce. At the other end of the marital spectrum is the practice of **polygamy,** or plural marriage, in which one person is allowed to have two or more spouses at the same time. Polygamy can take two basic forms, either polygyny or polyandry. By far the most common form of polygamy in all societies today is referred to as **polygyny,** which is the cultural practice that allows a man to have two or more wives at the same time. In contrast, **polyandry** is a rare form of polygamy that allows a woman to have two or more husbands at the same time.

As a cultural option, polygamy was far more common in ancient and more traditional societies and evolved as a survival mechanism and as a cultural adaptation. However, when various societies accepted plural marriages as a legitimate option, it usually took the form of polygyny, that is, the practice of allowing a man to have two or more wives at the same time. For example, polygyny was the only form of plural marriage allowed among the Aztecs. As a rule, polygyny was only practiced by powerful and wealthy men and served as an indicator of their social standing and prestige in the community. Therefore, the more wives that a man could have and support in Aztec society, the more power and prestige he had in the community. This is quite generally the case also in societies today where polygamy is a legitimate cultural form.

The most common form of polygyny in Aztec society, and in most societies where polygyny was allowed, was **sororal polygyny.** Sororal polygyny occurs when a man is married to two or more sisters. In their ethnographic studies of Mexican culture, anthropologists have found the existence of sororal polygyny in Chan Kom (Redfield & Rojas, 1962, pp. 87–98), Ojitlan (Weitlaner, 1951, pp. 441–451), Chalchihuitan (Guiteras-Holmes, 1961, pp. 199–206), and in Cancuc (Guiteras-Holmes, 1947, p. 12).[1]

Sororal polygyny usually results from the cultural provision known as the **levirate.** The levirate

© 2013, bikeriderlondon. Used under license from Shutterstock, Inc.

---

1) During the 19th century, sororal **polygyny** was also practiced in at least 40 native American cultures.

was a rather common cultural formation in preindustrial and traditional societies that required a widow to marry the brother of her deceased husband. In practice, the levirate was not only an acceptable custom but a cultural expectation among well-to-do Aztecs. In fact, the levirate accounts for most of the polygynous relationships that occurred in Mesoamerican societies (Soustelle, 1963, p. 112). In more recent times, anthropologists have discovered that the levirate is still practiced in certain areas of Mexico, as was true in Chalchihuitan (Guiteras, 1947, p. 204) and in the village of Cancuc (Guiteras, 1947, p. 12).[2] The social function of the levirate allowed a family to maintain its name, titles, and property over a longer period of time, that is, in spite of the demise of one of its male members. This practice also ensured that the members of his extended family would provide for the children of a deceased brother. The basis for this cultural adaptation was the socially accepted view that children were their father's property and should remain within his family's kinship structure for all time. All of these considerations were of vital importance in traditional societies that lacked state or national laws and social welfare structures to ensure the care and protection of children over the long term, and particularly in cases where one or both of their parents experienced an untimely death.

The rarest form of polygamy is polyandry. Polyandry is the cultural option that allows a woman to have two or more husbands simultaneously. Although polyandry has occurred historically and is an acceptable cultural practice in certain societies today, it is nonetheless a rather rare form of social bonding. For example, in his now classic study of marriage and the family in various cultures throughout the world, Murdock (1949, pp. 26–28) found that only two societies allowed for the practice of polyandry. Interestingly enough, when polyandry occurs, it is usually a societal reaction to an acute shortage of women. Ironically, the shortage of women in those societies where polyandry occurs is often the result of the practice of female **infanticide** (van den Berghe, 1979, p. 62). It is also true that when polyandry occurs, it most frequently takes the form of **fraternal polyandry,** in which case the woman's husbands are brothers.[3]

Fraternal polyandry will not only minimize the necessity of dividing the land and resources but also keep the brothers together; therefore, the growth of the family will be controlled. **Fraternal polyandry** was common for generations among families in Tibet, and the neighboring Himalayan areas of India (Pahari), Nepal, and Bhutan.

DESCENT, AUTHORITY, AND RESIDENCE PATTERNS

All known cultures have normative structures known as **rules of descent** that inform people regarding which of their biological relatives are to be considered as sociological relatives to whom they have reciprocal rights, duties, and obligations. Historically, **patrilineal descent** is the most common means of determining family origins, and in patrilineal descent, the family tree follows the male line of the family. In the long term, patrilineal descent is always assumed, while matrilineal descent is always a certainty. **Matrilineal descent** is traced along the female line of the family. **Bilateral descent** patterns occur in those societies where both families play an equally important role in the determination of descent patterns. This is the most common form of descent in American society today. In contrast, bilateral descent has symbolic value in the Mexican cultural tradition, and this is the reason that married Mexican women keep their family surname and simply add their husband's surname to their surname (Foster, 1961, p. 1178). In contrast, the use of hyphenated surnames is a relatively new idea in American society.

All known cultures, past and present, have normative structures, which sociologists and anthropologists term **rules of residence,** that inform people where it is preferred for a newly married couple to reside. The residential location of nuclear and extended families has always played an important role in determining the nature of social relationships within the family and the relationships that exist between related families. For example, in a traditional society such as

---

2) The practice of **Sororal polygyny,** known as **Levirate,** still exists in some rural areas of Middle East countries such as Iran, Pakistan, and Afghanistan.

3) It is difficult to explain the reason for the practice of **polyandry** but Westermarck (1894) suggested that when the population needs to be controlled and minimized to adapt to limited resources, polyandry would be practiced.

Feminist Theory on the Subordination of Women and Age at First Marriage, Descent, Authority, and Residential Patterns

As a normative structure, patrilocality requires brides to leave not only their birth homes but frequently the villages of their birth as well and to move, often as virtual strangers, into the homes of their husbands' parents or kin. Patrilocality, in other words, strips brides of social, emotional, and economic systems of support. Marrying young, these brides move into the households of their husbands' kin with the lowest rank and few, if any, social supports. According to the Population Council, an international research group, in the developing world, today, about one girl in seven gets married before her 15th birthday (Bearak, 2006), an institution known to sociologists and anthropologists as *child marriage*. So entrenched is the practice of child marriage that local and international attempts to eliminate it in many parts of the world have proven largely unsuccessful (Moghadam, 2003, p. 270). For example, in Nicaragua, 16% of the girls are married by age 15; and in the Jinotega region of the country, 25% are married by age 15. In the Dominican Republic, 11% of the girls are married by age 15 (Haberland, Chong, & Bracken, 2004, p. 7). In Mozamique, 21% of the girls are married by age 15, and 39% of the girls in Mali are married by age 15 (Population Council, 2004a, 2004b).

Feminist theorists (e.g., Charrad, 2001; Epstein, 2007) view the practices of child marriage, patrilocality, and patrilineality not as social practices that have evolved in human societies to help assure the survival of the group but as instruments central to the oppression of women. Thus, in her 2006 Address to the American Sociological Association, Cynthia Fuchs Epstein (2007, p. 12), in speaking about the global subordination of women, points to:

© 2013, Rob Marmion. Used under license from Shutterstock, Inc.

. . . the iron grip of patrilineal kin groups in North African societies. She notes how Islamic family law has legitimized the extended male-centered patrilineage that serves as the foundation of kin-based solidarities within tribal groups so that state politics and tribal politics converge. This supports the patriarchal power not only of husbands but also of all male kin over women so that the clan defines its boundaries through a family law that rests on the exploitation of women.

in Mexico, **patrilocal residence** is the most common residential pattern and usually occurs when newlyweds move into the groom's father's household (Beals, 1946, p. 178; Foster, 1948, pp. 264–265; Friedrich, 1965, pp. 193–195; Parsons, 1937, pp. 66–96). However, the most common residential pattern for newlyweds in American society today is **neolocal residence.** This residential pattern occurs when a committed couple establishes an independent household. See Box 8.1.

The least common residential pattern among newlyweds or committed couples today is **matrilocal residence,** which occurs when the young couple moves in with the bride's family (Carrasco, 1964, pp. 200–201; Murphy, 1976, p. 193–194; Nutini, 1968, p. 203–206). This residential pattern rarely occurs in traditional Mexican society or in American society and is often viewed negatively. Even greater opprobrium is reserved for those who enter **beena marriages.** A beena marriage is a nuptial agreement by which the groom is actually adopted into his wife's family, with the stipulation that any children and all property will ultimately remain with the wife's family.

As with residential location, the male lineage predominates in most cultures around the world, and so it is the case in the Mexican cultural tradition. This is particularly true in terms of the **sex roles** within the family as they relate to issues of authority and dominance. Historically, **patriarchy** has played a significant role in the growth and development of the Mexican-American family. It is from this heritage that the stereotype of male dominance within the family has evolved.

Matriarchy is the least common form of marital authority found in most societies around the world today. When matriarchy occurs, it is usually when the wife/mother becomes a single parent (usually following divorce) or when the eldest male of the extended family (usually the grandfather) dies and the eldest female (i.e., the grandmother) is the sole survivor. Under these circumstances, the grandmother assumes the position of authority in the extended family, at least symbolically (Murphy, 1976, p. 192). It is at this final stage in her life that she is treated as the matriarch of the family. In view of the ever increasing divorce rates in American society today, more families are assuming the single-parent matriarchal form (Elsasser et al, 1980).

SOCIAL STRUCTURE OF THE NUCLEAR FAMILY

It is an established fact that the nuclear family is a cultural universal and serves as the basis for all forms of social organization. Therefore, it is not surprising that the nuclear family was the basic unit of social organization among the Aztecs of ancient Mexico and all other preindustrial societies. For example, among the Aztecs, the independent nuclear household was used as the most fundamental source of tribute and social responsibility. The head of the household in Aztec society was the eldest male, and he was responsible for any land and property owned by the family. Of utmost importance, he was held responsible for the payment of the annual tribute to the state (Carrasco, 1964, p. 188).

For similar reasons, the nuclear family constituted the very basic unit of social organization during the Mexican colonial period. Invariably, the nuclear family in traditional Mexican society was patriarchal, patrilineal, and patrilocal in form. As is true in all traditional societies, Mexican society was strictly a male-dominated society where women and children were kept under the absolute control of the male head of the family.

In contrast to commonly held views and social stereotypes, the nuclear family in traditional Mexican society was actually small, as the family size ranged from four to five-and-a-half members (Nutini, 1967, p. 387). This means that, on average, there were two to three children per household. Undoubtedly, the small size of the nuclear family was related to the high infant mortality rates that were prevalent during this period. The probability of an infant surviving beyond the critical fifth year of life was no better than fifty-fifty. Women typically gave birth to six to eight children, but only three or four survived to adulthood (De Leon, 1982, pp. 28–29; Nutini, 1967, p. 387).

The most comprehensive distinction that can be made in terms of nuclear family types in a traditional society is to determine whether the nuclear family is independent or dependent. An **independent nuclear family** is one that has established its own independent living quarters and has demonstrated its economic and social independence. In most Mexican villages, slightly less than half of all nuclear families could be classified as independent nuclear family households (Nutini, 1968, p. 183). In contrast, **dependent nuclear families** reside within an extended family network and are dependent on the social and economic resources of the extended family for their day-to-day survival.

The determination of whether a nuclear family is dependent or independent is often a function of the family's developmental process. This is true because most nuclear families begin their existence as dependent families, and only after they accumulate sufficient resources to leave the protection and support of the extended family do they establish their independent households (Nutini, 1968, p. 203). This process stems from the Mexican custom and social expectation that newlyweds will move into the groom's father's household and will remain there until they can establish an independent residence. On average, 75–90% of all nuclear families can trace their origins to an extended family unit (Nutini, 1967, p. 388). It is estimated that between 20% and 30% of all families in Mexican society can be classified as extended families (Friedrich, 1965, p. 193; Lewis, 1951, p. 60; Nutini, 1965, p. 125; Redfield & Rojas, 1962, p. 91; Rojas, 1945, p. 81).

It should be clear that the independent nuclear family is a mature family structure, as it has had time to establish its economic independence, rear children, and develop social relationships in the community. This process of growth and development means that most young couples will spend several years with the groom's parents. With hard work and the accumulation of resources, the young couple will gradually gain their independence from the extended family and move out

1. Dating and Courtship (Ages 21–30)
2. Cohabitation (Ages 23–30)
3. Marriage (Male: 27, Female: 25)
4. Marriage and Child-Rearing Life Cycle:
A. Child-free Stage
B. Preschool Stage (Ages 1–5)
C. Grade School Stage (Ages 6–12)
D. Teen Years (Ages 13–18)
E. Young Adult Years (19–25)
5. Empty Nest Stage (Various Options) (Age 55–60)
A. Soul Mates and Lifelong Companions
B. Mid-Life Crisis: Resolved
C. Divorce and Remarriage/Cohabitation
D. Grandparent–Grandchildren
E. Return of "Boomerang Kids"
F. Care of Elderly Parents
6. Early Retirement Years (Ages 60–65)
7. Life Expectancy (Men: 74, Women: 80)
A. Retired Widows and Widowers (80 and older)

Table 8.2 Marriage and Family Life Cycle (Foster, 1961)

on their own, for this is the cultural expectation that has evolved over the years (Foster, 1961, pp. 1179–1180). (See Table 8.2.)

Types of Nuclear Families

© 2013, DNF Style. Used under license from Shutterstock, Inc.

Beyond the consideration of whether a nuclear family is dependent or independent, it is also possible to delineate five types of nuclear families that are commonly found in traditional and modern families around the world:

1. Incipient nuclear family
2. Simple nuclear family
3. Aggregated nuclear family
4. Complex nuclear family
5. Polygynous nuclear family

In turn, each of these nuclear families will differ in terms of (a) whether they are dependent or independent, (b) whether they have children living in the home or not, and (c) whether they have other relatives or nonrelatives living with them. Clearly, these structural characteristics can reveal a great deal of information about how each of these families is different in terms of its adaptation to a variety of social, cultural, and economic circumstances.

The first type of nuclear family structure is very common and is known as the **incipient nuclear** family. This nuclear family type consists of only the husband and wife. Because newlyweds typically follow the traditional patrilocal residential pattern, most incipient nuclear families are also dependent nuclear families. This pattern prevails in more traditional societies today, because it is unusual for newlyweds to establish neolocal residences (Carrasco, 1963).

Although patrilocal residence provides newlyweds with certain economic advantages, the most important of which is free housing, it also means that they must relinquish their personal freedom and social and economic independence. In the traditional setting, newlyweds are usually given a small bedroom, as space in the extended family household is at a premium. In practice, household accommodations are allocated according to the hierarchical principle within each family; that is, the eldest sons are given priority in the selection of rooms and the use of household facilities (Nutini, 1968, p. 178). In return for their accommodations, newlyweds are expected to perform a variety of domestic chores. In actual practice, this usually means that the daughter-in-law is under the direct supervision and control of her mother-in-law, and the daughter-in-law quickly discovers that her living conditions are less than ideal in this traditional family setting (Salovesh, 1976).

One aspect of life in the extended family that can make things difficult for the young couple is that the son is usually required to work for his father as long as they remain in his household. If the son is employed outside the family farm or business, he is expected to relinquish his earnings to his father. Because his father is the ultimate authority in the household, it is left to his best judgment to determine how the money will be spent and how much of an allowance he will give to his son (Nutini, 1968, pp. 206–207).

While the incipient nuclear family is dependent on the protection and resources of the extended family, this is not always the case for the **simple nuclear family.** The simple nuclear family also began as a dependent family, but these families have children and greater economic resources at their disposal and can afford to move out on their own. This familial transition represents the overall pattern of social maturity within the extended family and can be seen as a move along the continuum of social improvement and economic independence.

However, not all simple nuclear families leave the security of the extended family. In some situations, as the nuclear family matures and accumulates its own resources, adjustments are made by the head of the household to ensure greater freedom and independence for the nuclear family. For example, they may construct an additional room to the house for the growing family. By this time, their relationship has matured and the son is allowed to keep his earnings and he is only expected to give his father enough money to help cover the day-to-day household expenses. At the same time, his puerile spouse has had time to work out an amiable relationship with her in-laws and is learning to enjoy the closeness and security of the extended family.

However, the members of the simple nuclear family do not necessarily abandon the security of the extended family at the first opportunity, as the benefits of living in an extended family sometimes outweigh the disadvantages and inconveniences. This initial transition experience often sets the pattern for the other sons in the extended family. Usually, the members of the extended family join forces and build the next eldest son a separate room for his wife and children. In this manner, the process of assistance and accommodation continues and the extended family matures and grows over time (Lomnitz, 1977).

In contrast, the **aggregated nuclear family** has had time to assert its independence and no longer relies on the assistance or support of the extended family. The aggregated nuclear family consists of the parents, their children, and one or more close relatives. In many ways, this family structure is similar to the simple nuclear family, with the exception that it is more mature and has more economic resources from which to draw. The key characteristic of this family type is that these family members have invited one or more relatives to live with them. For example, the wife's widowed mother may move into the household, as she may have limited resources and may need a place to stay. The advantage for the family is that the resident grandmother can help with the child-care responsibilities and the domestic chores. Or it may happen that the aggregated nuclear family may take care of a cousin or a nephew in time of need, for it is a common practice for traditional families, such as Mexican families, to succor or otherwise "adopt" close relatives who have fallen upon hard times. In practice, these *informal adoptions* are not at all unusual when families must survive at the subsistence level of existence. Close relatives, like nephews and nieces, who are informally adopted by more stable family units may live in these households for a few months or, in some cases, for several years. These informal adoptions represent one way in which a more fortunate family can help another family in times of need. It would be most unusual for a family to deny a call for assistance from a relative in time of need (Lewis, 1959).

The *complex nuclear family* is similar to the aggregated family but with the difference that it also includes one or more nonrelatives. For example, the complex nuclear family might consist of five children, a paternal grandmother who takes care of the children and does most of the cooking, an orphaned cousin, and a widowed *comadre* (co-parent) of the grandmother. The complex nuclear family is always an independent nuclear family and has established itself as one of the more solvent families in the community. This family structure has evolved and matured over the years and is simply reacting to the basic needs of relatives and close friends.

An unusual nuclear family structure that is known to exist in certain preindustrial and traditional societies is the *polygynous nuclear family*. As revealed in our previous discussion, polygyny was practiced among the Aztecs and was also considered an acceptable cultural alternative during the colonial period. By definition, polygyny allows a man to take several wives, and his wives are expected to share the economic and social responsibilities of marriage and provide for any offspring resulting from these relationships. In general, when polygyny occurs in Mexico, a man usually only takes two wives, and this relationship is agreed to by all the parties involved. For example, one study of family life in a rural Mexican village found that 9% of the married men were involved in polygynous unions (Nutini, 1968, p. 305).

In terms of household arrangement, there are two types of polygynous structures. In the first type, the husband and his wives occupy a common household and they constitute one independent polygynous family. This structural arrangement usually occurs in sororal polygyny and is also typical of polygynous unions where only two wives are involved. In sororal polygyny, the co-wives are sisters, and they share all the domestic chores and child-care responsibilities. In the second type of arrangement, the husband continues to live with his first wife in their established household and then finds another house (a *casa chica*) for his second wife, which is usually located at a propitious distance from the main house. The first wife in these polygamous relationships is always considered the legal wife, while the second wife plays a less conspicuous role in the family and in the community. Naturally, these polygynous arrangements require the husband to have greater time and resources at his disposal in order to support two independent households (Lewis, 1959, pp. 202–203). But unfortunately, these domestic arrangements are not always as cordial or convenient as the relationships that exist in the independent polygynous households.

In view of its various forms, the nuclear family is obviously a very flexible and adaptable social structure that provides for the survival of individuals who are forced to live under some rather harsh conditions. From its inception, the nuclear family is given aid and assistance by the larger and more resourceful extended family. Eventually, the nuclear family achieves its independence from the extended family and as it gains in strength and resources, it, in turn, offers aid to the less fortunate members of the kinship lineage. In sum, the nuclear family ensures the survival of dependent family members who otherwise might not manage on their own.

SOCIAL STRUCTURE OF THE EXTENDED FAMILY

Without any doubt, the most adaptive social structure for long-term survival is the extended family. While the nuclear family can manage the day-to-day problems, it is the extended family that provides for the long-term survival of the family. For this reason, the extended family continues to play a very important role in more traditional social settings, such as those found in the rural areas of Mexico and the Spanish-speaking segments of the American Southwest.

While the nuclear family is essential for the procreation and survival of any society, the extended family is clearly a requisite for the survival of the family from one generation to the next. The historical record demonstrates that the nuclear family is too small and lacks the strength and resources to survive over the long term.

The extended family consists of three or more generations of individuals who are related by *consanguineous ties*. In its basic form, the extended family consists of the husband and wife, their unmarried children, married sons, their spouses, and their grandchildren. In the Mexican tradition, the extended family is most often based on *agnatic kinship* ties and as a result is primarily patriarchal, patrilineal, and patrilocal in its structure and orientation.

Almost without exception, the eldest male in the family lineage is considered the head of the extended family household and is ultimately responsible for the conduct and welfare of all the members of his family. The head of the household is the undisputed authority in the family and his orders must be obeyed (Nutini, 1968, p. 214).

The extended family is inherently hierarchical and requires that all family members play (depending on their position in the family) either a superordinate or a subordinate role. The role that an individual plays in the extended family depends, for the most part, on her or his age and gender. Adherence to these basic rules of age and gender stratification is of utmost importance for the survival of the family, as failure to observe these basic rules of conduct will eventually result in the demise of the extended family as a smooth and efficient social unit.

Within our structural and cultural consideration of the extended family, it is possible to describe four basic types of families. These four family types are

1. Simple extended family
2. Aggregated extended family
3. Complex extended family
4. Fraternal extended family

Each of these family structures is different in certain ways, primarily as a result of adaptation to diverse social and economic circumstances, but it is nonetheless true that each family type adheres to the established definition of the extended family. That is, all of these families are based on the existence of consanguineous ties and they all include at least three generations of family members.

The most common form of the extended family, and the least complex structurally, occurs in the *simple extended family* that consists of the grandparents, their unmarried children, married sons and their spouses, and their children. The simple extended family is usually patrilocal, patriarchal, and patrilineal in its orientation and social structure. Although the extended family can maintain its existence for more than three generations, it usually dissolves when the children from the third generation establish their own independent households. The demise of the extended family only means that the various nuclear families that once composed it have established independent households. These independent nuclear households will in turn serve as the basis for the creation of a new extended family structure. In this way, the process of growth and development continues.

Within the context of a traditional cultural environment, the extended family grows and develops out of sheer necessity. From a historical perspective, the extended family structure in Mexico represents a concrete response to the basic need to survive in what can sometimes be a very harsh environment. For example, boys and girls in Mexican culture mature at a faster rate and are given adult responsibilities at a much earlier age than is normally the case in the United States, but it is also true that their dependence on their parents and the support of their families is much greater. The closeness of these family relationships and their higher levels of dependency simply reflect the fact that life is much more difficult and tenuous at the subsistence level of existence. This is the reason that a young man must obtain his father's approval for marriage, as he understands that he cannot support his new bride from his own meager resources. From this basic relationship among social desires, needs, and stark economic reality, it is clear why the extended family is so important in a traditional cultural environment and why the extended family structure has survived for hundreds of years.

Obviously, the extended family will survive and proliferate because it meets the social and economic needs of the second and third generations who constitute its form and structure. Therefore, in our example, the head of household will determine if he can support an extra person, that is, his son's new bride, and he also has to consider what additional provisions have to be secured in order to accommodate the new couple and the children who will inevitably follow. But the head of the extended family understands because he also had to approach his father and ask his permission to marry, thereby placing an additional strain on the meager resources of his father's family. So the cycle of marriage, family expansion, and growth continues from one generation to the next. Economic necessity and family obligations fuel this cycle of petition and dependence.

The process of growth continues from one son to the next, and as each dependent nuclear family has children, the household accommodations of the extended family expand accordingly. With the passage of time and the accumulation of resources, the dependent sons, each in their turn, will build separate dwellings for their families on the *ancestral paraje* (ancestral plot). By so doing, they achieve economic independence from their father's household, but they still have all of the advantages of physical propinquity to his household (Nutini, 1968, p. 188). In view of this developmental pattern over three or four generations, it is not uncommon to see a large house (the main house) on the *ancestral paraje* surrounded by two or three smaller houses (Lomnitz, 1977, pp. 100–103).

If the sons are unable to build a house on their father's property, they will purchase a lot as close to the *ancestral paraje* as possible. In part, this residential pattern derives from the Mexican family custom of subdividing a large lot into smaller plots that are then given to each of the sons as they marry and start their own families (Foster, 1961, p. 1180; Taylor, 1933, pp. 28–31). This traditional residential pattern of building on the *ancestral paraje* also explains why many families living on a particular block in the Mexican-American community today are related to one another (Gonzales, 1985, pp. 21–27; Rubel, 1971, pp. 3–24).

In the economic structure of the extended family, two distinct patterns evolve: either the sons are totally dependent on their father for economic support or they lead an independent economic existence. The issue of economic dependence or independence in the extended family is a matter of degree, but most recently married sons do not have the economic resources to support a family. Consequently, they must depend on their fathers' economic support.

As each son matures and as his economic position improves, his dependence on his father decreases and his independence from the economic resources of the extended family increases. Over time, each of the dependent nuclear families, within the extended family, gradually asserts its economic independence. For as long as they reside in the extended family household, they are expected to contribute to the overall maintenance of the family by giving a portion of their earnings to their father and by making occasional contributions of food. In addition, they are expected to volunteer their labor and to participate in family construction projects.

It is clear that the extended family bonds people together and allows them to work for mutual support and survival. For this reason, the extended family is the epitome of social exchange and altruistic consideration in human relationships. It is the giving and sharing of scarce resources to ensure mutual survival that promotes the imprinting of *familism*, the importance of human relationships and kinship ties. This also explains why the extended family plays such an important role in the lives of those who have experienced traditional extended family bonds, for it represents the essence of life in the family and in the community.

THE MATE SELECTION PROCESS

Sociologists have devoted a great deal of attention to the mate selection process, the way that people select marital partners from the pool of individuals who are available in any given social group. There are two major norms of mate selection, endogamy and exogamy. *Endo-* is a root word that means "within," and *–gamy* is a root word that means "marriage." Hence, **endogamy** is a norm whereby people are expected to marry within some group or groups. Common bases

1. All Possible Dating Partners
2. Propinquity Filter (The Accident of Location, Location, Location)
3. Attractiveness Filter (Physical Beauty)
4. Social Background Filter (Education, Occupation, Income)
5. Consensus Filter (Agreement on a Variety of Key Issues)
6. Complementary Filter (Opposites Attract)
7. Strong Friendship (Results in a Committed Loving Relationship)
8. Readiness for Marriage (Inseparable)
9. Experiment with a Trial Marriage
10. Results in a Legal Binding Marriage

Table 8.3 Mate Selection Filters

of endogamy are social class, race, ethnicity, and religious affiliation. Some societies do require that their members marry within their groups, a practice that is known as endogamy. Other societies require their members to marry outside their group, a practice known as **exogamy.** *Exo-* is a root word meaning "outside" or "outside of," and *–gamy* is a root word meaning marriage. Hence, exogamy is a norm of mate selection that requires people to marry outside of a certain group or groups. Exogamous marriages are sometimes termed *intermarriages*, as in a religiously exogamous marriage wherein the husband is, say, a Southern Baptist and the wife is, say, a Buddhist. In the long term, both of these mate selection rules work hand-in-hand to produce a balanced distribution of potential marriage partners in any given society. See Table 8.3.

The cultural rule that sets a definite limit on endogamy is the **incest taboo.** The incest taboo is the major norm of exogamy, and it prohibits marriage or intimate sexual relations with persons within prohibited degrees of kinship. What those "prohibited degrees of kinship" are varies from one culture to another. In general, the incest taboo is limited to the *primary relationships* that exist in the nuclear family. The incest taboo places a strict prohibition on sexual relationships between fathers and daughters, mothers and sons, and brothers and sisters. See Figure 8.1. Some cultures extend the incest taboo to include all secondary relatives, and sometimes it even includes the more distant tertiary relatives. *Secondary relationships* encompass those consanguineous ties that include first cousins, aunts, uncles, and grandparents. *Tertiary relationships* include those blood ties that extend to second and third cousins, great aunts, great uncles, and great grandparents.

The incest taboo varies from one culture to another in its inclusion and exclusion of relatives from the connubial bond. For example, among the Aztecs, marriage was prohibited within the *calpulli* (a territorial sector) and was always prohibited among members of the same clan (Vaillant, 1948, p. 111). In most cases, the *calpulli*, clan membership, and *appellido* (or surname) overlapped and were synonymous in ancient Mexico, and they established the outer limits within which marriage was strictly prohibited (Carrasco, 1961).

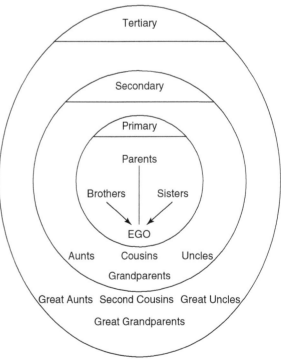

Figure 8.1 A Typology of Family Relationships

For example, in pre-Revolutionary Mexico, the incest taboo eliminated anyone with the same surname or anyone from the same *barrio* as a potential marriage partner. During this period, every barrio was associated with certain surnames, and these surnames were associated with barrio membership (Nutini, 1961, p. 71). In spite of these stringent rules of exogamy, it is nonetheless true that on a larger scale most marriages took place within the village or *municipio*, as most Meso-american communities exhibited a strong propensity for endogamous relationships. It is reported that at least three out of four of all marriages took place within the village or *municipio* (Diebold, 1966, pp. 47–48; Nutini, 1967, p. 399).

In addition to the territorial and clan considerations that served as the basis for the incest taboo, marriage was also prohibited between primary, secondary, or even tertiary relatives. Sometimes, the incest taboo extended to fourth cousins, as was true in Tepoztlan (Lewis, 1951, p. 76), Ojitlan (Weit-laner, 1951, p. 443), Tzintzuntzan (Foster, 1948, p. 249), and among the Maxatec Indians (Cowan, 1947, p. 252). To this day, the culture does not allow godchildren and godparents to marry or for god-siblings to marry without attracting social disapproval. This cultural prohibition on marriage between godchildren stems from the fact that the children of *compadres* (co-parents) cannot marry each other as they are considered spiritual brothers and sisters (Lewis, 1951, p. 76).

In contrast, in other societies, the preferred person to marry *is* one's cousin.

SOCIAL FUNCTIONS OF THE FAMILY

As demonstrated, the extended family is not static but is in a continuous state of flux, as this allows for the introduction of new members and the release of long-term members as the extended family ages and matures. As a result, most people live or have lived in an extended family at some point in their development and maturation (Diebold, 1966, pp. 41–45; Lomnitz, 1977, p. 102; Nutini, 1965, pp. 123–127). For example, Carrasco found that agnatic kinship ties determined the domestic residence of four of five dependent families in his study (Carrasco, 1964, p. 198). (See Table 8.4.)

When examined structurally, the primary difference between the simple extended family and the aggregated extended family is that in the latter type of family structure other relatives are present. Besides the grandparents and two or three dependent nuclear families, the aggregated

■ Emotional Fulfillment and Support
■ Sexual Adjustment
■ Dealing with Personal Habits
■ Gender Roles and Division of Labor
■ Marital Concerns: Finances and Housing
■ Work and Career Patterns
■ Social Life, Friends, Recreation
■ Extended Family and Relatives
■ Communication Patterns
■ Power and Decision-Making
■ Dealing with Conflict and Problem Solving
■ Values and Beliefs

Table 8.4 Marital Adjustment Tasks

extended family also includes other relatives who have taken up residence with the extended family, either on a temporary or a permanent basis. These relatives are usually lineage dependents who have agnatic ties with the head of the household and have called upon his altruistic feelings in their time of need. Usually, these dependents are older relatives who are beyond their productive years, or children and adolescents.

The term of residence of these older or younger extended family dependents is often permanent, as they tend to remain in the household until they expire, as in the former case, or until they assert their independence, as in the latter case. Relatives who are functioning adults are not as likely to attach themselves to a kinsman's extended family; and when they do, their stay is usually temporary. The one exception to this pattern of temporary residence of functioning adult relatives occurs when a close relative has a child out of wedlock and lacks any means of support. Under these circumstances, he or she will have few options but to call upon the largess of his or her kinsmen.

In a sense, the extended family can be viewed as an informal social services agency that is functioning in an environment that has very few sources of public assistance. Consequently, the permanent residents in the extended family tend to be older relatives who can no longer take care of themselves, or else they are the orphaned or abandoned children of close relatives. Other dependent relatives are the unfortunate widowed women with children or hapless unwed mothers.

Sometimes, these attached relatives are children who have been given to their kinsmen by their parents. This phenomenon occurs when a family has more children than it can support. They simply call upon the largess of relatives who have more resources at their disposal. In effect, an informal adoption takes place. These informal adoptions usually occur during infancy and the child is subsequently reared by an aunt and uncle, or by his or her grandparents. The child knows who his or her parents are but is simply told that due to some unfortunate circumstances his or her parents decided to allow another relative to rear him or her in their home. Once again, the social acceptability of these informal adoptions is a practical solution to the economic hard times in a society that offers few social services for orphans and the needy.

THE COMPLEX EXTENDED FAMILY

As with the other family types discussed thus far, the complex extended family evolved in response to a structural need in the family lineage. The complex extended family consists of three or more generations—the grandparents, their unmarried children, their married sons and spouses, their grandchildren, one or more primary relatives, and one or more nonrelatives. The fact that distinguishes the complex extended family from all other family types is that it includes nonrelatives as members of the family.

For the most part, these nonrelatives are treated as members of the family and are given the same consideration as any member of the extended family. These nonrelatives typically fall into one of three social categories: (a) **fictive kin** or family companion, (b) the *nana* (or nanny), and (c) the orphaned or attached poor. Anthropologists and sociologists use the term *fictive kin* to refer to the cultural practice of treating non-family members as if they were in fact members of the family.

In terms of their position and living condition in the extended family, the fictive kin have the best living situation, as they are often a contemporary of the matriarch of the family and are sometimes her *comadre*. Often, the family companion is a woman who has lost her husband and lacks any means of support; she has asked one of her close friends or *comadres* for support and is subsequently invited to move in with the extended family.

In those extended families with children and many chores to perform, it is not unusual for the family to have a *nana* to care for the children. The *nana* is usually permanently attached to the family, as she has no other means of support. For this reason, she often plays a dual role as a *criada* (a servant or maid) and as a member of the extended family, as she is never treated like a maid. Sometimes, *criadas* are drawn from the impoverished classes in the community, as they offer their domestic services in exchange for room and board. Once again, the extended family has adapted itself to the needs of certain unfortunate members of the community who might otherwise be relegated to a life of penury.

Perhaps, the most unfortunate of the attached nonrelatives are the orphaned or attached poor. For the most part, they have fallen upon hard times and in exchange for their labor they are treated as family members. If they are children or adolescents, the family, as a selfless act of altruism, usually adopts them.

MARRIAGE AND DIVORCE IN THE UNITED STATES

In the United States, both the composition of families has changed, and there has been substantively declining marriage rates since the 1940s. Alternatives to marriage such as cohabiting, and different forms of marriages such as gay and lesbian marriages have been more accepted by American society.

The median age at first marriage for both male and female has changed. Statistics show that individuals, regardless of their gender, get married for the first time at an older age. In the United States, the median age for females who marry for the first time in 2012 was 26.6 years versus 20.8 years in 1969. The same changes have happened for the male. In the United States, the median age for males who marry for the first time in 2012 has risen from 23.2 years in 1969 versus 28.6 years in 2012.

On the national level, a shrinking share of Americans is married—52% of males aged 15 and older and 48% of females aged 15 and older. Indeed, the proportion of Americans who are currently married has been shrinking for decades and is lower than it has been in at least half a century. The age groupings used in standard U.S. Census tabulations date back to a time when more people married as young teenagers. Among Americans aged 18 and older, the proportion currently married (but not separated) is 55% for males and 50% for females.

Among married Americans, the median duration of their married life in 2008 was 18 years. Among men, 9% are divorced; among women, 12% are divorced.

Year	Men	Women
2012	28.6	26.6
2011	28.7	26.5
2010	28.2	26.1
1972	23.3	20.9
1971	23.1	20.9
1970	23.2	20.8
1969	23.2	20.8

Median age at first marriage for both men and women the in United States from 1969 to 2012.
Source: Adapted from 2009 American Community Survey (Washington, DC: U.S. Census Bureau, 2009–2012).

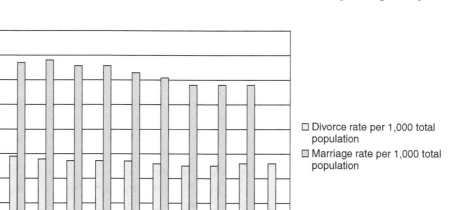

Figure 8.2 National Marriage, Divorce and Annulments Rate Trends in the United States From 2000 to 2011

*Some of the states were excluded from marriage, divorce and annulments rate. Populations for 2010 rates are based on the 2010 census.

Source: Adapted from CDC/NCHS National Vital Statistics System.

FAMILY TYPE

Undoubtedly, there is no single, absolute, or ideal family type that is the most appropriate for any and all groups of people, regardless of race, ethnicity, culture, or socioeconomic conditions in which they live. Traditionally, a family has been defined as an intact, biologically related system of two heterosexual parents in which the father is the sole or primary economic provider and the mother the sole or primary caretaker (Okun, 1996). Okun further posits that this definition of family was socially constructed and assumed to be the best way to raise children. As cited in Lemoge and Dickin (1992), however, a recommended alternative definition of family is that it is "any group of individuals that forms a household based on respect, the meeting of basic needs, as well as those of love and affection, and one in which assistance is freely given to maintain social, spiritual, psychological, and physical health." Some social critics have long suggested that the institution of the traditional family as we know it is crumbling. New types of families are emerging as social service agents attempt to provide displaced children with supportive homes, such as foster parents and grandparent guardians as well as with individuals previously discouraged by society from becoming parents, such as multiracial couples and gay and lesbian couples. Although these families usually provide a nurturing home life for the children in their care, the children of multiracial and gay and lesbian couples sometimes require acceptance of their families' different makeup and lifestyles, and often have need to seek reassurance that they are the same as their peers from more traditional families. This category of family style identifies several common types of nontraditional families and some of their diverse characteristics.

Non-Traditional Families

Families with Gay or Lesbian Parents. Children who are products of this family style are often adopted or the biological child of one of the partners. This family arrangement is often criticized and frowned upon by society in general and by the non-custodial, and often embittered, parent

© 2013, Dubova. Used under license from Shutterstock, Inc.

of the biological child. One of the expressed concerns centers on the children's development of their sexual preference during the critical years of growth and development. This concern for the children's social development and sexual preference sometimes results in bitter legal custody battles that denigrate the gay parent or instigate homophobic peer ridicule, resulting in stressful emotional consequences and internal conflict. According to Schwartz (1999), however, they have no more socio-emotional problems and are no more likely to be homosexual than children raised by heterosexuals.

Families With Grandparents as Parents. Families consisting of grandparents and their grandchildren, another of the diverse family structures, is growing. Rothenberg (1996) reported that between 1980 and 1990 there was a 40% increase in grandchildren living in their grandparents' homes, many without their parents. Research statistics presented by Rothenberg (1996), from a 1996 study of the National Center for Health Statistics, states that 3.735 million children under the age of 18 (5.4 %) lived in the home of their grandparent or grandparents and that Black children were more likely (13 %) to live with a grandparent than White (3.9 %) or Hispanic children (5.7 %). Most of these families reside in urban settings in the south.

The variety of reasons driving this trend, including the AIDS epidemic, parental abandonment, drugs, divorce of parents, unwed mothers, and death of one or both parents, has been impacted by recent legislative activity. The Kinship Care Act of 1996, introduced by Senator Wyden of Oregon, places grandparents first in line as potential foster care parents and adoptive parents for grandchildren who, for safety reasons, have been removed from their parents' home (Rothenberg, 1996). This legislation widens the scope of impact and, thereby, results in this phenomenon representing all socioeconomic and ethnic groups.

Being "saddled" with the responsibility of raising yet another family, particularly when many grandparents are looking forward to the freedom afforded through retirement looming ahead, grandparents are often faced with mixed feelings of love, anger, blame, guilt, and concern for finances. The children "sandwiched" in this triad of confusion between grandparents and parents must often deal with feelings of rejection, abandonment, and loyalty toward their parents paralleled with feelings of gratitude, imposition, and guilt toward their grandparents. Reconciling these feelings, frequently in a home away from their usual neighborhood, school, and friends, creates problems for social development and acquiring a positive sense of attachment to family and self-worth. Children thrust into this new and different routine must learn to deal with the shame and the feeling of being different from their peers. They must also learn to deal with new routines as well as different behavioral and academic expectations. The grandparents must learn to look for their grandchildren's strengths and build on them to provide a real sense of family acceptance and a stable home.

Single-Parent Families. In 1970, 85% of all children lived with two parents; in 1994, this figure had dropped to 69% (U.S. Bureau of the Census, 1996). Castro and Bumpass (1989) estimate that nearly one half of all children will live in a one-parent family before reaching age 18. Mothers are head of households in the majority of single-parent families; most fathers have little contact with their children. Increasingly, this lack of contact with the father results in children losing access to the social, economic, and emotional support fathers can provide. Thus, the role absent fathers play in the well-being of their children becomes critical because of the changes wrought in the family structure.

Father-Only Households. Until recently, fathers were the hidden parent in research on children's well-being; their importance to children's financial well-being was widely accepted, but their contribution to other aspects of children's development was often assumed to be secondary to that of mothers and was not usually examined (Nord, 1998).

Using longitudinal data, from both 1988 and 1992, on sibling pairs from the National Longitudinal Study of Youth, Teachman, Day, Carver, Call, and Paasch (1988) investigated the influence of father absence on behavioral and cognitive outcomes for children. The focus on fathers is derived from the fact that women head the majority of single-parent families. Many times in situations such as this, absent fathers have little to no contact with their children. The researchers examined sibling resemblance for three outcomes: the Behavior Problems Standardized Index (BPI) (an index of prosocial behavior and is indicative of the social adjustments a child is making as she or he matures), the PIAT mathematics standardized score PIATM, and the PIAT reading recognition standardized score (PIATR). The PIATM and PIAT are commonly used measures of cognitive achievement and have been tied to success in school according to the Center for Human Resource Research (Teachman et al., 1998).

The researchers' intent was to demonstrate, not to explain, differences in trajectories of child development between one-parent and two-parent families with respect to the three outcomes considered, they did not include background characteristics of families in their analysis. However, one exception was employed—the consideration of race. It was noted that other researchers (Peter & Mullis, 1997; Smith, Brooks-Gunn, & Klebanor, 1997) have noted sharp differences between Whites and Blacks on the used measured outcomes. The results of this study confirmed that there are differences between one-parent and two-parent families with respect to measures of behavioral and cognitive outcomes (Teachman et al., 1998). These researchers (1998) discovered that children in one-parent families have more behavioral problems and lower scores on mathematics and reading tests and that both older and younger siblings in one-parent families fall further behind their counterparts in two-parent families. It was also found that the same basic pattern of results appeared for both Blacks and non-Blacks, although race does have an effect. According to research by McLanahan and Sandefur (1994), children living in single-parent households are, on average, less successful in school and experience more behavioral problems than children living in two-parent households.

Homeless Children. Homelessness, among both rural and urban communities, is very prevalent today. Exact national figures are not available because 1990 census data on the homeless are doubtful, especially for rural areas; the census enumeration relied on the assumption that the homeless would be found in shelters (Vissing, 1999). Homelessness presents pressing challenges for families; families are denied the physical and emotional space needed for sustaining a private life, and children are deprived of the security they need to be themselves.

Transience, uncertainty, and emotional turmoil are factors that strongly undermine homeless children's school success. Failure to have access to appropriate education during these times can frustrate the growth of intellectual capacities of homeless children. Many, perhaps most, homeless students will develop physical, behavioral, and emotional problems including post-traumatic stress disorders, depression, and anxiety (Vissing, 1999). Some of the emotional problems arise from a feeling of guilt some children have about being the cause of the family's problem and some resent their parents for not providing for them. Self-destructive behaviors and psychic numbing are common; some act out to get needed attention, but withdrawal is more common (Vissing, 1999). Suicidal tendencies, unplanned pregnancies, and sexually transmitted diseases also increase.

Multiracial Families. This family group comprises both children whose parents have different ethnic heritages and those who themselves are different ethnically from their parents (Schwartz, 1999). The development of a multiracial children's identity will be determined in large part by how the family wants the children to be identified. Classifications range from "human" and "multiracial" to "monoracial," which indicates that the family has selected to designate only a single heritage for their children (Miller & Rotheram-Borus, 1994). These children's identities are also greatly influenced by society's attitudes, particularly racist attitudes, toward them.

Those families choosing the "human" classification oppose the concept of racial labeling altogether and argue that acceptance of any label—singular or multiple—other than "white relegates them to a lower status, given existing racism" (Pinderhughes, 1995). According to Weisman (1996), these consciously nonlabeled children often become better acculturated overall, identifying "with communities beyond the traditional racial group or even nation-state."

Families choosing the "multiracial" classification for their children believe that it is important for them to take equal pride in all their heritages, particularly if their physical appearance reflects their dual heritage, and they want the family's culture to embody that (Pinderhughes, 1995). There are, however, those multiracial individuals whose appearance in no way distinguishes them as a member of any of the individual groups they comprise and, thus, may believe that they cannot claim identification with those groups (Stephan, cited in Thornton, 1996). According to Weisman (1996), these people assert that the designation "multiracial" gives them membership in an entirely different community that is actually a new "race" or "ethnic group," and it is this group that evokes their feelings of solidarity.

According to Schwartz (1998a), other families foster their children's identification with only one race and classify them as "monoracial." This monoracial group can include single parents who choose to emphasize their own race as well as parents of children with African ancestry who assume that society will consider the children Black. Society often demands that these children identify with only the minority group in an effort to maintain the "racial purity" of Whites (Schwartz, 1998a). Conversely, some multiracial children may be urged to assume a White identity solely, on the assumption that if they can "pass" as White they can avoid experiencing racism (Miller & Rotheram-Borus, 1994). Unfortunately, however, when these multiracial children move outside of their acceptance group, either socially or geographically, they are frequently faced with confusion as to who they really are, and with rejection by others who are able to easily identify their "mixed" minority status and "call them out" or expose their fraud or "passing" to others.

Embedded in this multiracial culture are individuals whose ancestry is bicultural and their immediate family are not. However, the physical appearance of these individuals embodies the genetic makeup of their ancestry/heritage and results in them looking multiracial. This physical resemblance often creates problems for these individuals both within their dominant culture as well as within the majority culture, "blurring the physical categories upon which white status and power depend" (Wilson, 1987).

This situation is very prevalent in the Black culture as evidenced by the treatment of "light and almost white" Blacks who can "pass" as White or receive preferential treatment by Whites because they are of such close resemblance. Research studies have revealed that light-skinned African Americans are evaluated more favorably than dark-skinned African Americans. Hughes and Hertel (1990) found that the impact of skin color on socioeconomic status among Black Americans is as great as the impact of race (Black-White) on socioeconomic status in American society. Problems arise within the Black culture because of the residual thinking about beauty and how "lightness" transcends "darkness" in color and creates internal conflict for those who have the skin color of privilege versus those who do not. Some researchers have argued that Blacks having lighter skin identify less strongly with Black ethnicity and more with middle-class White culture and values (Hughes & Hertel, 1990). Positive characteristics such as higher class status, intelligence, and beauty have become associated with African Americans of lighter skin tones, whereas negative characteristics such as lower class status, lower intelligence, and unattractiveness have become associated with African Americans of darker skin tones (Averhart & Bigler, 1997). In 1991, Porter examined skin tone preference in African American school-age children and reported that skin tone was a salient personal characteristic and that regardless of age or gender, children preferred lighter over darker skin tones. The few studies of skin tone prejudice have consistently reported that African American children attend to skin color and show more positive attitudes toward lighter complexioned than darker complexioned individuals (Averhart & Bigler, 1997).

The role of heritage in a child's development is affected by history, as well as by social context and immediate environment (Schwartz, 1998b). Before the Civil War, social status among Black people in the United States was very strongly related to skin color (Hughes & Hertel, 1990).

The rejection-acceptance level of the community in which these individuals live often bombards the issues of self-esteem, self-confidence, and social development. As it is with all children, it is important to help multiracial children gain a positive self-concept. The variation in acquiring this positive self-concept and effectively impacting their social development drives the need to expose them to models of all the ethnicities they embrace. This exposure can help them understand the complexities of being multiracial and process ways to deal with culturally internal and external rejection, racism, and discrimination. To maintain a sense of balance in emotional well-being, individuals in this predicament must constantly reconcile within themselves to the decisions they make about the groups to which they can belong versus those groups in which they do belong.

Those individuals who choose to be, or are by parents and families, socialized as multiracial usually benefit from their heritage because they have an enhanced sense of self and identity, greater intergroup tolerance, language facility, appreciation of minority group cultures, and ties to single-heritage groups than do monoracial people (Thornton, 1996). According to Kerwin, Ponterotto, Jackson, and Harris (1993), these individuals often are able to identify multiple aspects of a situation where other people see only one. Additionally, they are also often able to see both sides of a conflict.

African American Families. It is necessary to write about Black American families because much of the research implies that there exists an authentic, monolithic Black family; however, there exists different family and parenting styles and social realities of Black families who have a common African heritage. According to Gibbs (1990), there is no single stereotypical "Black family," but rather a great diversity of families with different cultural backgrounds, socioeconomic levels, regional loyalties, political and religious affiliations, and levels of acculturation and assimilation into the dominant majority culture. Familial life, as an aspect of culture, continues to be an expression of a people's struggle to adapt, survive, and flourish in their physical and social milieu (Williams, 1990).

The resilience of Black families through the ages speaks in support of their survival of the hardships of slavery, the adjustment to emancipation, and the geographical separations of families during the great migration North. Rather than let these adversities tear them apart, Black families tended to draw closer together in order to survive. The strengths of Black families have been identified as (a) strong kinship bonds as manifested in the capacity to absorb other individuals into the family structure in informal adaptation, (b) a strong work orientation, (c) flexibility of family (members') roles, (d) high achievement orientation, and (e) religious orientation (Nobles, 1972). Bartz and Levine (1978) reported that Black families exhibited a combination of high support, high control, open *communication, and demands for mature behavior. These very traits enhance childrens' potential for successfully connecting with their peers in the world* of work.

According to Cheatham and Steward (1990), Black families are unlikely to be understood and appreciated as Black families unless and until research paradigms account for Blacks' cultural specificity. The authors (1990) further posit that work necessary to instate Black families as the critically important developmental units that they are has only begun.

INTERCULTURAL MARRIAGES AND CHILD REARING ISSUES

Amy Freeman and John Cripe

John Cripe and Amy Freeman are the parents of two children. Following is a narrative of their experiences as partners in a biracial marriage and members of a multicultural family. Throughout the discussion, the term Black and African American are used interchangeably, while the term White alludes to U.S. citizens of European descent. Much of the research is still quoted in this way, as well as the common language used between the married authors in their personal commentary regarding this subject.

John: Without warning a child once asked me, "Why would you marry someone Black?" The only answer I could come up at that moment is still the best one I have, "Because that was the only color she came in." You do not marry a race but an individual. The race and culture is included; it's a package deal, along with personality, habits, likes, dislikes, family, and everything else that makes one who one is.

Before I first met her, 20 years ago, I was from a monoculture environment with little access to other cultures. Even when other cultures were available, I rarely chose to go out of my way to interact with them. We were put together in a situation where neither of our cultures was prevalent. We learned about each other and each other's culture along with the dominant culture of another country at the same time. We learned much about the host country's culture, but because of language barriers between ourselves and the host country, we learned even more about each other. It has become a lifelong process of learning and adjusting to each other's culture. While we were dating, it mainly involved the two of us. When we decided to get married, our families became multicultural. After we were married, people we worked with, went to church with, or otherwise interacted with became more multicultural in their thinking. When we had children, the people with whom we interacted on their behalf had to deal with our multiculturalism. Our children alone, however, do not seem to evoke the same controversial diversity issues as we do. People who interact only with our children treat them as they would any other children of a "single-race" minority. Only when they have to interact with us as interracial parents does multiculturalism become a philosophical factor in the relationship, which must be evaluated in a new way.

Isolation is a condition we still deal with. It seemed for a long time that we were the only couple we knew that had our particular mix of races and genders; however, it seems to have changed over the past 20 years. Census data supports this; in 1980, only 1 of 1,000 couples had the same sex and racial makeup that we did. In 2000, the number had had risen to 1 in 500 according to the U.S. Census Bureau Current Population Survey, CPG, Report. Race itself is not hard to deal with; it is a label of one's ancestry. Differences in culture, which are sometimes associated with race, create some of the problems in intercultural marriages must deal with. It often defines choices they must make, both for themselves and their children.

Amy: I came from an African American family of 10. My parents migrated from the deep South to the steel belt and finally to the west coast where we were born and raised. Most of my childhood took place in rural eastern Washington State where a few African American people created small communities and churches. My father was a pastor who also worked for a potato processing plant to support his large family. My mother worked off and on throughout our childhood as needed. The larger community where we lived was a small White town where the high school of 1,200 students (from surrounding rural areas) contained only 12–15 African American students. We knew each other well. My primary connection to the African American community however was through the church. Because my father was a minister, the family traveled extensively, making sacrifices to interact with the larger African American community in cities all over the west coast. This kept us in touch with our culture.

I *learned early on to negotiate issues of culture to survive school and the* isolated town community. I learned quickly about racism. My conclusion early on was that intelligence was an incredible weapon against injustice at that time (but not always against deliberate vengeful stupidity). And, it was my experience that because I was Black, I needed three times the qualifications to receive the same credibility as my White counterparts. I attended a majority state university where I majored in a non-traditional technical field and, after enduring untold discrimination, graduated as the only African American and only female in my class in my field.

My marriage to a White man took me rather by surprise. We met in Germany in a very different cultural setting for both of us as Americans. Perhaps, it was this element that equalized the racial barriers/standards we had left in the United States. Both of us were equally foreigners trying to survive in the present, knowing our home country would present a very different set of circumstances. Once we returned to the United States, it was our intention to go our separate ways. When we did return, however, we found that things remained the same in our individual lives in the United States—just as predicted; but when we were together, our relationship was based on a mutual respect and the cultural freedom we had discovered in Europe. For me, there was no other person who offered this and I valued it greatly. For the first time, I wasn't put in someone else's box regarding who I should be. Eighteen months later, our friendship had turned into a marriage. This was not at all the way I had imagined it was supposed to happen.

THE FAMILY

We were married on New Year's Day of 1983. We were told that unlike other married couples who would become a beautiful blend of colorful unity, ours was destined to be one of vinegar and oil, up and down, Black and White, war and breaks in between. We were told that our marriage would be an ongoing uphill battle and we were constantly confronted with the never-ending question, "What about the children?"

Now, almost 20 years later, we're happy to say that things didn't turn out as bad as they said. We have two well-adjusted children, ages 6 and 14. We are still as Black and White as we were the day we married. When asked to reveal our philosophy regarding this issue, we had to think long and hard to dissect what we do everyday without thought. Our primary observation was that the multicultural views we perpetuate to our children are directly related to those we had developed as single individuals and later as a married couple before their births. In other words, we can only give them what we have and what we know. Having lived in the United States all of our lives, we come from opposite sides of a long-standing societal war. With this in mind, we both agreed that it was important to equip our children with tools to cope with contemporary American racial views and survival strategies that would ease their interaction with the local, national, and international community. The result of this is that publicly we refer to our children (and they refer to themselves) as African American. Privately, however, our home is a safe haven for our children to own all the parts of their combined heritage. This makes for a variety of jokes that only we understand, as well as a more tolerant and diverse perception of the world and all its cultural complexities. The unanticipated surprise of the whole adventure is that there have been several positive outcomes that we could not have imagined 20 years ago, as we listened to other people's version of our future.

For some of this, we have our families to thank. In our families, we both had one parent who was visibly pleased and one who had misgivings. However, all four attended the wedding. We both worked very hard to gain the acceptance of the other's parents and family. We did this out of concern for our unborn children in an effort to save them future trauma and to create for them a happy extended family in which to be born. We knew that all the in-law relationships were long term. If we wanted our children to have loving accessible grandparents, we knew that we were a factor in this relationship and in making both sets of grandparents comfortable with us. If they were afraid of us or our marriage, they would stay away from us and consequently, our children. We spent 5 years making this investment before having children.

By the time our first child was born, relatives flew thousands of miles to see her. For us, this was quite a sign of success and meant that despite all the negative commentary about the children of interracial marriages, it was possible for our children to have a balanced loving family and hence, become balanced loving adults. Both of our families (though not entirely in agreement with our decision to be married early on) ultimately became very supportive of us and worked hard to build healthy relationships with our children.

In the beginning, we had imagined that our children would be alone in their biracial "plight" as depicted to us 20 years ago. We initially explained to our children that in the United States many African Americans have ancestry of other races, but are recognized as Black whether the ancestor is a great, great grandparent or a father. We did not anticipate the growing numbers of biracial children with whom our children would eventually be able to relate. In our situation, we personally have met only a few, but just to be able to visibly see so many seems comforting for them. Our son pointed to a boy in a shopping mall and said, "Hey, he has hair just like me!" and proceeded to wave at the child who waved back in instant recognition. As an African American parent, it is easy to understand the solidarity brought about by just seeing another brown face across a room of hundreds of others.

Amy had nightmares of the children becoming grown and then deciding that they were White, disowning her forever. We were unsure of how they would respond to their own Blackness and their White father. But, they've responded very well and are very comfortable with it. They understand that their mother and they are Black and that their father is White and that they have a rainbow of extended family. When our oldest daughter was three, we overheard her explaining to another toddler, "That's my mom and dad. They don't match but they're very nice people." We can see that she still has a deep appreciation for both family heritages. But she still understands that socially she is recognized as African American.

One of the other positive outcomes we didn't expect from our children is the duality or the ease of cultural mixing that goes on in their lives. We expected that they would ultimately be raised as African Americans and perceive themselves as such based on the information we provided regarding their public and private identities. However, the ease with which they adapted to both sides was startling. For instance, our daughter, at 14, studies classical viola. Consequently, 2 days a week, she takes private lessons, plays with the youth orchestra, and aspires to attend Julliard—yet, on Sunday, she and her viola will freestyle with the best of the African American gospel musicians at our church with not a sheet of music in sight. This is but one example. The same is true when watching the children interact with relatives on either side of the family. They eat sourdough bread as easily as they'll eat collard greens.

CHALLENGES

© 2013, Roi Brooks. Used Under license from Shutterstock, Inc.

As rare as biracial marriages are in which the woman is Black and the man is White, we clearly deal with issues of isolation. We did, however, have the odd experience of being in a small church where at one point there were two other Black women married to the only other two White men in this predominantly African American church. We were the third couple who fit this description. We also have a biracial friend whose White mother would visit periodically. She gave us some encouraging words that have lasted for years. She married a Black man in the late 1940s and was disowned by her family. She was widowed some years later and continued to remain in the Black community to raise their five children. Her children who are adults now perceive themselves as African American. She too thought it best to give her children tools to navigate the present categorized society. We believe interaction with others in a similar position helped our family for that 3- or 4-year time period during its developmental stages. Since that time, we have not been personally involved with any other family with the racial mix as our own.

Our son will grow up to be a Black man. We are both conscious of this and go out of our way to surround him with positive African American male role models who by example teach him many survival strategies in the racially biased culture he is growing up in. This is primarily through family members, our church, and community. So far, we believe we're doing alright—he's just 6. He seems self-assured, has a good vocabulary, sensitive to the needs of others, and wants to be a super hero when he grows up. We reassure him that this is a very good thing and remind him that he is surrounded by so many of them. His godmother, a very big influence on him, is a Kenyan journalist. Both our son and daughter are familiar with all four grandparents and a 93-year-old great grandmother.

We have deliberately taken opportunities to render our children well traveled. It is important for them to know that the environment we live in is but a part of the world—not the whole world. So, when negative things happen, they know that the world is not made up entirely of negative things, but a variety. We hope they learn that negativity is actually in the eye of the beholder. Remember, we were told that our own marriage could become a negative event. (So, you can't listen to everybody.)

In the 1980s, we remember looking hard and paying well for children's books in which our daughter would see herself and her family, as so many other children do. African American books and single culture books were easier to come by when we left the small rural community we lived in to shop for them. We bought books with many cultural backgrounds and great illustrations paying as much as $25 for one children's book because we saw it as an investment in our child's future worldview. We felt it important to create an environment where the child saw herself in power and not alone. Finding books with pictures of biracial families was very difficult to come by. Two favorites were *More, More, More Said the Baby* and *Black is Brown is Tan*. In both cases, the families looked almost identical to ours. We've also taken our children to theaters and provided other cultural exposure. We have since left that small rural community with a population under 10,000 and moved to a neighboring town with a population over 100,000. We travel to larger cities several times each year.

THE FORMULA

There is none. Like all other parents, ours, too, is on-the-job training. Our child rearing is based on our separate and combined cultural views and a fair amount of improvising. The guidelines for how we raise our children are a combination of our personal experiences as children, information passed on by our parents and new discoveries in a world that our parents couldn't have imagined in 1983. At the end of the day, we just hope that our children take away three or four of the following survival tools we have tried to pass on.

1. Order is important. Knowing one's family and social history helps us define ourselves as a part of a continuum, while accepting our uniqueness at the same time. Adults receive the respect of children just because they have been here longer.

2. Our word is good. If we promise to do something, we go out of our way, even if it becomes inconvenient, to follow through later. We believe this builds trust and encourages them to be honest and trustworthy people. If, on rare occasions, we fail to follow through (like getting a dog), we acknowledge the event as a failing followed with an apology to the child. This teaches the child that all of us are fallible.

3. We teach them to identify publicly as African Americans because socially in the United States this simple explanation is not only true, but it also leaves options to later explain (or not explain) personal background details to outsiders who may eventually mean you political harm. Socially, people in the United States understand the categorizing that goes on and often feel entitled to an explanation of those answers like "other" that do not fall within the categorical boxes. Even as an African American, I am not always in the mood to explain my existence and political position on race relations in the United States Why put our biracial children through it? We tell them they can explain if they choose. They have the right to self name. It took Amy a long time to "make my Black peace with that," but the easiest answer in a pinch, evoking no questions, is Black, because they'll certainly not be recognized as White in this country at this point in time.

4. Just because people think they know doesn't mean that they do. The United States is a very myopic system and only believes in its own rendition of the world. This is true of many countries. It is up to each individual to travel and personally verify if what we are told is indeed true, and what parts of the world's historical process are being left out. Small exposures to one culture doesn't make one an expert. Ours' is not the only story of racism, there are many. It is important to hear each person's first hand story of himself before passing judgment based on hearsay. Learn about others and you'll see similarities to yourself within the human condition.

5. There are good and evil, friends and foes, on both sides of the racial line. People are not always their true selves when guests are present.

6. Reading and writing are revolutionary tools. Education is its own reward.

7. Be unafraid to question authority because they do not always know what is best for you, though they may know what is best for those like themselves. We live within a power structure, which is biased toward a European male value system advocating that all things are possible for everyone as long as the existing cultural system does not lose power. (This belief system is not unlike other power structures in the world. It is a common human failing.)

8. Home is a state of mind. Home is a place of peace, security, rest, respect, and freedom. Home is a place where fears can be vented (even if they are unfixable) and where victims are supported, encouraged, and loved. Parents defend children until they are old enough to defend themselves. Children will ultimately defend themselves by mimicking parents' methods. In our case, always non-violently. (*Amy:* I remember when my younger sister was unjustifiably fired from a local fast food restaurant. My older sister wrote an editorial to the local newspaper—just as my mother would have—evoking other letters complaining about the business establishment.)

9. Don't lie. Don't steal. Nothing replaces your own integrity.

10. Never become arrogant enough to believe that you are the only one controlling the Universe. No single individual knows or has everything. That's why we need each other.

We believe that multiracial people are the next silent majority soon to become vocal about their identities. When we talk to adult biracial people, they seem to want the right to self-name and claim all their parts as they see fit. We imagine that our children will become like these people, so we allow them the freedom to be who they are; however, much of it may or may not fit into the world view of our generation. We do appreciate the celebration of each of our heritages. Yet, we recognize that it is more difficult to celebrate both of them than it is to intensely concentrate on one. We sacrifice some of the intensity of each in favor of cultural mixing and sharing to create new philosophies that will guide the lives of our children into a future we can only imagine.

SUMMARY

When we evaluated the research on this particular subject, we found that we fit most of the typical findings for our family description. Our feelings of social isolation and tension early on are well founded. According to the U.S. Census, the overall number of interracial couples in the United States rose from 1 in 1,000 in 1980 to 1 in 500 in the 2000 Census. Although the numbers have doubled in the last 20 years, they are still low. Wehrly, Kenney, and Kenney (1999) showed that interracial couples married for 20 years or more have experienced more societal pressures than younger couples. However, in 1997, 14 years after our marriage, Nash's study of interracial dating couples shows that they still experience public rejection. Also, the western United States, where we were both raised, has the highest proportion of African American interracial marriages (Tucker & Mitchell-Kernan, 1990). The highest proportion of interracial marriage between two groups is White male and Asian female, whereas the lowest rate is ours, White male and Black female. (Grosz, 1997; Lind, 1998). Although Black/White unions formed only 24% of all interracial relationships in 1990 (Thornton & Wason, 1995), there is disproportionately more research on this combination than any other (Brown, 1987; Johnson, 1991; Robinson & Howard-Hamilton, 1994), and it is considered by U.S. society to be the most risky and controversial. Reasons for this involve issues of racial loyalty and psychological and sociological stereotypes. Spickard (1989) found that this societal concern is based on a racially stratified U.S. history. Another factor is the U.S. negative social view of multiracial adults and children (Nakashima, 1992).

Kenney and Cohen (1998) were able to disprove several social assumptions regarding harmonious and conflicting choices within interracial marriages when they interviewed 80 northeastern

Black/White couples who had been married between 1 and 35 years. The group was largely composed of highly educated, professionally employed, and middle-class individuals. Liu (1998) showed that it is typical of those in U.S. society to assume that the relationship of every mixed couple is based on political and racial motivation. Azoulay (1997) indicated that members of the Black and Jewish communities have the largest resentment of such relationships because it is a public show of disloyalty to the group because of the group's history of racism and oppression by others. In the Kenney and Cohen (1998) study, most couples contended that their reasons for marriage were not based on a desire to prove anything regarding race or culture to the outside world. Rather, racial and cultural questions did come to mind when deciding to make the trade-off between social, psychological, and emotional familiarity for new personal growth. The multiracial couples were found to be similar to same-race couples in that they had shared values, beliefs, and interests and attributed this to marital success. They concluded that the ability to counter negative social influences was directly connected to the self-esteem of both partners. Downey (1996) suggests that the success of an interracial marriage is also directly related to the couple's willingness to respect and learn each other's cultural background.

Once a couple is married, there is a social stereotype that *all* problems in the relationship are related to racial differences. Again, this is unfounded by the 80 interviewed couples who revealed that most problems associated with cultural and racial issues are only presented in a public forum with those outside the family. Typically, this conflict arises from the visual appearance of the family and the inaccurate assumptions that follow. Instead, the greatest areas of tension cited by the couples themselves were finances, parenting, employment, decision-making, and finding time for each other. The subjects of Kenney and Cohen's (1998) study were professional and middle class. This is an important factor when considering Solsberry's finding that the degree of racial difficulty experienced by biracial couples varies with socioeconomic level, educational background, and the community in which they live (Solsberry, 1994). A high level of income and education would give the parents increased ability to change the living environment and social exposure of the family.

It is common for a parent in an interracial marriage to be questioned by society when publicly alone with biological children who look visually different than the parent. People are unusually comfortable posing questions and making assumptions that they would not mention to visually similar parents and children (Wehr, Kenney, & Kenney, 1999). White members of interracial families also become acutely conscious of *White privilege* in society and develop what Kenney calls, *racial/cultural empathy.* This typically happens when they experience or witness the discriminatory plight of a minority spouse or child. This reinforces the need for parents to pass on successful survival strategies to their children.

There are many myths that center around the belief that biracial children will have more problems than other children based on visual identity issues and the belief that a child will somehow have more genetic material of one parent than the other (Gibbs, 1987; Melina, 1990; Wardle 1992). However, it was also found that stability of the children is based on having positive role models in the home who provide clear direction for dealing with societal problems (Brandell, 1988). It is typical for interracial parents to deliberately create a safe, multicultural environment for children where they are accepted, even if it means relocation or spending extra money and time. This is manifested through the selection of books they read, the schools they attend, and the population mix of the community in which they live. In the Kenney and Cohen (1998) study, parents wanted their biracial children to have an appreciation of all cultural backgrounds and would deliberately introduce this idea at an early age, believing that they were handing children additional tools to cope with present and future societal racism.

We conclude that at the bottom of it all, we, too, are just another set of parents trying to create joyous, productive human beings with all the challenges and rewards encountered in the journey. We choose not to view our interracial composition as a problem to be solved because it cannot be undone, neither would we want it to be. Instead, we see it as an asset that will better equip our children to think broadly and utilize more options as they negotiate their lives.

CHAPTER 9

Re-examining the Role of Religion and Spirituality in Cultural Communities

THE ROLE OF RELIGION IN AMERICAN SOCIETY

When compared to many of the other advanced industrial nations of the world, the United States is a very religious country. A recent study by the Pew Research Center finds that more than eight out of ten Americans (83.4 percent) report that they belong to an organized religious group. This compares to only about one out of four people in the major European countries (Pew Research Center, 2008). One out of six Americans (16.1 percent) is not affiliated with any particular religion. The overwhelming majority of Americans (78.4 percent) who are members of an organized religion indicate that they are Christians. Only 5 percent of the U.S. population says that they belong to a religious group that is not Christian (Pew, 2008: 10).

What is interesting is that while the United States does have high levels of membership in an organized religion compared with many other countries, the actual rate of church attendance is only in the mid-range when compared to these other countries. When Americans are asked if they attend church on a regular basis—this usually means once or twice a month—less than half (44 percent) say that they do. In contrast, in Ireland 84 percent of the people say that they attend church on a regular basis, and in the Philippines, seven out of ten (68 percent) people attend church on a regular basis (Pew Research Center, 2008).

In general, European nations have rather low rates of church attendance. The highest rates of church attendance in Europe are in Italy (45 percent). Much lower rates are found in the Netherlands (35 percent), Austria (30 percent), the United Kingdom (27 percent), Spain (25 percent), and France (21 percent) (Pew Research Center, 2008). The lowest rates of church attendance among European nations tend to occur in the Norwegian countries, where only 4 percent of the people say that they attend church on a regular basis. Russia is at the very bottom of the list. In Russia, only 2 percent of the people attend church services on a regular basis (Arts, Hagenaars, and Halman, 2009; Halman, et al., 2006).

Church Membership in the United States

When we consider the adult population of the United States today, we discover that about half of all Americans (51.3 percent) are Protestants. Among Protestants there is great diversity. About half of the Protestants belong to one of the Evangelical churches. One out of three Protestants is a member of one of the more traditional mainline Protestant churches (Pew Research Center, 2008).

Within the Protestant churches in the United States there is also great diversity by race, ethnicity, income, and education. Historically, Protestant churches have sorted themselves by race and social class. A close look at the Protestant denominations in the United States today certainly reveals the persistence of these differences.

The largest denomination among the Protestants in the United States is the Baptists, as they represent one-third of all Protestants in this nation. Many members of the Baptist church describe themselves as evangelical Christians. Within the Baptist churches, there are at least three dozen sub-groups. Some of the better known ones include the Southern Baptist Convention, the National Baptist Convention, and the large number of historically black Baptist churches located primarily in the southern part of the United States.

The second largest group within the Protestant churches in the United States is the Methodists, and most of the Methodists are members of the United Methodist Church. Other well-established groups among the Protestants are the Lutherans, the Pentecostals, and the Presbyterians. Overall, the groups that are growing the fastest among the Protestants are the Evangelicals and those Protestants who attend mega-churches and nondenominational congregations.

While church attendance among Protestants has remained at the same level for a couple of decades, the actual number of Americans who describe themselves as Protestants has declined since the early 1970s. During the 1970s and 1980s about two out of three of Americans described themselves as Protestants, but today only about half as many make this claim (Pew Research Center, 2008).

In contrast, the number of Catholics has remained about the same during this same period of time. About one out of four Americans describe themselves as Catholics. The consistency in the number of Catholics over time can be attributed to two important factors: the attraction of new converts to the faith and the continual influx of new immigrants who are Catholics into the United States. Recent studies on newly arrived immigrants reveal that nearly half of them are Catholics. Thus, much of the growth among Catholics can be attributed to the large influx of immigrants from Mexico, Central America, and South America. Most of these immigrants are Catholics (Pew Research Center, 2008).

Besides the larger numbers of Protestants and Catholics, there are other small Christian denominations, such as the Mormons (1.7 percent of the adult population), Jehovah's Witnesses (0.7 percent), and Orthodox Christians (0.6 percent). These denominations are still growing as a result of natural increase within their congregations and their concerted efforts to recruit and maintain new members (Pew Research Center, 2008).

In addition to the dominant Christian groups in American society, other major religious traditions and denominations are also represented in population of the United States. These other religious traditions remain in the minority, as the Jewish groups in the United States represent 1.7 percent of the adult population, Buddhists 0.7 percent, Muslims 0.6 percent, and Hindus 0.4 percent (Pew Research Center, 2008). In addition, there are other non-Christian groups that are even smaller in size in the United States today. It is interesting to note that much of the growth among these various non-Christian groups can be attributed to the recent influx of immigrants from the Middle East, Asia, and Africa (Pew Research Center, 2008).

Almost one out of six Americans (16 percent) is not a member of any church and/or is simply a nonbeliever. For a nation the size of the United States, this is a very significant figure. In fact, the number of nonaffiliated individuals in the United States today is about the same as the number of people who say that they are members of the mainline Protestant churches (Pew Research Center, 2008: 11).

The conclusion that we can draw from this overview of religious affiliation and church membership is that America is predominately a Christian society and the great majority of Christians identify with the Protestant church. On the other hand there is a great deal of diversity among Christians, Protestants, and other non-Christian denominations, and this is something that is accepted by the great majority of citizens. The belief in religious freedom is still strong in the arena of American democratic values.

What Is Religion?

Over the years, sociologists and philosophers have attempted to construct a succinct definition of religion. One interesting approach is to trace the Latin origins of the English word religion. The Latin word religare serves as the root of the English word religion. The Latin word religare refers to the ability to unite, bond, or obligate a group of individuals. Therefore, religion, in practical application means that a group of people are united in a common mission because of a strong sense of commitment and obligation to each other. Religion serves as a bond that holds a group of people together. It therefore serves as a basis for their organization as a group of people. This is exactly how Emile Durkheim developed his concept of religion.

Durkheim studied hunting-and-gathering societies (folk societies) to understand the role of religion in human social organization. In these early societies, humans were aware of the power of nature and of the many events that were beyond their understanding and control. In an effort to come to grips with the complexities of their natural environment, humans would often attribute the mysteries of the natural world to the unobtrusive workings of superior, unknown, or unseen beings.

Subsequently, many of these early human groups attributed all the unknown objects or events that they experienced in their natural environment to "the gods." This pantheistic interpretation of the natural world is what served as a basis for the organization of their societies.

It did not take very long for the leaders of these groups to realize that they could use their own personal connections with these unknown gods to influence the political decisions that were made by the members of their group. Soon a few key individuals in the tribe made it clear that they had established a direct connection to the gods and therefore their words must be respected and followed. And this is probably the first example of the symbiotic relationship between religion and politics.

An important part of this process was the fact that humans were forming and cementing long-term relationships with each other on the basis of their belief in a superior power. The various rituals and beliefs that they devised served to bring people together in new committed relationships. Their shared religious beliefs are what brought them together. Religion now served as a basis of solidarity. People used their religion to project their own feelings and beliefs about how they should organize themselves and how they should conduct themselves. Before long religion became a way of life.

When most people are asked for a definition of religion, they are most likely to give you their own (personal) definition of religion. And their definition of religion will more than likely be colored by their own personal religious beliefs and experiences. Since the dominant religious institution in the United States today is Christianity, most Americans would probably start by saying that religion is the belief in a supreme being. However, this aspect of the definition of religion would automatically exclude some of the major religious beliefs systems in the world. Some religions are polytheistic and others do not believe in a supreme being, as such. Thus, the common definition of religion might be tainted by personal experiences and therefore is of limited use in an unbiased or in-depth scientific study of the role of religion in society.

Emile Durkheim on Religion

Emile Durkheim is one of the founding fathers of modern sociology. Very early in his studies, Durkheim focused on the role of religion in everyday life. His efforts resulted in the publication of his now renowned book on religion, *The Elementary Forms of Religious Life* (1912/2001).

Following years of study, Durkheim came to a clear understanding of the relationship among humans, society, and religion. His simple definition of religion was to state that, ". . . religion is a unified system of beliefs and practices relative to sacred things, that is to say, things set apart and forbidden—beliefs and practices which unite into one single moral community, called a church, all those who adhere to them" (Durkheim, 1995: 44).

Durkheim's definition starts with the idea that religion is based on our beliefs about the sacred (Durkheim, 1912/2001). The sacred items in any society are those that demand respect, generate a sense of awe, and cause us to form strong emotional bonds with the sacred. The sacred can either be a tangible cultural item or an intangible cultural item that generates a sense of awe and respect. This simply means that sacred items in our environment and experiences can either be material or nonmaterial.

A tangible sacred item could be a crucifix hanging on someone's bedroom wall, or it could be a capsule located in a great cathedral containing a bone fragment of a long deceased prophet. On the other hand, a nonmaterial, or intangible, sacred item could be a spoken word or the recollection of a profound emotional experience with the sacred. But in all cases the sacred item provides a deep emotional experience for the believer. It therefore creates strong emotional bonds among all the true believers in a group.

The Importance of Shared Religious Beliefs

This type of deep emotional experience is what draws true believers to the (religious) group and unites them in a common cause. Therefore the sacred is the holy item or emotional experience that is at the core of any religious experience. In effect, the sacred, or the holy, is built upon the emotional experiences and the bonds that develop over time in any religious group. With the passage of time the religious group builds upon these sacred or holy experiences. This then creates and sustains a sacred culture that generates and builds its own history and traditions. Over time, true believers create a strong social network and vital emotional bonds among their members. The end result of these profound group experiences is an organized and often institutionalized religion.

Religion is not only a sacred and an emotional experience for the individual, but rather it is often a social or a group experience. In order for an individual to have the sacred or religious experiences, she or he must share the sacred experiences with others. Above all, the religious or sacred experience is usually a social experience. Although it is possible for the individual, in total isolation, to have a sacred or religious experience, it is more common for individuals who share the same system of beliefs to join together in common worship. Indeed, all of the major organized religions are based on the group experience. It is the members of the group who will develop and maintain the religion.

Religion and the religious group are bound together by their common beliefs and experiences. The religious experience is a social, psychological, and emotional experience. The religious group not only provides a system of social support, it also provides the individual with a sense of fellowship, a sense of well-being, and a sense of spiritual comfort. These are the cement that binds all religious groups. In short, religion provides the individual with a sense of peace and tranquility. Religion is the ointment that soothes the soul (Durkheim, 1912/2001; Marx, 1844/1970), which in essence is both the strength and attraction of all organized religions.

Religion and the Cosmic Questions

In addition to providing the individual with a sense of spiritual tranquility and inner peace, the major religions also provide answers to three of the most important questions facing all individuals in any organized society. We sometimes refer to these three questions as the cosmic questions. It is these questions that every organized religion must answer. These questions are (1) Where did we come from? (2) Why are we here? and (3) Where are we going?

By developing and building a strong background in *theology* and *cosmology*, all of the major religions have provided individual members with answers to these three cosmic questions. After all, these are the questions that seem to occur to all individuals living in any organized society. It is one of the major functions, or responsibilities, of any organized religion to provide plausible answers to these key questions. One of the major attractions of any organized religion is that it does provide meaningful answers to each of these cosmic questions.

In the process of providing answers to these cosmic questions, the major religions have all called upon their followers to have faith—that is, to believe in what the religion professes. Since the cosmic questions are difficult to answer on the basis of logical or scientific evidence, then faith must be introduced into the equation. Therefore the members of organized religions must also be believers; they must have faith. Hence they are often referred to as the faithful. It is this call to faith that gives organized religion its attraction and its power. This is what attracts people to the religion. For them, the religious experience provides the answers for which they are looking. Religion gives them the answers that they desperately need. This is what is all important in their lives.

CHARACTERISTICS OF ORGANIZED RELIGIONS

Now that we have given consideration to what religion is, by way of a formal definition and key examples, we should review the six major characteristics of all organized religions.

Religion Is a Group Experience

First, by taking the sociological perspective, we can say that religions are by their nature a social experience. Therefore the religious experience is a group experience. As we have said, people who share a common spiritual belief join together in worship and become members of a strong cohesive group. As members of a spiritual group they form strong social bonds. They extend a helping hand to others. They embrace their brothers and sisters. They share common experiences, common beliefs, and common goals. They are now part of a brotherhood. Humans are by their very nature social animals, and the religious experience and the religious bond are of utmost importance to their well-being. The religious community becomes the individual's support group, and this is one of the major attractions of organized religion today.

Religions Provide a Spiritual Connection

As we have mentioned, another important characteristic of all organized religions is providing their members with access to the sacred. Organized religions provide their members with spiritual meaning and a sense of spiritual connection. Religion provides a channel or direct connection to the creator or the supreme being. As Emile Durkheim pointed out years ago, religion divides the world into the sacred and the profane (1961). That which is sacred belongs to God, and those things that are of the material world are profane or secular. In addition to providing access to the sacred, religion also provides the answers to the three important cosmic questions.

Religions Provide a Belief System

A third important characteristic of all religions is that they are based on a body of beliefs. Every religion promulgates its beliefs. Historically, the major religions had established oral traditions to maintain their systems of beliefs and spiritual practices. Today all major religions have a "holy book" that clearly documents their beliefs and traditions. In many religions, the holy book is in fact considered the word of God. Sometimes the holy book is considered to be the interpretation of the word of God, and this can create problems for the faithful.

As a result of the teachings found in the various holy books, every religion has its list of do's and don't. All religions have a set of laws and specific rules for proper behavior. Attached to these rules of behavior are rewards and punishments. For example, most religions believe in a judgment day, in a life after death, and in the existence of a heaven and hell. These are powerful mechanisms of social control. These common religious beliefs serve to promote good behavior among the faithful.

Religions Provide Social Structure

A fourth characteristic of all organized religions is that they are highly structured. The major religions are like large government bureaucracies, with a strong leadership, a social hierarchy, and distinct positions and roles within the organization. What distinguishes the major religions from other bureaucracies is that they get their power and authority directly from God. In effect, what the church leadership says is in fact the "word of God." This is the unique characteristic that gives the major religions their power over their congregations. Sometimes this religious power and authority are transferred into the political arena. When a religion and a religious leader take complete political control of a society, we say that they have established a theocracy, where religion and the state are one and the same.

© 2013, Hung Chung Chih. Used under license from Shutterstock, Inc.

Religions Provide Important Rituals

A fifth characteristic of major religions is that they set forth a specific set of practices or rituals. Every major religion has its own rituals and religious observances. Every religion does things in a certain way and at a certain time. All religions have their own religious calendars. For example, a religious service must be conducted in a specific way or specific holy days must be observed in a certain way. The maintenance of rituals also means that ceremonies must be performed on a certain day and in a specific way. This may also mean that certain "sacred words" or phrases must be spoken at a certain time during a religious service or, for example, over the body of the deceased. The rituals and worship practices observed by the major religions give their religious ceremonies a sense of awe or grounded spiritualism. These rituals represent their way of communicating with God and provide the faithful a way to create the presence of God in their services. Their ability to communicate with God is their ultimate source of power and authority. This is what the faithful expect. This is why they dutifully attend religious services and why they are members of the religious community.

Religions Support Moral Entrepreneurs

A sixth characteristic of organized religions is that they are the moral leaders of the community. Religious organizations set the moral standards for proper social behavior. As sociologist Robert Merton pointed out years ago, religious leaders are the moral entrepreneurs of our society. This means that one of the roles of organized religions is to inform their flock of the good and evil in society. It is the role of organized religions to inform their flock of the good and evil in society—to tell their members what is right and what is wrong. Some religions believe that it is the moral obligation of their members to not only live good, moral, and righteous lives, but also to encourage others to do the same. In some cases, this can result in "moral activism" on the part of the membership. Their moral activism can turn into political activism, which is a major route by means of which they in fact become, as Merton predicted, moral entrepreneurs.

This drive to preserve the moral fabric of society in part explains why the Quakers started the abolitionist (anti-slavery) movement and why religious leaders from a variety of denominations marched in support of the civil rights movement. Their moral (religious) convictions forced the faithful to take direct political action to promote social change. We even see this type of religious political activism today, particularly among the religious right, in the great abortion debate that has consumed many religious activists.

All of these are key characteristics of organized religions and can be applied to all of the major religions in the world. This is one way to define an organized religion and evaluate the role of organized religion in society.

TYPES OF RELIGIOUS ORGANIZATIONS

One of the roles that sociologists accept as unbiased investigators is to stand back and critically analyze the social structure of any organization under study. Over an extended period of time sociologists have studied various religious organizations and have developed a classification system that allows for the careful analysis of each type of organization. These "types" are what Max Weber referred to as ideal types.

The use of ideal types in sociology today is common, and these types have proven to be very useful in contributing to our understanding of the complex nature of all social organizations. The ideal type is typically a composite of the key characteristics that are often associated with a specific social phenomena or social category. In the analysis of religious organizations, we typically find four types of religious organizations or structures. In general, most organized religions can be classified, from most complex to least complex, into one of the following four ideal types:

Churches
Denominations
Sects
Cults

Each of these organizational types has its own unique characteristics. In general, all religious organizations can be classified or ranked in order of: (1) their overall longevity or history, (2) their level of formality, and (3) the level of complexity in their organizational structure.

The Universal Church

The first of our ideal types is the Church, sometimes referred to as the Universal Church or *Ecclesia* (a Latin expression, from the Greek, for Church or "meeting of the called-out ones"). In the analysis of religious organizations, the Church is the most highly developed organizational form. The Church has a long and enduring history. This usually means that it has been in existence for several hundred years. The Church has a long track record and has had a long time to build up an extensive collection of church doctrines and documents, as well as its own cultural milieu.

As a result of its very long history, the Church in some cases has become a state institution, as it often holds a religious monopoly over the citizens of a particular state. Sometimes Church membership is associated with a specific group of people—with their own history, language, culture, and traditions. The Church also claims universality, as its influence and authority affect every aspect of daily life among its members. In effect, the Universal Church is often considered the official state religion. The boundaries between church and state are sometimes blurred. Therefore the decisions of Church leaders are often congruent with and directly affect state policies and political decisions. In these cases, religious decisions and practices are supported by state laws.

When a Church has this type of collegial relationship with the state, it is sometimes referred to as an Ecclesia. Examples of Ecclesias include the role of the Catholic Church during the period of the Holy Roman Empire and the role of the Anglican Church in England when it was declared the official state religion. The same can be said of the role of Islam in Saudi Arabia today, where it is truly a state religion. It is well known that Islam is certainly the national religion in many of the Middle Eastern countries today.

In its organizational structure, the Church is very formal and highly structured. The Church is also very hierarchical, with a complex ranking system with specific positions of power and authority. Each person in this hierarchy must play his or her role and follow the orders of superiors.

There is a complex division of labor in the Church's organizational structure. Power and authority always flow from the top down, and orders and policies are followed without question, for the leadership of the Church claims authority directly from God.

The clergy of the Church are highly respected by the church membership. The clergy demand respect. They maintain their social distance from the flock. The clergy in the Church are full-time professional clergy with many years of religious indoctrination, a formal theological education, and advanced clerical training. They are the true insiders and have access to church secrets. The clergy are charged with maintaining church history, culture, and traditions. They are committed for life and must devote all of their time and energy to the Church.

Church services and rituals tend to be very formal. They are lead by a priest or minister, while the congregation looks on. There is very little lay participation in these religious services. Much of what takes place in these religious services is a mystery to the church membership.

The Stability of Denominations

Just below the Church in terms of complexity of organizational structure is the denomination. Denominations are Churches, but they are not as formal or as complex in social organization and structure. Some would say that denominations are not as fully developed as a Church. Perhaps this is correct, as denominations have not had enough time to develop into a Church.

As a group, denominations are not as formal as Churches. They are also not as strict and as controlling as Churches tend to be. Denominations are more open to the new ideas of their parishioners. Usually they are more tolerant and more liberal in their overall philosophy and theology. One could say that denominations are not as rigid as Churches. Denominations are still building a track record. They are working on their history and traditions. Some would say that denominations are a work in progress.

In terms of their membership, denominations are smaller than Churches. In a sense this gives them a certain advantage over Churches, as the members of denominations experience a greater sense of community and a greater sense of personal involvement in their worship services and religious activities. Their rituals and religious services are also less formal. The religious services also allow for higher levels of participation and involvement by church members.

In this regard, the clergy in the denomination are also less formal and more often in direct contact with the people. The clergy are not as aloof or as distant as the clergy from the larger, more formal Church. Often denominational clergy are not full-time clergy. They have some formal religious education and theological training, but they have not had years and years of education or indoctrination, as is often the case with Church clergy. These are men and women "of the cloth." They come from the people and are with the people in their worship services and in their everyday lives. Some denominational ministers are actually part-time lay ministers who devote their lives to spreading the word among the common people.

Denominations offer religious services two or three times a week and expect regular attendance from their members. They also encourage their members to participate in church groups and activities. They expect that their members will be active and involved in all church activities. To be a member of the denomination means that you are always an active member of the congregation.

Denominations typically rely on the high fertility rates of their members to expand their ranks. For this reason denominations usually encourage their parishioners to have large families. By the same token, denominational members are encouraged to recruit new members from within their extended families, and from their neighborhoods and communities. Sometimes they are required to go out in small groups, on a regular basis, and bring in new members. Some denominations formalize their efforts by actually creating missions for their younger members. To take on a mission means that you must give up two or three years of your life to spread the word of God.

On a personal and social level, denominational members tend to have very close ties. Often denominational members see themselves as one large family and are very willing to offer a helping hand in time of need. The denomination involves its members in family and church activities.

The closeness and the strong social bonds that are created in the denomination's religious environment are one of its main attractions. In effect, denominations offer their members an instant family and a supportive group of friends. Therefore, denominations tend to be close-knit groups that encourage the cohesiveness and support of their members.

The Transformation of Sects

A group that is very different from either the Church or the denomination is the sect. A sect is a religious group that is formed out of protest, as its members break away from an existing denomination. Therefore, sects typically start as a protest movement or as a rebellion from a much larger established group.

In most cases sects are founded on the basis of a protest over some important theological point or a specific religious practice. These are splinter groups that see themselves as the "true believers" of the faith who break away in order to maintain the old, traditional ways of doing things. As rebels or reformers, they want to do things their way and they want to rid themselves of the old, traditional power structures of the church. This is why sects tend to be very informal. They want to dismantle the power structure, so they do rely on one-to-one relationships and remove all of the trappings of power and authority in the social hierarchy.

By their nature, sects are small, informal groups that shun class or status differences in their own personal relationships and in their worship services. Sect ministers are often self-appointed laypersons who have received "the calling" and lead their people in worship services and prayers. Their teachings place great emphasis on the original teachings of the church, and they rely on the original doctrines of the church. They often shun the material possessions of this world and place a great deal of importance on the ideas of salvation, deliverance, and the rewards of an afterlife or fears of the fires of hell.

Sect members are very conservative and are expected to spread the word among nonbelievers. While they are usually small congregations, they obtain most of their new members from religious conversions. They are adamant in their beliefs, and many aspects of their lives are very much a part of their religious beliefs and practices. Often sect members are from the lower and working classes in society and some have, over the years, established their own independent and self-sufficient religious communities. Sects that are established on the religious community model are strong in their religious indoctrination and have closed themselves off to the rest of society.

A couple of good examples of sects that you have probably heard of are the Amish and the Hutterites. They both have long histories as conservative religious communities that have shunned relationships with the greater society. Other well-known sects today, which are more community based, are the Jehovah's Witnesses, the Pentecostals, and the Christian Scientists.

Some sects fall in between sects and denominations in their structure and organization, and we refer to these as institutionalized sects. They are not as cloistered as the traditional sects and have received a higher level of recognition and acceptance by other religious groups and society in general. Two good examples of some well-known institutionalized sects today are the Mennonites and the Quakers.

The Growth and Acceptance of Cults

In general, we can say that religious cults are more out of the mainstream than sects, and they are less acceptable to the members of the general society. Cults are usually seen as anti-establishment groups that have turned away from the norms and expectations of organized societies. They not only reject the dominant society but they reject the formal organized religions around them. These are rebellious groups who want to create something new, something different.

Cults are usually started as a new religious movement and are often headed by a strong charismatic leader. The cult leader believes that he or she is in direct communication with God. Cult leaders often present themselves as the messengers of God, or as modern-day prophets. People are primarily attracted to cults because of the power and charisma of the leader and because they believe that the type of change that the leader promotes is needed.

People who are attracted to cults are often found on the fringes of society and are searching for something new. Cult followers are looking for a new way of life. They seek meaning in their own lives. Cults are usually small, isolated groups that avoid and fear outsiders. Admission into the cult is closely controlled and new members are forced to undergo stringent initiation rights. The social and religious practices of cults can range from the unorthodox to the strange. Cult rituals are sometimes viewed as unusual or bizarre. For this reason, a great deal of secrecy is usually associated with all cult activities.

One of the best known cults of recent times is the Branch Davidians, headed by David Koresh. Branch Davidians received national attention when the FBI raided their religious compound in Waco, Texas, in 1993. The Branch Davidians believed that David Koresh was their Messiah. He taught them that their final days would end in violence and that they would then be allowed to enter the Kingdom of Heaven. Koresh also convinced his members that he had to have sex with all of the women in his cult in order to populate his new religious community.

A more recent cult was known as Heaven's Gate. This cult was from southern California, and its members committed group suicide. They believed that after their deaths they would be taken up to spaceship that would take them to their eternal reward. The Reverend Jim Jones and the mass suicides that he orchestrated in Guyana are another example of a cult experience that ended in tragedy for hundreds of innocent victims.

RELIGIOUS TRANSFORMATION AND CHANGE

Now that we can give consideration to the characteristics of each of these types of religious organizations, it is clear that a process of change or transformation can occur very gradually as a religious group moves, over a long period of time, from being a cult, to being a sect, and then eventually becoming a new denomination. A number of the more acceptable sects today started as rebellious religious movements or fringe groups in society. In effect, they started out as cults and are now accepted into the greater religious and social community as sects.

Thus, the movement from one type of religious group to another is really a process of social change. As new religious groups are accepted by society, they tend to become more conservative and more mainstream. As their level of acceptance increases, their overall size and membership also increase.

THE GROWTH AND DIVERSITY OF WORLD RELIGIONS

It is clear that organized religions play a significant role in the lives of human beings, no matter where they are found around the world. Religion is omnipresent in the lives of many men, women, and children. Religion is also diverse, and a wide range of religions often is found in many societies—except, of course, in those societies where there is an established state religion. For these reasons, we now turn to a review of the impact of thousands of religious groups and denominations around the world.

Of the 6.6 billion people on the earth today, it is estimated that one out of three are Christians (Central Intelligence Agency, 2007). Christianity is therefore the single largest religious group among all men and women across the globe. But as we will make clear, there is also great diversity among the various Christian groups today. The second largest religious group worldwide is the Muslims; one out of five persons alive today is Muslim. And as with the Christian groups, there are also key differences in the beliefs and practices of people within the major Muslim groups. The third largest religious group worldwide is the Hindus; one out of seven people are members of this faith. See Figure 9.1.

In reviewing the data on the distribution of membership among world religions, it is also interesting to note that what would actually be the fourth largest religious group worldwide is

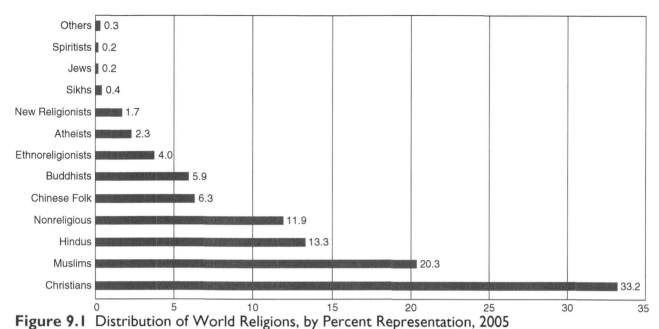

Figure 9.1 Distribution of World Religions, by Percent Representation, 2005

Source: Calculated from David B. Barrett, Todd M. Johnson, and Peter F. Crossing, "The 2005 Megacensus of Religions: Year in Review 2005," in Encyclopedia Britannica, Britannica Book of the Year 2006 (Chicago, IL: Encyclopedia Britannica, 2007), Table 1.

people who consider themselves to be nonreligious. This simply means that there are still significant numbers of people worldwide who do not belong to any organized religious group. In addition, there is another large group of individuals who do not believe in the existence of a God. The Atheists account for over 151 million people, which is 2.3 percent of the total world population. Taken together, this means that the nonreligious and the Atheists make up 15.2 percent of the world's population. To the members of organized religions who take the optimistic view, this only means that there is still a lot of work to be done.

The actual number of individuals who are members of organized religions around the world is very significant. As we have noted, Christians are the single largest group of believers in the world. Of the more than 2 billion Christians around the world today, almost half of them—more than 1 billion—are Roman Catholics. The second largest group Protestants, followed by Orthodox Christians and Anglicans. One of the fastest growing groups among Christians today are the Evangelicals.

The second largest single group of believers worldwide is the Muslims, with a membership of 1.3 billion. As is true of the Christians today, there are also certain key differences among the Muslim religious groups, which we shall discuss shortly. The Hindus are the third largest religious group, with over 860 million members, most of whom are concentrated in India. Buddhists are also a significant group, with a worldwide population of over 378 million.

THE VARIETY OF RELIGIOUS GROUPS

Since our nation was founded on the principle of religious choice and freedom of worship for all, we are a society of great religious diversity. Since the great majority of our founding citizens were WASPS (White Anglo-Saxon Protestants), it is not surprising that the majority of residents of the United States today are Christians, and most of these Christians are also Protestants.

Although the American Creed states that all religions are welcomed, this was not always the case. In the beginning of European settlement in America, America was very much a Christian nation and specifically a Protestant society. If you were not a Protestant you were likely to experience prejudice and discrimination. This is the primary reason that the Irish-Catholic immigrants,

	Religious Group	U.S. Population (Mid-2005)	Percent of U.S. Population	World Population	Percent of World Population
1	Christians (Total)	250,042,000	83.3	2,133,806,000	33.1
2	Affiliated Christians	200,614,000	66.9	2,020,184,000	31.3
3	Independents	78,786,000	26.3	425,170,000	6.6
4	Roman Catholics	65,900,000	22.0	1,118,991,000	17.3
5	Protestants	61,295,000	20.4	375,815,000	5.8
6	Marginal Christians	11,018,000	3.7	34,151,000	0.5
7	Orthodox	5,992,000	2.0	219,501,000	3.4
8	Anglicans	2,206,000	0.7	79,718,000	1.2
9	Evangelicals	44,800,000	14.9		
10	evangelicals	103,500,000	34.5		
11	Unaffiliated Christians	46,428,000	16.5		
12	Jews	5,764,000	1.9	15,073,000	0.2
13	Muslims	4,745,200	1.6	1,308,941,000	20.3
14	Black Muslims	1,850,000	0.6		
15	Buddhists	2,721,000	0.9	378,808,000	5.9
16	New religionists	1,509,000	0.5	108,131,200	1.7
17	Ethnoreligionists	1,158,000	0.4	256,332,000	4.0
18	Hindus	1,144,000	0.4	860,133,000	13.3
19	Baha'is	829,000	0.3	7,650,000	0.1
20	Sikhs	270,000	0.1	25,377,700	0.4
21	Spiritists	149,000	0.0	13,030,500	0.2
22	Chinese Universists	86,700	0.0	409,921,900	6.3
23	Shintoists	60,600	0.0	2,789,200	0.0
24	Zoroastrians	56,800	0.0	2,648,000	0.0
25	Taoists	12,000	0.0	2,734,000	0.0
26	Jains	7,700	0.0	4,589,800	0.1
27	Other Religionists	600,000	0.2	1,200,000	0.0
28	Nonreligious	29,390,000	9.8	769,379,000	11.9
29	Atheists	1,493,000	0.5	151,612,000	2.3
30	Total	301,888,000	100.00	6,453,628,000	100.00

Table 9.1 The Population of World Religions

Source: Derived from David B. Barrett, Todd M. Johnson, and Peter F. Crossing, "The 2005 Annual Megacensus of Religions: Year in Review 2005," in *Britannica Book of the Year*, 2006 (Chicago: Encyclopedia Britannica, Inc, 2007), Table 2, "Religious Adherents in the United States, 1900–2005," and Table 1, "Worldwide Adherents of All Religions, Mid-2005." As of June 28, 2007, available online at URL: http://search.eb.com/eb/article-9432655

who arrived in very large numbers during the nineteenth century, experienced such brutal forms of discrimination. Many believe that the real prejudice against Irish Catholics did not subside until President Kennedy, an Irish Catholic, took the oath of office.

Country	Number of Christians	Percent
USA	252,394,312	85.0
Brazil	166,847,207	93.0
China	110,956,366	5.7
Mexico	102,011,835	99.0
Russia	84,494,596	60.0
Philippines	73,987,348	93.0
India	68,189,739	2.3
Germany	61,833,042	83.0
Nigeria	61,437,608	40.0
Democratic Republic of Congo	53,370,662	70.0

Table 9.2 The Largest National Christian Populations

Source: Russell Ash, The Top Ten of Everything 2007 (New York: Sterling Publishing Company, 2006), p. 60; Central Intelligence Agency, CIA World Factbook 2007, as of July 1, 2007, available on the World Wide Web at URL: https://www.cia.gov/library/publications/the-world-factbook/index.html

CHRISTIANITY

The single largest religious group in the world today, and in the United States, is Christianity. Christianity is one of the oldest religions in the world and can trace its origins to the Middle East and the teachings of Jesus Christ. With the founding of the Catholic Church, the teachings of Christ spread far and wide. The fall of the Roman Empire enhanced the power of the Catholic Church and the influence of the Pope on the social and political life of Western Europe.

Christianity is a monotheistic religion and is based on the belief in the Holy Trinity, consisting of the Holy Spirit, God the Creator, and Jesus Christ. The congregants believe in a judgment day upon death, in life after death, and in the existence of heaven and hell.

Today Christianity is the dominant religion in many parts of Latin America and Europe. Because of its missionary efforts, Christianity is one of the fastest growing religions in the developing nations in Africa and Asia. See Table 9.2.

PROTESTANTS

Protestants are the largest multidenominational religious group in the United States today. However, at the same time, Protestants are, as we shall see, a very diverse group. Besides their common origins, there are also a set of common religious beliefs all Protestants hold in common. They are called, and they refer to themselves as, Protestants because they began as a separatist religious movement, or Reformation, that protested some of the basic teachings and beliefs of the Roman Catholic Church. The most famous leaders of the Protestant Reformation were John Huss (1369–1415), Martin Luther (1483–1546), Ulrich Zwingli (1484–1531), John Calvin (1509–1564), and John Knox (1513–1572). Of these most famous leaders of this religious movement, Martin Luther is the best know today.

As a group, Protestants believe that they can communicate directly with God, by means of personal devotion and prayers. They believe that they do not need any intermediaries, such as a priest or the Pope. Rather, Protestant ministers are viewed as guides and leaders in prayers and worship services. They also believe that the Bible is the primary source of their religious beliefs and theology. As Protestants, they are required to read and know the Bible and shape their lives to conform to the teachings of the Bible.

Religious Body	Membership
Catholic Church	66,260,000
Southern Baptist Convention	16,400,000
United Methodist Church	8,251,042
Church of Jesus Christ of Latter-Day Saints	5,503,000
Church of God in Christ	5,450,000
Evangelical Lutheran Church in America	5,038,000
National Baptist Convention, USA, Inc.	5,000,000
National Baptist Convention of America, Inc.	4,985,000
Presbyterian Church (USA)	3,241,000
Assemblies of God	2,730,000

Table 9.3 The Largest Christian Churches in the United States

Source: Calculated from National Council of Churches, 2005 Yearbook of American and Christian Churches (Nashville, TN: Abingdon Press, 2005).

Within the Protestant fold there are two main groups, the old mainline Protestants and the (newer) conservative or fundamentalist Protestants. The mainline Protestants include some thirty dif-ferent denominations. The best known of these Protestant denominations are the Baptist, Methodist, Lutherans, and the Presbyterians.

The fundamentalists, or the conservative Protestants, tend to be more dogmatic in their religious beliefs and teachings and they require a literal interpretation of the Bible (as they view the Bible as the "literal word of God") and hold that one can only be "saved" if Jesus Christ is accepted as his or her personal savior. Today these religious fundamentalists are often referred to as *Evangelicals*. As a group, the Evangelicals are one of the fastest growing religious groups in the nation. While many of the mainline Protestant churches are stagnant or losing members, the Evangelicals are experiencing a dramatic increase in the size of their congregations. See Table 9.3.

© 2013, Rob Byron. Used under license from Shutterstock, Inc.

ROMAN CATHOLICS

The single largest religious group in the United States today is Catholicism. As a group, Catholics are a very conservative and traditional religious group. Catholics trace their origins to St. Peter, the first Pope. America was founded as a Protestant nation, so Catholicism was initially viewed as an immigrant and minority religion. With the influx of large numbers of Irish and Italian immigrants during the nineteenth century, Catholics soon became a major force on the religious landscape of America.

The Catholic Church today is still a conservative force in American politics and has had a significant influence on the social and economic policies of this nation. And as in the past, the Catholic Church is still dependent on the influx of new immigrants to fill its ranks, and the two primary sources of new parishioners come from Latin America and Asian nations. (See Box 9.1).

Levels of Religious Involvement among Catholic Youth

It is always interesting to ask people which religious group they belong to or which church they attend. They will usually give you the name of the church or the group. This is how we often identify ourselves and it is also how we label and categorize other people. As with race or ethnicity, once someone knows what your religion is, then they know how to treat you. They often use labels to identify themselves or others and then they rely on all of the old stereotypes to deal with people. Unfortunately, this is just a fact of life in America.

The question of religious identity is an important one today, as most people do identify with one of the major religions. It is one thing to say that you belong to a certain religion, but you also must clarify how strong your identification and commitment are to that particular religious group. This is important because so many Americans today say that they are Christian, Catholic, or Jewish, but more often they are Christian, Catholic, or Jewish in name only. The better question, then, is to ask them how committed they are to their religious group and whether they actually practice their religion. Is their religion really a part of their daily lives? This is exactly what we did in a recent national study of Catholic youth.

In our study of Catholic youth we wanted to find out the true level of commitment and involvement of young adult Catholics in the church, not just the number of "name only" Catholics. According to national opinion polls, a significant number of Americans who identify with a particular religion are only members in name only. The rate of attendance at religious services has fallen dramatically for most religious groups in recent years.

After conducting 848 in-depth personal interviews with an equal number of Anglo and Latino young adult Catholics (who were all confirmed as youth and were now between the ages of twenty and thirty-nine) we were able to analyze their level of church attendance and church involvement. At the conclusion of our study we developed a rather interesting typology of church attendance and participation.

We came up with four (ideal) types of Catholics in our study. The first type we referred to as the "Parish Involved Catholics" (Type I). These individuals attended church services on a weekly basis and were also involved in at least one of the church organizations. Most were involved in religious education classes, in youth groups, or served on parish committees. It was clear that these Parish Involved Catholics had a high level of commitment to the church and were very active in the formal activities of the church. To quote the findings from our study, "In sum, these people are joiners who like their parishes, and they are personally religious persons with a strong, nourishing faith" (Hoge et al., 2000). But unfortunately the Parish Involved Catholics only represented a small proportion of all the young adult Catholics in our study, for only one out of ten of our interviewees could be classified as a Parish Involved Catholic.

The largest category of Catholics in our study was the group that we referred to as the "Regular Attending Catholics" (Type II). These parishioners said that they only attended church services two or three times per month. They also said that, for the most part, they were not involved in any Catholic groups or organizations. Two out of five (41 percent) of the Anglo and Latino young adult Catholics in our study were classified as Regular Attending Catholics.

The next group of Catholics in our study were the "Occasional Attenders" (Type III). These individuals said that they were not active in church groups or activities and that they only attended church services about once a month, or about once every other month. So it is clear that this group of young adult Catholics did not have a very strong level of attachment or involvement in the church. These individuals tended to have more of a cultural than a spiritual attachment to the Catholic church. These are Catholics who only attended mass or other church services on special occasions (like baptismals and funerals) and on the major holy days of the year. One out of four (23 percent) of the young adult Catholics in our study fell into the Occasional Attenders category.

The last of the groups in our typology of young adult Catholics were the "Non-Attending Catholics" (Type IV). For the most part these individuals rarely attended mass or any other church services. In effect they were Catholics in name only. They no longer followed the teachings of the church and had a very limited connection with the church. About one out six (16 percent) of our interviewees fell into the non-active category.

The message behind these ideal types is that although people identify themselves as a member of a particular religious group, this does not mean that they are committed to the group or that they are active members. Other sociological studies conducted among all of the major religious groups in the United States also confirm the findings of our national study of young adult Catholics—that is, the level of church attendance and religious participation among most of the major religions in the United States is low and has fallen off dramatically in recent years. Some of the more recent studies, however, do indicate that in some denominations the level of attendance and active participation is now on the increase. Researchers attribute this renewed interest in church attendance and participation to the events of September 11, 2001.

Source: Dean Hoge, W. Dinges, M. Johnson, and J. L. Gonzales Jr., *Young Adult Catholics: Religion in the Culture of Choice* (Notre Dame, IN: University of Notre Dame Press, 2001).

Nation	Percent of Population	Number of Catholics
Brazil	86.50	134,818,000
Mexico	95.30	86,305,000
United States	26.00	61,000,000
Philippines	83.60	58,735,000
Italy	97.20	55,599,000
France	82.10	47,773,000
Spain	94.20	36,956,000
Poland	95.40	36,835,000
Colombia	91.90	32,260,000
Argentina	90.70	31,546,000
Germany	34.80	28,403,000

Table 9.4 The Nations with the Most Roman Catholics

Source: Felician A. Foy, *Our Sunday Visitor's Catholic Almanac* (Huntington, IN: Our Sunday Visitor, 1997), pp. 333–367.

As an established religion, the Catholic Church is very influential around the world, and it is the single largest religion on the planet, with a membership of over 1 billion. (See Table 9.1). And as a result of the natural increase in its population and its well-organized missionary work, it is growing and well represented in a number of major nations around the world. The work of the Church is particularly important in many of the developing nations in Latin America, Asia, and Africa. (See Table 9.4).

Rank	Nation	Number
1	USA	5,764,208
2	Israel	4,772,138
3	France	607,111
4	Argentina	520,130
5	Canada	383,837
6	Palestine	451,001
7	Brazil	312,173
8	United Kingdom	244,719
9	Russia	222,689
10	Germany	222,689

Table 9.5 The Largest National Jewish Populations

Source: Russell Ash, *The Top Ten of Everything 2007* (New York: Sterling Publishing Company, 2006), p. 60.

The Basis for Jewish Religious Beliefs

It is interesting to observe that when most people think of Jewish Americans, they usually think of them in terms of their religion. This is true in that religion is the sociocultural cement that has bound the Hebrew nation throughout history. But only half of Jewish Americans today identify with a particular synagogue, and of these only about 15 percent attend religious services regularly (Mesinger and Lamme, 1985: 146).

One study of church/synagogue attendance in the United States reveals that only 20 percent of Jews, compared with 49 percent of Catholics and 41 percent of Protestants, attend church services weekly (Hoffman, 1989: 593). And a national survey of religious identification found that only two-thirds of the 6.8 million American Jews claimed to practice their religion (Johnson, 1992: 392). Therefore, the facts indicate that the level of religiosity (i.e., religious participation) is rather low among Jews. This finding contradicts the popular image of Jews as being highly religious (Glazer, 1990: 36–37).

In the United States today there are three distinct branches of Judaism, (1) Orthodox, (2) Conservative, and (3) Reformed. The development of each of these branches in United States can be related to distinct periods in Jewish immigration. The reason for this historic demarcation is that some groups held very traditional beliefs, such as the Sephardic Jews, who were Orthodox. The Eastern Jews were considered conservative in their beliefs, while the Ashkenazic Jews were seen as Reform Jews.

It is estimated that between 10 to 20 percent of Jewish Americans follow Orthodox beliefs. For Orthodox Jews, traditions, rituals, religious observances, and the teachings of the Torah (the first five books of the Bible) and the Talmud (rabbinic doctrines) form the basis for their lives in the secular world. Fundamentalism and sacred traditions constitute the religious orientation of Orthodox Jews (Danziger, 1989; Heilman and Cohen, 1989).

Some groups within the Orthodox community, such as the Hasidic Jews, Chassids, and the Satmarim, are religious fundamentalists who live in close-knit sectarian communities (primarily in New York City). They have limited contact with the outside world, dress in traditional garb, observe all the religious laws and rituals, send their children to religious schools, speak Yiddish, and live by the Holy scriptures (Kamen, 1985; Poll, 1969b).

The reform movement originated in Germany and was transported to America by the Ashkenazic Jews. Today about one-third of the synagogues in the United States follow the reform movement. The objective of the reform branch was to adapt Jewish religious beliefs to the changing American environment. Therefore strict adherence to Jewish rituals was not viewed as important; the substitution of English for Yiddish in religious services was allowed; and the strict observation of Jewish dietary restrictions were not considered essential. The secularization of Jewish religious beliefs was achieved by the turn of the century. Today some are of the opinion that the reform movement has made many services in synagogues as open and liberal as some Protestant churches (Feingold, 1982: 56–68).

Conservative Judaism was a reaction to the reform movement, as it represents the middle-ground position within Judaism. The conservative movement is associated with the massive influx of Eastern Jews during the late nineteenth century and early twentieth century. Members of the conservative movement found Orthodox beliefs far too restrictive for their secular goals in American society. In addition, they considered many of the changes promoted by the reform movement as far too radical for their beliefs, although most Conservative Jews are politically liberal. Today, from 40 to 50 percent of all Jewish Americans identify with the conservative movement.

In Jewish culture, the synagogue is the focus and the center of Jewish activity. Historically the synagogue was, (1) a Beth T'filoh (a house of worship), (2) a place were rabbinical students and laypersons gathered for religious study, and (3) a community center. The first synagogue in the United States was built two years after the arrival of the Sephardic Jews in New Amsterdam. By 1880, there were 270 synagogues in America. Ten years later there were 533, and by 1906 there were almost 1,800 (Rosenberg, 1985: 54). Today there are 3,416 synagogues in the United States (Hoffman, 1989: 591).

Jewish religious beliefs are derived from the Torah and the Talmud. For Orthodox Jews these sacred books contain the substance of life, as they guide individual behavior and require certain ritual observances. Perhaps the best known ritual observance is the Kashrut, which is the law that either permits or prohibits the consumption of certain foods. Kosher laws prescribe how the food is to be prepared and eaten (Poll, 1969a).

Jewish holidays play a very important part in the lives of all Jews, whether they are religious or not. Traditionally, Jewish holidays are considered days of rest, when work and economic exchange is prohibited. The observance of the Sabbath is the most common ritual restriction on Jewish activities. Most Jewish holidays mark important religious or historical events.

The Mitzvahs restrict the behavior and dress of traditional Jews. For example, among the Hasidic Jews, the yarmulke (the skullcap) is worn at all times and they usually dress in black clothes. On the Sabbath, they are in the synagogue for the entire day. Women are segregated from the men, they marry young, and they have large families. A college education is discouraged among Hasidic Jews, as the men devote their lives to the study of the Torah (Isaacs, 1977).

Today it is not unusual to find Jewish Americans who are not religious and who do not observe Jewish traditions. One study found that most fourth-generation Jews are Reform Jews (45 percent) or are nonreligious (31 percent), that is, in ritualistic terms (Cohen, 1988: 43–57). This observation is supported by several studies that demonstrate that the younger generations of Jewish Americans tend to be less religious, have more gentile friends, are less involved in the Jewish community, live in gentile neighborhoods, and have higher rates of exogamy. Generally, Jewish Americans only attend religious services on key holidays and only practice those religious rituals that preserve family ties, such as barmitzvah (Schoenfeld, 1988). In the end, the younger Jewish generations are more interested in symbolic ethnicity rather than true religious devotion (Bershtel and Graubard, 1992: 93–161).

Source: Juan L. Gonzales Jr., *Racial and Ethnic Groups in America,* Fifth Edition (Dubuque, IA: Kendall/Hunt, 2004).

JUDAISM

Judaism is considered by many to be the oldest organized religion in the world. Judaism can trace its origins to the prophet Abraham, who lived more than 4,000 years ago. As a people, the

Jews evolved in Mesopotamia and were enslaved by the ancient Egyptians, where one of their most influential prophets, Moses, led them to freedom in the Holy Land. Historically, the Jews have considered themselves the "Chosen People," as revealed in the Ten Commandments. Their holy book, the Torah, is the source of their religious and spiritual beliefs.

The influence of the Jews is significant in world history and in contemporary political affairs. In spite of their rather small size, much of their political power and influence can be attributed to the creation of their own nation-state of Israel following World War II.

Today it is estimated that there are about 15 million Jews worldwide, almost 5 million of whom are living in the United States. In fact, there are more Jews living in the United States today than in the state of Israel. Because of the Holocaust, and the resulting Jewish diaspora, Jews can be found living in most of the industrial nations of the world today. (See Table 9.5).

The religion and culture of the Jewish people are closely intertwined. As a result, most Jews see themselves both as a religious group and as a cultural or ethnic group. Many aspects of Judaism are reflections of the Jewish cultural experience; and, in a similar fashion, the Jewish culture is often represented in their religious practices and beliefs.

As with the various Christian groups, Jews can also be viewed as either being conservative or liberal in their religious beliefs and practices. In fact, Jews can be classified into at least three major branches, from the (1) Orthodox, and the (2) Conservatives, to the most liberal (3) Reform Jews. There is also a large group of Jews today who refer to themselves as Secular Jews, and also another, newer group of Jews who prefer to call themselves Reconstructionists. As a group, Secular Jews are working to adapt the teachings and practices of Judaism to the demands of modern urban society. For a review of the major branches of Judaism and a discussion of the religious beliefs and practices of Jewish Americans today, see Box 9.2.

ISLAM

It is interesting to note that the three major religions of Christianity, Judaism, and Islam share a rather common history and also follow the teachings of the major prophets of the Old Testament. The followers of Islam are called Muslims and their prophet is Muhammad, who was born in Mecca in the year 570. The Muslim holy book is the Qur'an, and every Muslim is required to read the Qur'an in Arabic, although the faithful are allowed to offer their personal prayers to Allah in their native languages.

All Muslims are required to follow the five basic teachings of the faith, which sometimes are referred to as the Five Pillars of Islam. First, they must believe in only one God and they must accept Muhammad as the true messenger of God. Second, they must pray to Allah five times a day. Third, they must fast during the holy month of Ramadan. Fourth, they must give alms to the poor. And fifth, they must make the pilgrimage to Mecca at least once in their lifetime. This pilgrimage to Mecca is called the Hajj.

With a membership of over 1.3 billion, Islam is the second largest religion in the world. And while many nations in the Middle East are Muslim nations, some of the largest concentrations of Muslims are found outside of the Middle East. It is also true that though most Arabs are Muslims (about 90 percent), Arabs can be members of any religion. There are thousands of Arab Christians living in the Middle East. And it is also interesting to note that the largest Muslim nation is not located in the Middle East, but rather is Indonesia. (See Table 9.6).

As with other major religions of the world, Islam is also made up of a number of different branches. The largest and most influential branch in Islam is the Sunni, with a membership of 940,000,000. The next largest group is the Shiites, who number over 120,000,000. The Ahmadiyya have a population of 10 million. And the smallest branch in Islam is the Druze, with a population of only 450,000.

HINDUISM

The Hindu religion has a following of more than 800 million people today and is clearly one of the major religions of the world. Hinduism is also one of the oldest religions in the world, as it can trace its origins to about 2,500 B.C. It started in the Indus Valley and brought forth one of the most advanced civilizations in the world.

Hinduism is very different from the other major religions of the world in that it is polytheistic. For the practicing Hindu there are many gods. In fact, there are perhaps as many as 330 million gods in the Hindu religion. But in actual practice there are really only three major gods in the Hindu faith: Brahma is the god who

© 2013, neelsky. Used under license from Shutterstock, Inc.

Rank	Country	Number of Muslims
1	Indonesia	167,606,358
2	Pakistan	154,563,023
3	India	134,149,817
4	Bangladesh	132,868,312
5	Turkey	71,322,513
6	Iran	67,724,004
7	Egypt	63,503,397
8	Nigeria	54,665,801
9	Algeria	31,858,555
10	Morocco	31,000,895

Table 9.6 The Largest National Muslim Populations

Source: Calculated from Russell Ash, *The Top Ten of Everything 2007* (New York: Sterling Publishing Company, 2006), p. 60.

created the universe, Vishnu is the god who sustains life in the universe, and Shiva is the god who will destroy the universe at the appointed time. Many of the Hindu gods take on human or animal forms, and the major gods are well known and recognized by the faithful.

Hinduism is based on three basic doctrines that must be followed by the faithful. The doctrine of Samsara refers to the transformation of souls. This is based on the belief in reincarnation, that the individual will return in another life or another form after death. The individual could return as either a human, hopefully at some higher level, or as an animal, at some lower level. In this way people are rewarded for their good works in this (their current) life, for this will affect their placement in the next life. This movement either up or down the social hierarchy is based on the principal of dharma. This was the basis for the caste system in traditional Indian society. The third principal is karma, which refers to the cycles of cause and effect in the world. Good karma, or good works and good feelings for others, will result in positive results and rewards. On the other hand, bad karma will have negative results in the lives of individuals.

As with the other major religions, Hinduism is broken into distinct groups or branches. The largest of these sub-groups or branches is the Vaishnavites, with a population of 580,000,000. The second largest Hindu group is the Shaivites, with 220,000,000 followers. The most liberal of the Hindu branches is the reform Hindus, with 22 million members. And the smallest of the Hindu branches is the Veerashaivas (Lingayats), with about 10 million followers.

Of the almost 900 million Hindus in the world today, most are found in their country of origin, India. The second largest group of Hindus resides in Nepal. (See Table 9.7).

© 2013, Lukasz Kurbiel. Used under license from Shutterstock, Inc.

BUDDHISM

Another world religion that can trace its origins to India is Buddhism. Buddha, Siddhartha Gautama, was born a Kshatriya in India in 563 B.C. The Buddha sought enlightenment and traveled far and wide to find peace, wisdom, and truth. The Buddha is referred to as the Enlightened One. The focus of Buddhism is personal enlightenment. Like Hinduism, Buddhists believe in reincarnation, and believe that all individuals will experience birth, death, and then rebirth. This is the natural cycle of life.

Today there are over 378 million Buddhists around the world. And although Buddhism originated as an alternative religion (to Hinduism) in India, most of the followers of Buddhism today live in various Asian nations. The single largest concentration of Buddhists is found in China, followed by Japan and Thailand. (See Table 9.8.)

Country	Percent	Number
Nepal	89	19,000,000
India	79	780,000,000
Mauritius	52	600,000
Guyana	40	300,000
Fiji	38	300,000
Suriname	30	116,000
Bhutan	25	400,000
Trinidad and Tobago	24	300,000
Sri Lanka	15	2,800,000
Bangladesh	11	12,000,000

Table 9.7 Countries with the Highest Proportion of Hindus

Figures are approximate.
Source: Adherents.com, http://www.adherents.com.

Rank	Country	Number of Buddhists
1	China	111,358,666
2	Japan	70,722,505
3	Thailand	53,294,170
4	Vietnam	40,780,825
5	Myanmar	37,151,956
6	Sri Lanka	13,234,600
7	Cambodia	12,697,958
8	India	7,596,701
9	South Korea	7,281,110
10	Taiwan	4,823,361

Table 9.8 The Largest National Buddhist Populations

Source: Calculated from Russell Ash, *The Top Ten of Everything 2007* (New York: Sterling Publishing Company, 2006), p. 61.

The Sikh Religion and Culture

The Sikhs are a distinct sociocultural group in India and are considered an ethnoreligious minority in their homeland. The Sikhs are physically distinct from other Asian Indians, as they are larger in body build, are taller, and their religion requires that they wear turbans and keep their beards (Fox, 1985; McGregor, 1970). The Punjab is the homeland of the Sikhs and they constituted 85 to 90 percent of the original Asian-Indian immigrants to America (Jacoby, 1956: 7; Latif, 1974; Millis, 1911: 75).

Much of the distinctive appearance and cultural uniqueness of the Sikhs can be attributed to their religious beliefs that require them to observe the tradition of the "five Ks," which means that they have to (1) wear their hair and their beard unshorn (*Kesh*), (2) carry a comb (*Kanga*), (3) wear a pair of shorts (*Kuchha*), (4) wear a steel bracelet (*Karah*), and (5) they must always carry a saber (*Kirpan*) (McLeod, 1989; Singh, 1964: 10, 1966). The reason that they are required to observe these religious requirements is that they were supposed to strive for the ideal of ascetic saintliness and were expected to be prepared to defend their families and their religion as soldier-saints (Cole and Sambhi, 1978: 122–129; Singh, 1963).

As a religion Sikhism dates back to the fifteenth century when their leader Guru Nanek first gathered his followers near Lahore in the Punjab. Guru Nanek's teachings held that there is only one God, that this world is an illusion, and that all ritual is a distraction (Wenzel, 1968: 247). Much of the theology of Sikhism is derived from the teachings of Hinduism and Islam. The *Granth Sahib*, the Sikh holy book, contains the writings of various gurus and the teachings of Hindu and Muslim saints of all castes and creeds (Cole and Sambhi, 1978; Singh, 1964). In addition to observing all religious and cultural beliefs, Sikhs are required to be courageous and militant, to avoid the use of tobacco, and to take the common name of "Singh" (literally "lion," Singh and Singh, 1950: 62, Stratton and Mann, 1993; Wenzel, 1966: 10).

Today the Sikhs number over 24 million and most of these are concentrated in India. The largest groups of Sikhs living outside of India are found in England (800,000), Canada (350,000), and the United States (251,000). These settlement patterns reflect the labor migration routes developed during the early part of the twentieth century.

SUMMARY

In order to study and analyze the role of religion in society we must agree upon a working definition of religion. The definition of religion must be broad enough to be all inclusive and at the same time it must be specific enough to allow for careful study and rigorous analysis. Over time, sociologists have agreed on a basic set of characteristics that should apply to all organized religions. The application and study of these key sociological characteristics can help us to understand the structure and organization of all religions and the role that they play in organized society.

From our review of the major world religions, it is clear that there is great diversity in the way that people relate to the Supreme Being. See Box 9.3. Though there are certainly some important differences among the major religions, it is particularly interesting to observe the many similarities that occur among organized religions today.

Christianity is the single largest religion in the world today and is still growing and creating new converts. In recent times, Islam has become the focus of world attention due to the events of September 11, 2001, but it is important to note that the great majority of Muslims (99.9 percent of them) are God- fearing people who only seek peace and tranquility in their lives. The Hindu religion is also a very significant world religion and has made important contributions to the civilization of humankind. But unlike many of the other major religions that have grown and expanded to all parts of the world, the Hindu religion has remained concentrated, for the most part, in its country of origin, India. Buddhism is the second major world religion to have started as a small religious sect in India. But unlike Hinduism, Buddhism has spread to other countries in the Far East and now has many more adherents outside of India than inside India.

What we now realize is that religion does play a very important role in the daily lives of the great majority of individuals around the world. And from the sociological perspective we can say that religion has been a positive force in the lives of most individuals and has contributed to the peace and stability of many societies around the world. The expectation is that religion will continue to play an ever-increasing important role in the lives of all individuals and will contribute to the inner peace of all citizens.

CHAPTER 10

Respecting the Culture of Health

INTRODUCTION

Many health problems are associated with biological factors such as age, gender, and ethnic or racial origin. In other cases, illness and injury correlate with sociocultural factors, including economic conditions such as poverty. Third, unsafe behaviors are more prevalent in certain populations, reflecting both biological and psychosocial origins. A few examples are drunken driving, smoking, and substance abuse. Two psychologically-based risk factors contributing to illness and injury are emotional problems and mental disabilities. This chapter ties together some of these disparate facts by examining biopsychosocial factors influencing health among diverse population groupings.

An effort was made throughout this textbook to be inclusive, so all chapters include references to the ways health issues specifically relate to gender, age, and ethnicity or race. Unfortunately, many populations are underrepresented in studies in behavioral medicine and health psychology so we know less about them. Exceptions are research projects specifically aimed at members of populations delineated by age, gender, income, race, ethnicity, national origin, or disability.

In this chapter the biopsychosocial approach of health psychology is used to understand health issues for populations affected by poverty, discrimination, and

Consider the use of the term "athlete." Would this individual be considered an "athlete" to you? Why or why not?

disabilities. The chapter especially focuses on biology-based health problems linked to psychosocial risk factors. Many health problems cluster within groupings in populations. An obvious gender example is that breast cancer is most often found in females, but only males experience prostate cancer. Members of both genders develop heart disease, but their symptoms, diagnoses, treatments, and prognoses are often different. Young people are at risk for some diseases partly as a result of the quality of care they receive while growing up. Adolescent health is affected by socially driven tendencies to use tobacco, alcohol, weapons, and drive recklessly. The health of older persons often reflects lifestyle choices they made earlier in their lives. Health risks also mirror the value system of the culture in which they exist. Prejudice and discrimination toward others are part of value systems and influence health. Health risks are influenced by poverty, ethnicity, race, age, gender, and disabilities, regardless of individual lifestyle patterns.

For example, individuals living at lower socioeconomic levels experience both poorer health and less safety from injuries. The United States prides itself on being tolerant of and welcoming to people from diverse origins, but the reality for many is a disadvantaged health status reflecting racial and ethnic background, immigration status, and national origin. Many people with mental and physical disabilities are also subject to discrimination. Variations in sociocultural status result in disparities in health and health care. A different conceptual model is the socio-psycho-physiological framework of health and illness (Rugulie, Aust, & Syme, 2004). This approach directs attention to the impact of social structure on physiological and psychological conditions and processes. The social and economic structure, particularly the distribution of wealth, is the overarching factor at the top of this framework.

© 2013, Warren Goldswain. Used under license from Shutterstock, Inc.

HEALTH AND SOCIOCULTURAL CHARACTERISTICS

Health and Income

Health problems are aggravated by lower levels of education, substandard housing, more dangerous occupations, and limited access to medical care. The most obvious health disparities reflect economic status. Epidemiologists have known for decades that health mirrors wealth. People with lower incomes are less likely to experience a long and healthy life compared to those with higher incomes. Earning power is an outcome of educational levels and hiring practices.

The government defines poverty for purposes of providing federal and state assistance, but the official poverty line underestimates the actual cost of living in the United States. Poverty statistics are based on definitions developed by the Social Security Administration. Poverty line thresholds vary by family size, number of children in the family, and, in some cases, ages of the adults in the family. Thresholds are updated annually by the United States Bureau of the Census to reflect changes in the Consumer Price Index for all urban consumers. In 2000, the average poverty threshold for a family of four was $17,603 (National Health Interview Survey, 2008). About 13% of all Americans live below this line, but millions more are economically disadvantaged. African Americans and Hispanic Americans have double the percentage of poverty of other racial and ethnic groups. Living on a lower income often means living in crowded, unsanitary housing in hazardous and polluted neighborhoods where stress levels are extremely high. Beliefs and behaviors also reflect socioeconomic status. Health beliefs and behaviors reflect social norms in neighborhoods and in the workplace (Kaplan, Everson, & Lynch, 2000). Low-income populations are less likely to eat healthily and exercise regularly, and are more likely to smoke (Emmons, 2000).

The most recent information from National Health Interview findings shows that the percentage of persons in excellent health increased with increased levels of education and family income (Adams, Lucas, & Barnes, 2008, pp. 5–6). Some highlights of the latest report are as follows:

- College graduates were more than twice as likely as persons who had not graduated from high school to be in excellent health.
- Persons with private health insurance were more likely than persons with other types of health insurance or uninsured persons to be in excellent health.
- Poor adults were three to four times more likely than those who were not poor to require help with activities of daily living and instrumental activities of daily living.

- Persons with the least education and the lowest incomes were the most likely to be unable to work due to health problems.
- Persons in the lowest income group were about four times more likely than persons in the highest income group to delay medical care due to cost and about eight times more likely to not get needed medical care. About 23 million persons delayed medical care in the last year due to cost.

Impoverished people are less likely to have health care insurance. They may not be able to afford to take time off from work to seek medical care. Both factors interfere with preventive health care services. People without resources often delay diagnoses and treatment for both illnesses and injuries. This postponement, based in socioeconomic conditions, increases the likelihood of chronic disease, disability, and premature death. Income influences the likelihood of stress including low job security, lack of control, and moods and emotions, including hostility and depression (Allgower, Wardle, & Steptoe, 2001). The distribution of wealth often reflects ethnic and racial minority status.

Health and Race, Ethnicity, and National Origin

Over the last 100 years the United States has become more diverse. About 30% of the population belongs to a racial or ethnic minority group (Census Bureau, 2001). American Indian and Alaska Natives, black or African Americans, Hispanic or Latino Americans, Native Hawaiian and other Pacific Islanders, and Asian Americans are more likely to be poor and less likely to be as healthy as European Americans (Office of Minority Health and Health Disparities [OMHHD], 2008). Members of these groups experience a disproportionate burden of preventable disease, death, and disability (OMHD, 2008). For example, low-income populations, minorities, and children living in inner cities experience more emergency department visits, hospitalizations, and deaths due to asthma than the general population (OMHD, 2008). Recent immigrants, especially illegal immigrants, experience even lower socioeconomic status and levels of education, greater language difficulties, and discrimination. As a result they are more likely to experience inequities in health care. An important point made in the introduction was that poverty and minority status are often related.

It is difficult for social scientists to separate and evaluate the impact of dual or coexisting factors on health and safety. **Life expectancy** is one calculation commonly used to assess health differences by race, ethnicity, and national origin (U.S. Department of Health and Human Services [DHHS], 2006). For example, life expectancy at birth for blacks is 73 years and 78 years for whites.

National statistics on causes of death are based on death certificates and make comparisons possible among groupings (National Center for Health Statistics, 2007). In the United States, the six major causes of death in descending order are heart disease, cancer, stroke, respiratory diseases, accidents or unintentional injuries, and diabetes, but these vary by ethnicity. Compared to other racial categories, Hispanic, American Indian/Alaska Native, and Asian/Pacific Islanders are more likely to die of accidents than other groupings. Death from diabetes is more common for blacks, Hispanics, American Indian/Native American, and Asian American/Pacific Islanders than for European Americans. Heart disease is the leading cause of death for all racial/ethnic groups except Asian or Pacific Islanders, who are more likely to die of cancer. In most instances death due to Alzheimer's disease is associated with being long-lived. Alzheimer's is the sixth leading cause of death for whites, but ranks 14th, 13th, and 12th for blacks, American Indian/Native American, and Asian American/Pacific Islanders, respectively. Scientists are still trying to sort out the influence on health risks of genetic susceptibility compared to suboptimal living conditions.

Biological Aspects of Race or Ethnicity

Some diseases are specifically associated with racial and ethnic groups. Three examples are osteoporosis, sickle-cell anemia, and type II diabetes. Osteoporosis is a greater risk for European and Asian American women than members of other racial and ethnic groups. First, members of these two populations are more likely to begin life with smaller bone size. Other factors implicated in osteoporosis are lack of calcium and vitamin D in the diet, limited exposure to sunlight, smoking, and lack of regular weightbearing exercise.

Sickle-cell disease is a group of genetic disorders characterized by the predominance of protein hemoglobin S (HbS) in red blood cells (Thompson & Gustafson, 1996). This blood disease occurs mostly in African Americans but also in some Mediterranean-origin populations. Red blood cells are especially important for carrying oxygen and storing iron. The term *sickle cell* refers to red blood cells being crescent-shaped, leading to anemia. Some symptoms of sickle-cell anemia are fatigue, weakness, headaches, joint pain, dizziness, and an enlarged spleen. When both parents carry the sickle-cell genetic trait, then a major concern becomes transmission to their children. Patients with sickle-cell disease may experience damage to bone marrow, heart, kidneys, spleen, and are at greater risk of stroke than others (Brown, Mulhern, & Simonian, 2002). Medical management is a lifelong issue.

Type II or adult-onset diabetes is associated with older age, obesity, history of gestational diabetes, inactivity, family history, and race or ethnicity. Complications of diabetes include heart disease and high blood pressure, blindness, kidney disease, and amputations (Wysocki & Buckloh, 2002). The prevalence rate for diabetes among American Indians in the southern United States and southern Arizona is about 27%, or nearly a third of that population. About 13% of blacks, 10% of Hispanic Americans, and 9% of whites are estimated to have diabetes (CDC, 2005a). Mexican Americans are 1.7 times as likely to have diabetes as non-Hispanic whites.

Psychosocial Aspects of Race, Ethnicity, and National Origin

Certain behaviors put people at risk regardless of genetic background, but some are also associated with income and minority status. For example, smoking puts people at risk of cancer, heart disease, and chronic obstructive lung disease (Fisher, Brownson, Heath, Luke, & Walton, 2004). Research on smoking among adults in the United States indicates that about 32% of American Indian and Alaskan Natives smoke. Data on other groups show 22% of whites and blacks currently smoke, as do 15% of Hispanics, and 13% of Asians (CDC, 2006a). The ratio may change, because recent data about smoking among teens indicate that about 26% of whites, 12% of blacks, and 22% of Hispanics begin smoking in high school (CDC, 2006b). If these percentage differences prevail over time, then higher rates of smoking-related diseases in some groupings are expected in the future.

HIV/AIDS frequently reflects poverty, lifestyle choices, gender, and minority status. Behavioral risks include unprotected sexual intercourse and intravenous drug use (Ironson, Balbin, & Schneiderman, 2002). In 2005, the CDC estimated that about 40,000 people become infected each year in the United States, and of those diagnosed with HIV/AIDS during 2005, 49% were black, 31% were white, and 18% were Hispanic (2005b).

Health and Gender

Gender, being female or male, is an important issue affecting health. Sexism, or prejudice and discrimination based on gender, continues to influence health and safety in addition to race, ethnicity, education, socioeconomic status, and age. Discrimination against people based on their gender is a pattern of behavior existing in most cultures and reflects enduring societal structures. **Social structure** refers to the existing order or the general social context within which people live out their lives. The term includes the organization of a society's historical, political, economic, family/kinship, religious, and educational systems. The social structure in the United States continues to be gender-biased, despite changes made in the 20th century including women being allowed to vote, to own property, and to seek certain types of jobs. In the United States women continue to be marginalized in many facets of life, including education, business, and sociopolitical processes. Pay inequities, inadequate child care arrangements, and restrictions on control of reproduction persist to plague women's physical and emotional health.

THINK ABOUT IT

You have a headache. How does your socioeconomic status, religious beliefs, educational background, gender, age, or health status affect what you will do to alleviate your headache? Discuss.

Gender discrimination adds to the impact of ethnic, racial, and economic inequalities. Women of African, Hispanic, Asian, Native, and European American background often experience lower levels of health and health care than males of the same ethnic and racial origins. About a third of women who head households live in poverty, which is a major contributor to illness and injury. The combined effects of poverty, discrimination, inability to provide for one's children, and fear of violence are sources of enormous stress for women (Ratcliff, 2002).

Domestic violence and sexual harassment continue to influence women's mental and physical health. Unrealistic beauty standards for women are common in our society. These expectations contribute to distorted body image, disordered eating practices, and excessive exposure to tanning, putting women at risk of skin cancer. Women are also exposed to hazards in their homes and workplaces. Up until very recently, no major longitudinal studies focused on women's health or health care. Variations in causes of illness and injury reflect biological, psychological, and sociocultural factors specific to gender.

Biological Aspects of Being Female

Women have a greater life expectancy than men: 81 years compared to 76 years (DHHS, 2006). Women have lower rates of injury, but higher rates of illness. Women are more likely than men to experience osteoporosis and some autoimmune disorders. Breast cancer in men is rare, but 1 in 8 women will develop the disease in their lives. Cardiovascular disease is the leading cause of death in women, but heart disease was considered a male disease up until about 1989. Heart attacks continue to be treated less aggressively in women and are more likely to be fatal for women than for men. Stress, mental health, and substance abuse are additional issues for women whose experiences with these health problems are different from men's. Due to the feminist movement in the 1960s and publications of the Boston Women's Health Collective in the 1970s and since, women's health is now being given more attention than ever before (Boston Women's Health Collective, 1973).

HIV/AIDS is a particular problem for poor minority women, who often contract it through heterosexual intercourse and needle sharing. Nevertheless, women were not included in HIV/AIDS clinical trials until 1993 (Ratcliff, 2002). Women are excluded from many health studies and are underrepresented in drug trials. Exclusion occurred partially due to fears about the side effects of the drugs if women were pregnant and also due to drug companies' concerns about the effects of menstrual cycles on research outcomes. In many cases it was assumed women were just like men, but with a smaller body size. During the previous century, the biology of women's health mainly included reproductive concerns. Hormones, menstruation, menopause, and maturation continue to be treated as medical problems requiring medical treatment. Two national women's health studies have brought women's health to the attention of both the general population and the medical community. The Nurse's Health Study is based on questionnaires completed by participating nurses who are women. The National Women's Health Initiative is an ongoing study that includes medical data, controlled experiments, and information about lifestyle and disease and accident occurrence. Women's health is gaining research recognition (Stanton & Gallant, 1995; Gallant, Keita, & Royak-Schaler, 1997; Etaugh & Bridges, 2004; Alexander, LaRosa, Bader, & Garfield, 2004).

Psychosocial Aspects of Being Female

On a worldwide basis, women still have less access than men to education, income, gainful employment, sports, and health care. For example, women were once limited to running only half the court in basketball games. It took legislative change for women to gain greater access to athletics, scholarships, and related rights (Tricard, 2008; Snooks, 2000).

Sexual Violence

Sexual violence is a specific health risk that is greater for women than for men. It is an important and emerging area of concern in the United States and throughout the world. **Sexual violence** refers to nonconsensual sexual activity and includes threats, intimidation, peeping, taking nude photos, unwanted touching, and rape (CDC, 2008a). Global sexual violence problems include gang rapes in wartime and in prisons, sexual trafficking, and child marriages.

In the United States, 1 in 6 women, and 1 in 33 men report experiencing an attempted or completed rape at some time in their lives (Tjaden & Thoennes, 2000). Sexual violence includes **sexual harassment** in schools, neighborhoods, and at job sites. An estimated 20% to 25% of college women experience attempted or complete rape during their college career (Fisher, Cullen, & Turner, 2000). Among high school students 11% of females and 4% of males reported having been forced to have sex (CDC, 2008a). Sexual violence contributes to a number of health problems, including unwanted pregnancy, chronic pain, stomach problems, and sexually transmitted diseases. Emotional effects include fearfulness, anxiety, anger, and stress leading to eating disorders and depression. Globally, sexual violence is a common and serious health problem affecting millions of people.

Health and Disabilities

One of every seven people in this country has a physical, intellectual, or emotional disability affecting quality of life. In many cases, disability is complicated by poverty. Health and health-related behaviors such as exercise and eating are affected by physical and mental limitations. Social isolation of people with disabilities further contributes to biopsychosocial difficulties. Public attitudes and environmental obstacles exacerbate quality of life. The Americans with Disabilities Act and recent court decisions have provided some relief, but many problems still exist in this country for persons with disabilities.

Now a disability and health team exists to support the development of guidelines for making emergency preparation, fitness and recreation sites, primary care, communication, and conferences more accessible to people with disabilities (CDC, 2008a). The team's web site is not controlled by the Centers for Disease Control, Department of Health and Human Services, or the Public Health Service. Some states have centers for universal design and the San Antonio Planning Department has a disability etiquette handbook. State and local governments provide disaster resources and emergency evacuation for people with physical disabilities. Disabilities may be physical, intellectual, emotional, or a combination of these difficulties.

Accessible is a term describing the suitability of a product or service for people with disabilities. **Universal design** describes products and environments that can be used regardless of body dimension, age, or disability status. Using universal design prior to construction is usually superior to retrofitting environments. Accessibility is a very important biopsychosocial issue.

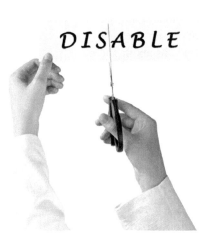

DISABLE

© 2013, arka38. Used under license from Shutterstock, Inc.

Biological Aspects of Disabilities

Problems with fatigue, balance, heat tolerance, sensory loss, muscle and skeletal weakness, tremors, and difficulty with vision, hearing, swallowing, and breathing may undermine overall health and prevent regular exercise among those with disabilities. For all people with disabilities, exercise should be modified or adapted to enhance health and prevent injury. Lower-limb amputations are usually due to diabetes, trauma such as war injury or automobile accidents, and congenital malformations. Exercise can be managed differently depending on the cause of the amputation (Pitetti & Pedrotty, 2003). For example, persons with diabetes should focus on cardiovascular exercise to prevent further deterioration in their health. Too-vigorous exercise may result in overuse injuries, joint pain, and falls that cause skin damage that may be slow to heal. Exercise is important for those with disabilities due to causes of amputations other than diabetes. For persons who have experienced trauma or congenital disability, exercise management may include aerobic, strength, flexibility, and functional exercises. Exercise may mean vigorous arm rather than leg movement for increasing aerobic capacity. Those with balance problems can use reclining or recumbent cycles, and guard rails when walking. When seizures are controlled, people with epilepsy may enjoy competitive contact sports. Muscle memory is affected by neurological diseases such as Parkinson's.

Exercises are usually modifiable for people with intellectual and emotional limitations. Attention deficits, motivation, and understanding may vary from day to day and require greater supervision. Some types of mental retardation are accompanied by heart defects. Co-ordination, along with difficulties in balance, weakness, and breathing may interfere with exercise (Fernhall, 2003). Alzheimer's disease is progressive and characterized by degeneration in both mental and physical health. Agitation, memory loss, depression, and incontinence may interfere with caregivers' efforts to maintain physical fitness in patients with Alzheimer's. A supervised short daily walk may be the maximum exercise possible. Exercise may improve mood and self-concept, and decrease depression and anxiety for people diagnosed with long-term or serious and persistent mental illness or psychiatric disability (Skrinar, 2003). Exercise is therapeutic in treating depressive disorders as well as beneficial to biological health. Some medications may interfere with exercising.

Psychosocial Aspects of Disabilities

Depression and deteriorating self-concept may follow losing control over one's life due to disabilities. The emotional state of those with a mental or physical disability can vary from day to day and include angry reactions. Structured supervision is usually important. When a culture idealizes physical beauty and perfection, then prejudice and discrimination are issues for many people with noticeable physical or mental disabilities. Children with disabilities are often discouraged early in life by well-meaning but overprotective parents and caregivers. Establishing and maintaining independence rather than dependence requires major effort on the child's part and on the part of the caregivers.

Health and Age

Illness and Injury in Children and Adolescents

The U.S. Department of Health and Human Services Healthy People 2010 includes goals specific to the health of children and adolescents (2007). Children's health issues interest health psychology researchers and developmental psychologists. Research topics include such

What does this picture suggest about human relationships in a culturally diversity society?

varied areas as prenatal counseling for couples at risk of infant birth defects, childhood obesity, learning disabilities, school-based problems, and effective therapies for child abuse. **Developmental disabilities** and birth defects are a diverse group of severe and chronic conditions resulting in mental and physical impairment. These can affect learning, language development, mobility, and self-help. Developmental disabilities include cerebral palsy, autism, hearing loss, vision impairments, intellectual disabilities, and traumatic brain injury (CDC, 2008).

Childhood obesity is another important area of research interest, because obesity is a major risk factor for diabetes, cardiovascular disease, and some cancers. Overweight children and adolescents are more likely to become obese as adults (CDC, 2008c). Eighty percent of children who were overweight at ages 10 to 15 were obese at age 25 years, and 25% of obese adults were overweight as children. Data from the National Health and Nutrition Examination Survey (NHANES) surveys show that the prevalence of people who are overweight is increasing. The most recent surveys show that 14% of children aged 2–5, 19% of children ages 6–11, and 17% of those 12–19 are overweight (CDC, 2008c).

Health promotion and injury prevention are additional areas of children's health research. The leading cause of death for people from ages 1–24 is accidents. Most are motor vehicle accidents for which adults are responsible, but playground injuries, poisoning, fires, and drowning are additional causes of injury and death (DHHS, 2006). Both children and teens tend to overestimate their physical abilities, resulting in injuries (Plumert, 2004). Personality traits such as being impulsive, aggressive, daring, and careless are also linked to higher rates of injuries in children. This is especially true of children diagnosed with ADHD or **attention deficit-hyperactivity disorder** (Schwebel & Plumert, 1999; Farmer & Peterson, 1995).

Violence is a serious threat to the health and well-being of children and adolescents in the United States. Each year hundreds of thousands of children suffer abuse or neglect. For ages 5–24, the third and fourth leading causes of death are homicides and suicides (CDC, 2008d). For adolescents, risk-taking behaviors are a major health and safety problem. The teenage years are burdened with tendencies to substance abuse, motor vehicle injuries, violence, stress, depression, suicide, pregnancy, eating disorders, and sexually transmitted infections. More than 3 million young women between the ages of 14 and 19 have a sexually transmitted disease (CDC, 2008a). These include the human papillomavirus (HPV), chlamydia, herpes simplex virus, and trichomoniasis. Adolescent health is also affected by delinquency, homelessness, and academic underachievement. Youth violence includes aggressive behaviors such as verbal abuse, bullying, hitting, slapping, and fistfighting. Adolescents with chronic diseases such as diabetes are at high risk for not following medical therapies, leading to potentially life-threatening consequences. Detrimental experiences in childhood increase the probability of health problems in later life.

The **Adverse Childhood Experiences Study (ACE)** is an ongoing investigation of the link between childhood maltreatment and later-life health and well-being (CDC, 2008f). Over 17,000 adult members of the Kaiser Permanente Health Maintenance Organization are participating in comprehensive physical examinations and providing detailed information about their childhood experiences of abuse, neglect, and family dysfunction. To date over 30 scientific articles have been published.

The study began when researchers recognized the fact that many risk factors for chronic illness tended to cluster together. That is, people who have one risk factor such as smoking tended to have other risk factors such as alcohol abuse. The ACE Study suggests that adverse childhood experiences are a major risk factor for the leading causes of illness, death, and poor quality of life. The conceptual framework for the study takes a whole-life perspective, suggesting that adverse childhood experiences lead to social, emotional, and cognitive impairment, followed by behaviors leading to disease, disability, social problems, and early death.

Illness and Injury in Older Adults

Gerontology is the science of aging and special problems of aged persons. **Geriatrics** is a medical specialty focusing on the diagnosis and treatment of diseases affecting the aged. It is sometimes difficult for medical personnel and researchers to distinguish between effects of aging and certain types of physical and persistent mental illness. By 2030 the number of Americans over 65 years of age will have more than doubled to 70 million, or 1 in every 5 persons (CDC, 2008c). This will increase demands on the public health system, including medical and social services Illness, disability, and premature death are avoidable with regular physical activity, healthy eating, avoiding tobacco use, and early detection for diseases through routine screening.

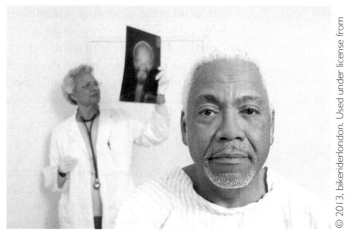

© 2013, bikeriderlondon. Used under license from Shutterstock, Inc.

Some studies suggest that **cohort effects** may be more important than the effects of aging (Satre & Cook, 2004). Cohort effects reflect differences between generations rather than aging per se. For example, later generations with more education may exhibit intellectual abilities superior to earlier generations. Culture change is reflected by research attention being given to newer cohorts such as "baby boomers" and "generation X." These studies suggest that cultural changes in society are more important than age in affecting cognitive capacity.

Ageism, or prejudice and discrimination based on age, is common in the United States. Some sociologists suggest that being young is more valued than having the wisdom of old age. Feeling, acting, and looking young are the ideal of many. Ageism affects the health and safety of all persons regardless of gender, race, ethnicity, education, or socioeconomic status. As life expectancy increases, more research will probably focus on biological, psychological, and sociocultural factors related to aging.

Biological Effects of Aging Age shapes types of illness and injury. Chronic physical disorders and pain are more common in elderly populations than in younger people. Multiple medications, drug interactions, and confusion about dosage sometimes require hospitalization for the elderly. Osteoporosis, arthritis, and back pain are more common at older ages. Some ailments and accidents can be prevented by home renovations, including increased lighting, non-slippery floor coverings, convenient locations for essential items, hand rails, and lift chairs. Preventive action should include discussions of ways to avoid accidents and falls. Deafness is more characteristic of older Americans. As more and more Americans live into old age, technology for hearing aids will probably improve. Many of the elderly experience lower incomes following retirement. This interferes with healthy nutritional practices and access to medical care and medications. Economic problems add to the health problems of aging populations, especially among widowed women who are dependent on spousal Social Security or pensions. In spite of lower incomes and declining energy and strength, it is important for the elderly to be encouraged to exercise and to follow nutritious eating patterns.

Psychosocial Aspects of Aging The elderly are vulnerable to ageism and elder abuse. Both are harmful to biological and psychosocial health. Examples of ageism in this culture include jokes made about sexuality in old age and jokes about disabilities such as deafness and feebleness. Many elderly people are psychologically at risk due to social isolation, which causes damage to both physical and mental health. Single elders are more likely to live in age-segregated communities such as retirement centers and nursing homes. This often has demoralizing effects. Quality of life issues are especially important for elderly people who have limited ability to drive themselves to medical care and for grocery shopping. Problems with activities of daily living such as dressing, bathing, and room cleaning are more problematic for the elderly than other age groupings. Insomnia is also more characteristic of older Americans. It is not the typical problem of trying to go to sleep, but rather of staying asleep. The following day they are tired and more likely to fall or eat inadequately. Help for this type of insomnia may be exercise by brisk walking during the day. Stress, depression, and suicide are additional hazards of aging. These often result from loss and loneliness due to deaths of spouses and longtime friends, as well as the loss of previous levels of physical activity.

SUMMARY

This chapter focused on disparities in health and health care related to poverty, race/ethnicity/national origin, gender, age, and disabilities. Poverty prevents easy access to health care services. Additionally, the poor are more likely to find themselves in dangerous jobs with little or no health care coverage. Racial and ethnic differences are frequently associated with disparities in wealth and result in inequality in health and health care. Some racial groups have specific health risks that may be genetic and/or consequences of day-to-day living conditions.

The social structure of the United States values females less than males. This results in disparities in health and health care. For centuries the main focus of medical care for women has been on reproductive health, rather than on other important causes of illness, injury, and death. People with physical, intellectual, and emotional disabilities may experience discrimination, affecting their emotional and physical health. In spite of limitations, those with a physical or psychiatric disability should be encouraged to exercise to maintain health and mobility. Age groups are also at particular risks for injury or illness. Children are at the mercy of their parents or caregivers with regard to health and health care. Adolescents are more likely than other age groups to take risks threatening to health and safety. Old age is often a time characterized by declines in income, health, energy, and even intellectual capacity. The very old are prone to falls, broken bones, heart disease, and cancers. Poverty, race/ethnicity, gender, age, and disabilities all impact biological, psychological, and social health.

CHAPTER 11

Recapturing Humanity

Intergroup human relations have been the central focus of this text. A variety of concepts have been introduced by social psychologists and sociologists to unravel the intensity of cultural dimensions involved in these interactions. The distinctions between the research done by psychologists and research done by sociologists point to the role that individual identities and social expectations play in intergroup relationships. Psychologists tend to examine the underlying mental and emotional experiences that lead people to think, act, and feel the way they do. On the other hand, sociologists explore the role that society plays in constructing group identities that can change, but are also resistant to change.

As both psychological and sociological research continue to examine how humans engage each other in social settings, many of the questions and concerns that were present since the beginning of humanity are not only relevant today, but will require investigation as long as there are humans. In her book, *Generation Me*, Jean Twenge (2006) explored changes in human behavior, cultural expectations, and consciousness through four generations. Her research explains how societal rules dictate human behavior (Grison, Heatherton and Gazzaniga, 2015). For instance, the culture of the "Baby Boomers" (those who were born in the 1940s) tended to focus on making significant changes in society by becoming more aware of their roles in it. It was these individuals who grew up as post-depression teens and World War II citizens. Psychologically, this cultural group valued hard work, but not at the expense of enjoying life. This generation saw the creation of television and the development of a Social Security system that would respect and take care of the underserved (i.e., mentally unstable; elders post-retirement).

The generation that came after the "Baby Boomers,"—"Generation X" or "Baby Busters"— were more interested in finding themselves and contributing through competition to the social order (Twenge, 2006) than to questioning authority and policies. This cultural group, born in the 1960s during the height of the "self-love" movement, saw the intensification of social justice and civil rights where the welfare of all was valued more than the experience of some. Sociologists were more interested in the group struggle for social order than psychologists who were most curious about how individuals responded to how the changes going on in society affected them. Not only were individuals responding to the change, but the value system of this group deviated from those of the previous generation to where internal conflicts erupted in households from the "Baby Boomers" who wanted the younger generation to participate in wartime efforts. Meanwhile, questions surrounding the "Baby Busters" centered around the uncivil and secrecy-laden reasons for warfare that prompted the drafting of soldiers into Vietnam, the Gulf War, and the Iran Conflict. Protests erupted not only on the streets, but in households where multigenerational cultures resided.

Generation	Era	Personality Traits	Influences
GI generation	1901–1924	Traditionalists; value hard work; cooperative work ethic	Born during war times and increasing industrialization and automation (i.e., TVs, cars)
Silent generation	1925–1945	Traditionalists; respect loyalty; extended family relationships valued	World War II; Korean War; segregation; social programs created; Great Depression; mafia
Baby Boomers	1945–1970	Social reformers; advocate change; do what feels right to them; peace; freedom; optimistic	Rebounding from the Great Depression; space exploration; birth control pills; Chicano Farm Workers movement
Generation X (Baby Busters)	1965–1985	Social negotiators; interested in health, wealth; value free time	Watergate; Vietnam; first to try computer technology; latchkey kids; higher divorce rates than previous generations
Generation Y (Millenials)	1980–2000	Globally sensitive; tech-savvy; confident; assertive; "entitled"	Increase in information super-highway; "the world is flat" phenomenon

Information obtained from University of Iowa School of Social Work - National Resource Center for Family Centered Practice. (2009). *Committed to Excellence Through Supervision*, USDHHS Grant # 90CT0111.

Table 11.1 Psychology and the Intergenerational Diversity

THINK ABOUT IT

How would you explain to someone who is not reading this textbook that "Baby Boomers," "Baby Busters," "Generation X," and "Millenials/ Generation Me" are cultures? What are some of the distinctive features of each group? How does what we know about these groups contribute to our understanding of multicultural psychology?

What can be seen in these intergenerational cultures is an expansion of the understanding about life and one's contribution to it. This is one of the reasons why books and research are continuing written about how human relations in the workplace, at home, and in the civil society are supposed to occur. While there is no conclusion that has been made, the evidence demonstrates that there are differing interpretations of standards, realities and values for different cultural groups. Even within the same work environment, people of different generations view the expectations of the work space, relationships with work mates, and benefits of things like working late in varying ways. How can this affect the work environment? Home environment? Romantic relationships?

MULTICULTURAL COMPETENCE

Throughout this textbook, we have reviewed answers to the question about the psychology of human interaction with people who are similar and dissimilar to them (Weiten, 2012; Mio, Barker, & Tumambing, 2013; Myer, 2007). While it may seem that the answer is grounded in a behavioral motivation to accomplish some task in order for the person to increase the chances of success and limit uncomfortable outcomes, the answer is not that simple. The world is made up of a complex society with complex people who have complex ideas about complex issues: love, values, relationships, success. Whether one is communicating with someone who has a hearing impairment, is four-years old, or is a carpenter, the format for how the message gets communicated and interpreted may be different. While we refer to this as *diversity,* there are those who have never considered that difference is just that—difference. Likewise, diversity is not *wrong*. In fact, when one is engaged in qualitative research, the difference is not as important as the fact that there is quality, richness, and depth to the difference.

Multicultural psychology as a branch of the science and profession of psychology has affected how psychology is utilized and understood. Throughout the previous two decades, it has invested in creating language, expectations, and delivery methods that require all those who are trained as psychologists to be multiculturally competent. What is **multicultural competence**? Multicultural competence is a behavior that requires a cognitive (thought) and affective (feelings) appreciation for cultural groups. In order for one to be multiculturally competent, one has to be able to appreciate the diverse values, thoughts, traditions, and other elements that make a culture what it is (APA, 2003 Stuart, 2004). Once that is accomplished, the person then goes on to learn more about the culture that can lead them to want to learn even more. Famed UCLA basketball coach John Wooden was once quoted as saying, "It's what you learn after you know it all that counts" (Weaver, 1982). The multiculturally competent person is a continual learner who realizes that there are as many reasons for individual behavior as there are individuals in the world. Going out of one's way to discover all the possible answers is when the real competence tends to reveal itself.

Knowledge does not always equate to behavior. Several researchers agree that culture influences psychological processes (Matsumoto & Juang, 2013; Bowman, 2009), but that there is also an enhanced cultural sensitivity that comes when an individual chooses to explore culture on purpose. In their research on the effect of diversity courses on cognitive skills, Hurtado, Mayhew, and Engberg (2003) found that students who took a diversity course demonstrated greater gains in moral reasoning than students completing a management course (Bowman, 2009).

In fact, when considering what psychologists now know about diverse groups, we see that the measure and scope of their knowledge is based on a reflexive view of worldview, personal understanding, complex social systems, and some things we do not yet know. This can be seen in a work by D'Andrea and Daniels (2001) in their RESPECTFUL model where R = religious/spiritual issues; E = economic/class issues; S = sexual identity issues; P = psychological development issues; E = ethnic/racial identity issues; C = chronological issues; T = trauma and threats to well-being; F = family issues; U = unique physical issues; and L = language and location of residence issues (D'Andrea & Heckman, 2008). When discussing a person's psychological experience, then, all of these factors are considered in a way that respects the multidimensionality and multiple identities that make the person an individual (Nettles & Balter, 2012).

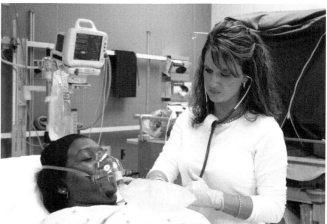

The ability to successfully interact with people from diverse cultures is the hallmark of multicultural compentence.

As was discussed in Chapter 4, "Communication and Civility," this same type of communication error is made when an individual tries to adapt cultural behaviors using previous experience as a guide. What usually happens is that there is discomfort between the two cultures that can result in unintentional miscommunication. Another classic example occurred in the political arena when Michelle Obama, First Lady of the United States, met Queen Elizabeth of England in 2009 (nbcnews.com). In an act that breached protocol, Mrs. Obama greeted the Queen with a handshake that led to an embrace during a photo shoot. While several onlookers who were unaware of aristocratic protocol simply smiled, those aware of the faux pas looked on in horror. That is, until the unconventional happened—the Queen responded with a hug around Mrs. Obama's waist (cnn.com).

In a world where diversity continues to increase and awareness of "difference" is frequently discussed and debated, there is a need to critically evaluate how individuals behave, feel, and think when they encounter someone who is not like them. The science and profession of psychology has recognized this as an issue that affects the human socialization process. As has been discussed in previous chapters, whether a conversation is held between a male and a female; a heterosexual male and a lesbian female; a teenager and a librarian; or a military veteran and a marathon runner, the fact that the individuals experience the world from different perspectives will affect their interaction. While they may attempt to find common ground, there may be topics in which they may not find common ground. Although the essence of their humanity should suffice to bring about a shared history, there may be certain areas on where they have little in common.

So, the question that sometimes is asked is, "What can I do so that I do not offend someone unintentionally?" This question is one that can be answered simply by explaining that it is not realistic to expect that someone will not be offended by something at some time. However, the question is better posed, "How can I become more aware of different cultural behaviors, traits, expectations, values, and the like?" This answer is simple: Never stop learning about human behavior. When Harrell discussed the "5 Ds of difference (Harrell, 1995; Harrell & Bond, 2006; Mio et al., 2013)" she explained that the reasons that people neglect to engage one another is because they assume that they are more different than they are similar, so they minimize opportunities to communicate with people who they believe are not similar to them (whether in values, tradition, age, or ability). The Ds are distancing, denial, defensiveness, devaluing, and discovery. See Table 11.2.

	Meaning	Examples
Distancing	Keeping distance from another	"Why are all the Black kids sitting together in the cafeteria?" (Tatum, 2003)
Denial	Acting as if differences do not exist	"All I said was, why are you so sensitive?"
Defensiveness	Asserting oneself against psychological harm by presenting arguments	"I was just trying to be friendly."
Devaluing	Using microaggressions to decrease another's value	"We can't have amputees compete in the real Olympics."
Discovery	Welcoming diversity and exploring opportunities to appreciate it	"I never knew that…"

Table 11.2 Five Ds of Difference (Harrell, 1995)

As was stated in chapter one (p. 6), the American Psychological Association (APA) believed that addressing the issue of multicultural competence was so important that in 2002 it revised the APA Ethics Code to include the "Guidelines on Multicultural Education, Training, Research, Practice, and Organizational Change for Psychologists" (APA, 2002). This document was created to give to psychological professionals (including psychologists and psychology teachers) a clearer understanding of the diverse social groups with which they would come into contact while providing psychological services. It was not enough to simply alert these professionals about cultural languages, values, traditions or history, but to seek to enhance the ability to effectively engage with individuals from diverse backgrounds. This includes in research, in understanding basic information about cultural nuances and organizational change necessary to broaden the skills required to meet the psychological needs of these groups.

ABC's OF MULTICULTURAL COMPETENCE

Just as in the ABCs of psychology, we could also consider the ABCs of the multiculturally competent. The core values of the multiculturally competent individual is one who seeks not only to find common ground with a person who has a different worldview or experience from one's own, but

- **A** = *Appreciates others.* "Appreciation" does not mean that there has to be agreement about the cultural behaviors, attitudes, or thoughts. Being multiculturally competent suggests that the individual understands that everyone is free to discover, divulge, discuss, and experience their own culture without evaluation from others who are not members of that culture.
- **B** = *Behaves in a way that respects the cultural rights and reservations of different groups.* When people are multiculturally competent, they can build relationships through the practice of civil behavior and attitudes. It necessitates that people conduct themselves in a way that allows others to have "breathing room" to be themselves without being concerned about others' motives for interaction.
- **C** = *Continuously seeks ways to learn more and educate others about diversity.* Multicultural competence requires that individuals take the time and desire to educate themselves about other cultures, worldviews, histories, and experiences. This is a lifelong learning process that allows the individual to continually be open to recognize, reconnect with, and recommit to being able to work with humans, not specific groups.

With an increasing look at how the global economy is affected by social diversity, it is clear that there has to be a more intentional eye on improved cultural relationships in order to advance a better understanding of those who share the planet. In their research on diversity, Cooper and Leong (2008) explored how diversity affects organizational consulting psychology. They consider that given the changing cultural landscape—including the increase in numbers of individuals from different cultural backgrounds—psychologists working with organizations who want to improve their efficiency in the global marketplace, better engage their customers and target markets, and increase their profits and professional competitiveness have to consider the role of an increasingly diverse workforce in their companies. What can be found in similar studies like Cooper and Leong's (2008) is that if a group of individuals (e.g., corporations, political groups, religious systems) is not motivated to integrate with other cultures, this can lead to what Crisp and Turner (2011) refer to as acculturative stress. Another way to view acculturative stress is cognitive dissonance (Festinger, 1957; Gawronski, 2012).

In research on what happens when a person adapts to social and cultural diversity, the person's cognitive functioning, as well as his/her behavior, is affected (Crisp & Turner, 2011; Searle & Ward, 1990). According to Crisp and Turner (2011), it was found that those who are able to be cognitively flexible – dually think in terms of their experience and the experience of others—were better prepared to question the "sociopolitical climate" (p. 261) and social "creativity strategies [necessary] to affect social change" (p. 261). This suggests that the person who is multiculturally competent will not necessarily have an easier time navigating social circles, nor will they be accepted in all social circles, but they will have the cognitive ability to assess stereotypical attitudes and discriminatory behavior. This is one of the reasons why students and professionals are required to gain a global perspective as long as they are engaging people of diverse backgrounds. It is also one of the reasons why research in this area continues to grow (Nelson, 2005; Leigh et al., 1996; Bowman, 2009; Esmiol, Knudsen-Martin, & Delgado, 2012).

There are those who wonder if being multiculturally competent means being insincere, unrealistic, or "dumbing down" one's value system. Quite the contrary. The multiculturally competent can acknowledge that a person who is hard of hearing or who was born into the deaf community may not desire to have cochlear implants even though this surgery would improve the person's ability to hear. Without a judgment base, the multiculturally competent individual would be able to appreciate that (a) everyone has and makes choices, (b) the assumption that hearing is better than not hearing is based on a discriminatory (audism) worldview, and (c) there is more than one way to "hear."

COMPETENCE IS MORE THAN AWARENESS

As discussed earlier, educational institutions have standardized practices for ensuring that students receive a well-rounded education. They do this by exposing students to science, language, music, and global citizenry. These types of practices make it possible for students to become aware of and

Simply learning a language is not sufficient to suggest understanding, appreciation and ability to work with a culture different from one's own. Awareness suggests knowledge; competence, the use of the "bottom-up" approach.

knowledgeable about of the diversity of experiences that people have in the world. That awareness, however, does not equate to competence. Simply taking one diversity course does not suggest that a person is multiculturally competent any more than standing in a garage makes one a car. **Awareness** is a conscious process that takes place in the brain where neurons interact with one another so that a message is relayed to the brain regarding a particular item, feeling, or thought. While multicultural competence is also a conscious process—one has to be intentional about wanting to effectively engage people who are similar to or different from them—the key is intentionality. Competence takes place once a person has decided that it is important enough to be given undivided attention.

Similarly, multicultural competence is not to be confused with knowledge. Attaining **cultural knowledge** is *the act of gaining insight, and even experience, about a culture.* Taking two semesters of a foreign language makes a person more conversant in the language, but not necessarily knowledgeable about other aspects of the culture. Use of manner and appreciation for high-context or low-context communication is not usually taught in introductory language courses. Instead, the focus is on word recognition and usage. Some people may consider themselves bilingual because they know some words or phrases in another language. The test of true bilinguality, however, comes in not simply knowing when to respond during conversation, but sometimes knowing when not to.

Neither is multicultural competence the same as being culturally sensitive. **Cultural sensitivity** is the next step in awareness where an individual is knowledgeable about and becomes careful about cultural taboos and expectations when interacting with someone from a particular cultural group. Sensitivity is what encourages someone to open the door for someone who is in a wheelchair, but that sensitivity does not equate to a desire to become invested in learning about and working with members from that population.

Multicultural competence does require that awareness, knowledge, and sensitivity are included in building relationships and working with people who are from diverse backgrounds. However, the challenge to becoming multiculturally competent has been discussed as obtaining and using the ABCs of multicultural competence: having an appreciation for diverse populations, showing respectful behavior among diverse groups, and being committed to intentionally learn more about other cultures.

WHERE DO WE GO FROM HERE?

At this point, there are those who would ask, "Now that I know all of this information, what am I supposed to do with it?" The basic assumption about multicultural psychology is that *behavior takes place within a cultural context.* The way that people act and even think and feel is the result of socialization and responses to those expectations. Therefore if one can learn to hold stereotypical views, engage in discriminatory practices, and revel in the 'isms, then one is capable of *unlearning* these behaviors. What is necessary is that (a) correct information be made available, (b) a desire to change one's belief model, (c) a willingness to adjust one's cultural mirror in order to correctly observe and understand the diverse community in which one lives, and (d) taking advantage of opportunities to learn and grow with the changing global landscape.

1. Conduct an honest self-assessment of you and your cultural group(s).

    Humans, typically, are not prone to assessing themselves. Whereas they may look at other people to determine a self-identity, it is rare that—without provocation—a person will honestly assess his or her own character, goals and desires, strengths and weaknesses. Where these self-assessments may sometimes be seen during psychology or sociology assignments and in preparation for job interviews. When one conducts a self-assessment, it is with the intent to find out more about oneself. Who is the individual? What does the individual know about her family of origin? What does the individual's name (first, middle, last) mean? How was the person nicknamed? What are the person's favorite colors, foods, entertainment, values? The overarching question for the latter questions is why?

    In conducting an honest self-assessment, the individual must come face-to-face with the reality that he (a) might not know the answers, (b) is not invested in finding the answers, or (c) has taken for granted that the culture into which he has been taught has indelibly determined his fate. This is not an exhaustive list, but one that is included to suggest that there are as many reasons for "why" as there are people to answer them.

2. Identify diverse cultural dynamics that can help to better understand the histories of disenfranchised groups.

    According to the WorldBank (2009), life expectancy rates are increasing, with U.S. citizens expecting to live an average of 78.7 years. Globally, that number decreases to 69.7 years. Because people are living longer in certain areas of the world, this allows more time for them to reevaluate their lives. Each day is replete with hints that prove that no one knows everything. Yet, with the advent of a more technological age comes access to information and materials that once took weeks or months or longer to acquire. In the new, "flat" world (Friedman, 2007), anyone can access information on the World Wide Web in less time than it would take to access hard copy materials in a library. Instead of remarking how unusual a particular culture's practice, why not perform a search on the culture using the computer to gain knowledge about it?

3. Expect to become more aware of practices, programs, procedures, and other systemic operations at work in politics, institutions, and the general society.

    Cognitive dissonance theory points to the fact that inconsistent thoughts about a subject leads to aversive arousal creating a desire to decrease the inconsistent in favor of a preferable outcome. It becomes important with respect to multicultural psychology when one considers its contribution to the stereotypes (thoughts) and prejudices (feelings) that serve as a basis for people's belief systems. For instance, if someone held the ableist belief that it is better to see than to be blind, what does that say about the talented intellectuals, entertainers and corporate moguls who had visual impairments (e.g., Helen Keller, Stevie Wonder, Ronnie Milsap, Marla Runyan, José Feliciano, Andrea Bocelli). David Paterson, former governor of New York, was once quoted as saying, "I'm blind, not oblivious" (*Meet the Press*, 2009).

In March 1988, hundreds of student and advocates for the deaf community engaged in a protest that would oust Gallaudet University President Elisabeth Zinser (Shapiro, 1988). Dr. Zinser, to the chagrin of the students, faculty, and alumni, at Gallaudet was not from the deaf community. In fact, for months leading to the selection of the president, many at Gallaudet had vocalized the desire to have a deaf president at the helm. In an act that shocked and perplexed

This man represents many cultures, but society mainly may recognize only one of them as being important.

the nation, Gallaudet students staged a very public protest that led to Dr. Zinser's separation from the university. Many in the hearing community who witnessed the protest via the media did not understand why such a demonstration would take place at the liberal arts college founded for the deaf in 1864. This type of change to an institutional (i.e., business, government, college) culture suggests that working within a culture is the best way to facilitate change (Kezar & Eckel, 2002). However, this work must take place from a position of understanding, appreciation, and willingness to cooperatively consider cultural values, norms, and expectations.

Guidelines on Multicultural Education, Training, Research, Practice, and Organizational Change for Psychologists (APA, 2002)

Guideline 1: Psychologists are encouraged to recognize that, as cultural beings, they may hold attitudes and beliefs that can detrimentally influence their perceptions of and interactions with individuals who are ethnically and racially different from themselves.

Guideline 2: Psychologists are encouraged to recognize the importance of multicultural sensitivity/responsiveness, knowledge, and understanding about ethnically and racially different individuals.

Guideline 3: As educators, psychologists are encouraged to employ the constructs of multiculturalism and diversity in psychological education.

Guideline 4: Culturally sensitive psychological researchers are encouraged to recognize the importance of conducting culture-centered and ethical psychological research among persons from ethnic, linguistic, and racial minority backgrounds.

Guideline 5: Psychologists strive to apply culturally appropriate skills in clinical and other applied psychological practices.

In an effort to better understand the world, explore (your assumptions; others' values) and grow.

FINAL WORDS

Throughout this text, you have been asked to consider the role and goal of understanding psychology from a cultural perspective. As a student, you are charged by an institution to consider what the institution has to offer, how the you can best utilize the available resources, and plan to maximize those resources in order to what? The goal of higher education is to become a better citizen; a more successful student; or a more proficient professional who is invested in training others to do likewise. What about being all three at once?

Most research on the psychology of culture has focused on individual questions about what makes a culture a culture. At the heart of the individual questions comes a need to better critically consider and understand how to improve group relations. In both cross- and multicultural psychology, the intent has been to present cultural research in a way that suggests that there are no "big I's and little U's." Instead, the media portrays the "us vs them" principle with popular television shows like "Survivor," "The Biggest Loser," in sports and entertainment, and even family game shows, demonstrating the importance of conquering over appreciating and learning about others.

Social psychology is replete with studies that examine the importance of social ties and relationships. It may surprise you that we have barely unlocked the adjoining doors that connect the totality of multicultural psychology. There is much more to be discovered, researched, and understood.

Since its early beginnings, multicultural psychology has continued to take an intentional look at how to raise awareness of the issues of race/ethnicity, age, class, ability, gender, sexual orientation, religion, and communication styles (D'Andrea & Heckman, 2008; Esmiol et al., 2012; Reichert, 2012). Simply consider the fact that research suggests that college students suffer disproportionately from depression (Reichert, 2012) and financial instability (Mahmoud, Staten, & Lennie, 2012). The college student culture is one that is often overlooked as a cultural group, although several research studies are undertaken each year to better understand the thoughts, attitudes, feelings, and behaviors of this group. Consider what other cultural groups go unnoticed or underecognized and why these stigmatizing behaviors continue. Then, take the next step to becoming multiculturally competent as you reflect on humanity.

SUMMARY

Several books have been written about the globalization of the world. Even Thomas Friedman's prolific book *The World Is Flat* (2007) opened the readers' eyes to see that what was previously perceived as impossible is now possible. The thought of communicating in "real time" with someone on the "other side of the world" has become a reality just as the increase in ability to forge relationships and global citizenry with those we previously saw as "weird" or "different." Yet, just as those in the time of Christopher Columbus were not sure whether they wanted to pursue the exploration of the world past its flatness, so many people cannot see past the values and assumptions they have made about people from cultures that differ from theirs.

In order to develop a better sense of humanity, multicultural psychology has accepted the challenge to explore cultural diversity from a psychological perspective; search past the unfamiliar and unattractive stigmas in society that keep discrimination and privilege alive; and welcome the possibility to improve social interactions between cultural groups. Whether walking across the street to speak to a neighbor who comes from a different experience from yours or flying across the world to discover that same wonder requires a decision to be made.

Multicultural competence, a practice that is required globally, seeks to ensure that a professional is able and willing to work effectively with people from various backgrounds. While it is not important for the professional to experience the values, history, customs or practices of the culture in order to be multiculturally competent, the person does have to demonstrate a willingness to be respectful and civil in interactions with other cultural groups.

Glossary

ABCs of multiculturally competent   Appreciates others; behaves in a way that respects others; continues learning.

ABCs of psychology   Affect (feelings), behavior (actions), cognition (thoughts) that describe what psychologists study.

accessible   Describes buildings and other facilities that may be easily used by people with disabilities such as those confined to a wheelchair.

ACE Study, the   Adverse Childhood Experiences Study; an ongoing investigation of the link between childhood maltreatment and health later in life.

acculturation   The contact between individuals from different cultures and the changes that take place as a result of that contact.

acquiescences bias   The tendency to agree rather than disagree with items on questionnaires.

affect   Feelings; emotions.

ageism   Discriminatory actions, thoughts, and statements directed against people based on their age.

allocentric   Philosophical view where an individual acts or feels that the needs of his or her group are more important than his or her individual needs.

allocentrism   How individuals may act in accordance with collectivistic cultural frameworks.

American Psychological Association (APA)   Scientific and professional organization that supports the study, research, and practice of psychologists.

arranged marriage   Practice where parents choose marital partners for their children.

attention deficit hyperactivity disorder (ADHD)   A developmental disability that interferes with learning due to short attention spans and other problems.

awareness   A conscious process that takes place in the brain where neurons interact with one another so that a message is relayed to the brain regarding a particular item, feeling, or thought.

Baby Boomer   Generation of people born post-World War II , between 1946–1964.

Baby Buster   (See "Generation X".)

back translation   A technique of translating research protocols that involves taking the protocol as it was developed in one language, translating it into the target language, and having someone else translate it back to the original.

behavior   Actions; things people do.

behaviorism   Psychological theory based on individual's desire to observe, control, and measure behavior; developed by John B. Watson. B. F. Skinner is another prominent behavioral theorist.

bias   Differences that do not have exactly the same meaning, within and across cultures; a lack of equivalence.

bilateral kinship system   Family heritage traced through both father and mother.

bilingual education   A program designed to allow students to learn academic concepts in their native language while they learn a second language.

bilingualism   The use of two or more languages in places of work or education and the treatment of each language as legitimate.

brain drain   Immigration to the United States of skilled workers, professionals, and technicians who are desperately needed by their home countries.

chain immigration   Immigrants sponsor several other immigrants who upon their arrival may sponsor still more.

civility   Formal politeness; demonstrating respect and showing manners in the presence of others.

cognition   Thoughts; the process of thinking.

cognitive dissonance   An uncomfortable feeling one gets when holding two or more contradictory beliefs about something.

cohabitation   Living together.

cohort effects   Influences on study participants' reflection generational differences. These may confound or interfere with conclusions when a study is complete.

collectivistic   Worldview that supports the value of the needs of the entire group instead of individuals within the group.

communication   The process by which information is exchanged.

conceptual bias   The degree to which a theory or set of hypotheses being compared across cultures is equivalent.

conflict perspective   Members of society function best when they are in competition with each other instead of in cooperation.

conscious   Aware; awake; ability to interact with the environment.

contextual factors   Any variable that can explain, partly or fully, observed cross-cultural differences.

context variables   Variables that operationalize aspects of culture that researchers believe produce differences in psychological variables.

cross-cultural comparisons   A study that compares two or more cultures on some psychological variable of interest, often with the hypothesis that one culture will have significantly higher scores on the variable than the other(s).

cross-cultural validation study   A study that examines whether a measure of a psychological construct that was originally generated in a single culture is applicable, meaningful, and thus equivalent in another culture.

cult   Social movement or group whose beliefs or practices are considered abnormal or bizarre by the society. Short for "culture."

cultural attribution fallacies   A mistaken interpretation in cross-cultural comparison studies. Cultural attribution fallacies occur when researchers infer that something cultural produced the differences they observed in their study, despite their not being empirically justified in doing so because they did not actually measure those cultural factors.

cultural knowledge   The act of gaining insight, and even experience, about a culture.

cultural sensitivity   The next step in awareness where an individual is knowledgeable about and becomes careful about cultural taboos and expectations when interacting with someone from a particular cultural group.

culture   The shared, patterned, and historically reproduced symbolic practices that facilitate meaningful human existence.

decenter   The concept underlying the procedure of back translation that involves eliminating any culture-specific concepts of the original language or translating them equivalently into the target language.

denomination (religious)   Subgroup of a particular religion that operates in name, beliefs, traditions, and practices.

developmental disabilities   A diverse group of severe and chronic conditions resulting in mental and physical impairment. May include learning, language development, mobility, and self-help.

diverse   Varied; having differences

domestic violence   Aggressive physical, social, or psychological coercion of a family member or partner. It includes child abuse and spousal abuse.

ecclesia   Latin for "the called out ones"; church group.

ecological- (cultural-) level studies   A study in which countries or cultures, not individuals, are the unit of analysis.

emic   An approach that assumes there is one way to do things because the particular "thing" comes from the perspective of members of the same group who have determined that their way is the right way.

ethnicity   A group of people who share a common trait like values, customs, language, traditions, beliefs, or rituals.

ethnoreligious groups   Extreme form of exclusive religious groups (e.g., Hasidic Jews, Amish) whose goal is to withdraw from society in order to maintain their distinctiveness.

equivalence   A state or condition of similarity in conceptual meaning and empirical method between cultures that allows comparison to be meaningful; a lack of bias.

etic   An approach that assumes the way to do something based on an "outsider's" view; attempts universal knowledge and application.

experiments   Studies in which researchers create conditions to establish cause–effect relationships.

exploratory studies   Studies designed to examine the existence of cross-cultural similarities or differences.

extreme response bias   The tendency to use the ends of a scale regardless of item content.

factor analysis   A statistical technique that allows researchers to identify groups of items on a questionnaire.

5 Ds of difference   Harrell's model that explains why people have a difficult time interacting with people who do not share their values, beliefs, traditions, or history.

FMLA Family Medical Leave Act of 1993; first law to recognize the need of families to care for their children and other dependents.

functionalism Theory based on how the human mind adapts to its environment; theory developed by William James in late 19th/early 20th century.

Generation X (also "Baby Buster") Generation of people born between 1965 and 1980.

geriatrics A medical specialty dealing with health problems of the aged.

gerontology The scientific study of aging or of old age.

globalization Worldwide integration of government policies, cultures, social movements, and financial markets through trade, movements of people, and the exchange of ideas.

heterogamy Mate preference between two people who are dissimilar in social and demographic characteristics.

homogamy Mate preference where the mates have similar social characteristics.

humanism Theory based on the assumption that the individual is the central focus of psychology and that human potential is possible in all individuals; developed by Abraham Maslow and Carl Rogers in the mid-20th century.

hypothesis-testing studies Studies designed to test why cultural differences exist.

idiocentric Philosophical view where an individual is more concerned with his or her interest being met than that of others.

idiocentrism Refers to individualism on the individual level. On the cultural level, individualism refers to how a culture functions.

indigenous See *native*.

indigenous cultural studies Studies that use rich, complex, and in-depth descriptions of cultures and cultural differences to predict and test for differences in a psychological variable.

individualistic Worldview that supports a cognitive appreciation for individual achievement and personal success that becomes a part of the behavior of the culture.

individual-level measures of culture Measures that assess psychological dimensions related to meaningful dimensions of cultural variability and that are completed by individuals.

intelligence Way of thinking that allows one to understand and apply knowledge to new situations.

internal reliability The degree to which different items in a questionnaire are related to each other, and give consistent responses.

interventions Strategies; ways to help do something get done differently.

kinship system Pattern of relationships that define people's family relationships to one another

level-oriented studies Studies that examine cultural differences in mean levels of variables.

liberation theology A belief system that focuses on unshackling those who are poor and oppressed in the world.

life expectancy Estimation of amount of time one has to live. It is a calculation commonly used to assess health differences by race, ethnicity, and national origin by the U.S. Department of Health and Human Services.

linguistic bias The semantic equivalence between protocols (instruments, instructions, questionnaires, etc.) used in a cross-cultural comparison study.

linkage studies   Studies that attempt to measure an aspect of culture theoretically hypothesized to produce cultural differences and then empirically link that measured aspect of culture with the dependent variable of interest.

macro   Big; large scale.

majority   The group that makes up more than half of a population.

matrilineal kinship system   Family heritage traced through the mother.

measurement bias   The degree to which measures used to collect data in different cultures are equally valid and reliable.

micro   Small; minor scale.

minority   The group that makes up less than half of the population.

mixed status   Families in which one or more members are citizens and one or more are noncitizens.

monogamy   Marriage practice of a sexually exclusive marriage with one spouse at a time.

multicultural   Belonging to more than one cultural group.

multicultural competence   A behavior that requires a cognitive (thought) and affective (feelings) appreciation for cultural groups

multicultural psychology   The scientific study of how groups identify, create, and engage in cultural activities and values when they are in the same group or in different groups.

multilevel studies   Studies that involve data collection at multiple levels of analysis, such as the individual level, context, community, and national culture.

native   Someone or something that was the original.

nativism   Beliefs and policies favoring native-born citizens over immigrants.

naturalization   Conferring of citizenship on a person after birth.

nuclear family   Family in which the parents and children live in the same household.

operationalization   The ways researchers conceptually define a variable and measure it.

paradigm   A philosophical assumption about something.

paradigm shift   A change in the philosophical assumption of something based on the acquisition of new or updated information.

patrilineal kinship system   Family heritage traced through the father.

polyandry   Marriage of a woman to two or more husbands.

polygamy   Marriage of one person to two or more people of the opposite sex.

polygyny   Marriage of a man to two or more wives.

priming studies   Studies that involve experimentally manipulating the mind-sets of participants and measuring the resulting changes in behavior.

procedural bias   The degree to which the procedures used to collect data in different cultures are equivalent to each other.

profane   That which is of the everyday world and is specifically not religious.

psychoanalytic   Theory based on the assumption that instinct, early childhood experiences, and the unconscious influence human behavior; developed by Sigmund Freud in the late 19th/early 20th century.

psychology   The scientific study of behavior and mental processes.

psychometric equivalence   The degree to which different measures used in a cross-cultural comparison study are statistically equivalent in the cultures being compared, that is, whether the measures are equally valid and reliable in all cultures studied.

quinceañera   The Latin American celebration of the transition from childhood to womanhood.

race   The arbitrary categorization of the human species based on observable physical differences.

racial identity   The degree to which one identifies with other people who have been socially categorized in the same racial group and how much one identifies with the different cultural aspects of his or her race.

reference group effect   The idea that people make implicit social comparisons with others when making ratings on scales. That is, people's ratings will be influenced by the implicit comparisons they make between themselves and others, and these influences may make comparing responses across cultures difficult.

refugees   People living outside their country of citizenship for fear of political or religious persecution.

reliability   The degree to which a finding, measurement, or statistic is consistent.

religion   An institutional system of symbols, beliefs, values, and practices by which a group of people interpret and respond to what they feel is sacred and provides answers to questions of ultimate meaning.

remittances   The monies that immigrants return to their country of origin.

RESPECTFUL   A model designed by D'Andrea and Heckman (2008) to describe factors to be considered when working with diverse populations: R = religious/spiritual issue; E = economic/class issues; S = sexual identity issues; P = psychological development issues; E = ethnic/racial identity issues; C = chronological issues; T = trauma and threats to well-being; F = family issues; U = unique physical issues; and L = language and location of residence issues.

response bias   A systematic tendency to respond in certain ways to items or scales.

sacred   That which is set apart from ordinary activity, seen as holy, and protected by special rites and privileges.

sample   A set or portion of a larger group.

sampling bias   The degree to which different samples in different cultures are equivalent to each other.

sexism   Discriminatory actions, thoughts, and statements directed against people based on their biological status as a female or male.

sexual harassment   Offensive and unwanted behavior directed toward a person, including words and actions that induce shame and fear.

sexual violence   Forced and violent assaults such as rate; usually committed by males against females.

sickle cell disease   A hereditary blood disease in which blood cells are abnormally shaped. It occurs mainly in people of African descent and cases a form of anemia.

Silent Generation   Generation of people born between the Great Depression (1925) and World War II (1942).

sinophobes   People with a fear of anything associated with China.

socially desirable responding   Tendencies to give answers on questionnaires that make oneself look good.

social majority   The group that holds the most social power.

social minority   The group that holds less social power.

social structure   The organizational components within which people live. The term includes the political, economic, family/kinship, religious, and educational systems of a nation or country.

structural equivalence   The degree to which a measure used in a cross-cultural study produces the same factor analysis results in the different countries being compared.

structuralism   Theory of the role of mind and consciousness; theory developed by Wilhelm Wundt in the late 19th/early 20th century.

structure-oriented studies   Studies that examine whether constructs are conceptualized the same way across cultures, the relationship of a construct to other constructs, or the measurement of a construct.

therapy   Interventions that lead a person to make changes in his or her behavior, thoughts, or feelings.

top-down approach   A process that uses previous experience or prior knowledge to form the basis for the person's knowledge.

transnationals   Mmigrants who sustain multiple social relationships that link their societies of origin and settlement.

unconscious   Unaware; inability to interact with the environment due to lack of attention or focus.

uniracial   Belonging to one race.

universal design   Design of products and environments to make them usable regardless of body dimension, age, or disability status.

unpackaging studies   Studies that unpackage the contents of the global, unspecific concept of culture into specific, measurable psychological constructs and examine their contribution to cultural differences.

validity   The degree to which a finding, measurement, or statistic is accurate, or represents what it is supposed to.

value orientations   Term coined by Kluckhohn and Strodtbeck (1961) that suggests the different cultures hold particular perspectives.

White privilege   Unearned societal benefits given to the Caucasian race that are not offered to those of other races.

worldview   Cultural perspectives that determine how people perceive and respond to what happens around them.

xenophobia   The fear or hatred of strangers or foreigners.

Bibliography

—. (April 2, 2009) http://www.nbcnews.com/id/30017148/ns/world_news-europe/t/michelle-obama-charms-britain-hugs-queen/#.U3S_CP3D85s

—. (2009, April 2). http://articles.cnn.com/2009–04-02/living/michelle.obama.queen_1_michelle-obama-britain-s-queen-elizabeth-ii-buckingham-palace?_s=PM:LIVING

Adams, P. F., Lucas, J. W., & Barnes, P. M. (2008). Summary health statistics for the U.S. population: National Health Interview Survey, 2006. National Center for Health Statistics. *Vital Health Statistics 10* (236).

Agronick, G. S., & Duncan, L. E. (1998). Personality and social change: Individual differences, life path, and importance attributed to the women's movement. *Journal Of Personality And Social Psychology, 74*(6), 1545–1555. doi:10.1037/0022–3514.74.6.1545

Alexander, L. L., LaRosa, J. H., Bader, H., & Garfield, S. (2004). *New dimensions in women's health* (3rd ed.). Sudbury, MA: Jones and Bartlett.

Allgower, A., Wardle, J., & Steptoe, A. (2001). Depressive symptoms, social support, and personal health behaviors in young men and women. *Health Psychology, 20,* 223–227.

American Anthropology Association Statement on Race (1998). Retrieved from http://www.aaanet.org/stmts/racepp.htm.

American Psychological Association. (2011). *Answers to your questions about transgender people, gender identity and gender expressions.* Washington, DC: Author. Retrieved from http://www.apa.org/topics/sexuality/transgender.pdf.

American Psychological Association. (2008). *Answers to your questions: For a better understanding of sexual orientation and homosexuality. Washington, DC: Author. Retrieved from www.apa.org/topics/sorientation.pdf.*

American Psychological Association (APA) (2003). Guidelines on multicultural education, training, research, practice and organizational change for psychologists. American Psychologist, vol. 58, pp. 377–402.

Ardilla, R. (2007). The nature of psychology: The great dilemmas. American Psychologist, vol. 62(8), pp. 906–912.

Arendale, M. (2008). Am I Still Latina? Retrieved from http://web.trinity.edu/Documents/student_affairs_docs/CCI_docs/Diversity/Am%20I%20Still%20Latina_%20An%20Immigrant's%20Path%20into%20White%20Habitus.pdf

Armstrong, T. L. and Swartzman, L. C, (2001). Cross-cultural differences in illness models and expectations for health care provider-client/patient interaction. In Kazarian, S.S. and Evans, D.R. (eds) Handbook of Cultural Health. CA: Academic Press, pp. 64–80.

Aronson, J., Burgess, D., Phelan, S. M., & Juarez, L. (2013). Unhealthy Interactions: The Role of Stereotype Threat in Health Disparities. *American Journal of Public Health, 103*(1), 50–56. doi:10.2105/AJPH.2012.300828

Associated Press (April 18, 2007). Deaf woman sentenced to life in prison. NBC News. http://www.nbcnews.com/id/18180658/ns/us_news-crime_and_courts/t/deaf-woman-sentenced-life-prison/

Beebe, S. A., Beebe, S. J., & Ivy, D. K. (2012). Communication: Principles for a lifetime (5th ed.). Boston, MA: Pearson, pp. 135–63

Bennett, M. J. (2008). Intercultural communication: A current perspective. In J. Q. Adams and P. Strother-Adams' Dealing with Diversity (2nd ed). Dubuque, IA: Kendall-Hunt, pp. 33–52

Berger, R. M. (1990). Passing: Impact on the Quality of Same-Sex Couple Relationships. *Social Work, 35*(4), 328–332.

Berry, J. W. (1997). Immigration, acculturation, and adaptation. *Applied Psychology: An International Review, 46*, 5–34.

Blankenship, M. (2006). Children of a Lesser God. Variety. 406(6), 57.

Blatchford, C. (1997). Many Ways of Hearing: 94 Multi-tasked Lessons in Hearing. ME: Walsh.

Boston Women's Health Collective (1973). *Our bodies, ourselves: A book for and by women.* New York: Simon and Schuster.

Bowman, N. A. (2009). College diversity courses and cognitive development among students from privileged and marginalized groups. *Journal of Diversity in Higher Education, 2,* 182–194.

Boysen, G. A.,Vogel, D. L., Cope, M. A., Hubbard, A. (2009). Incidents of bias in college classrooms: Instructor and student perceptions. Journal of Diversity in Higher Education, vol. 2, pp. 219–231.

Brewster, M. E., Velez, B., DeBlaere, C., & Moradi, B. (2012). Transgender individuals' workplace experiences: The applicability of sexual minority measures and models. *Journal of Counseling Psychology, 59*(1), 60–70. doi:10.1037/a0025206

Brown, R. T., Mulhern, R. K., & Simonian, S. (2002). Diseases of the blood and bloodforming organs. In S. B. Johnson, N. W. Perry, Jr., & R. H. Rozensky (Eds.), *Handbook of clinical health psychology* (Vol. 1, pp. 101–141). Washington, DC: American Psychological Association.

Cameroon News (March 9, 2013). Sodomy laws violate basic human rights. http://news.cameroon-today.com/cameroon-human-rights-news-sodomy-violation-of-basic-human-rights/5857/. Obtained March 9, 2013.

Carter, K., & Seifert, K. M. (2013). Learning psychology. Burlington, MA: Jones-Bartlett.

Carter, S. L. (1998). Civility: Manners, morals, and the etiquette of democracy. New York: Basic Books.

Cass, V. (1979). Homosexual identity formation: A theoretical model. *Journal of Homosexuality, 4*(3), 219–235.

Cauce, A. M. (2011). Is multicultural psychology a-scientific?: Diverse methods for diversity research. Cultural Diversity and Ethnic Minority Psychology, vo. 17, pp. 228–233.

Census Bureau, Census 2000 Brief: Overview of Race and Hispanic Origin, 2001.

Centers for Disease Control. (2005a). National diabetes fact sheet: General information and national estimates on diabetes in the United States, 2005. Atlanta, GA: U.S. Department of Health and Human Services.

Centers for Disease Control. (2005b). HIV Infection Reporting. Retrieved May 5, 2007 from http://www.cdc.gov/hiv/topics/surveillance/reporting.htm

Centers for Disease Control. (2006a). Cigarette use among adults—United States, 2005. *Mortality and Morbidity Weekly Report,* 55(42), 1145–1148.

Centers for Disease Control. (2006b). Cigarette use among high school students—United States, 1991–2005. *Mortality and Morbidity Weekly Report,* 55(26), 724–726.

Centers for Disease Control, National Center for Health Statistics. (2007). Deaths: Leading Causes for 2003. Retrieved May 5, 2007 from http://www.cdc.gov/nchs/products/pubs/pubc/hestats/leading

Centers for Disease Control. (2008a). Understanding Sexual Violence. Retrieved April 15, 2008 from http://www.cdc.gov/injury

Centers for Disease Control. (2008b). Disabilities, National Center on Birth Defects and Developmental Disabilities. Retrieved April 15, 2008 from http://www.cdc.gov/ncbddd

Centers for Disease Control. (2008c). Childhood Overweight. Retrieved April 15, 2008 from http://www.cdc.gov/nccdphp/dnpa/obesity/childhood/index.htm

Centers for Disease Control. (2008d). Healthy Youth! Health Topics: Youth. Retrieved April 15, 2008 from http://www.cdc.gov/Healthy Youth

Centers for Disease Control. (2008e). Healthy Aging for Older Adults. Retrieved August 29, 2008 from http://www.cdc.gov/aging

Centers for Disease Control. (2008f). Adverse Childhood Experiences Study. Retrieved October 26, 2008.

Chandra, A., Mosher, W., Copen, C., & Sionean, C. (2011). Sexual behavior, sexual attraction and sexual identity in the United States: Data from the 2006–2008 National Survey of Family Growth. *National Health Statistics Reports, 36*. Hyattsville, MD: National Center for Health Statistics.

Chung, Y. B. (2006). External-internal control. In Y, Jackson (Ed.) Encyclopedia of Multicultural Psychology. Thousand Oaks, CA: Sage, p. 209.

Ciccarelli, S., & White, N. (2011). *Psychology.* 3rd edition. Belmont, CA: Pearson/Prentice Hall. (ISBN-10: 0205832571)

Citizenship and Naturalization Services. (2013). Retrieved from WWW.USCIS.com Franklin, F. (1906). *The legislative history of naturalization in the United States: From the Revolutionary War to 1861.* Chicago: University of Chicago Press.

Clements-Nolle, K., Marx, R., & Katz, M. (2006). Attempted suicide among transgender persons. *Journal of Homosexuality, 51*, 53–69. doi:10.1300/J082v51n03_04

Comas-Diaz, L. (2009). Changing psychology: History and legacy of the society for the psychological study of ethnic minority issues. Cultural Diversity and Ethnic Minority Psychology, vol. 15, pp. 400–408.

Cooper, S. and Leong, F. T. L. (June 2008). Introduction to the special issue on culture, race, and ethnicity in organizational consulting psychology. Consulting Psychology Journal: Practice and Research, vol. 60, no. 2, pp. 133–138.

Crisp, R. J., and Turner, R. N. (2011). Cognitive adaptation to the experience of social and cultural diversity. Psychological Bulletin, vol. 137, no. 2, pp. 242–266.

Crooks, R., & Baur, K. (2002). *Our sexuality*. 8th edition. Pacific Grove, CA: Wadsworth. (ISBN: 0-534-57978-7).

Cross, W. E., Jr. (1971). Toward a psychology of Black liberation: The Negro-to-Black conversion experience. *Black World, 20,* 13–27.

Cross, W. E., Jr. (1991). *Shades of Black: Diversity in African-American identity*. Philadelphia: Temple University Press.

Curry, C. (2012). Rutgers Trial: Clementi May Never Have Seen Ravi's Apology. Retrieved from http://abcnews.go.com/US/rutgers-students-apology-suicide-written-minutes/story?id=15871532

D'Andrea, M. and Heckman, E.F. (2008). A 40-year review of multicultural counseling outcome research: Outlining a future research agenda for the multicultural counseling movement. Journal of Counseling and Development., Volume 86, Issue 3, pages 356–363.

Davetian, B. (2009). Civility: A cultural history (1st ed.). Toronto, Canada: University of Toronto Press.

Davis, S. (1999). The therapeutic use of androgens in women. *Journal of Steroid Biochemistry and Molecular Biology, 69,* 177–184.

Day, R. D., Peterson, G. W., & McCracken, C. (1998). Predicting spanking of younger and older children by mothers and fathers. *Journal of Marriage and the Family, 60,* 79– 94.

DeNavas, C., Proctor, B., & Smith, J. (2011). Income, Poverty, and Health Insurance Coverage in the United States: 2010. Retrieved from http://www.census.gov/prod/2011pubs/p60–239.pdf

Dreger, A. (1999). *Intersex in the age of ethics.* Hagerstown, MD: University Publishing Groups.

Dresser, N. (1996). Multicultural manners: New Rules of Etiquette for a Changing Society. New York, NY: Wiley Press.

Dykes, B. (2000). Problems in defining cross-culture "kinds of homosexuality"—and a solution. *Journal of Homosexuality, 38,* 1–18.

Eadie, W. F. (2010). In plain sight: Gay and lesbian communication and culture. In Samovar, L.A., Porter, R. E., & McDaniel, E. R. (Eds) Intercultural Communication: A Reader (13th ed.). Boston, MA: Cengage.

Ekman, P. E. (2009). Telling Lies: Clues to Deceit in the Marketplace, Politics, and Marriage. NY: W. W. Norton & Company.

Eliason, M. & Schope, R. (2006). Shifting sands or solid foundation? Lesbian, gay, bisexual, and transgender identity formation.

Emmons, K. M. (2000). Health behaviors in a social context. In L. F. Berkman & I. Kawachi (Eds.), *Social epidemiology* (pp. 242–266). NY: Oxford University Press.

Esmiol, E. E., Kndson-Martin, C., & Delgado, S. (2012). Developing a contextual consciousness: Learning to address gender, societal power, and culture in clinical practice. Journal of Marital and Family Therapy, vol. 30, no. 4, pp. 573–588.

Etaugh, C. A., & Bridges, J. S. (2004). *The psychology of women: A lifetime perspective* (2nd ed.). Boston: Pearson.

Fabes, R. A., m school competence: The roles of sex-segregated play and effortful control. *Developmental Psychology, 39*(5), 848–858. doi:10.1037/0012-1649.39.5.848

Farberman, R. (2011). Bridging the multicultural gap. *Monitor on Psychology* 42(4). Retrieved from http://www.apa.org/monitor/2011/04/multicultural.aspx

Farmer, J. E., & Peterson, L. (1995). Injury risk factors in children with attention deficit hyperactivity disorder. *Health Psychology, 14,* 325–332.

Fassinger, R. (2005). Paradigms, praxis, problems and promise: Grounded theory in counseling psychology research. Journal of Counseling Psychology, vol. 52, pp. 156–166.

Federal Bureau of Investigation (2009). Hate Crime Statistics, 2009. (Washington, DC: GPO, 2010), Table 1, http://www2.fbi.gov/ucr/hc2009/abouthcs.html.

Federal Trade Commission (2011). Consumer Fraud and Identity Theft Complaint Data January through December 2010 (Washington, DC: GPO, 2011), 13, http://www.ftc.gov/sentinel/reports/sentinel-annual-reports/sentinel-cy2010.pdf

Fenderson, D. A. (1984). Rehabilitation services as ideology: A response to Stubbins, Coudroglou, and Berkowitz. *Rehabilitation Psychology, 29*(4), 217–219. doi:10.1037/h0091012

Fernhall, B. (2003). Mental retardation. In J. L. Durstine & G. E. Moore (Eds.), *ACSM exercise management for persons with chronic diseases and disabilities* (2nd ed. pp. 304–310). Champaign, IL: Human Kinetics.

Fisher, B. S., Cullen, F. T., & Turner, M. G. (2000). *The sexual victimization of college women* (Publication No.: NCH 182369). Washington, 43828_CH14_5183.qxd 11/13/08 10:25 AM Page 365. DC: Department of Justice, National Institute of Justice.

Fisher, E. B., Brownson, R. C., Heath, A. C., Luke, D. A., & Walton, S., II. (2004). Cigarette smoking. In J. M. Raczynski & L. C. Leviton (Eds.), *Handbook of clinical health psychology: Vol. 2.* (pp. 75–120). Washington, DC: American.

Flowers, B. J. and Richardson, F. C. (1996). Why is multiculturalism good? American Psychologist. Washington, DC: APA

Fone, B. (2000). *Homophobia: A History.* New York: Metropolitan Books.

Forni, P. M. (2008). The civility solution: What to do when people are rude. New York, NY: St. Martin's Press.

Forni, P. M. (2003). Choosing civility: The twenty-five rules of considerate conduct. New York, N.Y: St. Martin's Griffin.

Franklin, A. J. (2009). Reflections on ethnic minority psychology: Learning from our past so the present informs our future. Cultural Diversity and Ethnic Minority Psychology, vol 15, pp. 416–424.

Freedman, V., Martin, L., & Schoeni, R. (2004). Disability in America. Population Bulletin 59, 3.

Friedman, T. (2007). The world is flat. NY: Picador.

Gallant, S. J., Keita, G. P., & Royak-Schaler, R. (Eds.). (1997). *Health care for women: Psychological, social and behavioral influences.* Washington, DC: American Psychological Association.

Gates, G., & Newport, F. (2012). Special Report: 3.4% of U.S. Adults Identify as LGBT. Retrieved from http://www.gallup.com/poll/158066/special-report-adults-identify-lgbt.aspx

Gawronski, B. (2012). Back to the future of dissonance theory: Cognitive consistency as a core motive. Social Cognition, vol 30, no. 6, pp. 652–668.

Gilligan, C. (1982). *In a different voice: Psychological theory and women's development.* Cambridge, MA: Havard University Press.

Goldberg, S. G., Killeen, M. B., & O'Day, B. (2005). The disclosure conundrum: How people with psychiatric disabilities navigate employment. *Psychology, Public Policy, And Law, 11*(3), 463–500. doi:10.1037/1076–8971.11.3.463

Goldblum, P., Testa, R. J., Pflum, S., Hendricks, M. L., Bradford, J., & Bongar, B. (2012). The relationship between gender-based victimization and suicide attempts in transgender people. *Professional Psychology: Research And Practice, 43*(5), 468–475. doi:10.1037/a0029605

Goldstein, M.C. (1979). Pahari and Tibetian polyandry revisited. Ethnology, 17, pp. 325–337

Goldstein, Z. (n.d.). Basic Laws. Retrieved from http://www.chabad.org/library/article_cdo/aid/367836/jewish/Basic-Laws.htm

Gone, J. P. (2011). Is psychological science a-cultural? *Cultural Diversity And Ethnic Minority Psychology, 17*(3), 234–242. doi:10.1037/a0023805

Grice, H. P. (1996). Logic and conversation in H. Geirsson and M. Losonsky (ed.) Readings in language and mind. NY: Wiley, pp. 121–133.

Grice, H. P. (1975). Logic and conversation. In Martinich, A. P. (ed). Philosophy of Language. New York, NY: Oxford University Press, pp. 165–175.

Grison, S., Heatherton, T. F., and Gazzaniga, M. S. (2015). *Psychology in your life.* New York: Norton.

Guan, M., Lee, F., & Cole, E. R. (2012). Complexity of culture: The role of identity and context in bicultural individuals' body ideals. *Cultural Diversity And Ethnic Minority Psychology, 18*(3), 247–257. doi:10.1037/a0028730

Gudykunst, W. B., Matsumoto, Y., Ting-Toomey, S., Nishida, T., Kim, K., & Heyman, S. (1996). The influence of cultural individualism-collectivism, self-construals, and individual values on communication styles across cultures. Human Communication Research, 22(4), 510–543.

Hall, E. T. (1976). Beyond culture. New York: Doubleday.

Hall, E. T., & Hall, M. R. (1990). Understanding cultural differences. Yarmouth, ME: Intercultural Press Inc.

Hall, G. C. N. (2010). Multicultural psychology (2nd ed.). Upper Saddle River, NJ: Prentice Hall

Hall, L. E. (2005). The dictionary of multicultural psychology: issues, terms and concepts. Thousand Oaks, CA: Sage.

Harrell, E., Ph.D., & M. Rand. 2010. Crime against people with disabilities, 2008. Washington, DC: U.S. Department of Justice, Office of Justice Programs, Bureau of Justice Statistics.

Harrell, S. P., & Bond, M.A. (2006). Listening to diversity stories: Principles for practice in community research and action. American Journal of Community Psychology, vol. 37; pp. 365–376.

Harrell, S. (1995, August). Dynamics of difference: Personal and sociocultural dimension of intergroup relations. Paper presented at the 103rd Convention of the American Psychological Association. New York.

Hayes, P. (2007). Addressing cultural complexities in practice: Assessment, diagnosis, and therapy (2nd ed.). Washington, DC: American Psychological Association.

Healthy People 2010. Retrieved May 10, 2007 from http://www.healthypeople.gov/data/midcourse/html/introduction.htm

Helms, J. E. (1984). Toward a theoretical explanation of the effects of race on counseling: A Black and White model. *The Counseling Psychologist, 12*, 153–165.

Helms, J. E. (1993). An overview of Black racial identity theory. In J. E. Helms (Ed.). *Black and White racial Identity*. Westport, CT: Praeger Publishers.

Herbert Adams, C. and Jones, P. D. (2011). Therapeutic communication for health professionals, (3rd ed.) New York, NY: McGraw-Hill.

Herek, G., Kimmel, D., Amaro, H., & Melton, G. (1991). Avoiding heterosexual bias in psychological research. *American Psychologist, 46*, 957–963.

Hixson, L., Hepler, B., & Kim, M. O. (2012). The Native Hawaiian and Other Pacific Islander Population: 2010. Retrieved from http://www.census.gov/prod/cen2010/briefs/c2010br-12.pdf

Hodge, M. (2007, December 14). The Matthew Shepard Act. *Anderson Edition*. Retrieved from http://www.samesexliving.com/matthew%20shepard%20act.jpg

Hofstede, G. (1980). Culture's Consequences: International Differences in Work-Related Values. Beverly Hills, CA: Sage.

Hornsby, B. W. Y. (2013). The effects of hearing aid use on listening effort and mental fatigue associated with sustained speech processing demands. Earing & Hearing. doi:10.1097/AUD.0b013e31828003d8 *homeostasis*. [Def. 1]. (n.d.). *Merriam-Webster Online*. In Merriam-Webster. Retrieved March 12, 2013, from http://www.merriam-webster.com/dictionary/homeostasis.

Hothersall, D. (1995). History of psychology. NY: McGraw-Hill.

Hughes, L. E., & Gartsman, A. (2007). Introduction to linguistics study guide. Honors Junior/Senior Projects. Paper 23.

Hurtado, S., Mayhew, M.J., & Engberg, M.E. (2003). *Diversity in the classroom and students' moral reasoning*. Paper presented at the Association for the Study of Higher Education. Portland: OR, November, 2003.

Hutcheon, E. J., & Wolbring, G. (2012). Voices of "disabled" post secondary students: Examining higher education "disability" policy using an ableism lens. *Journal of Diversity in Higher Education, 5*(1), 39–49. doi:10.1037/a0027002

Ironson, G., Balbin, E., & Schneiderman, N. (2002). Health psychology and infectious diseases. In S. B. Johnson, N. W. Perry, Jr., & R. H. Rozensky (Eds.), *Handbook of clinical health psychology* (Vol. 1, pp. 5–36). Washington, DC: American Psychological Association.

Jagger, M. (2008). The effects of race and ethnicity, both obvious and subtle. Retrieved from http://web.trinity.edu/Documents/student_affairs_docs/CCI_docs/Diversity/The%20Effects%20of%20Race%20and%20Ethnicity,%20Both%20Obvious%20and%20Subtle.pdf

Jones, M. A. (2002). Deafness as culture: A psychosocial perspective. Disability Studies Quarterly, vol. 22, no. 2, pp. 51–60.

Kaplan, G. A., Everson, S. A., & Lynch, J. W. (2000). The contribution of social and behavioral research to an understanding of the distribution of disease: A multilevel approach. In B. D. Smedley & S. L. Syme (Eds.), *Promoting health: Intervention strategies from social and behavioral research* (pp. 37–80). Washington, DC: National Academies Press.

Kezar, A. and Eckel, P. D. (July/August 2002). The effect of institutional culture on change strategies in higher education: Universal principles of culturally responsive concepts. The journal of Higher Education, vol. 73, no. 4, pp. 435–460.

Kich, G. K. (1996). In the margins of sex and race: Difference, marginality and flexibility. In M. P. P. Root (Ed.), The multiracial experience: Racial borders as the new frontier. NY: Sage; pp. 263–290.

Khosravizadeh, P. and Sadehvandi, N. (2011). Some instances of violation and flouting of the maxim of quantity by the main characters (Barry & Tim) in Dinner for Schmucks. 2011 International Conference on Languages, Literature and Linguistics; IPEDR vol. 26. Singapore: IACSIT Press

King, L. A. (2014). *The science of psychology: An appreciative view (3rd ed)*. New York: McGraw-Hill.

Kinsey, A., Pomeroy, W., & Martin, C. (1948). *Sexual Behavior in the Human Male*. Philadelphia: W.B. Saunders.

Kinsey, A., Pomeroy, W., Martin, C., & Gebhard, P. (1953). *Sexual Behavior in the Human Female*. Philadelphia: W.B. Saunders.

Kohlberg, L. (1973). Continuities in childhood and adult moral development revisited. In P. Baltes & K. W. Schaie (Eds.), *Life-span development psychology: Personality and socialization*. San Diego, CA: Academic Press.

Kohls, L. R. (1981). *Developing intercultural awareness*. Washington, D.C.: Sietar Press.

Kraybill, D.B. (2001). The riddle of Amish culture. Baltimore, MD: Johns Hopkins University Press.

Kulick, D. (2000). Gay and lesbian language. Annual Review of Anthropology 29:243–85.

Laney, G. (2004). Racial profiling: Issues and federal legislative proposals and options. CRS Report for Congress.

Lahey, B. B. (2011). Psychology: an introduction (11th ed.). Boston, MA: McGraw-Hill.

Laney, G. P. (2009). Racial profiling: Issues and federal legislative proposals and options. In S.J. Muffer (Ed), Racial Profiling: Issues, Data and Analyses. NY: Nova Science.

Lapour, A., & Heppner, M. J. (2009). Social class privilege and adolescent women's perceived career options. *Journal of Counseling Psychology, 56*(4), 477–494. doi:10.1037/a0017268

Lee, B. (1995, July). The wage effects of sexual orientation discrimination. *Industrial and Labor Relations Review*.

Leigh, I. (2012). Not just deaf: Multiple intersections. In R. Nettles & R. Balter (Eds.) Multiple Minority Identities: Application for Practice, Research and Training. NY: Springer.

Leigh, I. W., Corbett, C. A., Gutman, V., & Morere, D. A. (1996). Providing psychological services to deaf individuals: A response to new perceptions of diversity. Professional Psychology: Research and Practice, vol. 27, no. 4, pp. 364–371.

Leninger, M. M., & McFarland, M. R. (2006). Culture care diversity and universality: A worldwide nursing theory. Sudbury, MA: Jones Bartlett.

Lett, James (1996). Emic/etic distinctions. Encyclopedia of cultural anthropology.

Leuchovius, D (2003). ADA Q&A...The Rehabilitation Act and the ADA Connection. PACER Center.

Lindsay, C. (1994). Things that go wrong in diversity training: Conceptualization and change with ethnic identity models. Journal of Organizational Change Management, vol. 7, no. 6, pp. 18–33.

Lipkin, Arthur. (1999). Understanding Homosexuality, Changing Schools: A Text for Teachers, Counselors, and Administrators. Boulder, CO: Westview Press.

Liu, W. Pickett, T., & Ivey A. (2007). White middle-class privilege: Social class bias and implications for training and practice. *Journal of Multicultural Counseling and Development, 35,* 194–206.

Louderback, L. A., & Whitley, B. E. Jr. (1997). Perceived erotic value of homosexuality and sex-role attitudes as mediators of sex differences in heterosexual college students' attitudes toward lesbians and gay men. *Journal of Sex Research,* 34, 175–182.

Lunden, I. (2012). Analyst: Twitter passed 500M users in June 2012, 140M of them in US; Jakarta 'Biggest Tweeting City.' Retrieved from http://techcrunch.com/2012/07/30/analyst-twitter-passed-500m-users-in-june-2012–140m-of-them-in-us-jakarta-biggest-tweeting-city/

MacDonald, A., Jr. (1981). Bisexuality: Some comments on research and theory. *Journal of Homosexuality, 6,* 21–35.

Mahmoud, J. S. R., Staten, R., Hall, L. A., Lennie, T. A. (2012). The Relationship among Young Adult College Students' Depression, Anxiety, Stress, Demographics, Life Satisfaction, and Coping Styles. Issues in Mental Health Nursing, vol. 33, no. 3, pp. 149–156; doi:10.3109/01612840.2011.632708

Mahoney, J. (1975). An analysis of the axiological structures of traditional and proliferation men and women. *Journal of Psychology, 90,* 31– 39.

Markus, H. (2008). Pride, prejudice, and ambivalence: Toward a unified theory of race and ethnicity. *American Psychologist, 63*(8), 651–670. doi:10.1037/0003–066X.63.8.651

Martin, C. L., Ruble, D. N., & Szkrybalo, J. (2004). Recognizing the centrality of gender identity and stereotype knowledge in gender development and moving toward theoretical integration: Reply to Bandura and Bussey (2004). *Psychological Bulletin, 130,* 702– 710.

Matsumoto, D., & Juang, L. (2012). Culture and psychology (5th ed. Belmont, CA: Wadsworth.

Maxwell, J. A. (2005). Qualitative research design: An interactive approach (2nd ed.). CA: Sage.

McLoyd, V. C., Kaplan, R., Hardaway, C. R., & Wood, D. (2007). Does endorsement of physical discipline matter? Assessing moderating influences on the maternal and child psychological correlates of physical discipline in African American families. *Journal of Family Psychology, 21*(2), 165–175. doi:10.1037/0893–3200.21.2.165

Meet the Press (2009). David Paterson On Meet The Press: "I'm Blind, I'm Not Oblivious" http://www.huffingtonpost.com/2009/09/27/david-paterson-on-meet-th_n_301379.html

Mio, J. S., Barker, L. A., & Tumambing, J. (2012). Multicultural psychology: understanding our diverse communities. IA: Oxford University Press.

McBride-Chang, C., & Jacklin, C. (1993). Early play arousal, sex-typed play and activity level as precursors to later rough-and-tumble play. *Early Education & Development, 4,* 99–108.

McIntosh, P. (1987). White privilege: Unpacking the invisible knapsack. In S. Plous (Ed.), Understanding prejudice and discrimination (pp. 191–196). New York, NY: McGraw-Hill.

Meyer, I. H., & Dean, L. (1998). Internalized homophobia, intimacy, and sexual behavior among gay and bisexual men. In G. M. Herek (Ed.) Stigma and sexual orientation: Understanding prejudice against lesbians, gay men, and bisexuals (pp. 160–186). Thousand Oaks, CA: Sage.

Mio, J. S., Barker, L. A., & Tumambing, J. (2012). Multicultural psychology: understanding our diverse communities (3rd ed.). NY: Oxford Press.

Mooney, L. A., Knox, D., & Schacht, C. (2011). Understanding Social Problems (7th ed.). Belmont, CA: Cengage.

Morris, C. G., & Maisto, A. A. (1998). Psychology: An introduction. NJ: Prentice-Hall.

Morris, J., Waldo., C., & Rothblum, E. (2001). A model of predictors and outcomes of outness among lesbian and bisexual women. *American Journal of Orthopsychiatry, 71,* 61–71.

Mui, Y. (2012). *Wells Fargo, Justice Department settle discrimination case for $175 Million*. The Washington Post.

Myer, D. (2007). Exploring social psychology (4th ed.). Boston, MA: McGraw-Hill.

Myers, K., & Sadaghiani, K. (June 2010). Millennials in the workplace: A communication perspective on millennials' organizational relationships and performance. Journal of Business and Psychology; 25(2), pp. 225–238.

National Center for Transgender Equality (2009). *ENDA by the numbers*. Washington, DC: Author. Retrieved from http://transequality.org/Resources/enda_by_the_numbers.pdf

Nelson, T.D. (2005). Ageism: Prejudice Against Our Feared Future Self. *Journal of Social Issues, Vol. 61, No. 2, pp. 207—221*

Nettles, R., & Balter, R. (2012). Multiple minority identities: Applications for practice, research and training. New York, New York: Springer Publishing Company.

Nettles, R., & Balter, R. (Eds.) (2011). Multiple minority identities: Applications for practice, research and training. New York, NY: Springer.

Neuliep, J. W. (2012). Intercultural communication: A contextual approach (5th ed.). Thousand Oaks, CA: Sage; pp. 235–265.

Niles, K. A., Giles, H., & LePoire, B. (2003). Language and communication in Hogg, M. A. and J. Cooper (eds) The Sage handbook of social psychology. Thousand Oaks, CA: Sage; pp. 233–234.

Norwalk, K. E., Vandiver, B. J., White, A. M., & Englar-Carlson, M. (2011). Factor structure of the gender role conflict scale in African American and European American men. *Psychology of Men & Masculinity, 12*(2), 128–143. doi:10.1037/a0022799

Office of Minority Health and Health Disparities. (2008). Eliminating Racial and Ethnic Health Disparities. Retrieved April 15, 2008 from http://www.cdc.gov/omhd

O'Connor, E. (2001). An American psychologist. In APA Monitor on psychology. Washington, DC: APA.

Oyserman, D., & Lee, S. S. (2008). Does culture influence what and how we think? Effects of priming individualism and collectivism. *Psychological Bulletin, 13*(2), 311–342. doi:10.1037/0033–2909.134.2.311

Padden, C., & Humphries, T. (2009). Inside deaf culture. Boston, MA: Harvard University Press.

Padden, C., & Humphries, T. (1988). Deaf in America: Voices from a culture. Cambridge: Harvard University Press.

Parham, T. A. (2000). The psychology of Blacks: An African centered perspective (3rd ed.). Upper Saddle River, NJ: Prentice Hall.

Park, Y. S., & Kim, B. K. (2008). Asian and European American cultural values and communication styles among Asian American and European American college students. Cultural Diversity And Ethnic Minority Psychology, 14(1), 47–56. doi:10.1037/1099–9809.14.1.47

Patrick, E. (2000). Bi: We're not confused. *Ms.*, December 2000/January 2001, 11.

Pauketat, T. R. (March 2001). Practice and history in archaeology: An emerging paradigm. Anthropological Theory, vol. 1, no. 1, pp. 73–98. doi:10.1177/146349960100100105

Pettinicchio, D. (2004). The Disability Rights Movement: The Case of a Disabled Identity. Conference Papers—American Sociological Association, 1–28. doi:asa_proceeding_35223.PDF

Pew Research Center (2007). Major Religious Traditions in the U.S. Retrieved from http://religions.pewforum.org/reports.

Pitetti, K. H., & Pedrotty, M. H. (2003). Lowerlimb amputation. In J. L. Durstine & G. E. Moore (Eds.), *ACSM exercise management for persons with chronic diseases and disabilities* (2nd ed., pp. 230–235). Champaign, IL: Human Kinetics.

Plumert, J. M. (2004). Accidents. In A. J. Christensen, R. Martin, & J. M. Smyth (Eds.), *Encyclopedia of health psychology* (pp. 1–3). New York: Kluwer Academic.

Ponterotto, J. G. (2010). Qualitative research in multicultural psychology: Philosophical underpinning, popular approaches and ethical considerations. Cultural Diversity and Ethnic Minority Psychology, vol. 16, pp. 581–589.

Ponterotto, J. G., Casas, J. M., Suzuki, L.A., & Alexander, Charlene M. (1995). Handbook of multicultural counseling. CA: Sage.

Poteat, V. P., & Canderson, C. J. (2012). Developmental changes in sexual prejudice from early to late adolescence: The effects of gender, race, and ideology on different patterns of change. *Developmental Psychology*. Advance online publication. doi:10.1037/a0026906

Ramirez, D., McDevitt, J., & Farrell, A. (2000). A Resource Guide on Racial Profiling Data Collection Systems: Promising Practices and Lessons Learned. U.S. Department of Justice. Retrieved from https://www.ncjrs.gov/pdffiles1/bja/184768.pdf

Ramnerö, J., & Törneke, N. (2008). The ABCs of human behavior: Behavioral principles for the practicing clinician. Oakland, CA: New Harbinger Press.

Rand, M., & Harrell, E. (2009). Crime against people with disabilities, 2007. Washington, DC: Bureau of Justice Statistics, 1, http://bjs.ojp.usdoj.gov/content/pub/pdf/capd07.pdf

Ratcliff, K. S. (2002). *Women and health: Power,technology, inequality and conflict in a gendered world.* Boston: Allyn and Bacon.

Rayburn, C. A. (2004). Religion, Spirituality, and Health. *American Psychologist, 59*(1), 52–53. doi:10.1037/0003–066X.59.1.52c

Reichert, E. (2012). Reducing stigma barriers to help-seeking behavior among college students. Psychology, vol 3, no. 10, pp. 892–898. Retrieved from http://0-search.proquest.com.library.ccbcmd.edu/docview/128529505?accountid=3784

Reid, D. K., & Knight, M. G. (2006). Disability justifies exclusion of minority students: A critical history grounded in disability studies. Educational *Researcher, 35, 18–23.*

Roberts, M. C. (1985). A plea for professional civility. Professional Psychology: Research and Practice, 16(4), 474. doi:10.1037/0735–7028.16.4.474

Rosario, M., Schrimshaw, E. W., & Hunter, J. (2004). Ethnic/racial differences in the coming-out process of lesbian, gay, and bisexual youths: A comparison of sexual identity development over time. *Cultural Diversity And Ethnic Minority Psychology*, *10*(3), 215–228. doi:10.1037/1099–9809.10.3.215

Rosenblum, K. E., & Travis, T. C., 2008. The meaning of difference: American constructions of race, sex and gender, social class, sexual orientation, and disability. New York, NY: McGraw-Hill.

Rubin, J., Provenzano, F., & Luria, Z. (1974). The eye of the beholder: Parents' views on sex of newborns. *American Journal of Orthopsychiatry, 44*, 512–519.

Rugulie, R., Aust, B., & Syme, S. L. (2004). Epidemiology of health and illness: A socio-psycho-physiological perspective. In S. Sutton, A. Baum, & M. Johnson (Eds.), *The Sage handbook of health psychology*, (pp. 39–42). London: Sage Publications.

Rathus, S. A. (1999). Psychology in the new millennium. Orlando, FL: Harcourt-Brace.

Sanchez-Burks, J., Lee, F., Choi, I., Nisbett, R., Zhao, S., & Koo, J. (2003). Conversing across cultures: East-west communication styles in work and nonwork contexts. Journal of Personality and Social Psychology, 85(2), pp. 363–372.

Satre, D. D., & Cook, B. L. (2004). Aging. In A. J. Christensen, R. Martin, & J. M. Smyth (Eds.), *Encyclopedia of health psychology* (pp. 5–8). New York: Kluwer Academic.

Schaefar, Richard. (2012). Racial and ethnic groups (13th ed.). Boston: Pearson Education, Inc.

Scarborough, E., and Furumoto. F. (1987). *Untold Lives: The First Generation of American Women Psychologists.* NY: Columbia University Press, pp. 109–129.

Schwartz, S. J., & Zamboanga, B. L. (2008). Testing Berry's model of acculturation: A confirmatory latent class approach. *Cultural Diversity And Ethnic Minority Psychology, 14*(4), 275–285. doi:10.1037/a0012818

Schwebel, D. C., & Plumert, J. M. (1999). Longitudinal and concurrent relations between temperament, ability, estimation, and injury proneness. *Child Development, 70,* 700–712.

Searle, W., & Ward, C. (1990). The prediction of psychological and sociocultural adjustment during cross-cultural transitions. International Journal of Intercultural Relations, vol. 14, pp. 449–464. doi:10.1016/01471767(90)90030-Z

Sell, R. L. (1997). Defining and measuring sexual orientation: A review. *Archives of Sexual Behavior, 26,* 643– 658.

Setrakian, L., & Singh, N. (March 9, 2007). Should the deaf get death? ABC News. http://abcnews.go.com/wnt/legalcenter/story?id=2937917&page=1

Shapiro, J. (1988). Gallaudet president removed after protests. Washington, DC: National Public Radio.

Simmons, S. (2000). Organ Donation. Retrieved from http://www.aish.com/ci/sam/48936217.html

Siraev, E. B. and Levy, D. A. (2010). Cross-cultural psychology: Critical thinking and contemporary applications (4th ed). Boston, MA: Allyn & Bacon

Skrinar, G. S. (2003). Mental illness. In J. L. Durstine & G. E. Moore (Eds.), *ACSM exercise management for persons with chronic diseases and disabilities* (2nd ed., pp. 316–319). Champaign, IL: Human Kinetics.

Slusher, M. P. and Anderson, C. A. (1996). Using causal persuasive arguments to change beliefs and teach new information: The mediating role of explanation availability and evaluation bias in the acceptance of knowledge. *Journal of Educational Psychology, 88,* 1, 110–122.

Smith, L., Foley, P. F., & Chaney, M. P. (2008). Addressing Classism, Ableism, and Heterosexism in Counselor Education. *Journal of Counseling & Development, 86*(3), 303–309.

Smith, Ronald E., Sarason, Irwin G., & Sarason, Barbara R. (1982). Psychology: The frontiers of behavior (2nd ed.). NY: Harper & Row.

Snooks, M. K. (2000). Title IX of the Education Amendments of 1972. In A. M. Howard & F. M. Kavenik (Eds.), *Handbook of American women's history* (2nd ed., pp. 571–572). Thousand Oaks, CA: Sage Publications.

Socialbakers (2012). Facebook Statistics by Country. Retrieved from http://www.socialbakers.com/facebook-statistics/

Steele, C. M., & Aronson, J. (1995). Stereotype threat and the intellectual test performance of African Americans. *Journal of Personality and Social Psychology, 69,* 797–811. doi:10.1037/0022–3514.69.5.797

Stith-Williams, V., & Haynes, P. (2007). For cultural competence: Knowledge, skills and dispositions needed to embrace diversity. Virginia Department of Education.

Stanton, A. L., & Gallant, S. J. (Eds.). (1995). *The psychology of women's health: Progress and challenges in research and application.* Washington, DC: American Psychological Association.

Steele, C. M., & Aronson, J. (1995). Stereotype threat and the intellectualtest performance of African Americans. *Journal of Personality and Social Psychology, 69,* 797–811. doi:10.1037/0022–3514.69.5.797

Stoloff, C. (1973). Who joins women's liberation? *Psychiatry, 36,* 325–340.

Straus, M., & Gelles, R. (1986). Societal change and change in family violence from 1975 to 1985 as revealed by two national surveys. *Journal of Marriage and the Family, 48*, 465–479.

Stuart, R. B. (2004). Twelve practical suggestions for achieving multicultural competence. Professional Psychology: Research and Practice, vol. 35, no. 1, pp. 3–9.

Sue, D. W., Bingham, R.P, Porché-Burke, L., & Vasquez, M. (1999). The diversification of psychology: A multicultural revolution. American Psychologist, vol. 54, no. 12, pp. 1061–1069.

Sue, D. W. and Sue, D. (2003). Counseling the culturally diverse: Theory and practice. NY: Wiley

Sue, D. W., & Arredondo, P. (1992). Multicultural counseling competencies and standards: A call to the profession. Journal of Multicultural Counseling and Development; 70; pp. 477–486.

Tatum, B. (2003). Why are all the black kids sitting together in the cafeteria. NY: Basic Books.

Thomas, A. J. (1998). Understanding culture and worldview in family systems: Use of the Multicultural Genogram. The Family Journal, vol. 6, no. 24–32. doi:10.1177/1066480798061005

Thompson, R. J., Jr. & Gustafson, K. E. (1996). *Adaptation to chronic childhood illness.* Washington, DC: American Psychological Association.

Tjaden, P., & Thoennes, N. (2000). *Extent, nature, and consequence of intimate partner violence: Findings from the National Violence Against Women Survey* (Publication No.: NCJ 181867). Washington, DC: Department of Justice.

Triandis, H. C. (2000). Culture and conflict. The International Journal of Psychology, 35(2), pp. 18–28.

Triandis, H. C. (1995). Individualism and collectivism. Boulder, CO: Westview Press.

Triandis, H. C. (1989). The self and social behavior in differing cultural contexts. Psychological Review, 96(3), pp. 506–520. doi:10.1037/0033–295X.96.3.506

Triandis, H. C., & Gelfand, M. J. (1998). Converging measurement of horizontal and vertical individualism and collectivism. Journal of Personality and Social Psychology. Washington, DC: American Psychological Association, Inc., vol. 74, No. 1, pp. 118–128.

Triandis, H. C. and Suh, E.M. (2002). Cultural influences on personality. Annual Review of Psychology. 53, pp. 133–60.

Tricard, L. M. (2008). *American women's track and field, 1981–2000.* (pp. 1–2). Jefferson, NC: Mc-Farland.

Troiden, R. R. (1989). The Formation of Homosexual Identities. *Journal Of Homosexuality, 17*(1/2), 43–73.

Turkle, S. (2011). Alone together: Why we expect more from technology and less from each other. NY: Basic Books.

Turner, P. J., & Gervai, J. (1995). A multidimensional study of gender typing in preschool children and their parents: Personality, attitudes, preferences, behavior, and cultural differences. *Developmental Psychology, 31*(5), 759–772. doi:10.1037/0012–1649.31.5.759

Twenge, J. M. (2006). *Generation me: Why today's young American are more confident, assertive, entitled — and more miserable than ever before.* New York: Atria.

Tyler's Story (2012). The Tyler Clementi Foundation. Retrieved from http://www.tylerclementi.org/tylers-story/

United States Bureau of Labor Statistics. (2011, July). Highlights of Women's Earnings in 2010. U.S. Department of Labor.

United States Census Bureau (2011). USA Quick Facts. Retrieved from http://quickfacts.census.gov/qfd/states/00000.html

United States Department of Health and Human Services. (2006). *National Vital Statistics Reports,* June 28, 2006, 54(19).

University of Iowa School of Social Work (2009). "Committed to Excellence Through Supervision". USDHHS Grant # 90CT0111. National Resource Center for Family Centered Practice.

Ursula Burns. (2009, May 21). New York Times. Retrieved from http://topics.nytimes.com/topics/reference/timestopics/people/b/ursula_m_burns/index.html

U.S. Department of Commerce. (2014). "Welfare Statistics". US Department of Health and Human Services, CATO Institute.

U.S. Department of Health and Human Services (2006). Your Rights Under Section 504 of the Rehabilitation Act. Retrieved from http://www.hhs.gov/ocr/civilrights/resources/factsheets/504.pdf

Wade, C., & Tavris, C. (2011). Psychology (10th ed.). Boston, MA: Prentice-Hall.

Wade, J. C., & Coughlin, P. (2012). Male reference group identity dependence, masculinity ideology, and relationship satisfaction in men's heterosexual romantic relationships. *Psychology of Men & Masculinity, 13*(4), 325–339. doi:10.1037/a0026278

Wahl, O. F. (1999b). Telling is risky business: Mental health consumers confront stigma. New Brunswick, NJ: Rutgers University Press.

Weaver, E. (1982). It's what you learn after you know it all that counts. NY: Doubleday.

Wegeneck, A.R. and Buskist, W. (2010). The Insider's Guide to the Psychology Major: Everything You Need to Know About the Degree and Profession. Washington, DC: American Psychological Association.

Weinberg, M. S., Williams, C. J., & Pryor, D. W. (1994). Dual attraction: Understanding bisexuality. New York: Oxford University Press.

Weiten, W. (2012). Psychology: Themes and variations, Briefer version (8th ed.). Belmont, CA: Wadsworth

Weiten, W. (2011). Psychology: Themes and variations. 8th edition. Belmont, CA: Wadsworth.

Westermarck, E.R. (1894). The history of human marriage. NY: Macmillan; Vol. 3 (NOTE: Original work published in 1891)

Wilcox, S. (1989). American deaf culture: An anthology. Burtonsville, MD: Linstock Press.

Williams, D. R. (1993). Race in the health of America, problems, issues and directions. *Mortality and Morbidity Weekly Report, 42* (RR-10); 9.

Williams, J. (2005). "Robert V. Guthrie." San Diego Union-Tribune (Nov. 12). www.signsonsandiego.com

Wilson, D., & Sperber, D. (2002). Truthfulness and relevance. Mind 111: 583–632.

WorldBank (2009). The World Bank Annual Review. Washington, DC; The World Bank.

Worthington, R. L., & Reynolds, A. L. (2009). Within-group differences in sexual orientation and identity. *Journal Of Counseling Psychology, 56*(1), 44–55. doi:10.1037/a0013498

Würtz, E. (2005). A cross-cultural analysis of websites from high-context cultures and low-context cultures. Journal of Computer-Mediated Communication, 11(1).

Wysocki, T., & Buckloh, L. M. (2002). Endocrine, metabolic, nutritional, and immune disorders. In S. B. Johnson, N. W. Perry, Jr., & R. H. Rozensky (Eds.), *Handbook of clinical health psychology* (Vol. 1, pp. 65–99). Washington, DC: American Psychological Association.

Ying, Y., Lee, P., Tsai, J. L., Hung, Y., Lin, M., & Wan, C. (2001). Asian American college students as model minorities: An examination of their overall competence. *Cultural Diversity And Ethnic Minority Psychology, 7*(1), 59–74. doi:10.1037/1099–9809.7.1.59

Zosuls, K. M., Ruble, D. N., Tamis-LeMonda, C. S., Shrout, P. E., Bornstein, M. H., & Greulich, F. K. (2009). The acquisition of gender labels in infancy: Implications for gender-typed play. *Developmental Psychology, 45*(3), 688–701. doi:10.1037/a0014053

Index